**Direito Comparado
Perspectivas Luso-Americanas**

**Comparative Law
Portuguese-American Perspectives**

Direito Comparado
Perspectivas Luso-Americanas

Comparative Law
Portuguese-American Perspectives

2016 • Volume III

Coordenadores – Editors
Dário Moura Vicente
Marshall J. Breger

DIREITO COMPARADO
PERSPECTIVAS LUSO-AMERICANAS
COMPARATIVE LAW
PORTUGUESE-AMERICAN PERSPECTIVES

COORDENADORES
Dário Moura Vicente e Marshall J. Breger

EDITOR
EDIÇÕES ALMEDINA, S.A.
Rua Fernandes Tomás, nºs 76-80
3000-167 Coimbra
Tel.: 239 851 904 · Fax: 239 851 901
www.almedina.net · editora@almedina.net

DESIGN DE CAPA
FBA.

PRÉ-IMPRESSÃO
João Jegundo

IMPRESSÃO E ACABAMENTO
Pentaedro, Lda.

Maio, 2016

DEPÓSITO LEGAL
409917/16

Apesar do cuidado e rigor colocados na elaboração da presente obra, devem os diplomas legais dela constantes ser sempre objeto de confirmação com as publicações oficiais.
Toda a reprodução desta obra, por fotocópia ou outro qualquer processo, sem prévia autorização escrita do Editor, é ilícita e passível de procedimento judicial contra o infrator.

 | GRUPOALMEDINA

BIBLIOTECA NACIONAL DE PORTUGAL – CATALOGAÇÃO NA PUBLICAÇÃO

CONFERÊNCIAS LUSO-AMERICANAS, 2010-2013

Direito comparado : perspectivas luso-americanas = Comparative law : Portuguese-American perspectives / coord. Dário Moura Vicente. – v.
3º v.: p. - ISBN 978-972-40-6502-1

I – VICENTE, Dário Moura, 1962-

CDU   340

INTRODUÇÃO / INTRODUCTION

We are very pleased to offer this fourth volume of papers delivered as part of a unique collaboration between the Columbus School of Law, Catholic University of America and the Law School of the University of Lisbon. The collection consists of papers from conferences held between 2010 and 2013 alternately in Lisbon and Washington, D.C.[1]

The period between 2010 and 2013 was a time of great stress and turmoil in the United States and Portugal. The conferences, which discussed immigration policy, energy, and the financial "meltdown," raised issues central to the economic and political health of both countries. It should not be a surprise that both law and politics of these subjects have evolved considerably since the papers were given.

We note with sadness the passing of one of our contributors Ambassador Richard Williamson. Williamson was a distinguished lawyer and diplomat who served as *inter alia* as Assistant Secretary of State for International Organization Affairs and Special Presidential Envoy to the Sudan where he worked to prevent genocide. He was a senior foreign policy advisor to a number of Republican presidential candidates including John McCain and Mitt Romney.

These papers, in a sense, reflect a snapshot in time, providing an opportunity to understand some of the central legal and political issues of the

---

[1] Previously published volumes in this series include: Dário Moura Vicente and Marshall J. Breger *Comparative Law: Portuguese-American Perspectives,* vol. 1 (Coimbra, Almedina 2006); Marshall J. Breger and Markus G. Puder, "European Union Issues from a Portuguese Perspective" (Catholic University of America 2007); Dário Moura Vicente and Marshall J. Breger *Comparative Law: Portuguese – American Perspectives,* vol. 2 (Coimbra, Almedina 2010).

DIREITO COMPARADO / COMPARATIVE LAW

early 21st century. As importantly, they provide a still relevant introduction to US and Portuguese law in a variety of crucial fields. The specifics may well have changed but the fundamental issues endure.

Some of these papers are of particular interest. We note specifically George Garvey's paper on enviornmental cap and trade approaches in the US and the EU, a subject once popular, then practically discarded but relevant once more.[2] Other energy papers such as the late Ambassador Richard Williamson's analysis of Chinese influence on the oil economies of Africa, are particularly prescient in their analysis of geopolitical issues in Africa as well as petroleum economics. Maryellen Fullerton's paper on Portuguese and EU Asylum is of continuing interest.

The 2009 immigration conference lays out enduring issues of immigration policy in both the US and the EU with special attention to the situation in Portugal. Refugee and asylum policy in both the US and Portugal are reviewed (Stephen Legomsky, Maryellen Fullerton, Donald Kerwin, Carlos Ortiz-Miranda) as is the administrative reality of the immigration process (Carla Amado Gomes). Attention is paid, moreover, to the goals of immigration policy and the need for comprehensive immigration reform – issues high on today's political agenda in both Europe and the United States.

The 2010 discussion of the "Financial Crisis" of 2008 provides a unique vantage to review the greatest recession since World War II – *in media res*, as it were. Harris Weinstein's paper on the causes and the financial crises is uniquely informed by his work in resolving an earlier "bubble," the savings and loan crisis of the 1980s; Prof. David Lipton sagely analyzes the possibility of a long term solution to the threat of a future financial crisis. Prof. Andrea Boyack's contribution on the role of lax real estate regulation takes us through a government regulatory failure that many fear will return. Michael Taylor's study of the challenge of "too big to fail" as well as his review of standard setting procedures of the Bank for International Settlements (BIS) in Basel is also worth noting. His later career at the BIS makes his insights of particular interest. Prof. Miguel Moura e Silva provides a useful reminder that while antitrust enforcement does not seem

•

[2] Professor Garvey's paper, The U.S. Experience with Market-Based Emissions Regulations was delivered at the 2009 conference titled Environment and Development but his paper is published first in this volume.

to be a cause of the 2008 financial crisis, the impact of such financial crises on competition policy is a problem of the first rank.

The 2011 conference on energy law contains much information that, if not unique, is unlikely to be found in English in other than specialist studies. Antonio de Lecea reviews the structural relationships between EU energy law and Portuguese law. Luís Silva Morais analyzes the regulation of the energy sector in the EU. Donald Elliott addresses the still relevant question "Why does the United States not have a Renewable Energy Policy?" Richard Pierce deftly reviews the past, present and future of US energy regulation; Joseph Kelliher, a former Chairman of the Federal Energy Regulatory Commission (FERC), reviews the structure of energy regulation in the United States. Dário Moura Vicente discusses the arbitration process in the petroleum field and David Caron provides acute commentary. Other surveys of American law include Keith Larson's review of merger and restructuring developments in the energy sector.

We should make note, as we did earlier, of the late Ambassador Richard Williamson's study of Chinese influence in the geopolitics of African oil and Agostinho Pereira de Miranda's (and Rita Mota's) careful analysis of petroleum contracts in the Portuguese speaking countries of Africa.

Taken as a whole, these papers speak to the growing intersection between US legal interests and those of the EU, specifically Portugal. Together with the previous collections, they represent over ten years of Portuguese – US collaboration in legal scholarship. They are, we believe, a harbinger of increased transatlantic legal practice as well.

We wish to thank the Fundação Luso-Americana for their support of the entire Portuguese American legal project and of this volume in particular. The extraordinary work of the Foundation in bringing knowledge of, and indeed high regard for, Portuguese culture and law cannot be gainsaid.

Prof. Breger wishes, as well, to thank Dean Daniel Attridge of the Columbus School of Law, Catholic Univeristy of America for his encouragement and his former research assistant, John Passmore, for his assiduous efforts to bring this volume to fruition – efforts far beyond those detailed in his job description. Prof. Moura Vicente would also like to thank Ana Caras-Altas, of the Lisbon University Law School, for her help in revising and completing the final version of the manuscript.

DÁRIO MOURA VICENTE
MARSHALL J. BREGER

I Parte / Part I

IMIGRAÇÃO
IMMIGRATION

(8ª conferência, Washington, 2009
8th conference, Washington, 2009)

Refugees and Asylum in the United States

STEPHEN H. LEGOMSKY[*]

There will always be persecution in this world – even in what seem like times of relative calm, which at any rate is not how most people would describe today's turbulent world. Poor President Hoover learned this the hard way. In 1932, just as the Holocaust was first getting off the ground, he gave a campaign speech in which he declared: "With the growth of democracy in foreign countries political persecution has largely ceased. There is no longer a necessity for the United States to provide an asylum for those persecuted because of conscience."[1] The lesson is a sad one – human rights violations never take a holiday.

America has been a safe haven for political and religious dissidents since the colonial era, but the story of modern American refugee policy did not begin until the run-up to the Second World War. This paper will focus on current U.S. practice beginning with a primer on U.S. refugee and asylum law. The United States technically has never ratified the 1951 Refugee Convention[2]; however, in 1968 the United States did ratify the 1967 Refugee Protocol, and it is generally assumed that in doing so the United States was bound derivatively to the Convention.[3] Domestic legis-

---

[*] John S. Lehmann University Professor at Washington University School of Law in St. Louis.
[1] Herbert Hoover, Rear Platform and Other Informal Remarks in West Virginia, Ohio, and Michigan, 4 PUB. PAPERS 562 (Oct. 22, 1932) (Columbus, Ohio, Rear platform, 2:55p.m.).
[2] Convention Relating to the Status of Refugees, July 28, 1951, 189 U.N.T.S. 137.
[3] Protocol Relating to the Status of Refugees, Jan. 31, 1967, 606 U.N.T.S. 267.

DIREITO COMPARADO / COMPARATIVE LAW

lation comes mainly from the Refugee Act of 1980.[4] Even after 1980, and continuing until a few years after the end of the Cold War, U.S. refugee policy was famously preoccupied with Communism. The pattern was clear: Refugees from Communist countries were liberally admitted, while refugees from other totalitarian regimes enjoyed only rare success. Foreign policy still influences our refugee selection policies, but plays a much lesser role today than it did during the Cold War.[5]

Two different kinds of refugee programs need to be distinguished. Here, the common international terminology of offshore and onshore will be used. "Offshore" denotes programs in which the United States identifies refugees who are somewhere overseas – in refugee camps, living in the general population, but one way or the other the refugees are overseas – and brings them to the United States for permanent resettlement. Since 1980, the United States has operated by far the largest offshore permanent resettlement program for refugees in the world.[6] "Permanent" is used because there are many other countries, mainly in the developing world, that house far more refugees than does the United States, typically from within the same regions. At least in theory, and often in practice, those countries grant only temporary asylum, until the refugees can either return home safely or find permanent resettlement in the United States or other third country.

The "onshore" program is for people who make it to U.S. territory on their own, either at the frontier or in the interior, either legally or illegally. They may apply for any of three related remedies, described below:

The best of the remedies is asylum.[7] This is for people who meet the refugee definition, and do not fall within any of the criminal or national security exclusions, and receive the favorable exercise of administrative discretion. Once granted, asylum permits the asylee to remain in the United

---

[4] Refugee Act of 1980, Pub. L. No. 96-212, 94 Stat. 102.

[5] *See* Daniel L. Swanwick, *Foreign Policy and Humanitarianism in U.S. Asylum Adjudication: Revisiting the Debate in the Wake of the War on Terror*, 21 GEO. IMMIGR. L.J. 129, 144-49 (2007). While Swanwick acknowledges that War-on-Terror foreign policy has impacted asylum adjudications, he concludes that "today's asylum adjudication biases are relatively subtle when compared with those observed in the Cold War." *Id.* at 147.

[6] *See, e.g.*, UNHCR GLOBAL RESETTLEMENT STATISTICAL REPORT 3 (2008). In 2008, the United States accepted 48,828 refugees for permanent resettlement while Canada accepted the second most refugees for resettlement, accepting 5,663. *Id.*

[7] *See* 8 U.S.C. § 1158.

States and eventually receive permanent resident status. Similar treatment is granted to spouses and unmarried minor children of the asylee.[8]

The second remedy is meant to fulfill the U.S. non-refoulement obligations under the Refugee Convention and Protocol.[9] In the United States this remedy is called "withholding of removal."[10] This remedy is for certain refugees who fail to receive asylum for any of various reasons but who still need protection from persecution. This remedy avoids return to the country of persecution but does not result in permanent admission to the United States, so forced return to a third country remains possible. There is also no provision for the family members.

The third remedy, only briefly mentioned here, is relief under the Convention Against Torture, which the United States has ratified.[11] The Convention prohibits countries from returning people to places where they are in danger of torture.[12] This relief is useful for people who fear torture, but not on one of the Refugee Convention grounds, which are race, religion, nationality, social group, or political opinion. It is also useful for people who are ineligible for asylum and withholding because they have engaged in criminal or other disqualifying conduct, since the protection conferred by the Torture Convention is absolute; there are no exceptions.

The structure of the U.S. onshore program will now be discussed. In the United States, the refugee and asylum laws are part and parcel of the regulation of immigration. This is true in four senses. Formally and technically, the Refugee Act of 1980 is an amendment to the Immigration and Nationality Act, which continues to govern immigration.[13] Analytically, asylum seekers are non-U.S. citizens who hope to enter and remain in the

---

[8] *See* 8 U.S.C. § 1158(b)(3).

[9] *See* 1951 Refugee Convention *supra* note 2, art. 33 ("No contracting state shall expel or return ('refouler') a refugee in any manner whatsoever to the frontiers of territories where his life or freedom would be threatened on account of his race, religion, nationality, membership of a particular social group or political opinion.").

[10] *See* 8 C.F.R. § 208.16.

[11] Convention against Torture and Other Cruel, Inhuman or Degrading Treatment or Punishment, Dec. 10, 1984, 1465 U.N.T.S. 112 (1987).

[12] *Id.* art. 3 ("No State Party shall expel, return (*refouler*) or extradite a person to another State where there are substantial grounds for believing that he would be in danger of being subjected to torture.").

[13] Immigration and Nationality Act of 1952, Pub. L. No. 82-414, 66 Stat. 163, *as amended by*, Immigration and Nationality Act of 1965, Pub. L. No. 89-236, 79 Stat. 911.

DIREITO COMPARADO / COMPARATIVE LAW

United States because they are refugees, just as other people seek to enter and remain on the basis of family ties, or employment skills, or other valued attributes. Asylum seekers are different from most of the others, in that their migration is said to be "forced," or "involuntary." Functionally, refugees and asylum seekers face many of the same cultural challenges, have many of the same desires, and wrestle with some of the same bureaucracies and institutions, as other noncitizens.

In terms of public perception, the asylum process is associated by many with illegal immigration. Those who think of asylum in that way worry about asylum seekers abusing or manipulating the system, in the same way that they worry about other noncitizens violating the immigration laws. They see asylum mainly as a law enforcement issue. Others see it mainly as a human rights and humanitarian issue. Still others see it mainly as a foreign policy issue. Of course it is all of those things, in different measures.

The United States generally has one integrated procedure for applying for all three of the major onshore remedies simultaneously, but that procedure varies depending on the setting.[14] The main actors are "asylum officers" who work for the Department of Homeland Security and conduct non-adversarial interviews; immigration judges, who decide asylum claims during formal evidentiary hearings in which the opposing parties are the asylum seeker and the government; and the Board of Immigration Appeals, or BIA, an administrative tribunal that hears appeals from the immigration judge decisions. There is also an opportunity for judicial review in the general courts of appeals, subject to some limitations. In the case of most arrivals at the border, there is a special accelerated procedure, called "expedited removal."[15]

Created in the 1940s, the BIA reports to the Attorney General who appoints its members, may remove its members, and has the power to reverse its decisions.[16] The BIA performs only adjudicative functions.

---

[14] For a detailed description of the asylum process, see Jaya Ramji-Nogales, Andrew I. Schoenholtz & Philip G. Schrag, *Refugee Roulette: Disparities in Asylum Adjudications*, 60 STAN. L. REV. 295, 305-10 (2007).

[15] *See* 8 U.S.C. § 1225(b)(1)(A)(i); 8 C.F.R. § 235.3 (Inadmissible Aliens and expedited removal). Expedited removal was established in the Illegal Immigration Reform and Immigrant Responsibility Act of 1996, Pub. L. No. 104-208, 110 Stat. 3009-546. *See also* U.S. COMM'N ON INT'L RELIGIOUS FREEDOM, REPORT ON ASYLUM SEEKERS IN EXPEDITED REMOVAL (2005).

[16] *See* 8 C.F.R. 1003.1(a)(1); 5 Fed. Reg. 3503 (Sept. 4, 1940).

As a result of controversial "streamlining" inaugurated in 2002, the vast majority of BIA decisions are now made by single members rather than by three-member panels, and many of those are "affirmances without opinion" (AWOs).[17] These contain only one-paragraph boilerplate explanations reciting that the decision of the immigration judge is found to be correct.

In 2003, Attorney General John Ashcroft removed the more liberal members of the BIA and reassigned them to either non-adjudicative or lower level adjudicative positions.[18] That and other measures have left many immigration judges and BIA members fearful that ruling against the government can be hazardous to their jobs. That in turn poses a real threat to decisional independence. The concern is a serious one. An empirical study by Peter Levinson, former staff-counsel to the House Judiciary Committee, found that several BIA members did show sharply lower asylum approval rates starting immediately after the Attorney General's actions.[19]

There are many reasons that is a problem, but the most obvious is that judges and all other adjudicators must reach their decisions honestly. Their findings of fact should be based solely on the evidence before them, and legal conclusions based solely on honest interpretations of all the relevant sources of law – not on the basis of which outcome they think their boss, who can fire them, might prefer. Asylum claims that are overshadowed by the threat of loss of a job are not a recipe for justice.

Since the 2002 BIA streamlining, there has been a spectacular increase in petitions for judicial review of BIA decisions generally and their asylum denials in particular.[20] At the same time, a flood of judicial opinions have

---

[17] Executive Office for Immigration Review; Board of Immigration Appeals: Streamlining, 64 Fed. Reg. 56,135 (Oct. 18, 1999) (codified at 8 C.F.R. pt. 3) ("The rule recognizes that in a significant number of appeals and motions filed with the Board, a single appellate adjudicator can reliably determine that the result reached by the adjudicator below is correct and should not be changed on appeal.").

[18] *See* Stephen H. Legomsky, *Refugees, Asylum, and the Rule of Law in the USA, in* REFUGEES, ASYLUM SEEKERS AND THE RULE OF LAW: COMPARATIVE PERSPECTIVES 152-54 (Susan Kneebone ed., 2009); *see also* John D. Ashcroft & Kris W. Kobach, *A More Perfect System: The 2002 Reforms of the Board of Immigration Appeals*, 58 DUKE L.J. 1991 (2009).

[19] Peter J. Levinson, *The Façade of Quasi-Judicial Independence in Immigration Appellate Adjudications*, 9 BENDER'S IMMIGR. BULL., 1154, 1155-56 (2004).

[20] *See supra* note 18 and accompanying text.

excoriated immigration judges and the BIA for the quality of their decisions and sometimes for verbally abusing asylum applicants.[21]

In recent years, another controversy has erupted over the spectacular differences in the rates at which the various adjudicators grant asylum. A superb empirical study published in 2007 by Phil Schrag, Andy Schoenholtz, and Jaya Ramji-Nogales showed that, even for asylum seekers from the same country, the chance of winning varies dramatically depending on which asylum officer or which immigration judge decides the case.[22]

Importantly, the procedures described here are subject to one critical caveat: they are of no use unless one can access to them. Increasingly, there are more and more barriers to getting into the system. As Western nations struggle to reconcile refugee protection with national self-interest, they have been tempted to adopt a series of controversial strategies. Some of these reforms are specifically meant to cut off access to the asylum system entirely. Others permit potential asylum applicants to file claims but discourage them from doing so.

These strategies are more comprehensively categorized elsewhere, but they are briefly listed here. They include filing deadlines; presumptions that certain countries of origin or certain third countries are "safe"; accelerated procedures; preventive detention while the asylum claims are pending (which is used in the United States); criminal prosecutions of asylum-seekers for irregular entries; denial of permission to work; punishing individuals and/or their counsel for filing asylum claims later found to be "frivolous" or "manifestly unfounded"; pre-inspection at foreign airports; visa requirements combined with sanctions on commercial carriers who permit improperly documented passengers to land; and the interdiction of vessels on the high seas (mainly Haitians, but also Cubans and now a long list of other nationalities, in the Windward Passage between Haiti and Cuba, in the waters between Cuba and the Florida Keys, and even off

---

[21] Adam Liptak, *Courts Criticize Judges' Handling of Asylum Cases*, N.Y. TIMES, Dec. 26, 2005; *see* Benslimane v. Gonzales, 430 F.3d 828, 829-30 (7th Cir. 2005) ("Our criticisms of the Board and of the immigration judges have frequently been severe. ... [T]he adjudication of these cases at the administrative level has fallen below the minimum standards of legal justice."). In *Benslimane*, the U.S. 7th Circuit Court of Appeals noted that from September 2004 to September 2005, of the 136 petitions to review BIA holdings, a "staggering" 40% were reversed in whole or in part. 430 F.3d at 829.

[22] Ramji-Nogales et al., *supra* note 14, at 372-74.

the coast of Ecuador). The U.S. Supreme Court has interpreted the Refugee Convention and the U.S. statute as not applying on the High Seas, but UNHCR, the Inter-American Commission on Human Rights, NGOs, and scholars have roundly criticized the decision.[23]

Finally, here is a description of U.S. interpretations of the substantive criteria for refugee status. In two respects, the U.S. statute actually provides broader protection than the Convention requires. It includes internally displaced persons, not just people who have succeeded in fleeing their countries, and it allows refugee status solely on the basis of past persecution, even without a fear of future persecution, provided the past persecution was egregious enough.

Generally, both the Refugee Convention and the U.S. statute define "refugee" as a person who has "a well-founded fear of persecution on account of race, religion, nationality, membership in a particular social group, or political opinion."[24] Notice that gender is missing from both lists, and that is why women who fear domestic violence or other gender-related persecution have had to be inventive. They have often had to show that women, or some sub-category of women, constitute a social group, and thus attempt to define the meaning of "social group."[25]

Until very recently, the leading test in the United States and around the world has been the formulation laid out by the BIA in *Matter of Acosta*, in 1985.[26] The Board in that case defined a social group as a group in which membership is "immutable," a term the Board used broadly to embrace not only characteristics that are literally unchangeable, but also characteristics that the members "should not be required to change because [they

---

[23] *See* Sale v. Haitian Centers Council, Inc., 509 U.S. 155, 187-88 (1993). For a discussion of this case, see Dennis E. Wasitis, *Sale v. Haitian Centers Council, Inc: Closing the Golden Door*, 27 Akron L. Rev. 237 (1993).

[24] 8 U.S.C. § 1101(a)(42); 1951 Refugee Convention, *supra* note 2, art. 1, A(2) (as amended by 1967 Refugee Protocol, *supra* note 3, art. 1, ¶2).

[25] The BIA has held that "married women in Guatemala who are unable to leave their relationship" subject to domestic violence qualify for asylum as part of a "particular social group." In re A-R-C-G-, 26 I&N Dec. 388 (BIA 2014), Interim Decision #3811 (Aug. 26, 21014). *See* Alicia A. Caldwell, *US to Consider Spousal Abuse in Immigration Claims*, Associated Press (Aug. 27, 2014, 8:50 PM), http://hosted.ap.org/dynamic/stories/U/US_IMMIGRATION_AS YLUM?SITE=AP&SECTION=HOME&TEMPLATE=DEFAULT.

[26] In re Acosta, A-24159781, Interim Decision # 2986, 211 (Mar. 1, 1985).

are] fundamental to their individual identities or consciences."[27] Applying that test, the BIA and the U.S. courts have recognized a broad range of social groups. Women are clearly a social group under that definition because gender is immutable.

But since then, the Board in a series of cases has been superimposing additional requirements. Some courts have started deferring to those interpretations. This has posed terrific problems in domestic violence cases, explained below.

The issue is still unresolved. The BIA did not adequately defend immutability. It gave only a technical justification, invoking a venerable statutory interpretation technique known as "ejusdem generis."[28] The idea was that all four of the other persecution grounds – race, religion, nationality, and political opinion – have in common that they are *immutable* in the sense in which the Board was using that term. Therefore, the Board reasoned, the Convention drafters and Congress must have meant to link social group to immutability as well.

That is not the most satisfying rationale, the Board could have explained why immutability makes so much sense from a policy standpoint as well. The immutability test comes about as close to jurisprudential perfection as a test can get. Perfect asylum criteria should take account of both the reasons asylum is granted and the reasons it is limited. Therefore a perfect asylum system grants protection to those who need it and denies it to those who do not.

This is not an effective means of determination. For example, if one is going to be persecuted because of possessing attribute X, and attribute X is something that could easily be changed, thereby eliminating the risk of persecution, then attribute X should be changed rather than the United States expending immigration resources to grant one of the valuable asylum slots. If in contrast, attribute X is immutable in the *Acosta* sense, meaning either it literally cannot be changed it or that it is so fundamental to personal identity that the law should not require it to be changed, then there is no viable way to avoid persecution once sent home, and therefore asylum is necessary.

---

[27] *Id*. at 233.

[28] *Id*. ("We find the well-established doctrine of ejusdem generis, meaning literally, 'of the same kind,' to be most helpful.... That doctrine holds that general words used in an enumeration with specific words should be construed in a manner consistent with the specific words.").

The interpretation of this ideal test by the Board and the courts has created problems. Worse still, the particular requirements that have been superimposed make little policy sense. The most popular new requirement in the United States has been "social visibility," by which the Board means one must show that society in the home country perceives the alleged group as a group. The purpose of that requirement is unclear. Perhaps the Board's reasoning was that if society does not perceive the alleged group as a group, then it is not likely to target people just because they are members of that group. But if that is the idea, then the first question should be whether the persecutors perceive this as a group, not whether society generally does; and, more importantly, if the likelihood of persecution is the concern, that concern is already accommodated by insisting that the fear of persecution be objectively well-founded. If it is not, the claim fails anyway. But if it is, then why should it matter what the home society thinks? Most likely the Board was thinking purely in linguistic terms, visualizing a "social group" as a collection of individuals who come together in some recognizable way. The problem with interpreting the term in that purely linguistic manner is that the results end up bearing little resemblance to any rational combination of policy goals that one could realistically impute to either the people who drafted the Refugee Convention or the national legislators who passed legislation to implement it.

Portugal and European Union Asylum Policy

MARYELLEN FULLERTON[*]

This year's Conference on Portuguese and American Law highlights immigration law, a topic straight from the headlines in the press in both countries. The news stories generally feature desperate people from third-world countries, often denounced as economic migrants, illegal aliens, and bogus asylum seekers, and frequently portrayed as law-breakers and threats to society.[1] The real story, of course, is more complicated and nuanced. This paper will address one portion of this emotion-laden topic, specifically, the legal framework for migrants who seek asylum in Portugal. Accordingly, the Common European Asylum Policy and the legal standards it sets for Portugal and all other Member States of the European Union will be the focus here.

Portugal has long been a land of emigration and immigration. Indeed, from the mid-nineteenth century to the mid-twentieth century, more than two million Portuguese emigrated to the United States and Brazil.[2]

---

[*] Professor of Law, Brooklyn Law School. I appreciate the generous support of the Brooklyn Law School for my research on asylum in Europe.

[1] *E.g.*, Scott Sayare, *In Paris Without Papers, and Seeking Visibility*, N.Y. TIMES, Oct. 11, 2009, at A12; Caroline Brothers, *Afghan Youths Seek a New Life in Europe*, N.Y. TIMES, Aug. 28, 2009; Nadim Audi & Caroline Brothers, *French Officials Move to Close Camp of Migrants Headed to Britain*, N.Y. TIMES, Sept. 22, 2009; *The Breakdown: Where Migrants' Journeys Began, and How They are Faring in the European Squeeze*, N.Y. TIMES, Apr. 28, 2002.

[2] Jorge Malheiros, *Portugal Seeks Balance of Emigration, Immigration*, MIGRATION POLICY INST., (Dec. 1, 2002), http://www.migrationpolicy.org/article/portugal-seeks-balance-emigration-immigration.

During the 1960s and early 1970s, 1.5 million Portuguese emigrated to other European countries.[3] After the decolonization process of the 1960s and the Carnation Revolution in 1974,[4] the tide shifted from emigration to immigration, and foreigners became a noticeable phenomenon in the Portuguese landscape.[5] When Portugal joined the European Union (EU) in 1986,[6] the numbers of migrants arriving in Portugal continued to increase.[7]

I. Shift in Power from Member States to Brussels

At the time Portugal joined the European Union, the Member States viewed migration as a matter of national sovereignty and successfully fought efforts by the European Commission headquartered in Brussels even to collect data about immigrants from outside the European Union.[8] In 1987 the European Court of Justice (ECJ) ruled that the European Commission had acted beyond its competence and infringed on the rights of Member States when the Commission had instituted a policy requiring Member States to provide information about workers from non-Member States who had entered their territory.[9]

---

[3] *Id.*

[4] In April 1974 a coup led by military officers whose symbol was the red carnation deposed the Portuguese dictatorship, which had been led by Oliveira Salazar from 1933 to 1968 and subsequently by Marcelo Caetano. In April 1975 free elections were held to create a new Constitution, which was adopted in 1976, followed by the election of a democratic government led by Mario Soares.

[5] Malheiros, *supra* note 2.

[6] Portugal became a Member of the European Union (then known as the European Economic Community) in 1986. Documents Concerning the Accession of the Kingdom of Spain and the Portuguese Republic to the European Communities, 1985 O.J. (L 302).

[7] Malheiros, *supra* note 2.

[8] In 1985 the European Commission, the executive agency of the European Union (then known as the European Economic Community), established a policy requiring Member States to inform the Commission and other Member States about the numbers of workers entering from non-Member States and of proposed legislation or administrative policies that would affect these migrants. Commission Decision 85/381/EEC of 8 July 1985, 1985 O.J. (L 217) 25. Five Member States – Denmark, France, Germany, the Netherlands, and the United Kingdom – challenged the Commission's competence over matters relating to migration from non-Member States.

[9] In 1987 the European Court of Justice, the judicial branch of the European Union, agreed that the European Commission had overstepped its authority. The ECJ ruled that the Commission could collect information only regarding the integration of immigrants into the workforce of Member States, but could not require the member States to supply any addi-

The tide was about to shift, however. Less than five years after the ECJ judgment limiting the Commission's power concerning migration-related issues, the Treaty on European Union, known as the Maastricht Treaty, was negotiated.[10] The Maastricht Treaty expanded the scope of the European enterprise, and it created a legal framework supported by three pillars.[11] The first pillar concerned matters of the internal market; the second focused on foreign and security policy; and the third centered around policies involving justice and home affairs.[12] Asylum and migration policy fell within the third pillar,[13] which, together with the second pillar, was inter-governmental in nature. Thus, the Maastricht Treaty expressly identified migration and asylum policy as a matter of common interest to the EU Member States, but considered it an area where the Member States would make policy.

In 1997, only ten years after the ECJ ruling, the Treaty of Amsterdam transferred asylum and migration policy to the first pillar, placing it squarely under control of the EU institutions.[14] Subsequently, in 1999, the heads of state of the Members of the European Union met in Tampere, Finland and called for a common European asylum law.

> The European Council reaffirms the importance the Union and Member States attach to absolute respect of the right to seek asylum. It has agreed to work towards establishing a Common European Asylum System . . . .
>
> This System should include, in the short term, a clear and workable determination of the State responsible for the examination of an asylum applica-

tional information about migrants. Joined Cases 281, 283, 284, 285 & 287/85, Fed. Republic of Germany v. Comm'n, 1987 E.C.R. 3203.

[10] Treaty on European Union, Feb. 7, 1992, 1992 O.J. (C 191) 1 (entered into force Nov. 1, 1993) [hereinafter Maastricht Treaty].

[11] Prior to the Maastricht Treaty, the official name was the European Economic Community. The Maastricht Treaty expanded the scope beyond the economic sphere, giving rise to the broader European Community, and European Union titles. OLGA FERGUSON SIDORENKO, THE COMMON EUROPEAN ASYLUM SYSTEM: BACKGROUND, CURRENT STATE OF AFFAIRS, FUTURE DIRECTION 19-20 (2007).

[12] *Id.*

[13] To achieve the objectives of the European Union, in particular the free movement of person, "Member States shall regard the following areas as matters of common interest: asylum policy. . . ." Maastricht Treaty, *supra* note 10, art. K.1.

[14] Treaty of Amsterdam Amending the Treaty on European Union, the Treaties Establishing the European Communities and Certain Related Acts, Oct. 2, 1997, art. 2, ¶15, 1997 O.J. (C 340) 1 (entered into force May 1, 1999).

DIREITO COMPARADO / COMPARATIVE LAW

tion, common standards for a fair and efficient asylum procedure, common minimum conditions of reception of asylum seekers, and the approximation of rules on the recognition and content of the refugee status. It should also be complemented with measures on subsidiary forms of protection offering an appropriate status to any person in need of such protection. To that end, the Council is urged to adopt, on the basis of Commission proposals, the necessary decisions according to the timetable set in the Treaty of Amsterdam . . . .

In the longer term, Community rules should lead to a common asylum procedure and a uniform status for those who are granted asylum valid throughout the Union.[15]

Thus, in little more than a decade after Portugal joined the European Union, the EU Member States did an about face and expressly granted the central EU institutions the power to develop a common European law on asylum. This willingness to re-think the national sovereignty concepts that Member States held dear – and the consequent shift in power from the nation state to the supra-national European Union – was remarkable.

II. The Common European Asylum System

The European Council's endorsement of the creation of a Common European Asylum System expressly called on the European Commission to formulate legislative proposals. Jose Manuel Barroso,[16] the former Prime Minister of Portugal, has led the European Commission since 2004. Under Barroso and his predecessors, the Commission played a central role in drafting the five pieces of legislation that comprise the Common European Asylum System (CEAS).[17] As would be expected, the Commis-

---

[15] Tampere European Council 15 and 16 October 1999 Presidency Conclusions, Oct. 15-16, 1999, ¶¶ 13-15, *available at* Official Website of the European Parliament, www.europarl.europa. eu/summits/tam_en.htm [hereinafter Tampere Conclusions].

[16] Jose Manuel Durao Barroso, a former law professor at the University of Lisbon, served as the Minister of Foreign Affairs of Portugal from 1992 to 1995 and as the Prime Minister of Portugal from 2002 to 2004. He became the President of the European Commission in 2004; the European Parliament re-elected him in September 2009 to serve a second five-year term.

[17] Proposals become law when they garner a qualified majority vote of the European Council, which includes the head of government of each Member State. The Treaty of Nice of 2001 established qualified majority voting. Treaty of Nice Amending the Treaty on European Union, the Treaties Establishing the European Communities and Certain Related Acts, Feb.

sion's proposals generated substantial negotiations; compromises between Member States frequently altered the Commission's original vision of the appropriate common asylum policy for the European Union. Nonetheless, the Commission's work, after modification, ultimately created the CEAS.

The CEAS includes the Temporary Protection Directive of 2001,[18] the Reception Directive of 2003,[19] the Dublin II Regulation of 2003,[20] the Qualification Directive of 2004,[21] and the Asylum Procedures Directive of 2005.[22] Together these laws define who qualifies for asylum in the European Union, the procedures for evaluating their claims, how they should be treated during the asylum process, which country has responsibility for determining an asylum claim, and an EU-wide approach that can be employed in emergency situations when individual examination of asylum claims is not possible.

26, 2001, 2001 O.J. (C 80) 1 (entered into force Feb. 1, 2003) [hereinafter Treaty of Nice]. A qualified majority consists of the backing of more than 50% of the EU Member States, plus approximately 74% of the weighted votes assigned to the Member States (74% represents the required number of votes after enlargement of the Union in 2007, which resulted in a requirement for 255 out of 345 weighted votes). Furthermore, a Member State may request that the "Member States constituting the qualified majority represent at least 62 % of the total population of the Union" which would then be required in order to adopt the resolution. Treaty of Nice, *supra*, Protocols, art. 3.

[18] Council Directive 2001/55/EC, on Minimum Standards for Giving Temporary Protection in the Event of a Mass Influx of Displaced Persons and on Measures Promoting a Balance of Efforts Between Member States in Receiving Such Persons and Bearing the Consequences Thereof, 2001 O.J. (L 212) 12, 12–23 [Temporary Protection Directive].

[19] Council Directive 2003/9/EC, Laying Down Minimum Standards for the Reception of Asylum Seekers, 2003 O.J. (L 31) 18, 18–25 [Reception Directive].

[20] Council Regulation (EC) No. 343/2003 of 18 February 2003, Establishing the Criteria and Mechanisms for Determining the Member State Responsible for Examining an Asylum Application Lodged in one of the Member States by a Third-Country National, 2003 O.J. (L 50) 1 [Dublin II Regulation].

[21] Council Document 8043/04 on Minimum Standards for the Qualification and Status of Third-Country Nationals or Stateless Persons as Refugees or as Persons who Otherwise Need International Protection and the Content of the Protection Granted, 27April 2004 [Qualification Directive].

[22] Council Directive 2005/85/EC, on Minimum Standards on Procedures in Member States for Granting and Withdrawing Refugee Status, 2005 O.J. (L 326) 13 [Procedures Directive]. The Directive was adopted on 1 December 2005, entered into Force on 2 January 2006, and established a transposition deadline of 1 December 2007.

The CEAS employs a minimum standards approach, a traditional method of EU law-making. The EU legislation sets forth standards, which all the Member States must, at the least, adopt in their implementing laws. The Member States may, however, assume greater obligations toward refugees and asylum seekers than the EU laws mandate. This, in fact, is the approach that Portugal took as it modified its laws in order to implement the standards of the CEAS. Examining the terms of the new EU requirement of subsidiary protection and comparing them with the provisions of the 2008 asylum legislation adopted by the Portuguese Parliament illustrates one Member State's decision to afford more protection to asylum seekers than the minimum required. [23]

A. Subsidiary Protection in the Common European Asylum System

The Qualification Directive, the fourth of the five laws that comprise the CEAS, defines those who qualify for protection in the Member States and the content of the protection they must be afforded. Enacted in April 2004, the Qualification Directive provided that Member States must enact implementing legislation by October 2006.[24] The Qualification Directive requires the Member States to grant asylum to those defined by international law as refugees – individuals with a well-founded fear of persecution on account of race, religion, nationality, political opinion, and membership in a particular social group.[25] But it also goes a step further. In addition, the Qualification Directive requires Member States to provide asylum to those who would face a real risk of suffering serious harm – though not persecution – if returned to their homeland.[26] For example, an individual fleeing the lethal bombardment of her city in an insurrection might not qualify as a refugee because she is unable to show a well-founded fear of persecution. Nonetheless, if she can show that she will experience a real

---

[23] The pertinent Portuguese legislation is embodied in Law 27/2008 of 30 June 2008 Establishing the Conditions and Procedures for Granting Asylum and Subsidiary Protection and the Statuses of Asylum Applicant, Refugee and of Subsidiary Protection, Transposing into Internal Juridical Order Council Directives ns. 2004/83/CE of 29 April and 2005/85/CE of 1 December.

[24] Qualification Directive, *supra* note 21, art. 3.

[25] *Id*. art. 13.

[26] *Id*. art. 18.

risk of serious harm if she returns to her home country, she will be eligible to receive legal status and remain in the European Union.

Specifically, the Qualification Directive requires Member States to grant legal rights to those non-EU citizens who satisfy the subsidiary protection definition:

> an individual who does not qualify as a refugee but in respect of whom substantial grounds have been shown for believing that the person concerned, if returned to his or her country of origin . . . would face a real risk of suffering serious harm as defined in Article 15. . . . [27]

Article 15 of the Qualification Directive defines serious harm:

> (a) death penalty or execution; or
> (b) torture or inhuman or degrading treatment or punishment of an applicant in the country of origin; or
> (c) serious and individual threat to a civilian's life or person by reason of indiscriminate violence in situations of international or internal armed conflict. [28]

During the debates concerning the terms of the proposed Qualification Directive, many argued that the same legal status should apply to those granted subsidiary protection and to those granted asylum as refugees. For example, the Office of the United Nations High Commissioner of Refugees (UNHCR), now headed by António Guterres, another former Prime Minister of Portugal,[29] strongly asserted that the legal rights granted to noncitizens should be based on need, not on the reason justifying the grant of protection.[30] As a consequence, the UNHCR urged that there

---

[27] *Id.* art. 2(e).

[28] *Id.* art. 18.

[29] 29 António Guterres founded the Portuguese Refugee Council in 1991, was a member of the Socialist Party in Portugal, and served as the Prime Minister of Portugal from 1996 to 2002. He became the 10th United Nations High Commissioner for Refugees in 2005. *Interview with António Guterres, UN High Commissioner for Refugees*, MIGRATION POLICY INST. (Aug. 1, 2005), http://www.migrationpolicy.org/article/interview-antonio-guterres-un-high-commissioner-refugees/.

[30] UNHCR's Observations on the European Commission's Proposal for a Council Directive on Minimum Standards for the Qualification and Status of Third Country Nationals and

were no valid reasons for treating individuals granted refugee status differently from those granted subsidiary protection status.[31] Other groups, such as the Select Committee of the House of Lords (U.K.), noted that a two-tier system would create an unjustified distinction and would also likely increase the numbers of appeals because those granted subsidiary protection, but refused refugee status would have a reason to litigate.[32] The European Parliament also objected to the two-tier approach,[33] as did many nongovernmental organizations[34] and scholars.[35]

In the end, however, the political compromise embodied in the Qualification Directive specifies a two-tier system of protection.[36] The Member States must at a minimum grant three-year renewable residence permits to those determined to be refugees,[37] but need only provide a one-year renewable residence permit to those entitled to subsidiary protection.[38] Refugees must have access to travel documents,[39] but those receiving subsidiary protection are entitled to receive travel documents only "when serious humanitarian reasons arise that require their presence in another

---

Stateless Persons as Refugees or as Persons Who Otherwise Need International Protection, 14109/01 ASILE 54 (16 Nov. 2001).

[31] UNHCR, Note on Key Issues of Concern to UNHCR on the Draft Qualification Directive (Mar. 2004) 1.

[32] Select Committee on the European Union, Defining Refugee Status and Those in Need of International Protection, 2001-2, H.L. 156, ¶ 111 (U.K.).

[33] European Parliament, Report on the Proposal for a Council Directive on Minimum Standards for the Qualification and Status of Third Country Nationals and Stateless Persons as Refugees or as Persons Who Otherwise Need International Protection, 8 Oct. 2002, Final A5-0333/2002, PE 319.971.

[34] Amnesty International Irish Section, The Case for Complementary Protection, Jan. 2003; *Refugee Council's Response to the Home Office Consultation on Changes to the Policy of Issuing of Certificates of Identity*, Refugee Council (U.K.) (Feb. 2003), http://www.refugeecouncil.org. uk/assets/0001/6325/cid_traveldocs.pdf.

[35] Guy S. Goodwin-Gill & Agnès Hurwitz, Memorandum in Minutes of Evidence Taken Before the European Union Committee (Sub-Committee E), 10 Apr. 2002, 19 *in* Select Committee on the European Union, *supra* note 32.

[36] For a discussion of the political disagreements and compromises, see Jane McAdam, *The European Union Qualification Directive: The Creation of a Subsidiary Protection Regime*, 17 INT'L J. REFUGEE L. 461 (2005).

[37] Qualification Directive, *supra* note 21, art. 24(1).

[38] *Id.* art. 24(2).

[39] *Id.* art. 25(1).

State."[40] Refugees receive employment authorization,[41] while the state may limit employment opportunities based on the national labor situation for those accorded subsidiary protection.[42] Refugees are entitled to social assistance,[43] but those with subsidiary protection may see their welfare reduced to "core benefits."[44]

In sum, the Qualification Directive requires the Member States to adopt a more robust definition of individuals entitled to protection and lawful status. Simultaneously, though, the EU asylum law permits the Member States to offer a lower level of protection to those who need subsidiary protection.

B. Subsidiary Protection in Portuguese Legislation

With the enactment of the Qualification Directive in April 2004, followed by the Asylum Procedures Directive in December 2005, the EU put into place the final elements of the CEAS. Under the terms of these Directives, the Member States had two years to transpose their standards into national law.[45] Accordingly, the Portuguese Parliament drew up new asylum legislation. Law 27 of June 30, 2008, establishes the conditions and procedures for granting asylum and subsidiary protection,[46] and it defines subsidiary protection more broadly than the Qualification Directive requires. First, the Portuguese legislation provides beneficiaries of subsidiary protection with two-year renewable residence permits, in contrast to the one-year permit mentioned in the Qualification Directive.[47] Second, those receiving subsidiary protection who are unable to obtain national passports may request a Portuguese national passport for foreigners, if they wish to travel

---

[40] *Id.* art. 28(2).

[41] *Id.* art. 26(1).

[42] *Id.* art. 26(3).

[43] *Id.* art. 28 (1).

[44] *Id.* art. 28(2).

[45] Procedures Directive, *supra* note 22, art. 43.

[46] Law 27/2008 of 30th June, Establishes the Conditions and Procedures for Granting Asylum and Subsidiary Protection and the Statuses of Asylum Applicant, Refugee and of Subsidiary Protection, Transposing into Internal Juridical Order Council Directives ns 2004/83/CE, of 29th April and 2005/85/CE, of 1st December.

[47] *Id.* art. 67(2).

outside Portugal;[48] there is no requirement that they show serious humanitarian reasons that require their presence in another State.

More significantly, Portugal grants subsidiary protection to those who lack a fear of persecution but are unable to return to their homeland either "due to the systematic violation of human rights" or on account of the risk of suffering severe harm.[49] Human rights violations as a predicate for subsidiary protection are not mentioned in the Qualification Directive, but Portugal has listed them as an alternative basis for protection. Furthermore, the Portuguese legislation expressly adopts a broader view of "serious harm" than the Directive. In addition to threats from indiscriminate violence and the other circumstances categorized as "serious harm" in the Qualification Directive, Portugal's law includes "a generalized and indiscriminate violation of human rights."[50]

Most important, the Portuguese asylum law guarantees equal substantive rights to those needing protection. Refugees and those provided subsidiary protection have the same access to the labor market and the same right to work.[51] Refugees and those granted subsidiary protection also have identical rights to social assistance.[52] They have equal rights to health care,[53] education,[54] housing,[55] integration programs,[56] and freedom of movement within Portugal.[57] Other than the length of the original residence permit, the Portuguese legislation treats the two statuses in an identical fashion.

III. Conclusion

In the early part of the twenty-first century a new CEAS is unfolding. As a member of the European Union, Portugal must comply with the new EU minimum standards on asylum. Portugal's initial response to the EU asylum law – at least on paper – is to establish protections that exceed the

---

[48] *Id.* art. 69.
[49] *Id.* art. 7(1).
[50] *Id.* art. 7(2)(c).
[51] *Id.* art. 71.
[52] *Id.* art. 72.
[53] *Id.* art. 73.
[54] *Id.* art. 70.
[55] *Id.* art. 74.
[56] *Id.* art. 76.
[57] *Id.* art. 75.

minimum required. The Portuguese asylum law is only one year old, and the CEAS has only been existence for a short while longer. It is too soon to be able to evaluate the implementation of these new provisions. We must watch how the law develops in Portugal as well as in the European Union as a whole to know whether the guarantee of subsidiary protection makes an appreciable difference to people fleeing serious threats of harm in their homelands.

Creating an Effective, Humane U.S. Immigration Enforcement Policy As a Pillar of Comprehensive Reform

DONALD KERWIN[*]

President Obama has agreed to begin the push for immigration reform legislation in 2009. His vision includes many of the components of "comprehensive" legislation that have been supported by groups as diverse as the Catholic Church, the American Bar Association, and organized labor. Under this view, legislation should include:

- a legal immigration system that furthers U.S. economic competitiveness and reflects its labor needs;
- a family-based immigration system that privileges timely family reunification and recognizes the central role of family in integrating immigrants in U.S. society;
- a commitment to attracting foreign-born students in science, mathematics, and engineering, and professionals who pursue careers in related fields;
- earned legal status and ultimately citizenship for unauthorized persons who meet certain strict requirements;
- enforcement policies that promote the rule of law, protect national security, and honor human rights;

[*] Executive Director, Center for Migration Studies of New York (CMS).

- strategies to address the root causes of immigration in migrant-
-sending nations;
- the establishment of cooperative, mutually supportive relationships
with migrant source nations (particularly Mexico); and
- integration policies that seek to incorporate the nation's historic
number of foreign-born persons fully into the nation's life.

The new administration, of course, faces more pressing priorities than immigration, including the economic crisis, health care reform, and the wars in Iraq and Afghanistan. In addition, it wants to avoid the furious public reaction that greeted the last serious attempt at broad immigration legislation. Comprehensive legislation collapsed in 2007 due, in large part, to the widespread belief that the United States first needed to establish its credibility in enforcing its borders and establishing the rule of law. In fact, immigration enforcement spending has risen dramatically since the establishment of the Department of Homeland Security (DHS) in 2003.[1] The budgets of the two DHS immigration enforcement agencies, Customs and Border Protection (CBP) and Immigration and Customs Enforcement (ICE), have nearly doubled in the six years since their creation.[2] More to the point, a system characterized by regulated, legal immigration would contribute to immigration enforcement and national security.

This article will attempt to outline the contours of an effective, humane immigration enforcement policy that could be part of a comprehensive shift in U.S. immigration policy. It will pay particular attention to enforce-ment within the "interior" of the nation, drawing extensively on a report released in February 2009 by the Migration Policy Institute (MPI) titled *DHS and Immigration: Taking Stock and Correcting Course.*[3] The MPI report identified the 18 goals set forth below as key to an effective, humane immi-gration enforcement policy.

---

[1] Homeland Security Act of 2002, Pub. L. No. 107-296, 116 Stat. 2135.

[2] DORIS MEISSNER & DONALD KERWIN, MIGRATION POLICY INST., DHS AND IMMIGRATION: TAKING STOCK AND CORRECTING COURSE 8-9, 100 (2009), *available at* http://www.migrationpolicy.org/pubs/DHS_Feb09.pdf.

[3] *Id.*

1. Development and assessment of a broad U.S. immigration enforcement plan

The MPI report proposed that the Obama administration establish a task force comprised of relevant federal agencies to develop, modify, and evaluate a comprehensive immigration enforcement plan. Each year, the task force should assess the effectiveness of the plan and recommend adjustments in the mix and level of enforcement strategies and resource allocations. The participating agencies should also monitor and review DHS's performance in carrying out its border enforcement, investigative, detention, and removal functions. An early responsibility should be to assess the enforcement benefits of DHS/ICE work-site raids, state and local immigration enforcement agreements, and mandatory employer verification programs as compared to the costs to U.S. families, businesses, and local communities.

The task force could be convened by the Homeland Security Council (HSC). Established by the Homeland Security Act, the HSC coordinates the activities of the federal agencies and departments that contribute to homeland security.[4] The Obama administration has announced that it is considering folding the HSC into the National Security Council (NSC) in order to better coordinate domestic and foreign-policy national security responsibilities.

2. The need to control U.S. borders

The need to control U.S. borders and to enforce its immigration laws may be the only area of consensus in the U.S. immigration debate. This consensus has been reflected in significantly increased enforcement along the U.S.-Mexico border, including funding for 20,019 Border Patrol agents (up from 3,638 in 1986), 670 miles of fencing, and a border surveillance system.[5] In 1994, the Immigration and Naturalization Service (INS) established a border control policy of "deterrence through detention" that concentrated agents and enforcement resources in traditionally heavy crossing routes.[6] In response to post-9/11 threats, DHS developed a new

---

[4] Homeland Security Act § 901, 116 Stat. at 2258 (codified as amended at 6 U.S.C. § 491); § 904, 116 Stat. at 2259 (codified as amended at 6 U.S.C. § 494).

[5] MEISSNER & KERWIN, *supra* note 2, at 10-12.

[6] *See* DONALD KERWIN & SERENA YI-YING LIN, MIGRATION POLICY INST., IMMIGRANT DETENTION: CAN ICE MEET ITS LEGAL IMPERATIVES AND CASE MANAGEMENT RESPONSIBILITIES? 6 (2009).

border enforcement strategy with five objectives: (1) to establish the "substantial probability of apprehending terrorists and their weapons as they attempt to enter illegally"; (2) to deter illegal migration through improved enforcement; (3) to detect, arrest, and deter human, drug, and contraband smugglers; (4) to use "smart border" technology as a force- and deterrent-multiplier; and (5) to reduce crime in border communities.[7]

An effective, humane, and integrated enforcement plan will need to address the root causes of forced migration to strengthen multilateral security and enforcement arrangements, to reform the U.S. immigration system, and to combine domestic immigration and labor enforcement measures. The success of immigration control policies will depend on close collaboration within DHS, between DHS and other federal agencies, between federal, state, and local agencies, and with migrant sending nations. Dismantling international criminal networks, for example, will require multilateral law enforcement and security strategies, including financial and technical assistance to partner nations.

3. Targeting the criminal infrastructure that underlies large-scale, illegal migration, that preys on migrants, and that could facilitate terrorist infiltration

The international criminal networks that facilitate illegal migration and employment, often abuse migrants in transit, abandon them in the desert, hold them hostage in safe houses, and even sell them into involuntary servitude.[8] Sophisticated smuggling enterprises may also serve as a vehicle for terrorist infiltration.[9]

ICE's mission is "to detect and prevent terrorist and criminal acts by targeting the people, money, and materials that support terrorist and criminal networks."[10] ICE has repeatedly defined its responsibilities in terms of national security and public safety. According to its 2007 annual report,

---

[7] ALISON SISKIN ET AL. CONG. RESEARCH SERV., RL 33351, IMMIGRATION ENFORCEMENT WITHIN THE UNITED STATES 53 (2006).

[8] *Id.* 26 ("[A]lien smuggling can lead to collateral crimes including kidnapping, homicide, assault, rape, robbery, auto theft, high speed flight, vehicle accident, identity theft, and the manufacturing and distribution of fraudulent documents.").

[9] *Id.* 28.

[10] U.S. IMMIGRATION & CUSTOMS ENFORCEMENT, ICE FISCAL YEAR 2007 ANNUAL REPORT: PROTECTING NATIONAL SECURITY AND UPHOLDING PUBLIC SAFETY 1.

the agency targets "criminal networks and terrorist organizations that seek to exploit vulnerabilities" in the U.S. immigration system, financial networks, U.S. borders, and federal facilities.[11] Its performance should be measured based on its success in targeting the "people, money, and materials that support terrorist and criminal networks."[12] As with any effective law enforcement agency, its priority should be to dismantle organized criminal enterprises and to prosecute high-level criminals, rather than their victims or otherwise law-abiding, hard-working persons.

4. Creation of a viable employer verification system

DHS's principal interior enforcement goal should be to ensure compliance with the U.S. law that requires employers to verify identity and eligibility to work, and to punish "bad-faith" employers who prefer to hire and exploit unauthorized workers. In FY 2008, DHS removed (deported) 349,041 persons,[13] up from 50,924 in 1995.[14] However, total removals in FY 2008 still represented less than three percent of the nation's more than 11 million unauthorized persons. DHS cannot remove even a large percentage of the nation's unauthorized population, and this should not be its goal. Nor should its goal be to crack down on all employers who hire unauthorized workers in order to remove the "magnet" to illegal migration created by available jobs.

ICE will never be successful in enforcing the law without widespread compliance by the great majority of the nation's 7.6 million business establishments and 6 million business organizations (firms).[15] Most employers want to comply with the immigration laws, just as they customarily obey tax, minimum wage, and workplace safety laws. However, employers need

---

[11] *Id.* at iii.

[12] *Id.* at 1.

[13] Press Release, U.S. Immigration & Customs Enforcement, ICE Multifaceted Strategy Leads to Record Enforcement Results: Removals, Criminal Arrests, and Worksite Investigations Soared in Fiscal Year 2008 (Oct. 23, 2008), *available at* https://www.ice.gov/news/releases/ice-multifaceted-strategy-leads-record-enforcement-results.

[14] Office of Immigration Statistics, U.S. Dep't of Homeland Security, 2007 Yearbook of Immigration Statistics 95 (2008), *available at* http://www.dhs.gov/xlibrary/assets/statistics/yearbook/2007/ois_2007_yearbook.pdf.

[15] U.S. Census Bureau, Number of Firms, Number of Establishments, Employment and Annual Payroll by Employment Size of the Enterprise for the United States and States, Totals – 2006, *availabe at* http://www.census.gov//econ/susb/data/susb2006.html.

a reliable, efficient way to identify prospective employees and to determine their eligibility to work. This will require fraud-resistant identification and work-eligibility cards, accurate government databases, and the ability of workers to correct database errors expeditiously.

Once "customary compliance" with the law is established among good-faith employers, ICE will be able to direct its resources to the criminal infrastructure that facilitates illegal hiring and employment, and at those corporations whose business model depends on the exploitation of unauthorized laborers to the detriment of all U.S. workers.[16]

DHS's employer verification system rests on a legal framework created by the Immigration Reform and Control Act of 1986 (IRCA).[17] IRCA sought to foster permanent reductions in the U.S. unauthorized population in three ways. First, IRCA offered unauthorized immigrants two principal paths to legal status, which ultimately benefitted nearly three million persons. Second, it attempted to eliminate the "magnet" of employment by making it unlawful "to hire, or to recruit or refer for a fee ... knowing the alien" is ineligible to work.[18] Third, it sought to increase U.S. border control activities.

Of all the forms of immigration enforcement, employer verification has the potential to be the most humane, efficient, and effective. If successful, it lessens the need for more expensive, dangerous, and restrictive types of enforcement. It also enlists employers as a force-multiplier in its attempt to reduce or eliminate illegal migration.

The U.S. Government Accountability Office (GAO) reported that:

> [D]ocument fraud (use of counterfeit documents) and identity fraud (fraudualent use of valid documents or information belonging to others) have made it difficult for employers who want to comply with the employment verification process to ensure that they hire only authorized workers and have made it easier for unscrupulous employers to knowingly hire unauthorized workers.[19]

---

[16] MEISSNER & KERWIN, *supra* note 2, at 27.

[17] Pub. L. No. 99-603, 100 Stat. 3359 (1986).

[18] *Id.* § 101, 100 Stat. at 3360 (codified as amended at 8 U.S.C. §1324a).

[19] U.S. GOV'T ACCOUNTABILITY OFFICE, GAO-05-813, IMMIGRATION ENFORCEMENT: WEAKNESSES HINDER EMPLOYMENT VERIFICATION AND WORKSITE ENFORCEMENT EFFORTS 5 (2005).

To address this concern, the Illegal Immigration Reform and Immigrant Responsibility Act of 1996 (IIRIRA) directed DHS to create a voluntary, electronic verification program that would allow employers to match information from an employee's I-9 form with the DHS and Social Security Administration (SSA) databases.[20] As of 2008, 88,116 employers had enrolled in the E-Verify program.[21] Some states have made the program mandatory for all state employers or for state employers and contractors. The Obama administration has delayed the implementation of a rule requiring federal contractors with contracts in excess of $100,000 to participate in the program pending a broader review of E-Verify.[22]

The E-Verify program has been criticized for its high-rate of "false negatives" (employees incorrectly found to be ineligible to work), the high error rates in the SSA and DHS databases, its improper use by employers, and its inefficiency.[23]

DHS has reported that 3.9 percent of employees screened by E-verify receive "tentative non-confirmations" of work eligibility, with .37 percent of those employees able to prove their eligibility to work and 3.5 percent ultimately determined to be ineligible to work "because they are either not authorized to work in the United States, did not know that they had the opportunity to challenge an initial mismatch (or TNC), or choose not to follow the necessary procedures to prove work authorization after receiving an initial mismatch."[24]

---

[20] Pub. L. No. 104-208, 110 Stat. 3009, 3009-546 (1996).

[21] U.S. Citizenship & Immigration Servs., U.S. Dep't of Homeland Sec., History and Milestones, http://www.uscis.gov/e-verify/about-program/history-and-milestones (last visited Nov. 15, 2014).

[22] Federal Acquisition Regulation; FAR Case 2007-013, Employment Eligibility Verification, 74 Fed. Reg. 26981 (June 5, 2009) (delaying implementation until September 8, 2009); *see* Federal Acquisition Regulation; FAR Case 2007-013, Employment Eligibility Verification, 73 Fed. Reg. 67651 (Nov. 14, 2008).

[23] NAT'L IMMIGRATION LAW CTR., NOT READY FOR PRIME TIME AND NOT A MAGIC BULLET: NEW EXECUTIVE ORDER AND PROPOSED RULE REQUIRE FEDERAL CONTRACTORS TO USE BASIC PILOT/E-VERIFY (July 2008), *available at* http://www.immigrationpolicy.org/sites/default/files/docs/e-verify-exec-order-TPs-2008-07-15.pdf

[24] U.S. Citizenship & Immigration Sers., E-Verify Statistics, http://www.uscis.gov/portal/site/uscis/menuitem.5af9bb95919f35e66f614176543f6d1a/?vgnextoid=f82d8557a487a110VgnVCM1000004718190aRCRD&vgnextchannel=a16988e60a405110VgnVCM100000471 8190aRCRD (last visited Nov. 16, 2014).

DIREITO COMPARADO / COMPARATIVE LAW

The E-Verify program can assist good-faith employers to detect counterfeit documents, but has been less successful in identifying persons who use valid documents belonging to other persons. As a result, it has not solved the significant problem of "false positives" (persons who appear work-eligible but who are not), as has been illustrated by high-profile raids at businesses participating in the program.[25]

Employer verification constitutes the linchpin of an effective, humane enforcement regime. However, reauthorization and expansion of E-Verify should be based on DHS's progress in meeting several conditions, including: (1) the establishment of a secure, biometric, machine – readable card that establishes both identity and work eligibility; (2) improved accuracy rates in SSA and DHS databases; (3) lowered "false negative" rates and an explanation of discrepancies between DHS "false negative" rates and the "rates" found in employer studies; (4) analysis of why 3.5 percent of the persons who receive tentative non-confirmations fail to correct their records; and (5) expansion of DHS program compliance mechanisms.

DHS should also continue to pursue less costly and burdensome alternatives to E-Verify. In the interim, E-Verify should remain a voluntary program. To encourage employers to join, participation in the program should create a rebuttable presumption of compliance with the law. In addition, because IRCA definitively established employer verification as a federal function, state verification rules should be developed only at the direction of the federal government. The program should grow at a pace that DHS can accommodate.

5. Use of the Social Security Administration's no-match program to enforce immigration law

The Social Security Administration's (SSA's) "no match" program was created to credit the estimated $586 billion posted in the SSA's "earnings suspense file" (which includes payments that cannot be matched to social security numbers) to the accounts of the workers who paid into the system.[26] Each year, SSA receives roughly 245 million wage reports, cover-

---

[25] INDEPENDENT TASK FORCE ON IMMIGRATION & AMERICA'S FUTURE, MIGRATION POLICY INST., IMMIGRATION AND AMERICA'S FUTURE: A NEW CHAPTER 49 (2006), *available at* http://www.migrationpolicy.org/research/immigration-and-americas-future-new-chapter.

[26] SOCIAL SECURITY ADMINISTRATION OFFICE OF THE INSPECTOR GENERAL, SOCIAL SECURITY NUMBER MISUSE FOR WORK AND THE IMPACT ON THE SOCIAL SECURITY ADMINISTRATION'S

ing 153 million workers.[27] When an employee's name cannot be matched with a social security number, SSA posts the earnings to its earnings suspense file.

In August 2007, DHS issued a final regulation that would require employers who receive no-match letters to follow certain steps to avoid being found to have "constructive knowledge" that they are employing unauthorized immigrants.[28] On October 10, 2007, the U.S. District Court for the Northern District of California enjoined implementation of the rule.[29] On March 26, 2008, DHS issued a supplemental proposed rule that attempts to re-promulgate the earlier rule, with only minor changes.[30] On October 28, 2008, DHS issued a supplemental final regulation which largely tracks the March 2008 proposed rule.[31] At this writing, the preliminary injunction remains in effect.

Because it undermines the program's very purpose, the SSA no-match program should not be used as an immigration enforcement tool. In addition, the no-match program will be increasingly redundant with E-Verify, relying on the same SSA database. It will also be subject to the same inaccuracies as E-Verify and burdened by the same problem of "false negatives." It would also create significant costs and inefficiencies for employers and employees.

6. Strategies to enforce compliance with employer verification requirements: employer prosecutions, raids, and sanctions

ICE's work-site enforcement program consists of three complementary sets of tools meant to police the employer verification system. First, ICE can

MASTER EARNINGS FILE i (2008), *available at* http://oig.ssa.gov/sites/default/files/audit/full/pdf/A-03-07-27152_0.pdf.; Pia Orrenius, *'No Match,' No Sense*, WALL ST. J., Aug. 13, 2007.

[27] Steffanie Bevington, *Giving Employers Guidance: The Proper Response to No-Match Letters under* Aramark Facility Services v. Service Employees International Union, Local 1877, 39 GOLDEN GATE U. L. REV. 387, 387 (2009) (citing U.S. Social Sec. Admin., Overview of Social Security Employer No-Match Letters Process, http://www.ssa.gov/legislation/nomatch2.htm (last visited Mar. 20, 2009)).

[28] Safe-Harbor Procedures for Employers Who Receive a No-Match Letter, 72 Fed. Reg. 45,611, 45,623 (Aug. 15 2007) (to be codifed at 8 C.F.R. Pt. 274a).

[29] Am. Fed'n of Labor v. Chertoff, 552 F.Supp.2d 999, 1015 (N.D. Cal. 2007).

[30] Safe Harbor Procedures for Employers Who Receive No-Match Letter: Clarification; Final Regulatory Flexibility Analysis, 73 Fed. Reg. 15,944 (Mar. 26, 2008) (Supplemental Proposed Rule).

[31] Safe Harbor Procedures for Employers Who Receive a No-match Letter: Clarification; Final Regulatory Flexibility Analysis, 73 Fed. Reg. 63,843, 63,867 (to be codifed at 8 C.F.R. Pt. 274a).

investigate an employer in cooperation with law enforcement and regulatory partners, and refer employers for criminal prosecution. Second, it can audit employers' I-9 forms, fine employers, and refer them for criminal prosecution. Third, it can conduct work-site enforcement "actions" (raids). The *purpose* of these tactics is to enforce the employer verification provisions of the law and to punish non-compliant employers.

Once a reliable verification system is in place, ICE can use its work-site enforcement tools to promote "voluntary" compliance with its requirements by good-faith employers and can try to make non-compliance a prohibitive risk for bad-faith employers. An effective employer verification system would put ICE in a better position, consistent with its mission, to target the criminal networks that facilitate large-scale illegal migration and the employers who intentionally hire and exploit undocumented workers for competitive advantage.

From 2006 through 2008, ICE carried out a succession of high-profile raids at a variety of locations, against many targets. During this period, according to statistics compiled by Centro Legal, Inc., ICE raids included actions against individual employers in 21 states that led to extensive arrests (more than 100 people arrested in a raid).[32]

ICE's work-site actions have targeted sites deemed to be of national security significance, including military facilities, airports, seaports, nuclear plants, and chemical plants.[33] ICE has also pursued employers whose business models rely on unauthorized workers.[34] ICE should target employers who flagrantly violate immigration, labor, work-place protection, and other laws. As early as 1998, an INS memorandum stipulated that because "the purpose of worksite enforcement is to deter the unlawful employment of aliens ... worksite enforcement investigations that involve alien smuggling, human rights abuses, and other criminal violations must take precedence."[35]

---

[32] CENTRO LEGAL, INC., COMPREHENSIVE DOCUMENTATION OF IMMIGRATION ENFORCEMENT OPERATIONS (2008), *available at* https://tunkas2009.files.wordpress.com/2009/02/comprehensive_raid_list.pdf.

[33] U.S. Immigration & Customs Enforcement, U.S. Department of Homeland Security, Worksite Enforcement, https://www.ice.gov/worksite (last visited Nov. 16, 2014).

[34] Michael Chertoff, *Myth vs. Fact: Worksite Enforcement*, LEADERSHIP JOURNAL (July 9, 2008) http://www.dhs.gov/journal/leadership/2008/07/myth-vs-fact-worksite-enforcement.html.

[35] Immigration & Naturalization Ser., Immediate Action Directive for Worksite Enforcement Operations, (May 22, 1998) (reprinted in 75 INTERPRETER RELEASES 987, 987-96 (July 17, 1998)).

Raids can serve as a warning to otherwise law-abiding employers on the need to meet their employer verification responsibilities. However, they likely have little impact in their primary goal of "disrupting the infrastructure that supports illegal immigration."[36] Rather than uprooting human smuggling syndicates, false document rings, and scofflaw employers, ICE has linked undocumented *employees* to the criminal "infrastructure" that supports illegal migration, characterizing the mere *use* of false documents as "identity theft" or "aggravated identity theft."

7. Measuring level-of-effort and the success of enforcement measures
It is difficult to evaluate the success of ICE's work-site enforcement strategies, given its spotty and inconsistent record-keeping. ICE needs to establish mission-appropriate performance metrics. As it stands, ICE reports no activity in key work-site enforcement areas. In addition, "administrative arrests" constitute the only carried-over enforcement metric from the transition from INS to DHS/ICE. However, the available data suggest that while ICE's work-site enforcement activities have increased in its short existence, they fall well below historically high levels of INS enforcement.

By the one consistently tracked indicia of work-site enforcement ("administrative" arrests), ICE enforcement levels have not come near pre-DHS rates. By way of comparison, INS arrested an average of 6,625 persons per year between 1988 and 1994, 13,911 persons on average between 1995 and 1998, and 1,255 on average between 1999 and 2002.[37] Between 2003 and 2008, ICE administrative arrests rose steadily from 445 to 5,173, but still fell well below historic highs.[38]

Criminal prosecutions based on work-site activities increased steadily between 2001 and 2008, rising from 72 to 1,092.[39] Work-site related prosecutions peaked in the aftermath of a raid at a meatpacking plant in Postville, Iowa, in which 389 people were arrested and 306 were criminally charged. Prosecutors used the threat of aggravated identity theft,

---

[36] Chertoff, *supra* note 34.
[37] Office of Immigration Statistics, U.S. Department of Homeland Security, Employer Investigation Activities of the INS and ICE Immigration Investigations Program Fiscal Years 1986-2008 (2008).
[38] *Id.*
[39] *Id.*

DIREITO COMPARADO / COMPARATIVE LAW

a crime with a minimum two-year sentence, to pressure immigrants to plead to lesser crimes.

8. National security and immigration enforcement

ICE has too often located its work-site raids and other enforcement activities within a national security paradigm. ICE plays an important, mission-appropriate role in enforcing compliance with the law by good-faith employers and by punishing employers who flagrantly violate immigration, labor, work-place protection, and other laws. However, it undermines its credibility and its legitimate role in protecting the homeland when it exaggerates vulnerabilities to terrorism, identifies risk where it does not exist, or mischaracterizes its work.

ICE has applied a security paradigm to unlikely security risks like, for example, Maya women from Guatemala who worked in a factory (raided by ICE) that made backpacks for the U.S. military in New Bedford, Massachusetts. It has framed all of its work-site enforcement activities in terms of security, either personal (e.g., identity theft), corporate, or national. It has argued that unauthorized persons would be subject to terrorist coercion due to their lack of status.[40]

Such a scenario assumes that persons who work in secure facilities would not report terrorist plots, that terrorists would know the immigration status of employees in these facilities, and that they would enlist the assistance of strangers who might otherwise come to the attention of law enforcement officials. On the latter point, terrorists have proven far more likely to limit planning for attacks and to recruit persons who do not have criminal records or who would not otherwise draw attention from law enforcement.[41]

---

[40] Statement of Julie L. Myers, Assistant Secretary, U.S. Immigration and Customs Enforcement, Before the House Appropriations Committee, Subcommittee on Homeland Security, Mar. 27, 2007, at 14 ("Unauthorized workers employed at sensitive sites and critical infrastructure facilities – such as airports, seaports, nuclear plants, chemical plants, and defense facilities – pose serious homeland threats. Not only are the identities of these individuals in question, but these aliens are vulnerable to exploitation by terrorists and other criminals given their illegal status in this country."), *available at* http://www.ice.gov/doclib/news/library/speeches/070327budget.pdf.

[41] Donald Kerwin & Margaret Stock, *National Security and Immigration Policy: Reclaiming Terms, Measuring Success, and Setting Priorities,* 1 HOMELAND SECURITY REV. 131, 183-184 (2007).

9. Guidelines on whether and how to conduct work-site raids

In 2008, ICE devoted two percent of its total budget to worksite enforcement investigations.[42] In 2009, it arrested 5,187 persons during raids, less than two percent of the 349,041 persons it removed and only a fraction of a percent of the nation's unauthorized population.[43] Yet raids have an oversized impact on local communities and immigrant families.

In 2007, the Urban Institute concluded that for every two immigrants arrested in a raid, a U.S. child lost a parent (to arrest and deportation) and that two-thirds of the affected children were U.S. citizens.[44] The report detailed the hardship worked on newly fragmented families and the emergency-response role assumed by charitable and social service agencies in the wake of raids.

In November 2007, ICE released humanitarian guidelines on the conduct of raids that provided for the release of sole caregivers arrested during raids; toll-free hotlines for the family members of arrested persons; notification to non-governmental organizations (NGOs) once a raid is underway; coordination with federal, state, and local officials on humanitarian release decisions; and access to legal counsel.[45]

ICE should affirm, strengthen, and adhere to its protocols. It should extend its protocols to provide that arrested workers be screened for information on human smuggling rings and on employer violations of immigration, labor, and workplace protection laws. Arrested workers should be considered for "U" and "T" non-immigrant visas for their cooperation in the investigation and prosecution of criminal violations.

Finally, ICE should centralize its process for approving raids and adopt guidelines on whether to conduct a raid. Relevant considerations should include whether the raid will further an ICE work-site enforcement priority and whether its benefits will likely be outweighed by the damage to local communities and to U.S. families.

---

[42] MEISSNER & KERWIN, *supra* note 2, at 32.

[43] U.S. Immigration and Customs Enforcement, News Release, *ICE multifaceted strategy leads to record enforcement results: Removals, criminal arrests and worksite investigations soared in fiscal year 2008* (October 23, 2008), *available at* http://www.ice.gov/news/releases/ice-multifaceted-strategy-leads-record-enforcement-results.

[44] RANDY CAPPS ET AL., THE URBAN INSTITUTE, PAYING THE PRICE: THE IMPACT OF IMMIGRATION RAIDS ON AMERICA'S CHILDREN 15-20 (2007), *available at* http://www.urban.org/UploadedPDF/411566_immigration_raids.pdf.

[45] MEISSNER & KERWIN, *supra* note 2, at 33.

10. The use of criminal prosecution as an immigration enforcement strategy

Over the last 20 years, criminal prosecution for immigration-related offenses has sharply increased. As reported by the Transactional Records Access Clearinghouse (TRAC) at Syracuse University, immigration-related referrals for criminal prosecution have grown from 8.6 percent of all federal criminal referrals in 1987, to 9.9 percent in 1997, to 27.2 percent in 2007.[46] By contrast, FBI referrals have sharply declined as a percentage of total federal referrals, from 36 percent in 1987, to 33.4 percent in 1997, to 16.4 percent in 2007. Between 2000 and 2008, federal criminal prosecutions for immigration-related crimes increased nearly five-fold, from 16,724 to 79,400.[47]

Immigration-related criminal cases are heard in U.S. Magistrate Courts and U.S. District Courts. In August 2008, 64 percent of immigration convictions took place in Magistrate Courts, which handle less serious offenses, with the most frequent charge being illegal entry.[48] By contrast, re-entry of a deported alien was overwhelmingly the most common, immigration-related offense in U.S. District Courts.[49] Most immigration-related prosecutions continue to occur in border districts, but with significant increases in non-border communities.[50]

U.S. attorneys have not adopted consistent standards related to the severity of immigration violations that merit prosecution, and practices vary. Under Operation Streamline and other "zero tolerance" prosecution programs, DHS refers for criminal prosecution all immigration-related violations in particular Border Patrol sectors.

Because illegal crossings have diminished in the targeted areas during periods of intensive prosecution, DHS maintains that the program has had a deterrent effect.[51] However, no evidence exists that this strat-

---

[46] *Shifting Enforcement Priorities*, TRAC Reports (Mar. 6, 2008), http://trac.syr.edu/tracreports/crim/186/.

[47] *Federal Criminal Prosecutions Filed by Selected Program Areas*, TRAC Reports (2007), http://trac.syr.edu/tracreports/crim/184/include/table_1.html.

[48] Meissner & Kerwin, *supra* note 2, at 40-41.

[49] *Id.*

[50] *Id.*

[51] U.S. Department of Homeland Security, Press Release, *Remarks by Homeland Security Secretary Michael Chertoff and Attorney General Mukasey at a Briefing on Immigration Enforcement*

egy has deterred illegal crossings across the entire U.S.-Mexico border. It may simply be that "zero tolerance" strategies move or temporarily displace illegal migration streams. In addition, DHS has not addressed the widespread suspicion that the prosecution of relatively minor immigration offenses diminishes the resources available to prevent and prosecute more serious crimes.

11. Placing non-citizens who have been arrested and are serving prison time in removal proceedings

It has long been an INS/DHS priority to initiate removal proceedings for non-citizens serving criminal sentences prior to their release from prison. At present, ICE screens prisoners at all federal and state prisons, and at 10 percent of the nation's 3,100 jails.[52] Its goal is to screen all foreign-born persons in every federal, state, and local institution in the nation.

DHS ultimately plans to provide federal, state, and local law enforcement officials with access to its databases during the booking process.[53] This raises a risk that localities with Inter-governmental Service Agreements will arrest non-citizens for minor violations of the law, including traffic violations, as a way to generate additional revenue. At present, police officers check fingerprints against the Federal Bureau of Investigation's (FBI's) database, but not DHS databases. Once the FBI and DHS systems become inter-operable, DHS databases will be automatically checked for immigration history at the time that FBI databases are checked for criminal history.

In FY 2008, ICE initiated removal proceedings against 221,000 persons in federal, state, and local jails, more than triple the number from FY 2006. ICE should pursue its plans: (1) to provide federal, state, and local law enforcement officials with access to its database; (2) to screen non-citizens serving criminal sentences; (3) to place non-citizens into removal proceedings prior to the completion of their criminal sentences; and, (4) to secure travel documents for those persons serving criminal sentences

---

and Border Security Efforts (February 22, 2008), *available at* Am. Immigration Lawyers Ass'n, http://www.aila.org/infonet/dhs-secretary-chertoff-and-attorney-general-mukase.

[52] U.S. Immigration & Customs Enforcement, Fact Sheet, Secure Communities (March 28, 2008).

[53] U.S. Immigration & Customs Enforcement, News Release, Department of Homeland Security Unveils Comprehensive Immigration Enforcement Strategy for the Nation's Interior (April 20, 2006).

DIREITO COMPARADO / COMPARATIVE LAW

who are ultimately ordered removed. It should also ensure that inmates in removal proceedings or those who may face prolonged civil detention upon completion of their prison sentences have access to legal counsel.

12. Prosecution of national security risks and dangerous criminals

DHS should be particularly vigilant in identifying removable persons who threaten security or public safety and in initiating removal proceeding against them. It should also refer dangerous criminals for prosecution.

The numbers and percentages of persons DHS has charged on criminal, national security, and terrorist grounds have decreased from pre-DHS levels.[54] In a study of immigration court data from 1992 to 2006, TRAC found that INS charged an average of 61 persons per year with national security and terrorism grounds of removal between 1992 and 2001. However, between 2003 and 2006, DHS initiated removal proceedings against an average of 41 persons per year on national security and terrorism-related grounds. Individuals charged in immigration court on criminal grounds peaked in 1997 at 52,750, and declined steadily to 32,142 in 2006.[55]

DHS has argued that it occasionally opts to charge immigrants for routine immigration violations, rather than on more complex security and terrorist grounds. However, this practice would presumably have been in place pre-DHS as well. Despite the expanded criminal grounds for removal, only 36 percent of those removed by ICE between 2003 and 2007 were removed on "criminal grounds" *or* had been identified by DHS as "criminals" but were removed on other grounds.

TRAC also analyzed the cases referred for *criminal* prosecution on terrorist grounds in the two years following 9/11.[56] It found that prosecutors opted not to prosecute in 64 percent of the 6,472 "terrorism" or "anti-terrorism" referrals during this period, and charges were dismissed or the individuals were found not guilty in 9 percent of the cases referred.[57] Of the 1,329 persons convicted over a five-year period, 14 persons (one per-

---

[54] *Immigration Enforcement: The Rhetoric, The Reality*, TRAC REPORTS (May 28, 2007), http://trac.syr.edu/immigration/reports/178/.

[55] *Charged in Immigration Court by Charge Category FY 1992-2006*, TRAC REPORTS (2007), http://trac.syr.edu/immigration/reports/178/include/timeseries.html.

[56] *Criminal Terrorism Enforcement in the United States During the Five Years Since the 9/11/01 Attacks*, TRAC REPORTS (Sept. 4, 2006), http://trac.syr.edu/tracreports/terrorism/169/.

[57] *Id.*

cent) received a sentence of 20 years or more, 67 (five percent) received sentences of five or more years, 327 received sentences of one day to less than one year, and 704 received no prison time.[58]

During the same period, federal investigative agencies referred 1,391 persons for prosecution as "international terrorists," an expansive category that encompasses 80 crimes.[59] Prosecutors filed charges against 335 of the persons referred, but declined to prosecute in 748 cases.[60] Of the 213 persons convicted, 123 were sentenced to prison, with 90 receiving no prison sentences, 91 receiving sentences of one day or less than one year, 18 receiving sentences of one to five years, eight receiving sentences of five to 20 years, and six receiving sentences of 20 years to life.[61]

13. Prioritizing the arrest of persons ordered removed on criminal and national security grounds

The National Fugitive Operations Program (NFOP) has been one of ICE's most highly touted, fastest growing enforcement initiatives. Despite the name, the NFOP does not pursue "fugitives" in the sense of persons who have committed crimes and eluded arrest. Instead, the NFOP targets noncitizens who have been ordered removed, but have not left the country. Estimates of the number of "fugitives" or "absconders" have ranged from 314,000 in January 2002, to 623,292 in August 2006, to 560,000 at the end of FY 2008.[62] These figures seem to be highly elastic and suspect.

The NFOP had its genesis in post-9/11 "absconder removal teams" which were tasked with arresting and removing persons who had been ordered removed. In January 2002, the Department of Justice introduced the Absconder Apprehension Initiative with an initial focus on "priority" absconders from countries with an "Al Qaeda terrorist presence or activity."[63] In June 2002, Attorney General John Ashcroft announced the National Security Entry/Exit Registration System (NSEERS) program,

[58] *Id.*

[59] *Id.*

[60] *Id.*

[61] *Id.*

[62] U.S. DEP'T OF HOMELAND SECURITY, OFFICE OF INSPECTOR GEN., OIG-07-34, ASSESSMENT OF DEPARTMENT OF HOMELAND SECURITY'S FUGITIVE OPERATIONS TEAMS, 3-4 (2007).

[63] Memorandum from Larry Thompson, Deputy Attorney Gen., to the INS Comm'r, the FBI Dir., the U.S. Marshals Serv., and U.S. Attorneys, Jan. 25, 2002, *available at* FindLaw, http://fl1.findlaw.com/news.findlaw.com/hdocs/docs/doj/abscndr012502mem.pdf.

which attempted to track and ensure the timely departure of non-immigrants from terrorist producing countries.[64] In its detention and removal plan for 2003 to 2012, ICE identified the removal of "all removable aliens" to be a critical pre-condition to national security.[65]

By the end of FY 2008, ICE had 95 Fugitive Operations Teams (FOTs), up from just eight teams in FY 2003.[66] Apprehensions by FOTs increased from 6,584 in FY 2003 to 34,155 in FY 2008.[67] Funding for the program grew from $9 million in FY 2003 to $219 million in FY 2008.

Until August 2008, FOTs relied on DHS's 24-year-old Deportable Alien Control System (DACS) for information on persons ordered removed. In 2006, DHS's Office of Inspector General (OIG) concluded that the DACs database was "not always accurate and up to date."[68] Exacerbating database problems, persons ordered removed frequently move and are not likely to register changes-of-address with DHS. As a result, FOTs have consistently sought absconders at past or inaccurate addresses, and have arrested the unauthorized persons that they encounter at these residences.

Consistent with its mission, ICE has set the following "fugitive" apprehension priorities: (1) persons posing a threat to the nation; (2) persons posing a threat to the community; (3) persons with a violent criminal history; (4) persons with criminal convictions; and, (5) persons with no criminal convictions.[69] However, an MPI study found that 73 percent of the persons arrested by FOTs between 2003 and 2008 did not have criminal

---

[64] John Ashcroft, Att'y Gen., U.S. Dep't of Justice, Prepared Remarks on the National Security Entry-Exit Registration System (June 6, 2002), *available at* http://www.justice.gov/archive/ag/speeches/2002/060502agpreparedremarks.htm.

[65] U.S. Dep't of Homeland Sec., Immigration & Customs Enforcement, Endgame: Office of Detention and Removal Strategic Plan, 2002-2012: Detention and Removal Strategy for a Secure Homeland 2-2 (2003).

[66] U.S. Immigration & Customs Enforcement, *99 Aliens Arrested by Fugitive Operations Teams in the Dallas Area* (October 10, 2008).

[67] U.S. Immigration & Customs Enforcement, ICE Fugitive Operations Program (November 19, 2008).

[68] U.S. Dep't of Homeland Sec., Office of Inspector Gen., OIG-06-33, Detention and Removal of Illegal Aliens 24 (2006).

[69] U.S. Dep't of Homeland Sec., Office of Inspector Gen., OIG-07-34, Assessment of United States Immigration and Customs Enforcement's Fugitive Operations Teams 8 (2007).

records.[70] In 2007, "fugitive aliens" with criminal convictions represented only 9 percent of FOT arrests, down from 32 percent in 2003.[71]

The MPI report recommended that the program should target the population it was created to target, that is, persons ordered deported who threaten national security, public safety, or who have a criminal history. However, 80 percent of ICE "fugitives" do not have criminal histories.[72] Thus, ICE cannot expect FOTs to arrest a high percentage of "criminals" unless it narrows the program's focus.

14. The role of state and local law enforcement agencies in immigration enforcement

One of the most contentious issues in the U.S. immigration debate has been the role that state and local law enforcement should play in assisting ICE. Immigration is an area of federal authority. However, DHS views state and local police and correctional officials as a potential "force multiplier." IIRIRA created a formal mechanism, which had long existed in practice, to partner with local police forces and sheriffs' offices to perform certain immigration functions.[73] To date, ICE has entered 67 "287(g)" agreements (named after the relevant section of the Immigration and Nationality Act) with states and localities, and has trained 950 local officers and prison officials to enforce immigration laws.[74]

Many police chiefs and trade associations have opposed taking on immigration enforcement functions that conflict with their core responsibilities to protect and defend the public. They argue that community cooperation will flag if police officers routinely screen community members for immigration status violations. In addition, state and local officials lack expertise in federal immigration law and do not want to enforce areas of the law beyond their jurisdiction, competence, and resources. At the same time,

---

[70] MARGOT MENDELSON ET AL., MIGRATION POLICY INST., COLLATERAL DAMAGE: AN EXAMINATION OF ICE's FUGITIVE OPERATIONS PROGRAM 11-13 (2009), *available at* http://www.migrationpolicy.org/pubs/NFOP_Feb09.pdf.

[71] *Id.*

[72] U.S. Immigration & Customs Enforcement, News Release, New ICE program gives non-criminal fugitive aliens opportunity to avoid arrest and detention: Aliens and families to benefit from coordinated removals (July 31, 2008).

[73] SISKIN ET AL., *supra* note 7, at 56.

[74] U.S. Immigration and Customs Enforcement, Fact Sheet, The ICE 287(g) Program: A Law Enforcement Partnership (November 19, 2008).

most recognize the importance of determining the identity of persons that they stop and arrest, of ensuring that they do not release dangerous criminals, and of assisting in the process of placing non-citizen criminals in removal proceedings prior to their release from prison.

ICE should limit its 287(g) agreements and its working relationships with local law enforcement agencies to three areas which respect the missions and resource limitations of both ICE and the local agencies. First, local officials should be trained and deputized to identify non-citizen criminals who are serving time in their prisons and jails, assuming that DHS/ICE cannot perform this role. This type of arrangement will assist ICE in initiating removal proceedings against non-citizens prior to their release from prison and serve both federal and local interests in protecting the public.

On the other hand, ICE should not enlist state and local police to check the immigration status of those they routinely stop, customarily protect, or arrest for minor infractions. Immigrants will not report crimes, come forward as witnesses, or otherwise cooperate with the police if it might lead to their deportation or the deportation of a family member.

Second, state and local police need to be able to *identify* persons that they arrest for their own safety and for the protection of the community. In most cases, identification should not lead to placing people in removal proceedings. However, it will prevent the release of dangerous criminals posing as others. Along these lines, the Law Enforcement Support Center (LESC) allows federal, state, and local officers to secure identity, immigration status, and criminal history about foreign-born persons they are investigating or have arrested. ICE has made it a priority to add the records of certain immigration violators (including absconders) to the FBI's National Crime Information Center (NCIC) database.[75]

Third, ICE should formalize working relationships with states and localities to investigate and prosecute state and local crimes that can assist immigration enforcement efforts. For example, state "nuisance abatement" violations might be pursued as a way to close down smuggler safe houses in certain communities. Similarly, local police should continue to provide

---

[75] *Vulnerabilities in the U.S. Passport System Can Be Exploited by Criminals and Terrorists Before the S. Comm. on Homeland Sec. and Governmental Affairs*, 109th Cong. 22 (2005) (statement of Thomas E. Bush III, Assistant Director, Criminal Justice Information Services Division).

logistical support to ICE during operations that pose a risk to the public or to ICE officers.

15. Prioritizing programs based on mission and impact, and exercising prosecutorial discretion in individual cases

ICE's detention and removal activities seek to ensure that persons ordered removed actually depart and that their countries of origin permit them to return.[76] Nearly one-half of its ICE's 2009 budget (roughly $2.5 billion in total) supports its detention and removal operations. Because ICE cannot remove the more than 11 million unauthorized persons in the United States or even every removable person it encounters, it must set priorities on who it investigates, arrests, places in removal proceedings, and detains.[77] Thus, it should develop a formal policy on prosecutorial discretion, building on past guidelines by INS and ICE.

Prosecutorial discretion refers to the authority of law enforcement officials to investigate, arrest, charge, prosecute, detain, and otherwise exercise their coercive power. While some have argued that ICE should not pick and choose enforcement targets, in fact every successful law enforcement agency prioritizes and calculates how most effectively to use its resources. No law enforcement agency can ensure total compliance with the laws they enforce. In the circumstances, ICE must assess the meaningful differences in culpability and equities among millions of people who have violated the law. Its failure to establish priorities would, in fact, prioritize haphazard and standard-less law enforcement.

IIRIRA and the Anti-Terrorism and Effective Death Penalty Act (AEDPA) expanded the crimes for which non-citizens could be removed, diminished their ability to contest removal and to remain in the United States, and expanded the categories of persons subject to mandatory detention. Following passage of these laws in 1996, lawful permanent residents with longstanding family and equitable ties to the United States could be (and were) removed for relatively minor crimes.[78] Congress should restore

---

[76] U.S. Dep't of Homeland Sec., Budget-in-Brief, Fiscal Year 2009 33 (2008), *available at* http://www.dhs.gov/xlibrary/assets/budget_bib-fy2009.pdf .

[77] U.S. Gov't Accountability Office, GAO-08-67, Immigration Enforcement: ICE Could Improve Controls to Help Guide Alien Removal Decision Making 3 (2007).

[78] Catholic Legal Immigration Network, Inc., The Impact of Our Laws on American Families (2000), *available at* ILW.com, http://www.ilw.com/corporate/about_us.shtm; Am.

discretion to immigration judges to provide relief from removal for immigrants with strong equitable ties to the United States. In the meantime, ICE should exercise its discretion and refrain from putting such persons into removal proceedings, assuming they do not threaten national security or public safety.

In developing its policy guidelines, DHS could productively build on prior INS/DHS instructions. In 2000, for example, the INS issued a memorandum directing officers "to exercise discretion in a judicious manner at all stages of the enforcement process."[79] The memorandum recognized that, given "finite" resources, law enforcement officers cannot investigate or prosecute all violations and must decide on the most effective way to enforce the law. The memorandum instructed officers that they could "decline to prosecute a legally sufficient immigration case if the Federal immigration enforcement interest that would be served by prosecution is not substantial."[80] It detailed several factors that should be considered in assessing whether to exercise discretion: (1) immigration status; (2) length of U.S. residence; (3) criminal history; (4) family ties, medical conditions, and other humanitarian issues; (5) immigration history; (6) likelihood of removal; (7) eligibility for other immigration relief; (8) military service; (9) community attention; and, (10) law enforcement resources.[81]

In October 2007, the GAO analyzed the use of discretion by ICE agents over six phases of the apprehension and removal process: (1) the initial encounter with the non-citizen; (2) apprehension; (3) charging; (4) detention; (5) removal proceedings; and (6) actual removal. It concluded that ICE should develop guidance on exercising discretion related to the apprehension and removal process, including on "humanitarian issues and aliens who are not investigation targets."[82]

BAR ASS'N, AMERICAN JUSTICE THROUGH IMMIGRANTS' EYES 23-44, 59-71 (2004), *available at* http://www.americanbar.org/content/dam/aba/publications/commission_on_immigration/ americanjusticethroughimmigeyes.authcheckdam.pdf.

[79] Memorandum from Doris Meissner, Comm'r, Immigration & Naturalization Ser., to Regional Directors, District Directors, Chief Patrol Agents, Regional & District Counsel, HQOPP 50/4 (Nov. 17, 2000).

[80] Memorandum from Dorris Meissner, Comm'r, Immigration & Naturalization Servs., to Regional Dirs., District Dirs., Chief Patrol Agents & Regional and District Counsel, Exercising Prosecutorial Discretion 5 (Nov. 17, 2000), *available at* Legal Action Center, http://www. legalactioncenter.org/sites/default/files/docs/lac/Meissner-2000-memo.pdf.

[81] *Id.* at 7-8.

[82] U.S. GOV'T ACCOUNTABILITY OFFICE, *supra* note 77, at 34.

16. Enforcement of detention standards

Under the law, ICE *can* detain all non-citizens in removal proceedings. However, since passage of IIRIRA, ICE *must* detain virtually all persons who are removable on criminal or national security grounds, asylum-seekers in the "expedited removal" process until they can demonstrate a credible fear of persecution, arriving aliens who appear inadmissible for other than document-related reasons, and persons ordered removed for at least 90 days following their removal orders.[83]

Between 1994 and 2008, the average daily population in INS custody rose from 6,785 to 31,771.[84] ICE's FY 2009 budget funds 33,400 detention beds per night.[85] Between FY 2003 and FY 2007, the total number of persons detained by ICE per year increased from 231,500 to 311,213.[86]

DHS/ICE detainees may technically be in "civil" proceedings, but they are held in prisons or prison-like facilities that are governed by standards that "are identical to, and modeled after, correctional standard for criminal populations."[87] ICE holds 65 percent of its detainees in state prisons and local jails under Intergovernmental Services Agreements (IGSAs), 19 percent in for-profit prisons known as "Contract Detention Facilities" (CDFs), 14 percent in its own "Service Processing Centers," and 2 percent in the federal Bureau of Prisons (BOP) system.[88] Over the years, credible reports have catalogued severe problems related to the treatment of diverse detainee populations.[89] Recent press reports, for example, have

---

[83] *See generally* Donald Kerwin & Charles Wheeler, *The Detention Mandates of the 1996 Immigration Act: An Exercise in Overkill*, 75 INTERPRETER RELEASES 1433 (1998).

[84] ALISON SISKIN, CONG. RESEARCH SERV., RL32369, IMMIGRATION-RELATED DETENTION: CURRENT LEGISLATIVE ISSUES 13 (2012); ALISON SISKIN, CONG. RESEARCH SERV., RL32369, IMMIGRATION-RELATED DETENTION: CURRENT LEGISLATIVE ISSUES 12 (2004).

[85] STAFF OF H. APPROPRIATIONS COMM., 110TH CONG., CONSOLIDATED SECURITY, DISASTER ASSISTANCE, AND CONTINUING APPROPRIATIONS ACT, 2009, (H.R. 2638; P.L. 110-329) DIVISION D – DEPARTMENT OF HOMELAND SECURITY APPROPRIATIONS ACT, 2009 636 (Comm. Print 2008).

[86] *Id.*

[87] U.S. COMM'N ON INT'L RELIGIOUS FREEDOM, REPORT ON ASYLUM SEEKERS IN EXPEDITED REMOVAL, VOLUME I: FINDING & RECOMMENDATIONS 48-49 (2005).

[88] Eleanor Stables, *ICE Official Wants to Expand 'Alternatives to Detention' Programs*, CQ.COM (March 16, 2007).

[89] Donald Kerwin, *Revisiting the Need for Appointed Counsel*, MPI INSIGHT 6-7 (April 2005).

DIREITO COMPARADO / COMPARATIVE LAW

described sub-standard medical care and detainee deaths.[90] These factors argue for particular vigilance in ensuring the humane treatment of those in ICE's custody.

DHS/ICE has made substantial progress in establishing and enforcing credible detention standards. In September 2000, INS issued 36 "national detention standards" which cover security, the exercise of religion, medical services, visitation, telephone access, legal rights presentations, and transfers.[91] The standards have been applied in phases, first to DHS/ICE Service Processing Centers, followed by for-profit contract facilities, and finally to state and local jails. Developed in conjunction with the American Bar Association, the standards respond to the unique needs of immigrants in "civil custody." They should also apply to BOP prisons that hold ICE detainees.

In January 2010, ICE will implement performance-based standards which will include new standards on media interviews and tours, detainee searches, sexual abuse, and staff training.[92] A performance-based approach identifies and focuses on "the results or outcomes" that the standards are intended to achieve.[93]

ICE has established two entities to ensure compliance with its standards. The Detention Standards Compliance Unit contracts with private corporations to conduct annual monitoring visits at all facilities with ICE detainees and on-site compliance verification at SPCs, CDFs, and state/local prisons with significant numbers of detainees.[94] In 2007, ICE created the Detention Facilities Inspection Group (DFIG) under its Office of Professional Responsibility to review "critical incidents, detainee allegations

---

[90] Dana Priest & Amy Goldstein, *System of Neglect: As Tighter Immigration Policies Strain Federal Agencies, The Detainees in Their Care Often Pay a Heavy Cost*, WASH. POST, May 11, 2008; Nina Bernstein, *Few Details on Immigrants Who Died in Custody*, N.Y. TIMES, May 5, 2008.

[91] DHS subsequently added two more standards, bringing the total to 38.

[92] *See* DORA SCHRIRO, IMMIGRATION & CUSTOMS ENFORCEMENT, IMMIGRATION DETENTION OVERVIEW AND RECOMMENDATIONS (2009), *available at* https://www.ice.gov/doclib/about/offices/odpp/pdf/ice-detention-rpt.pdf.

[93] Letter from Stewart Baker, Assistant Sec'y for Policy, Dep't of Homeland Sec., to Felice Gaer, Chair, U.S.Comm'n on Int'l Religious Freedom (Nov. 28, 2008).

[94] U.S. IMMIGRATION & CUSTOMS ENFORCEMENT, PROTECTING THE HOMELAND: SEMIANNUAL REPORT ON COMPLIANCE WITH ICE NATIONAL DETENTION STANDARDS, JANUARY – JUNE 2007 (2007), *available at* http://www.ice.gov/doclib/about/offices/opr/pdf/semiannual-dmd.pdf.

of employee misconduct, and allegations of detainee mistreatment."[95] In June 2008, DHS's Office of the Inspector General (OIG) reported that "routine oversight of facilities has not been effective in identifying certain serious problems at facilities."[96]

17. Expansion of alternatives to detention

Several factors encumber ICE in meeting its detention and removal responsibilities. First, "mandatory detainees" do not invariably represent a threat to the community. By definition, all ICE detainees have already served any criminal sentences they might have received. Many "criminal aliens," even "aggravated felons," are not violent. Some committed only misdemeanors. For this reason, the DHS's OIG has warned that a sharp increase in mandatory detainees could limit "ICE's ability to detain high risk/high priority aliens" who "pose a potential national security or public safety risk."[97] It recommended that ICE "intensify efforts to obtain the resources needed to expedite the development of alternatives to detention to minimize required detention bed space levels," and urged it to "move forward in the development of cost-effective alternatives to detention."[98]

Second, ICE cannot control or even predict CBP's programmatic needs; CBP is not required to notify ICE of its apprehension initiatives and its projected need for additional detention bed space.[99]

Third, ICE has not moved expeditiously to develop and expand cost-effective "alternatives to detention" for non-mandatory detainees or attempted to extend its current programs to mandatory detainees. Yet, as discussed below, alternative programs have proven successful in ensuring court appearances and are far less expensive than detention.[100]

---

[95] Letter from Stewart Baker, *supra* note 93.

[96] U.S. DEP'T OF HOMELAND SEC., OFFICE OF INSPECTOR GEN., OIG-08-52, ICE POLICIES RELATED TO DETAINEE DEATHS AND THE OVERSIGHT OF IMMIGRATION DETENTION FACILITIES, 19 (2008).

[97] U.S. DEP'T OF HOMELAND SEC., OFFICE OF INSPECTOR GEN., OIG-06-33, DETENTION AND REMOVAL OF ILLEGAL ALIENS, 6 (2006).

[98] *Id.* 23, 25.

[99] SISKIN ET AL., *supra* note 7, at 24.

[100] For a description of several modest, but successful "alternative to detention" programs, see CATHOLIC LEGAL IMMIGRATION NETWORK, INC., THE NEEDLESS DETENTION OF IMMIGRANTS IN THE UNITED STATES 26-28 (2000).

DIREITO COMPARADO / COMPARATIVE LAW

IIRIRA expanded the categories of immigrants who are subject to mandatory detention, particularly those facing removal on criminal grounds. However, it took several years after the Act's passage for the immigrant detention population to tilt decisively to mandatory detainees. "Criminal aliens" made up only about 43 percent of the increase in INS detention between FY 1994 and FY 2001.[101] In FY 2002, 51 percent of detainees had criminal records.[102] By mid-2005, however, mandatory detainees accounted for 87 percent of the persons ICE's custody.[103] As these figures indicate, significant expansion of alternative programs can only occur if they are open to mandatory detainees.

Successful "alternative to detention" programs invariably include the same ingredients, family sponsorship, legal representation, meaningful supervision, and screening that excludes persons who threaten public safety.[104] Because flight risk increases after a removal order has been entered, supervised release program should primarily be available during the pendency of removal proceedings.[105]

Several "alternative to detention" models have proven successful. Between February 1997 and March 31, 2000, the Vera Institute for Justice administered a pilot project designed to ensure appearances by immigrants in removal proceedings who would otherwise have been detained. The project included screening, home visits, reporting requirements, legal referrals, and accompaniment to court hearings. Ninety-one percent of the participants appeared for all of their required hearings, compared to 71 percent in control groups.[106] Asylum-seekers and lawful permanent resi-

---

[101] U.S. Dep't of Justice, Office of the Fed. Detention Trustee, Detention Needs Assessment and Baseline Report: *A Compendium of Federal Detention Statistics* 14 (2002).

[102] Siskin, *supra* note 84, at 12.

[103] U.S. Dep't of Homeland Security, Office of Inspector Gen., *supra* note 97, at 5-6.

[104] Megan Golden, Oren Root, David Mizner, Vera Inst. for Justice, The Appearance Assistance Program: Attaining Compliance with Immigration Laws Through Community Supervision (1998) *available at* http://www.vera.org/sites/default/files/resources/downloads/aap.pdf.

[105] *Id.*

[106] Oren Root, Appearance Assistant Program Dir., Vera Inst. for Justice, Speech, The Appearance Assistance Program: An Alternative to Detention for Noncitizens in U.S. Immigration Removal Proceedings (Apr. 4, 2000), *available at* http://www.vera.org/sites/default/files/resources/downloads/aap_speech.pdf.

dents with minor criminal records appeared at even higher rates, leading program administrators to conclude that these populations did not need to be detained throughout the removal process. The program cost $12 per participant per day, compared to the $61 average daily cost ($95 today) to detain an immigrant.[107]

At present, ICE administers two programs which would best be characterized as "alternative forms of detention." The first, the Intensive Supervision Appearance Program (ISAP), begins with a period of electronic monitoring, home curfews, in person reporting, and unannounced home visits. ICE gradually eases and eliminates restrictions as participants demonstrate compliance with the program. The second, the "enhanced supervision" program, offers electronic monitoring (by itself) and a more intensive program with electronic monitoring, home visits, in-person reporting and other requirements.[108] "Mandatory detainees" are currently ineligible to participate in either of these programs. Instead, ICE offers them to asylum-seekers and to others who might otherwise be released from detention.

ICE's FY 2009 budget includes $63 million for "alternatives to detention," which amounts to less than three percent of its detention and removal budget.[109] ICE should extend its "alternative" programs to non-violent "mandatory detainees" and should develop and expand "supervised release" programs (modeled on the Vera Institute project) for discretionary detainees who would not otherwise be released. Again, such programs satisfy the purpose of detention are cost-effective and humane, and reserve detention space for high-risk, dangerous immigrants.

18. Adjudication of "extreme hardship" waivers for persons approved for family-based visas

Most U.S. "immigrant" (permanent) visas are awarded based on close family ties to a U.S. citizen or a lawful permanent resident. Between FY 2003 and FY 2007, family-based visas constituted 64 percent of all visas granted.[110] While there is no ceiling on the number of visas available for the immediate relatives of U.S. citizens (spouses, parents, and minor chil-

---

[107] *Id.*

[108] *Id.*

[109] STAFF OF H. APPROPRIATIONS COMM., *supra* note 85, at 637.

[110] U.S. DEP'T OF HOMELAND SEC., OFFICE OF IMMIGRATION STATISTICS, 2007 YEARBOOK OF IMMIGRATION STATISTICS 18-19 (2008).

DIREITO COMPARADO / COMPARATIVE LAW

dren), caps on "preference" category visas (those based on less immediate family ties), combined with ceilings on admission by nationality, have led to multi-year visa backlogs. Particularly affected are persons from common migrant sending nations who have been approved for heavily subscribed visas. For example, a Mexican spouse or minor child of a lawful permanent resident would currently need to wait more than seven years for his or her visa to become available.[111] Depending on the preference category and nationality, backlogs can span decades.

In 2009, U.S. Department of State (DOS) reported that 4.9 million persons who had been approved for visas had not yet received them, including 2.2 million U.S. residents.[112] Immigrants approved for visas who opt to wait for them in the United States must ultimately leave the country when their visas become available, with no guarantee that they will be able to return. This is because persons "unlawfully present" for at least 180 days are subject to a three-year bar on admission, and those unlawfully present for more than one year are subject to a ten-year bar.[113] The bars can be waived, but only upon a showing that the immigrant's exclusion would create "extreme hardship" to his or her U.S. citizen or lawful permanent resident spouse or parent, but not to her or her child.[114]

Under INA § 245(i), certain persons approved for permanent visas who have entered illegally or overstayed non-immigrant visas can apply to "adjust" to lawful permanent resident status without leaving the country by paying a $1,000 penalty.[115] However, the provision now applies only to the beneficiaries of visa petitions filed by April 30, 2001.[116] Others must leave the country to obtain their visas at a U.S. consulate, triggering the three- or ten-year bars based on "unlawful presence." For persons ultimately granted waivers, processing times can take months and even years; in Ciudad Juarez, for example, they average 13 to 14 months.[117] Many per-

---

[111] U.S. Department of State, Bureau of Consular Affairs, *Visa Bulletin for November 2008* (2008), http://travel.state.gov/content/visas/english/law-and-policy/bulletin/2009/visa-bulletin-for-november-2008.html.

[112] MEISSNER & KERWIN, *supra* note 2, at 65.

[113] INA § 212(a)(9)(B)(i)(I)-(II).

[114] INA § 212(a)(9)(B)(v).

[115] INA § 245(i).

[116] LIFE Act Amendments of 2000, Pub. L. No. 106-554 app. D, §1502, 114 Stat. 2764, 2763A-324.

[117] MEISSNER & KERWIN, *supra* note 2, at 66.

sons approved for visas opt to forego the possibility of legal status, rather than to risk permanent separation from their families.

Congress should pass legislation to extend in-county "adjustment" to all visa beneficiaries. However, DHS can further these goals in the interim by adjudicating "extreme hardship" waivers for persons approved for family-based visas *prior* to their departure from the United States. As with section 245(i), an additional fee or fine for a waiver application could support DHS enforcement and examinations functions. Most importantly, these reforms will reduce pressure on DHS enforcement agencies by ensuring that a population that is already approved for legal status can actually receive it.

Conclusion

It remains uncertain whether President Obama will be able to make good on his pledge to pass comprehensive immigration reform legislation over the next two years. However, it is certain that the need for effective, humane enforcement policies will be crucial to pursuing broader reform objectives.

At the heart of a viable immigration enforcement plan must be programs to address the root causes of migration in immigrant-sending communities. In addition, DHS should expand its programs to uproot human smuggling enterprises and to punish exploitative employers who hire large numbers of unauthorized workers. ICE should also exercise its prosecutorial discretion, opting not to place into removal proceedings non-citizens who have been approved for family-based visas or who will otherwise be able to obtain legal status in the United States.

An effective, humane enforcement plan must be coupled with a program to legalize a significant percentage of the nation's unauthorized immigrants and to reform the U.S. legal immigration system. The need is for comprehensive immigration reform, not "enforcement only" legislation that cannot succeed even on its own terms.

Employment Eligibility and Mobility of Workers in the United States

CARLOS ORITZ MIRANDA[*]

I. Introduction

This paper will review two general topics of U.S. immigration law: employment eligibility and mobility of workers. The statutory provisions covering these topics are contained in the Immigration and Nationality Act (INA), the basic statute governing immigration law in the United States, as well as other legislative amendments to the INA.[1]

II. Employment Eligibility

A. *Employment-based visas and immigration categories*

There are two general categories under which foreign nationals are admitted into the country on account of employment. The first category consists of immigrants, or permanent residents, and the INA provides for

---

[*] Associate General Counsel, U.S. Conference of Catholic Bishops. Carlos Ortiz Miranda received a B.A. from the University of Puerto Rico; a J.D. from the Antioch School of Law; and an LL.M. from Georgetown University Law Center. He is an adjunct professor of immigration law and policy at Catholic University, and served as Chair to the American Immigration Lawyer's Association's Committee on Religious Workers. Ortiz is a member of the District of Columbia and New York State Bar Associations, and has lectured and written extensively on various immigration topics. © United States Conference of Catholic Bishops (2009).

[1] Immigration and Nationality Act of 1952, §§ 101-507, 8 U.S.C. §§ 1101-1778 (2008) (as amended).

DIREITO COMPARADO / COMPARATIVE LAW

some 140,000 employment-based visas per year for immigrants.[2] These employment-based visas are divided into four preference categories, most preference categories require skilled labor and two preference categories require a pre-approved labor certification by the Department of Labor before the basic employment-based petition can be submitted for adjudication by the USCIS. Labor certifications essentially attest that there are no domestic workers who are qualified, able, and willing to accept the particular position, and that hiring the foreign national will not adversely affect the wages and working conditions of similarly situated domestic workers. Once the labor certification is approved, if needed, the basic employment-based petition is filed with the immigration authorities. If the foreign national is already in the United States and otherwise qualifies, the basic employment-based petition is filed concurrently with an application to adjust status to permanent residency.

The second main category for employment eligibility concerns non-immigrants who are granted temporary visas that are valid for varying time periods ranging from several months to multiple years. There are approximately a dozen nonimmigrant categories, including subcategories, which allow the visa holder to work in the country, and a good number of these have annual limitations. Included in this general category are "treaty nationals" that come from countries with which the United States has free trade agreements, or other nonimmigrant categories that the law classifies in alphabetical order starting with A visas and ending with V visas (not all of the A through V classifications are allocated for employment eligibility). Government statistics for 2007 indicate that 1,118,138 temporary workers (including trainees) were then admitted in the United States.[3] Of these, most come under the H classification covering skilled workers, agricul-

---

[2] *See generally* INA § 203 (allocation of immigrant visas); INA § 203(b) (preference allocation for employment-based immigrants). An immigrant may gain that status by being sponsored as an immediate relative of a U.S. citizen, based on a qualifying family relationship (approx. 480,000 per year), an employment-based sponsorship (140,000 per year), or winning the visa lottery (55,000 per year). There are four employment-based preference categories and most are reserved for high-skill employment; at least two of the employment based categories require a labor certification which tests whether there are sufficient domestic workers that are able, qualified, and willing to accept the job, and whether domestic worker in similar positions will be adversely affected by hiring the foreign worker.

[3] U.S. DEP'T OF HOMELAND SEC., OFFICE OF IMMIGRATION STATISTICS, 2009 YEARBOOK OF IMMIGRATION STATISTICS 65 (2010).

tural workers, non-agricultural workers, nurses, and industrial trainees. The H nonimmigrant classification for temporary workers in general, and the H1b nonimmigrant subcategory covering skilled workers in particular, is used heavily by United States businesses.[4] The same 2007 statistics showed that 461,730 persons and their families residing in the United States were temporary workers in specialty occupations under the H1b visa category.[5] Specialty occupations for which at least a baccalaureate degree is required fall under the H1b visa category.[6]

Foreign nationals that are either permanent residents or nonimmigrants authorized to work in the United States fall under the three classes discussed below. The first class includes workers authorized to work as an incident of their immigration status, examples include permanent residents, refugee, asylees, nonimmigrant fiancés of U.S. citizens, citizens of the Federated States of Micronesia, persons granted withholding of removal, persons granted temporary protected status, and persons in temporary immigration status as victims of trafficking or certain crimes (qualifying family members may also fall within this class). There are twenty members of this class under the applicable federal regulation.[7]

The second class includes workers authorized to work under a specific employer incident to their immigration status and encompasses most of the nonimmigrant work-based categories. Examples include foreign government officials, foreign students working on campus and in curricular practical training, representatives of international organizations, temporary workers in specialty occupations and other workers under the H nonimmigrant category already mentioned, trainees, information media representatives, exchange visitors, certain persons working in sciences, arts, athletes, entertainers, intracompany transferees, and religious workers. All in all, the applicable federal regulation specifies another twenty

---

[4] There is a 65,000 annual cap on H1-b visas; excluded from this cap are persons who work at universities and non-profit research facilities, 1,400 Chilean nationals and 4,500 Singapore nationals pursuant to free trade agreements, and 20,000 foreign nationals holding a master's degree or higher degree from U.S. universities. *See also* U.S. Dep't of Homeland Sec., Office of Immigration Statistics, 2007 Yearbook of Immigration Statistics 63-84 (2008). *See generally* INA § 214 (admission of nonimmigrants).

[5] U.S. Dep't of Homeland Sec., *supra* note 3, at 65.

[6] INA § 214(i)(1)(B); *see also* Stephen H. Legomsky, Immigration and Refugee Law and Policy 362-67 (4th ed. 2005) (discussion of the H1b visa category).

[7] 8 C.F.R. § 274a.12(a).

distinct members of this class of workers. Most, but not all, of the workers under this second class correspond to specific nonimmigrant categories. A common feature of the majority of workers that fall under this second class is that they must be sponsored by an entity in the United States.[8]

The third class includes workers who must apply for an employment authorization document from the immigration authorities. Examples of members of this class include spouses of those in the second class, foreign students engaging in certain off-campus employment or performing optional training, adjustment-of-status applicants to permanent residence status, and certain business travelers. There are approximately twenty-five categories of members in this particular class.[9]

B. Employment Authorization
(1) Employment authorization verification system

Once the foreign national qualifies for employment in the United States, he or she joins U.S. citizens in being required to prove they are authorized to be employed in the country.[10] With limited exceptions, U.S. citizens and foreign workers must be authorized to engage in employment. An employer must not knowingly hire a person who is not authorized to work in the country.[11] This statutory requirement is an effort by the federal

---

[8] 8 C.F.R. § 274a.12(b).

[9] 8 C.F.R § 274a.12(c).

[10] INA § 274A; 8 C.F.R. 274a.2 (implementing regulations); *see also* AMERICAN IMMIGRATION LAWYERS ASS'N, AILA's GUIDE TO WORKSITE ENFORCEMENT & COMPLIANCE (2008). *See generally* U.S. CITIZENSHIP & IMMIGRATION SERV., M-274, HANDBOOK FOR EMPLOYERS: INSTRUCTIONS FOR COMPLETING FORM I-9 (EMPLOYMENT ELIGIBILITY VERIFICATION FORM) (Rev. 04/03/09).

[11] The "knowing" standard is actual or constructive knowledge. Constructive knowledge is defined as "knowledge which may be fairly inferred through notice a certain facts and circumstances which would lead a person, through the exercise of reasonable care, to know about a certain condition." Some examples include: (1) conflicting information is provided by the employee when completing the I-9; (2) employer ascertains from other sources (another employer or the Basic Pilot program) that the person is not authorized to work; (3) information is obtained from government enforcement personnel that the person is not authorized to work; (4) a document presented seems to be altered or forged; (5) no completion, or incomplete completion of the I-9; (6) failure to reverify the I-9 after the expiration date of a document; and (7) no-match letters are received from the Social Security Administration and the employers takes no action. If there is a need to further investigate the employee's status, there should be a careful and consistent approach on the part of the employer (discount rumors

government to prevent the economic magnet that has attracted undocumented workers to enter and reside in the country in the past. The employment authorization verification system requires all employees to provide certain information and employers to review the information for employment authorization at the time of hire by inspecting certain documents and complying with the employment authorization verification system.[12] There are three main exceptions to this general rule: (1) independent contractors; (2) individuals who engage in casual, sporadic or irregular work in a private household; and, (3) and those individuals hired before November 6, 1986 (the date that the law became effective).

If the employer has not done so already, it is permissible to have a policy that would limit employment hiring to those who are currently authorized to work by inquiring if a job candidate is currently authorized to be employed in the United States. If the candidate answers in the negative, there would be no need to consider them. Some employers have a policy that informs all job applicants that they are subject to provide proof of employment eligibility under federal immigration law. A policy for hiring only citizens of the United States is not permitted under any circumstances.

(2) Compliance and Form I-9

Compliance is accomplished by the presentation and verification of certain documents and by the completion of the I-9 Form, Employment Eligibility Verification, and record retention. While there is a Spanish language version of the I-9 From, in the United States, it can only be used for explanatory purposes. Official use of the Spanish language version is only permitted in Puerto Rico.[13] The I-9 Form has three sections. Section one requires employee information and verification that the employee is authorized to work in the United States. It is completed by the employee at the time

---

or hearsay). There a several recent cases that would not shield an employer from 3rd party liability if the employer knows that use staffing agencies or independent contractors used unauthorized workers. (Wal-Mart, $11 million fine; Mohawk Indus. v. Williams, 411 F.3d 1252 (11th Cir. 2005), *vacated*, 547 U.S. 516 (2006) (remanded for consideration in light of *Anza v. Ideal Steel Supply Corp.*, 547 U.S. 451 (2006)).

[12] 8 C.F.R. § 274a, Subpart A.

[13] The Form I-9 with instructions may be found at www.uscis.gov following the toolbar for immigration forms.

of hire.[14] Section two consists of the employer review of documents presented by the employee and requires verification of those documents be completed within three days of the hire date. The employer verifies the documents and completes either List A or List B and List C of the documents listed on the I-9 Form.[15] Section three is used by the employer for updating and re-verification of documents on or before the expiration date of each document, when applicable.[16] Photocopying of documents is

---

[14] If a preparer or translator completes section 1, certification must be completed by the preparer or translator.

Section 2: Employer review of documents and verification must be completed within 3 days of the dire date.

Employer verifies documents and completes either List A or List B and List C of the documents listed on the Form, I-9. List A is for documents that demonstrate both the identity and employment eligibility of the individual, and 4spaces must be completed: (1) document title, (2) issuing authority, (3) document #, (4) expiration date, any; if List A is not applicable. The employer must examine one of the documents under List B and one from List C, record the title, number and expiration date, if any. The employer has to complete the signature block contained in Section 1 regardless of the documents verified. Special rule on receipt for application of missing documents: if the person hired does not have a needed document to establish identity and work eligibility, he/she may present a receipt within 3 days of the hire indicating that the document is being obtained, and has 90 days to provide the original document.

Section 3: Updating and reverification on or before the expiration date, if applicable, in Section 1

Block A to be completed if there is a name change at the time of re-verification Block B should be completed if the person is rehired with 3 years of the original hire, or if a current work authorization is about to expire and the employer examines the new document for re-verification purpose Bock C should be completed with information on the new document, including the do document title, document #, and expiration date, if any. The signature block in Section 3 should also be completed.

[15] List A is for documents that demonstrate both the identity and employment eligibility of the individual, and 4spaces must be completed: (1) document title, (2) issuing authority, (3) document number, (4) expiration date, any; if List A is not applicable. The employer must examine one of the documents under List B and one from List C, record the title, number and expiration date, if any. The employer has to complete the signature block contained in Section 1 regardless of the documents verified. Special rule on receipt for application of missing documents: if the person hired does not have a needed document to establish identity and work eligibility, he/she may present a receipt within 3 days of the hire indicating that the document is being obtained, and has 90 days to provide the original document.

[16] Block A to be completed if there is a name change at the time of reverification. Block B should be completed if the person is rehired with 3 years of the original hire, or if a current work authorization is about to expire and the employer examines the new document for re-verification purpose. Block C should be completed with information on the new document,

permitted, but if this done, the photocopies must be retained with the I-9 Form. Many employers create a tickler system to anticipate the dates of those documents that have an expiration date. Employers may complete and retain the I-9 Forms electronically, including the use of handwritten or electronic signatures.

Immigration and Customs Enforcement (ICE), a federal agency housed in the Department of Homeland Security, in coordination with the Department of Labor, has the authority to inspect the I-9 Forms for compliance.[17] If there is an inspection, federal authorities provide three days notice to employers, and when they arrive at the place of employment, they typically ask for a copy of the payroll ledger and the I-9 Forms for comparison. Defenses available to employers include a good faith effort to comply with verification requirements, but employers may still be subject to penalties for noncompliance.[18]

including the document title, document number, and expiration date, if any. The signature block in Section 3 should also be completed.

[17] Either agency must provide at least 3 days notice. The Department of Labor usually provides notice to inspect I-9's when they conduct other investigations such as reviewing EEOP affirmative action plans for federal contractors. The government's audit will review the I-9's and the payroll records that reflect current and terminated employees for a certain time period. Then the government determines the I-9s that should be made available for inspection. If you match the I-9s with those on the payroll, you can determine if there are any missing I-9s.

[18] If federal authorities find violations through compliance inspections, there are several levels of penalties may be imposed, which includes different levels of civil penalties, criminal penalties, and even incarceration for certain members of management. Violations for noncompliance with are subject to civil penalties using a three-tier approach covering first, second and third violations for hiring each unauthorized person. There is a schedule of fines for pre- and post-1999 violations. Let me give some examples, for post-1999 first-time violations the fines range from $275 to $2,200 for each unauthorized hire, and if there is a third violation, the fines range from $3,300 to $11,000. One or more violation for a single adjudication or proceeding constitutes one violation for determining the level of violations for imposing fines. In addition, civil fines can be imposed for failure to comply with the verification system, and these range between $100 to $1,100 for each employee concerned. Employers found to engage in a pattern or practice is subject to criminal fines of up to $3,000 for each unauthorized employment and/or up to 6 months in jail. If there is an inspection and the employer is charged with violations, the employer has 30 days to respond to the Notice of Intent to Fine by requesting a hearing before an ALJ located in the Department of Justice's Office of Chief Administrative Hearing Office (OCAHO). If the employer loses at the administrative level, he may appeal to the Court of Appeals for the particular circuit under which the action took place. Defenses to violations may include good faith attempts to comply for technical or procedural violations. Substantial compliance has been tried as a defense, but federal

The employment authorization verification system has lead to increases in document fraud whereby workers buy work-related documents, including using fake or stolen social security cards, or social security numbers from real persons, many of whom are unaware that their social security number is being used in this manner. Depending on the facts of cases, workers caught using fraudulent documents are prosecuted under both immigration proceedings at the administrative level, typically leading to removal since they were probably unauthorized to reside in the United States, and under federal criminal laws before federal district courts on charges such as document fraud or aggravated identity theft.[19]

(3) E-Verify

As a complement to the employment eligibility process, the federal government is urging employers to use a voluntary program known as the E-Verify program. This legislative program has been in place since 1997 and is administered by the United States Customs and Immigration Service (USCIS). E-verify is free to employers. By signing a Memorandum of Understanding with USCIS and the Social Security Administration, the employer registers for the program and is allowed to perform a check on federal databases (provided by the Department of Homeland Security and the Social Security Administration) to verify the employment eligibility of new hires. Checks have been completed either instantly or within one day in 96.1 percent of cases. That leaves 3.9 percent with tentative non-confirmations. The workforce in the United States is about 140 million and a 3.9 percent tentative non-confirmation could affect millions of workers.[20]

According to statistics compiled by the Migration Policy Institute, as of early 2009 more than 100,000 employers were registered to use E-Ver-

courts have rejected such a defense, at least when copies of documents have been made, and attached to incomplete Forms I-9.

[19] Enforcement against employers has increased significantly in recent years. Charges brought against employers include violations for knowingly hiring unauthorized workers and violations of the harboring provisions under federal immigration law. Forfeiture of profits is also a possibility. *See* U.S. Immigration & Customs Enforcement, News Release, Alabaster Construction Company Owner Charged with Employing Illegal Aliens (Jan. 29, 2009), *available at* http://www.ice.gov/news/releases/alabaster-construction-company-owner-charged-employing-illegal-aliens.

[20] *See* DORIS MEISSNER & DONALD KERWIN, MIGRATION POLICY INST., DHS AND IMMIGRATION: TAKING STOCK AND CORRECTING COURSE 80-81 (2009), *available at* http://www.migrationpolicy.org/pubs/DHS_Feb09.pdf.

EMPLOYMENT ELIGIBILITY AND MOBILITY OF WORKERS IN THE UNITED STATES

ify out of more than approximately seven million employers in the United States, and some 1,000 employers are signing up to use e-verify each week.[21] Approximately 15 individual states within the United States have passed laws requiring public agencies or public contractors to participate in E-Verify. The federal government has attempted to require E-Verify for most federal contractors through a 2008 Executive Order and subsequent federal regulation.[22] The federal regulation has been the subject of a lawsuit challenging the President's authority to impose E-Verify on government

---

[21] *Id.*

[22] 20 Federal Acquisition Regulation; FAR Case 2007-013, Employment Eligibility Verification, 73 Fed. Reg. 67651 (Nov. 14, 2009) (to be codified at 48 C.F.R. pts. 2, 22, 52). On November 14, 2008, the Civilian Agency Acquisitions Council and the Defense Acquisitions Regulations Council (Councils) published the final rule requiring certain federal contractors to verify employment eligibility of certain employees under the E-Verify program. More than 1,600 comments were submitted to the Councils during the rule-making process including comments submitted by U.S. Conference of Catholic Bishops. *Id.*
The final rule amends the Federal Acquisition Regulation (FAR) and will be effective for all new contracts awarded after January 15, 2009, that are subject to FAR system. It requires all federal contractors awarded contracts after the effective date to enroll in the E-Verify program, if not enrolled already, within 30 calendar days of the contract award. The employer then has 90 calendar days to verify all new hires who are working in the United States regardless if the new hires are assigned to the government contract. Actual verification must be performed within 3 business days after the hires. The final rule further stipulates that the employer must initiate verification for each employee assigned to the contract within 90 calendar days of enrollment, or within 30 calendar days of the employee's assignment to the contract, whichever date is later. Subcontractors are also subject to the new FAR requirements described above if the subcontract is for more than $3,000 for services or construction. *Id.*
Employees assigned to the contract are defined as hired after November 6, 1986, and who are directly performing work on the contract. The final rule exempts an employee who performs support work such as indirect or overhead, and does not perform any substantial duties applicable to the contract. Employers have the option to verify all employees hired after November 6, 1986, rather than only those employees assigned to the contract. If this option is chosen, the employer has the responsibility to notify E-Verify Operations. *Id.*
The final rule allows institutions of higher learning, a state or local government or the government of a federally recognized Indian tribe, or a surety performing under a takeover agreement with a federal agency pursuant to a performance bond to enroll in the E-Verify program and limit the use of E-Verify to those employees assigned to the contract defined above (as opposed to the entire workforce). There are specific conditions for federal contractors that are already enrolled in the E-Verify program. Exempt from enrollment in the E-Verify program are contracts that are for less than $100,000, contracts that have a period of performance of less than 120 days, work performed outside of the United States, and contracts that are for commercially available off-the-shelf items. While the final rule permits contracting officers

contractors.[23] The Obama administration has put a hold on the regulation and is currently reviewing it.[24] The program itself has been reauthorized by Congress four times, most recently in March 2009.[25]

According to certain accounts, some employers have misused the verification program by: (1) verifying the employment status of only foreign-looking job applicants *before* hiring them; and, (2) by reducing the pay or even firing employees who challenge the Social Security Administration's finding that they are working illegally. Some have suggested that these abuses can be corrected by enacting tough civil and criminal penalties for employers who misuse the program, by educating employers on the proper uses of the program, and by more frequently enforcing labor laws.[26]

A mandatory nationwide verification program would have to expand from its current size of around 100,000 employers to about seven million employers. Many believe that the Social Security Administration and the Department of Homeland Security should significantly reduce the error rates in their databases before E-Verify is made mandatory for all employers, a possibility currently debated in the U.S. Congress. Others have suggested that should E-Verify become mandatory, it should be phased-in at a reasonable rate with objective benchmarks regarding database accuracy, privacy, and employer compliance.[27]

II. Mobility of Workers
A. *Permanent Residents*
Foreign nationals who are permanent workers have no restrictions on changing employment, though it is expected they remain a part of the sponsoring employers workforce for a reasonable period.[28]

---

to waive the E-Verify program use in exceptional cases for a contract, a subcontract, or a class of contracts or subcontracts, it does not define what might constitute exceptional cases. *Id.*

[23] Chamber of Commerce v. Chertoff, No. 8:08 cv-03444-AW (S.D. Md. Dec. 23, 2008).

[24] *See* Elise Castelli, *Obama Again Delays E-Verify Requirement*, FED. TIMES (Apr. 17, 2009, 6:00 AM), http://www.federaltimes.com/article/20090417/ACQUISITION03/904170301/Obama-again-delays-E-Verify-requirement.

[25] The program has been criticized on a number of grounds including providing false negatives, improper use by employers, inefficiency, false positives on account of identity theft, and loss of privacy subject to cyber-thieves.

[26] MEISSNER & KERWIN, *supra* note 20, at 83-84.

[27] *Id.* at 82-84.

[28] 8 C.F.R. § 274a.12(a)(1).

B. *Applicants for Permanent Residency*

For applicants who have applied for adjustment of status to permanent residency based on an underlying petition for an employment-based visa as one of three employment-based preference categories, U.S. immigration law allows certain mobility if two conditions are satisfied: (1) an employment-based adjustment of status application for permanent residency has been filed and has been pending for six months or more and (2) the new job is the same as, or similar to, the job described in the labor certification or the employment-based petition. Immigration lawyers advise individuals who change employment under this legal provision to notify immigration authorities to avoid future problems. If the individual complies with the above requirements, the government may not deny their application for adjustment of status to permanent residency based on a change of employment.[29]

C. *Nonimmigrants*

Nonimmigrants who are sponsored in employer-specific positions may change employers or obtain new employment as long as they submit the change of employer or new employment petition while they are in a valid nonimmigrant immigration status and the petition is approved before they change employment.[30] There is a unique rule for workers in specialty occupation known as portability between employers. These workers can move to another employer as long as their current H1b immigration status is valid, and the new employer files a new petition to acquire the H1b immigration status with government before the current status expires.[31]

---

[29] American Competitiveness in the Twenty-First Century Act of 2000, Pub. L. No. 106-313, § 106, 114 Stat. 1251, 1253 (codified as amended at 8 U.S.C. 1184 note). However, if USCIS finds that the individual does not meet these requirements, they must issue a "Notice of Intent to Deny" pursuant to the American Competitiveness in the Twenty-First Century Act; instead of immediately denying the pending I-485. USCIS can, however, deny pending I-485s before first issuing a "Notice of Intent to Deny" where the beneficiary is ineligible for the benefits of the I-485 by statute, or the I-140 is withdrawn before the I-485 was pending for 180 days.

[30] *See* 8 C.F.R. § 274a.12(b) (foreign nationals authorized to for employment with specific employer incident to status); *id.* § 248 (change of nonimmigrant classification).

[31] American Competitiveness in the Twenty-First Century Act § 105.

III. Conclusion

United States immigration and employment law allows for the mobility of workers within prescribed procedures, but the fundamental question is whether the foreign national is authorized to work in the first place. The mobility of workers for those not authorized, such as the undocumented population, is certainly limited with the government trying to stop any employment through the employment authorization verification system. This system will remain part of landscape for employment and immigration law in the United States for the foreseeable future. Whether and to what extent the E-Verify program will be part of that landscape is less certain, although the executive branch of the United States government is pushing hard for its use. As far as the legislative branch is concerned, the future is less certain, and the struggle will be part of the effort related to comprehensive immigration reform.

The Administrative Condition of Immigrants
General Aspects and Topic Remarks

CARLA AMADO GOMES[*]

Introduction

At the end of 2007, there were 434,000 legal immigrants in Portugal. Statistical analysis of this number shows the huge increase in immigration that occurred over the last three decades. In 1980, 50,751 immigrants had legal residence in Portugal. Ten years later, the number doubled to 107,767[1]. Between 1991 and 2001, there was a further growth of 83% of immigrants in Portugal, which has contributed to a 22% increase in the total Portuguese population. Today, the number of legal immigrants is four times what it was in the beginning of the 1980s. However, compared to the rest of the population, immigrants comprise, less than 5% of the total, a small percentage compared to other European Union member States – 3.6% of immigrants in Portugal compared to the European average of 6.8%[2].

These numbers may seem surprising, considering Portugal has traditionally been envisaged as a country of emigration. The discoveries of the fifteenth and sixteenth centuries and the colonization that followed

---

[*] Professor of Law, University of Lisbon.
[1] See Jorge GASPAR, A autorização de permanência e a integração do imigrantes (Uma análise político-jurídica), *in OD*, 2001/IV, pp. 959 ff., 983 (supported by data provided by the Foreigner and Borders' Board).
[2] Source: Site of the Portuguese Presidency – *www.presidencia.pt*.

exemplified the adventurous character of the Portuguese people, searching for better living conditions in Africa, India and Brazil. In the late 1960s, the Portuguese political regime's antidemocratic nature and the poverty experienced by the domestic population in the less developed interior of the country justified a new wave of Portuguese emigration to European countries, the majority of emigrants settling in France, Switzerland and Germany. Portugal's political stabilization throughout the 1980s, and the accompanying economic development, drastically reduced the emigration flux.

Conversely, the 1970s introduced Portugal to the new reality of immigration, resulting from the grant of independence to some Portuguese colonies and subsequent large-scale expatriate return to Portugal from the colonies. Favorable conditions in Portugal and unrest in some of the former colonies also prompted many African people searching for stability and peace to immigrate. Throughout the 1990s, Portugal began to see the arrival of increasing numbers of citizens from within the European Community, benefiting from the freedom of circulation provided by Portugal's ratification of the Treaty of Rome and adhesion to the European Community.

The fall of the Berlin Wall in 1989, and *Perestroika* in the U.S.S.R. were also responsible for the arrival of citizens from Eastern Block countries such as Romania, Ukraine, and Moldova, attracted by the heavy investment and opportunities resulting from major public works in Portugal such as the *Vasco da Gama* bridge, completed in 1998, and public events including *Expo 1998*[3]. In addition, the strong cultural ties and privileged relations with Brazil contributed to the strong presence of Brazilian people in Portugal – presently the biggest resident foreign community[4].

---

[3] See Júlio CARNEIRO PEREIRA, Direito à emigração e imigração com direitos, *in RMP*, nº 90, 2000, pp. 113 ff., 115-116.

[4] According to the information provided in the site of the Portuguese Presidency mentioned above, 55% of immigrants come from States part of CPLP (*Comunidade dos Países de Língua Portuguesa* = Portuguese (language) speaking countries), 28% from the EU member States, 11% from South American States, 5% from Asian States and 4% from other countries.
The "Relatório de Actividades 2007 – Imigrantes, Fronteiras e Asilo" (*Report of 2007 Activities – Immigrants, Borders and Asylum*), made by the Foreigner and Borders' Board (see http://www. inforpress.publ.cv) concludes that Brazil is the biggest immigrant community in Portugal, with 66.354 persons (15%). Cape Verde is on second place, with 63.925 persons and Angola occupies the third place, with 32.728 residents (the numbers refer to legal immigrants).

THE ADMINISTRATIVE CONDITION OF IMMIGRANTS GENERAL ASPECTS AND TOPIC...

Despite the immigrant increase from so many sources, overall immigration numbers have decreased since 2004, largely due to the worldwide economic crisis' effects on Portugal, and the drastic reduction of employment that has resulted. An increase in people seeking to profit from recent economic development in Angola has contributed to a simultaneous slow rise of immigration to the former colony of Angola, now that the civil war has ended.

Accommodating immigrants who wish to stay for relatively long periods, working, studying or involving themselves in charitable tasks, has necessitated the existence of immigration laws and immigration policies[5]. States are not required to welcome immigrants; a general principle of International Law authorizes States to simply forbid the entrance of non-citizens; to place restrictions on their entrance; and to establish reasons to order their expulsion from the country as long as due process is given[6]. States might not grant foreign people the same rights allowed to their own citizens, even if a minimum standard is mandatory, for instance, access to justice, prohibition of arbitrary discrimination, or respect for human dignity[7]. Nonetheless, historically, foreign people – mainly traders – have been entitled to a right to hospitality or a right of natural partnership and communication, which encompasses the right to travel, the right to reside in the receiving country, the right to trade, the right to acquire citizenship and the right not to be arbitrarily expelled[8].

Portuguese immigration regulation is based on two primary foundations: (1) the obligations assumed towards the European Union, concerning both guaranteeing freedom of circulation and right of residency to EU citizens, and controlling entrance and permanence of citizens from third

---

[5] About the Portuguese policy for immigrants' integration, see the Resolution of the Council of Ministers 63-A/07, of the 3rd May.

[6] See Rui MOURA RAMOS, Estrangeiro, *in Polis*, II, Mem Martins, 1984, cc. 1215 ff., 1217.

[7] See the proposal of a "Chart on a minimum standard of rights for foreigner and minorities", *in* José Joaquim GOMES CANOTILHO (org.), Direitos humanos, estrangeiros, comunidades migrantes e minorias, Oeiras, 2000, pp. 27 ff.; *idem*, Enquadramento jurídico da imigração, *in Actas do I Congresso sobre Imigração em Portugal – Diversidade, Cidadania, Integração*, Lisboa, 2004, pp. 152 ff., 160 [which would comprehend obligations of *facere* (adopting protective measures) and of *non facere* (not adopting arbitrary discriminatory measures)].

[8] José MARTÍNEZ DE PISÓN, Derechos de la persona o de la ciudadania: los inmigrantes, *in Persona y Derecho*, nº 49, 2003, pp. 43 ff., 51.

countries[9]; and (2) the universal dimension of fundamental rights in the Portuguese Constitution, anchored in article 12, founded in the principle of human dignity (article 1), and echoing the Universal Declaration of Human Rights (article 16/2)[10].

In the following text, we will try to review the main aspects of the administrative condition of immigrants going through the Law of Immigration presently in force (Law 23/07, of the 4th July (LI)[11])[12] – more precisely, Foreigner Law (*Lei dos Estrangeiros*). This is a necessary remark because the Law doesn't define immigrants – and hardly mentions the word. To achieve that goal, there are some preliminary steps we have to take to circumscribe our subject and object (I.). Once establishing those operative concepts, some words on the constitutional status of immigrants are also required (II.). Then we can go ahead to explaining the powers of administrative authorities concerning the admission, the permanence and the expelling of immigrants (III. and IV.). We will summarise some conclusions at the end (V.).

I. Preliminary delimitation of the communication's subject

This presentation's theme demands some introductory remarks. First, we must establish the meaning of the term "immigrant" (**1.**). Second, we must explain what aspects are going to be focused under the expression immigrants' "administrative condition" (**2.**).

1. Who is an *immigrant*?

The LI doesn't provide any definition for *immigrant*. The law uses the expression *entrepreneurial immigrant* once (in article 60/2), and mentions

---

[9] On the international and European framework for human rights' protection within the European Community, both towards European citizens and third countries' citizens, Maria Concepción Pérez Villalobos, La cultura de los derechos fundamentales en Europa. Los derechos de los inmigrantes extracomunitarios y el nuevo concepto de ciudadania, *in Derecho Constitucional y Cultura. Estudios en homenaje a Peter Häberle*, coord. Francisco Balaguer Callejón, Madrid, 2004, pp. 701 ff.

[10] In this sense, José Martínez de Pisón, Derechos de la persona..., *cit.*, p. 47 and 71 ff.; José Alberto de Melo Alexandrino, A nova lei de entrada, permanência, saída e afastamento de estrangeiros, *in http:// www.fd.ul.pt / ICJ/ Iuscommunedocs*, pp. 24-27.

[11] The practical aspects of the regime are regulated in Decree 84/07, of the 5th November.

[12] Extensively on the legal framework established by this Law, José Alberto de Melo Alexandrino, A nova lei de entrada..., *cit., passim*.

THE ADMINISTRATIVE CONDITION OF IMMIGRANTS GENERAL ASPECTS AND TOPIC...

the term *illegal immigration* in only one Section (V.), leaving no clues to their content. So, one is forced to build an operative notion of immigrant to the purpose of this presentation. And this task will be performed on a *negative basis*, gradually excluding some categories of people until we reach the universe with which we are going to work.

a) First of all, immigrants are not Portuguese citizens. An immigrant is an alien, a stranger, someone who is not "one of us"[13] – the other[14]. This doesn't mean immigrants cannot turn into Portuguese citizens. The acquisition of Portuguese citizenship by immigrants is possible on the terms of Law 37/81, of the 3rd October (altered by the fourth time and republished by Organic Law 2/06, of the 17th April[15]), in the following situations:

    i.) Originally: by birth in Portuguese territory [article 1/1/d), e)[16] and f)];

    ii.) Not originally: by declaration, adoption or naturalisation [articles 2, 3 and 4; 5; and 6, respectively].

---

[13] On the historic perspective of the relation between State and aliens, see Cecilia CORSI, Lo Stato e lo straniero, Milan, 2001, pp. 1 ff.

[14] A doubt may arise in what concerns stateless persons, but as long as they are not Portuguese citizens [which they will automatically turn into if they are born in Portugal (see article 1/f) of Law 37/81, of the 3rd October), or if they apply to the attribution of Portuguese citizenship, on the basis of the same law], they are strangers and so can become immigrants.

[15] This law greatly enlarged the legal possibilities of naturalisation, and is envisaged as a contribute to immigrants' integration (through the loss of their condition of strangers) – see Jorge PEREIRA DA SILVA, "Culturas da cidadania" – Em torno de um acórdão do TC e da nova lei da nacionalidade, Anotação ao Acórdão do TC 599/2005, *in Jurisprudência Constitucional*, nº 11, 2006, pp. 81 ff., spec. 85 ff.

One must remark that this integration is firstly aimed towards Portuguese society, but also and secondly, because of EU citizenship, a way to penetrate in other member States' societies, benefiting from the status of European citizen.

[16] The proposition described in this sub-heading is really a mix between recognition and acquisition, because the individual has to declare she/he wants to be recognised as Portuguese since the day he was born – which means that, if no one (his parents, namely) makes this declaration for her/him, only when she/he reaches legal majority can this declaration occur and the Portuguese citizenship be registered – see article 21/5 (with the effects determined by article 11: since birth) and see also article 211 of LI (communication to the Board for foreigner and borders' matters). We should underline, however, that a foreign person who was born in Portugal and has residence in the country cannot be expelled, according to article 135/a) of LI – a similar (and exclusive) guarantee to the one Portuguese citizens have (article 33/1 of the Constitution).

Though we don't want to go into details, it should be mentioned that there are time-based premises that have to be verified previous to the citizenship's acquisition: for instance, if by marriage, three years must pass after the wedding day[17], assuming the marriage lasts (article 3/1)[18]; if by naturalisation, the foreigner must maintain legal residence in Portugal for at least six years (among other things: see article 6/1[19])[20]. The knowledge of the language is also an issue, at least if the person has reached majority [article 6/1/c)]; if not, the fact that the minor has had contact with the country or with the education system – as stated in article 6/2/a) and b) – establishes the presumption that the connection is strong enough for the bond of citizenship to be established.

b) Secondly, citizens of EU member States are not subject to LI – so, they are neither considered foreigner nor, truly, immigrants. The reason for this differentiation derives from the Union Treaty, which recognised the EU citizenship for economic and political purposes [see Part II of the European Community Treaty, which will turn into Part II of the Treaty on the functioning of the European Union, when (and if...) the Treaty of Lisbon enters into force]. Only the Portuguese State has the power to establish the criteria for citizenship's attribution[21]; but the subjective extension of this power is slightly disturbed by the existence of a *double link of citizenship*[22] that, nevertheless, depends on the previous attribution of a national link. In other words, and appealing to a George Orwell image: in Portugal

[17] Article 186 of Law 23/07, of the 4th July, punishes anyone who gets married just in order to obtain a visa, an authorization of residency or Portuguese citizenship. Imprisonment may go from one to four years.

[18] The civil partnership is equivalent to the traditional marriage, according to article 3/3. The situation has to be judicially recognised, though, prior to the request for Portuguese citizenship made by the foreigner's spouse.

[19] Comparing article 6/1 of the Law of Citizenship with article 126 of LI, concerning the attribution of long-time residency status, we conclude that the latter is much more demanding than the former – in other words, it is easier to become Portuguese than to get the long-time residency permit.

[20] But see the exceptions to the six years residence rule in numbers 3, 4, 5 and 6 of article 6.

[21] About the basis of this State's competence, see Emilio CASTORINA, Introduzione allo studio della cittadinanza, Milan, 1997, pp. 7 ff.

[22] Cfr. José Joaquim GOMES CANOTILHO, Enquadramento..., *cit.*, p. 162.

(as in any other EU member State), there are foreign people more foreign than other[23]...

The need to grant special conditions of freedom of circulation, residency and access to work justifies the existence of an autonomous legal framework applicable to EU citizens: Law 37/06, of the 9th August (which transposes directive 2004/38/CE, of the European Parliament and the Council, of the 29th April). We must underline that this regime is extended to Switzerland's citizens and to the citizens of States that are part of the Economic European Space Agreement (Iceland, Norway and Liechtenstein), according to article 3/4 of Law 37/06, and also to any member of a Portuguese citizen's family, regardless of her/his citizenship (article 3/5 of Law 37/06).

Basically, the difference of treatment between foreigner from third countries and foreigner from the EU and equivalent categories relies on:

i.) the fact that the latter don't need a visa to enter Portugal (a document of identification is sufficient)[24] – the former do;

ii.) the fact that EU citizens and family members may have residency in Portugal for three months without any formality[25] – foreigner from third countries need to obtain a short term visa or a residency visa. Brazilian citizens have a special prerogative, under article 217/5 of LI and article 6/2 of the *Agreement for reciprocal contracting*, signed in Lisbon between Portugal and Brazil on the 11th July 2003: they don't need to obtain the short term visa, once these requests are transformed in requests for temporary residency authorizations[26] (see article 75 of LI)[27];

---

[23] This happened since 1993, the year in which Decree-Law 60/93, of the 3rd March first regulated the framework of entry, permanence and leave of Portuguese territory by EU citizens (now substituted by Law 37/06, below mentioned in the text).

[24] Article 4 of Law 37/06.

[25] Article 6 of Law 37/06.

[26] According to article 84 of LI, the residency permit substitutes the identification card, having in mind, however, the regulation inscribed in the Treaty of Porto Seguro, signed on that city between Brazil and Portugal, in 2000 (approved for ratification by Resolution of the Republic Assembly nº 83/2000, of the 28th September, and ratified by the Presidential Decree nº 79/2000, of the 14th November). Decree law 154/03, of the 15th July gives execution to this Treaty and states the same equivalence between residency authorizations and identity cards (article 5/1). Nevertheless, the political rights involved in this Treaty, namely

iii.) the fact that EU citizens and family members can obtain long-term residency permits of five years either if she/he works in Portugal, or has enough means to support herself/himself (and family), and has health insurance (if demanded of Portuguese citizens staying in her/his State of origin under identical circumstances); or is studying in a public or private education establishment, legally recognised, and has enough means to support herself/himself and family, and has health insurance (if demanded of Portuguese citizens staying in her/his State of origin under identical circumstances [28]) – foreigners from third countries need to fulfil more demands to get (temporary and permanent) residency permits[29];

iv.) the fact that EU citizens and family members gain the right to live permanently in Portugal after five consecutive years of stay[30], and from then on benefit from a special protection against banishment, which then allows banishment only if based on serious reasons of public order or public security[31] – and if they had residency in Portugal in the past ten years or are minor, authorities can only invoke imperative reasons of public security to banish the person[32]. Rather differently, citizens from third countries with permanent residency authorisations are in a more fragile situation, although they can't be arbitrarily expelled – as article 134 of LI demonstrates. As to the immigrants with long-term residency status, the situation is identical to EU citizens (see article 136/1 of LI).

These brief notes show that foreign citizens in Portugal are not all alike, and that EU citizens (and those equivalent) have a special status compared to citizens from third countries. But, are we in condition to affirm that all citizens from third countries staying in Portugal, not Portuguese, not EU

---

the right to vote and be elected in local elections, demand a period of stay of at least three years (article 5/2 of the Treaty), which means the equivalence isn't immediate in all cases.

[27] In what concerns dispensing the visa, we should also pinpoint the special situations referred to on articles 122 and 123 of LI. See *infra* note 71.

[28] Articles 10, 7/1 (and 2), and 14 of Law 37/06.

[29] See LI, articles 77 e 80.

[30] Articles 10 and 13 of Law 37/06.

[31] Article 23/2 of Law 36/07.

[32] Article 23/3 of Law 36/07.

citizens or those equivalent, are (according to the law) immigrants? The answer is no, for three reasons:

i.) The condition of immigrant involves a *free will* to leave the country of origin in order to go to another State that provides employment, education or another kind of experience which constitutes a value to the individual. In other words, it is a *voluntary choice* – even if it's sometimes hard to affirm, given the extreme poverty situation faced by people in the country of origin. So, a refugee or a beneficiary of political asylum – or a victim of human trafficking – would not be considered an immigrant[33];

ii.) The will to leave the country of origin must be a *product of self-determination, not a duty*. That's why LI excludes diplomats and members of international organizations (and families, and staff) from the obligation to obtain an authorisation of residency (article 87)[34];

iii.) Being an immigrant implies a *detachment from the country of origin and the establishment of a connection* – stronger or weaker – *to the new welcome community*. That connection takes form within a certain period of time, certainly superior to a short visit. In other words, tourists aren't immigrants because they don't come with the purpose of staying: like Paul Bowles puts it, in *The Sheltering Sky* (contrasting tourists with travellers), a tourist generally hurries home at the end of a few weeks or months.[35]

So the last question would be: how much time should the stay last and what kind of objectives must an immigrant pursue in the receiving country? Looking at the kinds of visas LI regulates, we would say that an immigrant is someone who is granted a permanent residency authorisation [LI, articles 74/1/a), 76 and 80], or someone who is given the status of long-term resident, according to articles 125 and ff. of LI (see specially 126) – or, if we think on illegal immigrants, someone who is living in the country for at least five years, although illegally. Precisely, both the former cases demand a *five year period of stay in Portugal* previous to the attribution

---

[33] LI supports this analysis: see articles 4/2/b) and 109/2 and 5 (for victims of human traffic).
[34] See other examples of "forced immigration" *in* Jorge GASPAR, A autorização..., *cit.*, pp. 966-967.
[35] PAUL BOWLES, THE SHELTERING SKY (1949).

DIREITO COMPARADO / COMPARATIVE LAW

of the permit, that has no time limit [although it must be revalidated every five years: articles 76/2, 129/8 and 130/2 of LI] – the same period of time within which EU member States' citizens may obtain the right of living permanently in Portugal. The difference between the two statuses concerns mainly a language requirement: *basic knowledge* to get the authorisation; *fluency* to be recognised as a long-term resident (see articles 80/1/e) and 126/1/e) of LI).

In order to limit the subjective universe of this presentation, we are going to assume that *an immigrant is a foreign citizen who has lived (legally) in Portugal for at least five years, not necessarily working but having enough means of self-subsistence for herself/himself (and her/his family, if applicable) so not to rely on the national security system, and therefore has been given a permanent residency authorisation or has been attributed the status of long-term resident*. Before that, either she/he is a tourist or a visitor (even if a long-time one).

Three last remarks: first, the condition of immigrant is gradual – one isn't an instant immigrant, *one becomes an immigrant* (see III.); second, from the perspective we just adopted, *the time factor is decisive* to qualify an immigrant, more than the administrative process – because one can be an immigrant from a *material* perspective but not from a *formal* one: that's why there are legal and illegal immigrants[36]; third, *being an immigrant* – and not a mere visitor – involves time and connection to the welcome community but *doesn't imply a perpetual state*, because immigrants may stay for as long as they live, but they may also acquire Portuguese citizenship and no longer be immigrants. And, of course, they may go back home.

2. What aspects does the immigrants' *administrative condition* involve?

Immigrants are persons who can be viewed in multiple ways. Considering the work division of this VIII Conference and also our academic skills, the

---

[36] This point is debatable, since we must admit that, from a certain point of view, an immigrant is someone to whom the State has recognized a right to stay – in that case, it would be better to talk about illegal visitors, who never reached the formal status of immigrants. And if so, illegal immigrants would only be the ones who lost the status, after having achieved it. In practice, though, we talk about illegal immigrants as much as meaning any foreign citizen who has illegally entered in Portugal as referring to legal immigrants who turned illegal (because their authorizations were cancelled, or because they lost the long-term residency status, or they were expelled). In this text, although we depart from a restrictive concept of (legal) immigrant, when we deal with expulsion, we will also have illegal *visitors* in mind (see IV.).

analysis will focus on the legal framework provided by LI, leaving aside problems such as social integration of immigrants or economic effects of immigration[37]. More reluctantly, we will also exclude a deep incursion on the political condition of immigrants – restricting ourselves to brief notes on Constitutional norms on the subject (II.). Finally, a controversial dimension of immigrants' status relies on the problem of which fundamental rights they should be attributed/recognized[38], namely, in what way can their rights be diminished or reformatted in order to coincide with the moral and juridical values of the receiving country – which alone could well be the theme of another conference...

The object of our presentation will then be circumscribed to the brief description of the legal framework in what concerns admission, concession of long-term residency permits and expulsion by the administrative authorities and, in what relates to expulsion, also by the judicial power (towards legal immigrants).

II. Immigrants in the Constitution
Like LI, the Portuguese Constitution (PC) hardly mentions the word "immigrant". The PC states the right to leave (article 44), but not the right to enter[39]. In fact, besides article 74/2/j), founding the State's duty to grant immigrants' support to ensure their children's right to education, there's no other reference. It is a common absence in other constitutional texts, though. The protective norms towards immigrants don't appear as such but instead as guarantees provided to foreigners (that they are, essentially)[40]

---

[37] On this side of the problem, see António CLUNY, Multiculturalismo, interculturalismo e imigração em Portugal no início do séc. XXI, *in RMP*, nº 97, 2004, pp. 103 ff.

[38] On the various "masks" immigrants may be envisaged with by the welcome community, José Joaquim GOMES CANOTILHO, Enquadramento..., *cit.*, pp. 152 ff.

[39] That's why José Joaquim GOMES CANOTILHO (Enquadramento..., *cit.*, p. 159) affirms the PC consecrates the right to *emigrate*, not the right to *immigrate*.

[40] It is, for instance, the approach of the French *Conseil d'État* – see the note to Décision nº 2003-484 du 20 novembre 2003, by Nicolas FERRAN: La politique de maîtrise des fluxs migratoires et le respect des droits et libertés constitutionnels, *in Revue du Droit Public et de la Science Politique*, 2004/1, pp. 275 ff. – as well as of the Italian *Corte Costituzionale*: Paolo PASSAGLIA and Roberto ROMBOLI, La condizione giuridica dello straniero nella prospettiva della Corte Costituzionale, *in II Jornadas Italo-españolas de Justicia Constitucional. Problemas constitucionales de la inmigración: una visión desde Italia y España* (coord. by Miguel Revenga Sánchez), Valencia, 2005, pp. 11 ff., spec. 27 ff. –, and of the Spanish *Tribunal Constitucional*: J. Luis García Ruiz, La

DIREITO COMPARADO / COMPARATIVE LAW

or to minorities (because they usually keep their cultural and religious traditions, sometimes confronting those of the receiving country)[41] – or even, as happens in the U.S. Constitution, their relevance to the legislator derives from article 1, section 8, which deals with the Congressional power to legislate on naturalization matters[42].

In the PC, the principle of equivalent protection of foreigner's civil rights is stated in article 15/1. It derives from the principles of human dignity (article 1) and of fundamental rights' universalism (article 12): men are born free and equal, independently from their place of birth, and should be recognised as having equal rights. This statement echoes article 1 of the Universal Declaration of Human Rights, the basic catalogue received by our Constitution in article 16/2, to help to interpret and to complete the norms related to fundamental rights, in order to achieve the best level of protection. One should also add article 12 of the International Pact about Civil and Political Rights, where the rights to leave the country of birth, of legal entrance and of free circulation in a welcome State are established. Last but not the least, one must mention the prohibition of expulsion except for relevant reasons and the right to a due process, with contradictory hearing and judicial review, stated in article 13 of the IPCPR: both enter the catalogue of our Constitution through the open clause of article 16/1.

The principle of equivalent protection, received in article 15/1 of the PC, is central to grant the effectiveness of immigrants' fundamental rights – at least civil and social rights[43]. If we join the imperatives of universal and

---

condición de extranjero y el Derecho Constitucional español, *in II Jornadas Italo-españolas de Justicia Constitucional. Problemas constitucionales de la inmigración: una visión desde Italia y España* (coord. by Miguel Revenga Sánchez), Valencia, 2005, pp. 489 ff., spec. 500 ff.

[41] Justifying the nearness between the concepts *immigrants* and *minorities*, Ana Luisa PINTO e Mariana CANOTILHO, O tratamento dos estrangeiros e das minorias na jurisprudência constitucional portuguesa, *in Estudos em homenagem ao Conselheiro José Manuel Cardoso da Costa*, II, Coimbra, 2005, pp. 231 ff., 234.

[42] "It would not make sense to allow Congress to pass laws to determine how an immigrant becomes a naturalized resident if the Congress cannot determine how that immigrant can come into the country in the first place" – http://www.usconstitution.net/constnot. html#immigration (accessed on the 1st February 2009).

[43] In the United States, there's the leading case *Plyler v. Doe*, of 1982, where the Supreme Court affirmed that the right to education must be granted equally both to American children and to immigrants' children.

equal protection established in articles 12 and 13 to article 15/1, we conclude that, as a matter of principle, the Portuguese State cannot differentiate citizens from immigrants, as long as these latter are legally staying in the country. In the words of Mário TORRES, "in what concerns the general rights granted to Portuguese citizens, the Constitution admits only one position: whether full equivalence, *without restrictions*, between citizen and foreigner, or *exclusivity* of certain rights to Portuguese citizens"[44]. And it goes without submitting the extension to any condition of reciprocity, if not expressly affirmed.

This equivalence admits exceptions – which contributes to the creation of several categories of foreigners[45] – but only with regard to political rights and the exercise of certain functions[46]. These constitute the truest expression of the connection to the values and policies developed by the State, and are reserved to Portuguese citizens – one is even exclusive of the original citizens: the right to be a presidential candidate (article 122 of the PC). As much as the sovereign State can limit the entrance of foreign persons into its territory[47] based in a principle of national independence, so does sovereignty also justify the power to restrict certain rights to a State's citizens – those which reflect a will to participate in the community's main choices and so demand a stronger bond (of citizenship).

Sensing the need to integrate immigrants within their welcome subcommunities, the PC allows the legislature, since 1989[48], to regulate their rights to vote and to be elected in municipal elections[49]. This norm also

[44] Mário TORRES, O estatuto constitucional dos estrangeiros, *in SI*, n.º 290, 2001, pp. 7 ff., 22.

[45] As the Constitutional Court affirms – A jurisprudência constitucional sobre o cidadão estrangeiro, *Report of the 10th trilateral conference Portugal, Spain, Italy, which took place in Madrid, from the 25th to the 27th September 2008*, p. 2 (available at http://tribunalconstitucional.pt/tc/textos0202html).

[46] As the Constitutional Court puts it, "the exceptions to the principle of equivalence of rights between foreigner and Portuguese citizens established in the Constitution are easy to understand, once they rely on foreigners' relationship with the *institutionalized political community* – with which foreigners have, most certainly, a fragile bond (...)" – A jurisprudência constitucional sobre o cidadão estrangeiro, *cit.*, p. 5.

[47] See Charles P. GOMES, Les changements juridiques dans les cas d'immigration en France et aux États-Unis, *in RFSP*, 200/3, pp. 413 ff., 413.

[48] The 2nd constitutional revision introduced number 4 in article 15, which was altered in 1992, assuming the actual redaction.

[49] Immigrants' right to vote in municipal elections is regulated in Law 56/98, of the 18th August, altered by Law 23/00, of the 23rd August and by Organic Law 1/01, of the 14th

DIREITO COMPARADO / COMPARATIVE LAW

applies, naturally, to EU citizens, whose *enlarged citizenship* justifies the extension – and they have the right, likewise, to vote in the European Parliament's elections, based on reciprocity (article 15/5 of the PC, introduced in the constitutional revision of 1992).

The Constitutional Court has been called to analyse some situations concerning foreigners' rights (not necessarily immigrants, in the restricted sense we have defined). Most of the decisions concern judicial rights of defence: access to justice in matters of asylum and extradition, financial assistance, due process of expulsion, right to judicial review – and have been oriented by the principles of equal protection and prohibition of nonproportional restrictions[50]. There are decisions about access to public functions (because article 15/2 of the PC restricts the access to public charges that don't have a "predominantly technical dimension"[51]) and to social security as well.

Perhaps the most important group of judgements are the ones involving expulsion: on the one hand, the Constitutional Court denies the automatic effect of expulsion based on a penal condemnation, when the offender is a legal resident – appealing to the prohibition of penalties' automatic effect and also based on the freedom of circulation (articles 30/4 and 44 of the PC, respectively)[52]. On the other hand, the High Court for constitutional

---

August. Article 2 attributes the right to vote, dividing non-Portuguese citizen voters in three categories: EU citizens, citizens from Portuguese speaking countries (part of CPLP) and other citizens – all of them based in reciprocity and subordinated to an inscription in the local area census services. As to the first, however, the right is automatically attributed. As to the second, the right exists if they have residency in the municipality for at least two years. As to the third, if they have residency in the municipality for at least three years previously to the electoral act.

Article 5 allows them the possibility to be elected to municipal charges, assuming the same division mentioned above, and based on reciprocity: EU citizens, automatically; citizens from Portuguese speaking countries, if they have legal residency for at least four years, and as to the others, if they have legal residency for at least five years.

[50] For the detailed references, see Ana Luisa PINTO e Mariana CANOTILHO, O tratamento dos estrangeiros...., *cit.*, pp. 238 and ff.

[51] The Constitutional Court has considered these to comprehend professions like judge, policeman or high charges at the public administration that involve the power to unilaterally define subjective situations – see A jurisprudência constitucional sobre o cidadão estrangeiro..., *cit.*, p. 5.

[52] See cases 359/93 and 288/94 (see also case 442/93, involving an offender whose entrance in Portugal was illegal – the automatic effect was not considered unconstitutional in that situation).

matters decided several cases of constitutional incidents related to norms which allowed the expulsion of foreigners condemned by crimes committed in Portugal not considering the fact that they had minors at charge. These norms were considered unconstitutional on the basis that they lead to the expulsion of the offender's children with Portuguese citizenship – who can't be expelled, according to article 33/1 of the PC, and couldn't be left behind[53]. One must add that family protection (article 36/6 of the PC) and the jurisprudence of the ECJ and the ECHR concur in the prohibition of a foreign offender's expulsion whenever she/he has children at charge in Portugal, even if they are not Portuguese[54] – the LI conforms to that, as we can see in article 135/c).

III. Becoming an immigrant

As we said above, a foreign person in Portugal isn't necessarily an immigrant – she/he *might become one*. In fact, apart from tourists and (longer or shorter term) visitors, there are persons who stay for considerable periods of time and grow a connection to the country that ends in the attribution of a status: the long-term resident status[55]. The LI regulates these aspects, following very closely ten European directives and one framework decision of the Council (see the list in article 2)[56]. The transposition of these directives practically empties the power of the Portuguese legislator on the subject. In other words, he is strictly bound by a superior framework, due to the fact that the entering and staying of third-country citizens in

[53] On this jurisprudence, see Anabela LEÃO, Expulsão de estrangeiros com filhos menores a cargo (Note on the decision 232/04 of the Constitutional Court), *in JC*, nº 3, 2004, pp. 25 ff..
[54] See Carla AMADO GOMES, Filiação, adopção e protecção de menores. Quadro constitucional e notas de jurisprudência, *in RCEJ*, nº 13, 2008, pp. 7 ff.,
[55] Jorge GASPAR (A autorização..., *cit.*, p. 963) departs from a similar concept: an immigrant is an alien who arrives in the receiving country and seeks to install there on the basis of labour or economic motivations.
[56] On the European policy for immigration, see Miguel GORJÃO-HENRIQUES, A Europa e o «estrangeiro»: Talo(s) ou Cristo?, *in Temas de Integração*, nº 6, 1998, pp. 23 ff.; Henry LABAYLE, L'Union Européenne et l'immigration. Une véritable politique commune?, *in Mouvement du Droit Public, Mélanges en l'honneur de Franck Moderne*, Paris, 2004, pp. 1217 ff.; Helena PÉREZ MARTÍN, Libertad de circulación y de residencia: ciudadania e inmigración en la Constitución Europea, *in Colóquio Ibérico: Constituição Europeia. Homenagem ao Doutor Francisco Lucas Pires*, Coimbra, 2005, pp. 593 ff., spec. 604 ff

DIREITO COMPARADO / COMPARATIVE LAW

Portugal is a way to penetrate into a territory beyond Portugal's borders and a way to access a market much larger than Portugal's market alone..

This said, how can one become an immigrant[57]?

First, the foreigner has to enter the country legally[58] – or, exceptionally, benefit from an extraordinary legalization period[59] – which means obtaining a visa. In the case of someone who wishes to stay for a long period, working or studying, she/he needs a *residency visa* [article 45/e) of LI]. Portuguese consulates in the country of origin are competent to emit the visas [article 48/1/b) of LI], within 60 days after the presentation of the request (article 58/4 of LI)[60], but they must previously consult the Portuguese Foreigner and Borders' Board (*Serviço de Estrangeiros e Fronteiras, SEF*)[61], which has 20 days to respond – the silence means a favourable answer [article 53/1/a) and nº 6 of LI]. The visa must be denied if one of the situations mentioned in article 52/1, 3 and 4, occur: if the person was expelled from the country (and is still within the period of non-readmission[62]); if the person is included in the European[63] or in the national

---

[57] To consult practical data on the numbers of residence permits given by the Foreigner and Borders' Board up to 2007, go to http://www.sef.pt/portal/vl0/PT/aspx/estatisticas.

[58] See the conditions of entrance refusal in article 32 of LI – which partially correspond to the reasons of visa denial (article 52 of LI). We underline the fact that Portuguese authorities can't refuse the entrance to foreign citizens in the cases described in article 36 of LI: foreign people who were born in Portuguese territory and there usually reside; foreign people who are in charge of minors with Portuguese citizenship; and foreign people who are in charge of minors with a third State citizenship legally residing in Portugal.
See also *infra* note 71, about article 122/1/j) e n) of LI.

[59] In Portugal, there have been three extraordinary legalisations: in 1992 (Law 212/92, of the 12th October), in 1996 (Law 16/96, of the 24th May) and in 2004 (see article 71 of Decree 6/04, of the 26th April, referring to article 52/3 of Decree Law 244/98, of the 8th August, altered by Decree Law 34/03, of the 25th February).

[60] But see the exception in nº 3 of article 53, concerning the urgency of a residency visa's concession for independent professional activity.

[61] For the structure and competences of the Board, see Decree-Law 252/00, of the 16th October.

[62] This period should be fixed in the decision of expulsion. The LI fixes five years as a maximum period (article 144), which doesn't mean, of course, that after that lapse of time, the foreigner has automatically the right to re-enter.

[63] The European system of surveillance is the *Schengen System*. It was developed after the Schengen Agreements of 1985/1990 that aimed to abolish the internal controls within the frontiers of the EU members and establish common rules on visas, on the right of asylum and on external controls towards citizens of third States. The *Schengen System* is a compensatory

system of nonadmission[64]; if the person, even if not (yet) spotted in these systems, constitutes a serious menace to public order, to public security or to public health[65]; if the person was sentenced for a crime that, in Portugal, would involve a period of imprisonment for longer than one year; if the person doesn't have means of self-subsistence; if the person doesn't possess a valid travel document; and if the person didn't subscribe a travel insurance. Apart from the right of personal data rectification (article 52/5 of LI), these decisions are not subject to judicial review.

Residency visas are the first step to obtain a residency authorisation and are valid for four months (article 58/1 and 2 of LI). There are six types of residency visas[66]:

i.) in order to the exercise of subordinate labour (article 59 of LI). The concession of this visa depends on a contingent – fixed annually by the Government – of labour opportunities neither taken by Portuguese workers nor by workers from EU countries and equivalent nor, finally, by foreign workers already resident in Portugal (article 59/1). The only exception is the one described in nº 7: in that case, the foreign worker may get the job if she/he has a contract and is

measure to counterbalance the freedom of dislocation in the European space and consists on a data base that collects information on people and goods, in order to fight organized crime. The *System* is passing through a technical evolution, aiming quicker information transmission, which gave birth to several decisions of the Council that created SIS II (*Schengen System II*). Nowadays, only Cyprus, Romania and Bulgaria are out of the *Schengen System,* among EU members. Norway, Iceland and Switzerland, though not EU members, are linked to the *Schengen System* through a cooperation agreement.

For further details, see http://europa.eu/scadplus/leg/pt.

[64] See articles 32 and 33 of LI: the situations concern reasons of public security (internal or external), and may rely on suspicions (though these must be "strong") about the possible practice of acts contrary to the public order and public internal and external security. The protection of public health can also be invoked as a reason for not allowing the foreigner's entry – according to José Alberto de MELO ALEXANDRINO, A nova lei de entrada..., *cit.*, p. 15, article 32/2 is too vague when it refers to "other contagious infectious or parasitic illnesses detected in national territory".

[65] Even if the visa is emitted, the person may not be allowed the entrance if s/he became a public health menace afterwards. In this case, the refusal of entrance must be founded in the existence of an illness recognised by the WHO or specially identified by the national authorities. The foreign citizen may be invited to go through medical tests in order to prove s/he doesn't suffer from any of those illnesses – see article 32/2 and 3 of LI.

[66] See also articles 10 ff. of Decree 84/07, of 5th November.

DIREITO COMPARADO / COMPARATIVE LAW

able to prove that the offer was rejected by the workers mentioned in nº 1;

ii.) in order to the exercise of an independent profession or willing to create an enterprise (article 60 of LI);

iii.) in order to developing scientific investigation or a highly qualified activity (article 61 of LI);

iv.) in order to study at the secondary level, within students' interchange, or to develop training or doing voluntary work (article 62 of LI);

v.) in order to study at the university level (article 63 of LI); and

vi.) in order to regroup a family (article 64 of LI). The request is presented to the Portuguese Foreigner and Borders' Board by the foreign person who's already living in Portugal on the basis of a permanent residency authorisation or has been already recognized the status of long-time resident – see article 103 of LI. The decision is taken by the Director of the Board (article 102 of LI), within three months[67], must conform to the conditions prescribed in article 101 (basically, demanding that the foreigner who lives in Portugal has lodging and means of subsistence to support the family), and cannot violate article 106 of LI (that is to say, the resident does not fulfil the conditions of article 101, or the family member is refused entrance in the country for public security or public health reasons). We must add that LI considers *family members* all the categories of persons listed in article 99, and is extended to the partner of a civil partnership and her/his children, if the requester had their legal custody.

---

[67] Note that article 105/1 and 3 is equivocal. On the one hand, nº 1 says that the decision is notified "as soon as possible and in any case, within three months"; on the other hand, nº 3 states that if after six months no decision surges it means the request has been deferred. So, only six months after the presentation of the request is the requester admitted to ask the Board to certify the silent approval and communicate it to the Consulate competent to the visas' emission. Before that, whether he gets a favourable answer or he must wait for the passing of time (this solution is repeated in articles 117/4 and 7, and 129/3 and 5 of LI).
This solution raises at least two questions:
– Is the Board allowed to refuse the request after three months?
– After three months, is the requester allowed to propose an action in order to condemn the Board to the emission of the decision (favourable or not), on the terms of articles 66 and ff. of the Administration Judicial Process Code?

THE ADMINISTRATIVE CONDITION OF IMMIGRANTS GENERAL ASPECTS AND TOPIC...

After this first step, foreign persons are ready for the second phase: to get the temporary residency authorisation [article 74/1/a) of LI][68]. The authorisation is valid for one year and is renewable for periods of two years[69] (article 75/2 of LI). Besides the general principles to which administrative powers are subdued[70], the conditions for this authorization's concession are established in article 77 of LI and deal both with *positive* premises (valid visa[71]; presence in Portuguese territory; lodging; means of subsistence) and with *negative* ones (not having committed crimes to which correspond imprisonment superior to one year; not being prohibited to enter Portuguese territory; not constituting a menace to public security or to public health). The request is extendable to minors at charge of the requester (article 81/2 of LI).

---

[68] See also articles 51 and ff. of Decree 84/07, of 5th November.

[69] In the case of students at the university level, article 91/2 of LI states that this authorization is valid for one year and renewable for periods of another year. We must also mention the exceptional case of persons victim of human traffic to whom is allowed, on the basis of Section V of Chapter VI, the permanence in the country strictly for investigations' purposes (if the person so wishes), for periods of one year, renewable for equal time (as long as the circumstances justify the stay).

[70] Among which the equality principle, forcing authorities to observe equal criteria in giving authorizations to immigrants whose situations are objectively similar to precedent ones which benefited from favourable decisions – see case 080/02, of the 6th November 2003, decided by the Portuguese Administrative Supreme Court.

[71] Section VII deals with special cases, which don't require a valid visa previous to the authorization's concession. Article 122 includes seventeen very different situations, from foreign people's children born in Portugal, to sick people that need local medical assistance, to foreign citizens (who lived in the ancient colonies) who have actually paid service to the Portuguese Army, among others. Since LI is in force (September 2008), 8312 authorizations have been given on the basis of this article (source: http:// www.portugal.gov.pt / PORTAL/ PT/ Governos/ Governos_Constitucionais/ GC17/ Ministerios/MAI/Comunicacao/Notas_ de_imprensa/281105_mai_com_legalizacao_imigrantes_htm,accessed on the 4th February 2009).

The case described on n) is particularly relevant, because it concerns foreign persons victim of labour exploitation, who entered the country illegally, on the basis of false promises of work – as long as they have denounced the situation to Portuguese authorities and cooperate with them in order to punish the employers. This exception, as well as the one mentioned in j) is, in the end, a way of continuous (extraordinary?) legalisation.

Article 123 is even more special – in fact, it mentions an "exceptional regime" – because it applies to cases of humanitarian interest and others based on arguments of national interest or public interest, namely the fact that the person exercises relevant activity on a scientific, cultural, sportive, economic or social area.

DIREITO COMPARADO / COMPARATIVE LAW

The authorizations' renewal is submitted to the same prescriptions, and also to the proof of fiscal and social security obligations' compliment (see article 78 of LI). In the special case of imprisonment, the foreign citizen may still ask for renewal, but only if he wasn't subject to an order of expulsion (article 79 of LI).

Portuguese Foreigner and Borders' Board is competent to decide on the request of residency authorizations (article 81 of LI). The first request must be deferred within 60 days – 30 days for the renewal. In this last case, if the answer isn't communicated to the applicant in the delay of six months, the decision is considered favourable (article 82/3 of LI)[72]. In case of denial, the applicant may ask the administrative court to review the act (article 82/4 of LI). There is, likewise, judicial review if the authorization is cancelled by the Board based either on the foreign person's expulsion, or on the fact that she/he has become a menace to public security or public health, or because she/he has been away from Portuguese territory for a considerable period of time (see article 85/1 and 2 of LI – especially 7, for judicial review). We must underline that to these general conditions of cancellation (and refusal of renewal requests) some others may join, like the ones mentioned in article 95 of LI (concerning authorizations for studying at the superior level, or for developing professional training or charity activities) and the ones referred to by article 108 of LI.

After being in the country for at least five years, foreign citizens may apply, either to a permanent residency authorization[73] or to the long-term resident status[74] – that's the third step. In fact, the only difference between

---

[72] The law doesn't refer to silent approval of the first request – it only admits it for renewal. Which leaves two possible interpretations:
– when the Board doesn't answer a request for residency (temporary or permanent), the applicant should use the special administrative action for the authorities' condemnation on the emission of a lawful act (articles 66 ff. of the Administrative Process Judicial Code), within one year after the end of the six months. The applicant's situation will be, nonetheless, illegal until the Administrative Court decides. A possible corrector of this law hole would be to admit the use of the urgent remedy established in article 109 of the Administrative Process Judicial Code;
– when the Board doesn't answer a request for residency (temporary or permanent), the rule of article 82/3 also apply to the case, which means a silent approval, in order to a better protection of immigrants' expectatives.

[73] See also articles 64 and ff. of Decree 84/07, of the 5th November.

[74] See also articles 74 and following of Decree 84/07, of the 5th November.

the prerequisites defined for each is the knowledge of Portuguese language (see articles 80/1/e) and 126/1/e) of LI). So, after the *first* step, visa, and the *second*, temporary residency authorisation[75], at the *third* moment, the visitor finally (and formally) becomes an immigrant.

Permanent residency authorizations and long-term residency status allow the immigrant a rest on bureaucratic procedures. They have no time limit (see articles 76/1 and 129/8 of LI), though the titles[76] must be renewed every five years (articles 76/2 and 130/2 of LI). It doesn't mean they can't be lost: as we saw above, authorizations may be cancelled. And, concerning the long-term residency status, it may also be revoked, on the basis of: fraud on the obtaining; judicial expulsion; acquisition of a long-term residency status in another State of the EU; or leave of the EU or the Portuguese territory for a period of 12 consecutive months or for six consecutive years, respectively (see article 131/1 of LI). These decisions, as well as the authorizations' refusals or the status' concessions, are subject to judicial review by administrative courts, though LI grants a special protection on the cases of long-term residency denial and revocation: the judicial process automatically suspends the efficacy of the measure (article 132/3 of LI)[77].

We can be tempted to say that, in practice, this difference doesn't amount to much, because judicial administrative process grants interim protection through immediately suspending the act's effects, according to article 128/1 of the Administrative Judicial Process Code. Once we give it a second look, though, things may not be that simple:

- *Primo*, when judicial action doesn't suspend, on its own, the act's effects, the defendant forcibly needs to present a request for interim protection, which doubles the means and the costs, and leaves suspension on the hands of the judge (first, when he analyses the reasons presented by the Board to continue execution; second, when he decides the request for interim relief). The solution of article

---

[75] The special situation of Brazilian citizens must be remarked, because of the 2003 Lisbon Agreement – see *supra*, I.1. b) *ii.*).

[76] *Título de residência* and *Título CE de residente de longa duração*, respectivelly.

[77] This solution differs from the ones prescribed on article 85/7 of LI (and unnecessarily on articles 96/4 and 106/7 of LI): these actions don't suspend the acts effects by themselves. Curiously, articles 106/8 and 108/7 of LI, concerning family regrouping, have a different approach, probably in order to provide a stronger protection when family values are at stake.

132/3 of LI relies on a *unique process* and leaves the judge *no margin to reject the denial/cancellation's effects suspension*;

- *Secundo*, when the law talks about a process that immediately suspending the act's effect, it points to a special procedure, because, in principle[78], judicial action in the administrative courts doesn't work like that. On the other hand, as we just saw, if the defendant doesn't benefit from a special clause, he must use the general means of defense regulated in the Administrative Judicial Process Code, which involve two actions: the request for interim relief (suspension) and the request to annul the act.

The special process LI points to, when referring to the immediate suspension of the act's negative effects may well be the injunction for civil rights and liberties' protection, established on article 109 of the Administrative Judicial Process Code. First, because it is an urgent process that specially adjust to the values at stake in a process of this type. Second, because it is abnormally quick (theoretically, the problem would be solved in about a week). And third, because the efficacy of the protection provided makes interim relief measures much less useful.

As we saw above, the Constitution grants foreign citizens in Portugal equal rights as if they were nationals, except for the exercise of sovereign powers (judges; deputies to the Republic Assembly; members of Government; Chief of State) and for public jobs that don't concern strictly technical aspects (see article 15/2 of the PC). So, norms like articles 83 and 133 of LI are basically useless and may induce in error, for one may think that the rights there enunciated are the only ones attributed to the immigrant (like education, work, professional training, health care and access to justice). Even if it is more or less consensual that these lists relate to the rights more commonly exercised by immigrants, there's a risk of seeing them as closed lists – an interpretation contrary not only to the principle of equality resulting from article 15/2, but also to the principle of the rights' universality, founded in article 12 (both of the PC).

---

[78] We must remind the actions previewed in urban planning laws, promoted by the Public Attorney, which adopt the same solution of immediate suspension (though they accept the judge may review the suspension's "concession"). About this solution, see Carla AMADO GOMES, A tutela urgente no Direito do Urbanismo – algumas questões, *in Textos dispersos de Direito do Património Cultural e de Direito do Urbanismo*, Lisboa, 2008, pp. 181 ff., spec. 225 ff.

So, except for the impossibility of exercising some sovereignty charges and public functions, and for the possibility of expulsion[79], (legal) immigrants are just like Portuguese citizens and EU citizens and those equivalent, and must receive absolute equal treatment by the Administration. True, their status (both the ones who are given authorizations and the ones who retain the long-term residency status) is somewhat precarious because the statuses may be revoked anytime by the Administration. But the revocation's motives are listed and judicial review is granted in all cases (as well as free legal assistance).

IV. The expulsion of immigrants

There are two types of expulsion: the one determined by the Administration and the one determined by the judge. This difference has its roots in the guarantee established in article 33/2 of the PC[80]: foreign citizens who are legally in the country can only be expelled by judicial order.

Let's give a quick look at both, signalling the premises they stand in. Before that, however, we would like to leave three previous remarks:

1. There are four categories of immigrants who can't be expelled in any case[81]: those born in Portugal and live here; those who have children with Portuguese citizenship living in Portugal at charge; those who have children without Portuguese citizenship living in Portugal *effectively* at charge; and those who have been living in Portugal since before they were ten years old (article 135 of LI);

2. The decision of expulsion, when it comes from the Administration, is not considered a political act: it can be judicially reviewed by the administrative courts[82]. This is especially important because leaving the interpretation of concepts like "a menace to public order"

---

[79] Once again, we remind, however, the rule stated in article 135 of the LI, forbidding foreign citizens' expulsion in some cases.

[80] On the meaning of article 33/2 of the PC, see Jorge MIRANDA and Rui MEDEIROS, Constituição da República Portuguesa, Anotada, I, Coimbra, 2005, pp. 366-367.

[81] These categories were introduced by Law 244/98, of the 8thAugust, which was replaced by the present LI.

[82] Specifically on due process and access to justice by immigrants in Portugal, André Gonçalo DIAS PEREIRA, Garantias processuais e acesso ao direito e aos tribunais. A protecção específica dos estrangeiros, *in* José Joaquim GOMES CANOTILHO (org.), Direitos humanos..., *cit*, p. 201 ff.

DIREITO COMPARADO / COMPARATIVE LAW

(even more if it's just a presumption), or "a menace to State's dignity" solely in Administration's hands could imply a totally arbitrary analysis[83];

3. According to article 143 of LI – that echoes article 33/6 of the PC, concerning extradition[84] – expulsion cannot involve sending the foreign citizen to a country where she/he can be subjected to torture or degrading treatment (on the terms of article 3 of the ECHR). The immigrant must prove the fear of persecution in order to avoid being sent to that country. In cases as such, the administrative measure or the sentence that decrees the expulsion must mention the alternative destination.

1. The administrative expulsion of illegal immigrants

The expulsion authority of the Foreigner and Borders' Board is limited. Only illegal immigrants without a prior pronouncement of their status by a judge can be expelled by the Administration (articles 140/2 and 145 of LI). Illegal immigrants are those who entered in Portugal without a valid visa[85], who are staying in the country without valid authorization (temporary or permanent) – either because they never managed to get it or because it was cancelled – or, finally, who have seen their long-term residency status revoked.

When a foreign citizen is found illegally staying in Portugal, she/he can be detained by police authorities (article 146/7 of LI) and delivered to the Board, though he should be presented to a criminal judge within 48 hours. This judge may impose either a periodic obligation of presentation before the Board until the process is concluded, the obligation of staying in the residence with electronic surveillance or the confinement in a temporary shelter centre, if security reasons so require (see articles 142/1, 146/2 of LI, and 3 of Law 34/94, of the 14th September, about shelter

---

[83] Ultimately, one would be very near the XIXth century's doctrines which considered that if a State couldn't freely expel a foreigner it wouldn't truly be independent, like the US Supreme Court affirmed in the *Chinese Exclusion Case* of 1889 (*Chae Chan Ping vs. United States*) – see Charles P. GOMES, Les changements juridiques..., *cit.*, pp. 426-427.

[84] In this sense, José Joaquim GOMES CANOTILHO and Vital MOREIRA, Constituição da República Portuguesa Anotada, I, 4ª ed., Coimbra, 2007, pp. 531-532.

[85] Remember that the visa is dispensed in the 17 cases mentioned in article 122 of LI – see *supra* note 71.

centres[86]) – in this last case, the sheltering may never exceed 60 days (articles 146/3 of LI and 3/2 of Law 34/94)[87]. Preventive custody is expressly excluded (article 142/1 of LI). If the foreign person expresses her/his will to voluntarily abandon national territory and has documents to do so, she/he must be delivered by the judge to the Board and conducted to the border within the minimum period. Note that, in this case, no decision of expulsion is pronounced and the foreigner is forbidden to re-enter the country (only) for one year (article 147/2 LI).

Celerity characterises the process of expulsion; nevertheless, it necessarily involves a contradictory hearing and other instruction measures (see, above all, articles 32/10 of the PC, and 148 of LI)[88]. The project of decision is transmitted to the Director of the Board and must make the bedding clear, likewise it must establish that the expelled person's legal obligations, the period for which she/he will be forbidden to re-enter the country, and must mention the countries to which the person cannot be sent to, on the basis of article 143 (article 149/3 of LI). Immigrants who have obtained long-term residency status and who lost it can only be administratively expelled after some aspects have been considered, like the extent of their permanence in the country, their age, their personal and familial consequences of the expulsion, and their strength of the bond established with Portugal (or the lack of ties with the country of birth) – article 136/2 of LI.

The Board is also empowered to recognize and execute banishment decisions originating in other EU member State against a third country's citizen. The conditions for the recognition are established in article 169, and must involve the authorities of the State who took the decision of banishment and the authorities of the State that issued a residency authorization to the foreigner – if not the same and whenever the authorization was issued (nº 4). We underline that LI aims to harmonize the obligation of

---

[86] See also Decree-Law 85/00, of the 12th May, turning sheltering spaces in airports equivalent to shelter centres, on the basis of Resolution of the Council of Ministers 76/97, of the 17th April.

[87] Article 4/3 of directive 2008/115/EC, of the European Parliament and the Council, of the 16th December, on illegal immigrants' return to their home countries, recognizes member States the option to determine more favorable rules than the one establishing a maximum period of six months for illegal immigrants' confinement in shelter centers (see article 15/5 and 6).

[88] On the right to a contradictory hearing in this context, see case 01176/06, of the 15th May 2007, decided by the Portuguese Administrative Supreme Court.

DIREITO COMPARADO / COMPARATIVE LAW

recognition with the faculty of envisaging the banishment decision *within the national and the European context*. Looking at article 169/2, this purpose becomes very clear: when the banishment was decreed on the basis of a serious menace to public order or to public security, the Board must double check *the clear and present danger* the person may constitute to Portugal or to the EU. Proportionality is at stake here, considering the adequacy of the measure and balancing its most restrictive aim to the foreigner's freedom of circulation.

Curiously, and once more demonstrating the idea that this recognition must be an *ultimo ratio* decision, article 169/5 excludes it whenever the State that decreed the banishment postpones or suspends its effects. This alerts us to the possibility of revision of an expulsion's decision – by the Administration only, we think, so not to affront the principle of *res judicata*. The postponement/suspension has, we think, an external dimension only: once the foreigner wants to re-enter in Portugal, the expulsion regains its effects.

These decisions are subject to judicial review: by administrative courts, whenever the Board makes the recognition (article 171/3 of LI); by the Court of Second Instance, when the recognition is made by the judicial courts (article 169/3, sending to articles 152 to 158 of LI).

This decision can, as we have already mentioned, be subject to judicial review, in administrative courts. However, article 150 of LI says that the claim's presentation doesn't suspend the execution. Therefore, apparently, LI makes the defence excessively costly, because the foreign person might have to leave the country before proving her/his right. It must be emphasized, though, that the Portuguese Constitutional Court never admitted that the automatic suspension of administrative acts' effects generated by a judicial impugnation of their validity is part of the right to effective judicial protection (although article 268/4, *in fine*, of the PC, states that this right includes the possibility to *ask for* injunctive relief measures)[89].

One must remember, nonetheless, that article 128 of the Administrative Judicial Process Code establishes that the presentation of a claim for suspending an administrative act's effects automatically provides tempo-

---

[89] On the contrary, the U.S. Supreme Court decided that the guarantee of automatic suspension of an expulsion order is inherent to the principle of due process [in the *Japanese Immigration case* of 1903 (*Kaoru Yamataya vs. Fisher*)], stating that the person must be recognized the right to defend herself before being expelled from the territory.

rary relief, at least until the Administration proves the public damage of suspension, through convincing the judge to order the continuity of the execution until the final decision on the injunction process is taken. In other words, suspension is not automatic, it must be required. But the placing of the injunction before the court immediately suspends the execution of the expulsion's order, at least until the Administration convinces the judge of the necessity of its continuity.

2. The judicial expulsion of legal immigrants
When the immigrant is legally staying in Portugal, the expulsion can only be decreed by a judge. There are two types of situations in which a judicial expulsion may raise:

i.) The expulsion can be accessorily imposed to an immigrant condemned for a crime to which corresponds a punishment superior to one year of imprisonment. One must underline that several aspects should be considered before decreeing this extreme measure, like the gravity of the crime, the offender's personality, the time for which she/he is staying in Portugal, the social background, among others. Above all, the fact that the immigrant has permanent residency (meaning she/he is in the country for at least five years prior to the condemnation) implies that the expulsion can only be determined if her/his conduct represents a serious danger to public order or to public security (see article 151/2 and 3, and also article 136/1 of LI).
The execution of the order of expulsion is commanded by the judge of punishments' execution, after two-thirds of the punishment is completed or, if the good behavior of the offender so allows, when half of the punishment is completed (article 151/4 and 5 of LI).

ii.) The expulsion should be submitted to the judicial courts by the Foreigner and Borders' Board – articles 152/1 and 153/1 of LI. The reasons are listed in article 134/1 of LI and concern mainly national and European security[90] (however, there's a clause [d)] that relates to

---

[90] One can affirm that when the immigrant becomes a menace to European security and is listed in the Schengen information system (indicated by any member State), the Portuguese Foreigner and Borders' Board is obliged to expel her/him. See case 0473/02, of the 7th November 2002, decided by the Portuguese Administrative Supreme Court (a legalisation was at stake there, but the principle is also applicable in our context).

"the abusive interference in the exercise of political participation's rights reserved to nationals" whose significance is a mystery). These cases must consist on a serious breach of confidence in the immigrant's conduct that justifies the request for expulsion[91, 92].

The Board decides to initiate a judicial process of expulsion after investigating the immigrant's conduct and reuniting the necessary elements of proof (article 153 of LI). Once the claim is presented to the competent judge, the audience is appointed to the next five days, thus notifying both the immigrant, the witnesses identified in the process and the regional director of the Board (article 154/1 of LI). This audience can only be delayed once, for ten days, on the basis of one of four reasons (article 155/1 of LI): (1) if the defendant so asks, to prepare the defense; (2) if the defendant is absent (the immigrant's presence in the audience is mandatory – article 154/2 of LI); (3) if some indispensable witnesses is missing; or, (4) if the court needs some days to develop extra diligences in order to discover the truth.

If the court decides to expel the immigrant, the sentence must contain the same elements as the equivalent administrative measure: the bedding; the immigrant's legal obligations (namely, the delay she/he is given to leave the country); the mention of entrance interdiction and the period for which it will last; and the indication of the countries to which she/he cannot be sent to, on the basis of article 143 of LI (see article 157/1 of LI). Immigrants who have been attributed the long-term residency status can only be expelled after some aspects have been considered by the court (as well as by the Board, in the cases of administrative expulsion), like the duration of their permanence in the country, their age, the personal and familiar consequences and the strength of the bond established with Portugal (or the lack of ties with the country of birth) – article 136/2 of LI. Pondering these aspects reveal, of course, a need to observe proportionality parameters[93].

---

[91] In this sense, Jorge MIRANDA and Rui MEDEIROS, Constituição..., *cit.*, p. 367.
[92] If the Board suspects the immigrant may attempt to escape before the judgment, a request must be presented to the judge so special surveillance measures will be adopted, as set in article 142/1 of LI.
[93] See Jorge MIRANDA and Rui MEDEIROS, Constituição..., *cit.*, p. 367.

The appeal is made to the Court of Second Instance (*Tribunal da Relação*) but does not suspend the effects of the decision – so the immigrant must leave the country in the shortest period. The Board may give the immigrant the option to leave the country voluntarily, or ask the Court to determine: the sending of the immigrant to a temporary shelter centre[94]; the obligating of the immigrant to stay indoors or to use means of electronic surveillance; or the requiring of the immigrant to periodic appearances before the Board or police authorities (article 160 of LI). We must remark the diminishing of protection this process reveals in the phase of appeal when compared to the administrative expulsion. The point is, once the effects of the decision are not suspended until the appeal is decided, this solution is much more penalizing than the temporary relief provided by the administrative courts on the basis of article 128/1 of Administrative Judicial Process Code.

This decision is communicated to the country of destination's authorities and also to the Schengen Information System – whenever the immigrant is considered a menace to European security (if the reasons for expulsion concern only national security, the communication is restricted to the national list of nonadmissible persons), according to article 157/2 of LI. During the period for which the expulsion lasts, the immigrant cannot re-enter the country; if he does so, he may be subject to imprisonment up to 2 years or a penalty up to 100 days (see article 187 of LI).

V. Conclusions

After this quick overview of the immigrants' administrative condition in Portugal, we can conclude that:

1. The Law ignores the concept "immigrant"; it prefers to talk about "foreigner". Bearing in mind that an immigrant is someone who willingly leaves her/his country of origin in search of new opportunities of work, study or personal fulfilment in another country where she/he will join a new community for a considerable time, we've drawn a concept that has its basis on a time period of at least a five years stay in Portuguese territory;

---

[94] If the immigrant disobeys the order of expulsion, she/he can be detained by police authorities and presented to a judge who, if the expulsion is not possible within 48 hours, sends her/him to a temporary shelter centre until the order can be executed (article 161 of LI).

2. Considering the extended citizenship provided by the Union Treaty and the need to enforce the freedoms of circulation, establishment and residency within the European space, EU citizens benefit from a special regulation and are not qualified as foreigner – nor immigrants – by Law 23/07, of the 4th July (*Foreigner Law*, known as *Immigration Law*, although the word immigrant is mentioned only once...);

3. A foreigner who enters in Portugal isn't immediately an immigrant; she/he might become one, depending on the purpose and on the time of the stay. There are, so to speak, three steps to reach the immigrant level: a visa, a temporary residency authorisation, and a permanent residency authorisation or a long-term residency status. Once the last step is achieved, the legal immigrant is no longer in a precarious situation and she/he can only be forced to leave the country in given situations – and some immigrants can't be expelled at all (article 135 of LI) – and by a judge's order;

4. Expulsion is the natural consequence for a foreigner who is found illegally staying in Portuguese territory – that is to say: who entered illegally or who entered legally but lost the title of permanence. In this case, the Foreigner and Borders' Board is empowered to expel her/him, following a due process which includes contradictory hearing and legal assistance. The administrative decision may be judicially reviewed by administrative courts;

5. Legal immigrants can also be expelled, but in this case, the Portuguese Constitution demands a judicial process. There's a list of reasons which can be on the basis of the judicial expulsion, and the sentence is subject to review by a higher court – in this case, civil law courts are competent to decide. The time of permanence in the country, the person's age, the family situation and the bond with the country of origin are factors to be considered before the expulsion is decreed;

6. When expelled, a foreigner can't re-enter Portuguese territory for at least five years. And if the expulsion's motive relates to European security, the immigrant is identified as a menace in the Schengen Information system and will likewise be *persona non grata* in all EU States.

Lisbon, March 2009

II Parte / Part II

CRISE FINANCEIRA
FINANCIAL CRISIS

(9ª conferência, Lisboa, 2010
9th conference, Lisbon, 2010)

Easy Money, High Leverage, and the Burst Bubble

HARRIS WEINSTEIN[*]

Introduction

This paper is derived from a talk presented in March 2010 in Lisbon, Portugal. The subject is whether the causes of the financial crisis of 2008-2009 trace to a failure of U.S. government legal and regulatory controls.

In fact the crisis resulted from a chain of events. Any one of those events may properly be called a cause of the crisis. The significance of some of these events, may not, however, have been recognized or understood until well after their occurrence. Our focus, fully armed by hindsight, is a search for root causes – those links in the causal chain that were significant prerequisites to or amplifiers of other events that marked the road to financial collapse. We address only legal and regulatory events that appear to have opened the door to financial practices that may now be more readily recognized as among the roots of the financial collapse of 2008-2009.

Before we address this most recent financial calamity, however, we examine the history of systemic financial disasters. The history of centuries past teaches important lessons to those who seek to understand what

---

[*] Distinguished Lecturer, Columbus School of Law, The Catholic University of America; Retired Partner, Covington & Burling LLP. The views expressed in this paper are exclusively those of the author. The author greatly appreciates the assistance of a colleague, Jesse A. Gurman. To the extent this paper has merit, it is significantly Mr. Gurman's doing. The faults are entirely the author's.

befell us in 2008 and 2009. Once understood, economic history illuminates the governmental missteps most likely to have been among the significant roots of the recent collapse. That understanding, moreover, may be an important aid in assessing what should be done to lessen the potential for similar events in the future.

I. The Lessons of History: Debt and Real Estate Speculation as Producers of Financial Collapse

Crises such as that of 2008-2009 have been recurrent phenomena throughout the past – indeed, for at least 800 years. The crucial economic facts of many past crises bear a startling resemblance to those of today, both in their general economic pattern and in the real estate bubble that played so prominent a role in the 2008-2009 collapse.

This paper first summarizes conclusions respected economists have drawn from the crises of the past. It then discusses whether, and if so how, the 2008-2009 crisis fits within the understanding developed from study of the past. The conclusion is that the recent crisis offers nothing new in the generic nature of its origins and results – although its financial magnitude and geographic scope, and the practices that ultimately provoked the collapse, have been truly unusual.

II. The (Unlearned) Lessons of Economic History

Over 30 years ago the economist Charles Kindleberger addressed the origins of financial crises in his classic work, *Manias, Panics and Crashes*.[1] In late 2009, two contemporary economists, Carmen Reinhart and Kenneth Rogoff, published their more numerical study of crises, titled *This Time is Different*, a title heavily coated with irony.[2] As Professors Reinhart and Rogoff demonstrate, this time was not different.

We proceed in several steps. We first review the common elements of past financial crises, as analyzed by these leading economic historians. We then consider whether the most recent crisis fits into the historical pattern.

---

[1] Charles Kindleberger, Manias, Panics and Crashes: A History of Financial Crisis (1st ed. 1978). Charles Kindleberger was an international economic expert at the University of Chicago.

[2] Carmen Reinhart & Kenneth Rogoff, This Time is Different: Eight Centuries of Financial Folly (2009).

Common Elements of Financial Crises

Financial crises tend to follow familiar cycles and have at least some common elements. In his classic study, Kindleberger extensively documented the various stages of financial crises of the last four centuries, drawing parallels among the Dutch Tulip Bulb Bubble of 1636, the stock bubbles in the late 1920s and late 1990s, and various other commodity bubbles in Latin America, Asia, and Europe.[3]

Borrowing from a model developed by Hyman Minsky, Kindleberger describes a cycle that begins with a "displacement," or exogenous shock, to the macroeconomic system (such as a technological innovation or other unexpected event) that increases confidence in profit-making opportunities in some sector of the economy.[4] This displacement, fueled by a corresponding expansion of credit, leads to a "mania," or "euphoria," during which investors become overly optimistic about the potential magnitude of future returns.[5] Prices of the investment rise to reflect these heightened expectations, eventually exceeding the real, long-term economic value of the asset or commodity underlying the expansion. "Outsiders" to the specific business join in on the speculative fad, further inflating the bubble-like growth in prices.[6]

History teaches that both the relevant regulators and the investors themselves tend to turn a blind eye to the resulting bubble, convincing themselves – erroneously – that "this time is different." The resulting euphoric rally may spread across sectors, asset types, and, in an increasingly globalized economy, international borders.

Inevitably, some subsequent event triggers a pause in the mania, followed by panic among participants, and a resulting crash in the prices of the investment that spurred the run-up. The precise triggering event varies – it may be some government policy change or unexpected failure of a prominent firm, or, as in our case, a weakening of demand in the face of rapidly escalating housing prices, coupled with a rising default rate in real estate mortgages.

---

[3] *See* CHARLES KINDLEBERGER & ROBERT Z. ALIBER, MANIAS, PANICS, AND CRASHES: A HISTORY OF FINANCIAL CRISES 302-11 (6th ed. 2011) (Appendix, Outline of Financial Crises, 1618 to 2008).

[4] *Id.* at 26-28.

[5] *Id.* at 29-30.

[6] *Id.* at 30-32.

DIREITO COMPARADO / COMPARATIVE LAW

The broad financial outlook quickly swings from unduly optimistic to irredeemably bleak. As Nobel Prize winning economist Paul Krugman noted in August 2005, "bubbles end when people stop believing that big capital gains are a sure thing."[7] Firms, individuals, and households that jumped on the profit train fear the worst and jump off in droves. The panic to flee accelerates the decline in price. The flight from the market produces, and is motivated by, a self-fulfilling prophecy of lower prices. As prices fall, the value of real estate shrinks. Credit becomes dramatically restricted, as banks and other lenders who were irrationally eager to lend during the boom freeze up and hesitate to finance even more routine business as they await the market bottom. Bank runs and bankruptcies often ensue, and governments, as lenders of last resort, try to restore confidence or mitigate the fallout.

Reinhart and Rogoff's more recent account, *This Time Is Different*, builds on Kindleberger's narrative and provides a comprehensive, quantitative assessment of the role of debt in driving major swings of financial systems throughout history. The authors argue that pre-crisis periods are frequently marked by sizeable buildups in aggregate short-term borrowing to finance long-term investments.[8] This debt buildup may occur in the private sector, with bursts of expansive credit driving mania-like asset and commodity bubbles such as those identified by Kindleberger. Reinhart and Rogoff particularly point to real estate as a common subject of the debt that leads to the crisis.[9] It can also occur in the public sector. Global trade or currency imbalances may promote inexpensive government borrowing, which can in turn be used to finance levels of public spending that would normally require increased taxation.

When confidence shifts, and mania turns to panic and crash, the effects can be widespread and difficult to contain. On the private side, bank runs can cause bank failures and freeze the short-term lending upon which many individuals and firms relied during the euphoric build-up that preceded the crash. The resulting breakdown of the lending system can significantly damage the real economy.

---

[7] Paul Krugman, *The Hissing Sound*, N.Y. TIMES, Aug. 8, 2005.
[8] REINHART & ROGOFF, *supra* note 2, at 143.
[9] *Id.* at 157.

Reinhart and Rogoff extensively document these private and public sector debt cycles, which have occurred with remarkable frequency across many countries over the past *eight* centuries.[10] Their empirical analysis shows that the (debt-related) symptoms of these damaging cycles should not be difficult to identify in the early stages, but the "syndrome" of rationalization – the frequent, mistaken claim that "this time is different" – is so pervasive that, a long history of crises notwithstanding, we still have not learned our lesson.

This Time is (Not) Different

As Reinhart and Rogoff discuss, the financial crisis of 2007-2009 did largely follow the familiar pattern.[11] A significant buildup in private debt occurred in the years preceding the crisis, fueling a large bubble in residential real estate.

This buildup was driven by a combination of factors. It may have begun somewhat modestly, when the Asian financial crises of the 1990s resulted in substantial capital inflows into the United States as shaken investors looked for safer returns. At much the same time, the U.S. Federal Reserve was pursuing an accommodative monetary policy, holding interest rates low to counter the stock market crash that followed the dot-com equities bubble of the late 1990s and the events of September 11, 2001.

The increase in foreign-source investment and the eased lending resulted in significant pools of capital in search of new and higher returns. At the same time, innovations in the securitization process led many in the financial sector to believe that they could divest themselves of risks more effectively than had been possible in the past. This led many banks and mortgage originators to aggressively (and in some cases predatorily) loan to riskier borrowers, knowing that they could securitize the debt and pass the increased risk on to other actors.

This combination of increased money flow and easy lending, expanded use of securitization, and longstanding policies promoting housing finance, led to mania-like investment in housing and in mortgage-backed securities (MBSs).[12]

---

[10] *See generally id.* at 128-38.

[11] *Id.* at 203-22.

[12] MBSs are complex derivative instruments that were originally designed to spread risk.

During the buildup to the crisis, MBSs found extensive use in expanding credit to "sub-prime" borrowers who could not afford to borrow money to finance home acquisitions under customary "prime" lending standards. Instead, a herd-like investing class, seeking higher investment returns, acquired an ever-increasing appetite for MBSs (and related products such as credit default swaps), which were (mistakenly) viewed as investment-grade assets with stable, contained downside risk. This view was thanks in part to optimistic ratings bestowed on these products by credit rating agencies.

Average household debt grew as more borrowers acquired mortgages supported by MBS investors, often with little or no money down, since default risk was supposed to be dispersed to those who could bear it. Large financial companies, importantly including investment banks and others who operated outside the regulated, federally insured banking sector, took advantage of easy credit in the marketplace and increased their own leverage levels, creating, underwriting, and owning MBSs that continued to thrive as housing prices soared.[13]

Eventually, defaults on mortgage loans began to pick up, triggering the Kindleberger "confidence shift" away from housing and MBSs.[14] Panic set in as lending and MBS trading froze, followed by precipitous declines in both home prices and the securities whose value depended on them. As a consequence of these asset crashes, the value of recently-euphoric investments quickly became difficult to appraise. This in turn spurred a wider credit freeze, as lenders sought to limit their loss exposure by declining to extend loans in the amounts, and at the terms, that borrowers had come to expect.

Gary Gorton offers an additional and more historical perspective into the mechanism of the panic phase of the recent crisis. He argues that the panic involved a run on various "shadow banking" institutions – that is,

---

[13] As Reinhart and Rogoff show, this significant buildup in private debt was consistent with similar buildups preceding financial crises throughout history. REINHART & ROGOFF, *supra* note 2, at 216-20. They note that public debt levels were also on the rise, due to high levels of public spending financed by debt purchases by China and others. However, according to Reinhart and Rogoff, United States debt was not particularly high by historical standards in the run-up to the sub-prime crisis, and inflation levels correspondingly stayed under control during the crisis. *Id.*

[14] KINDLEBERGER & ALIBER, *supra* note 3, at 32-33.

the investment banks and other financial entities that were beyond the regulatory purview of the federal banking regulatory agencies – that was structurally very similar to the runs on conventional banks of the nineteenth and early twentieth centuries.[15] In short, many banks and hedge funds became accustomed to depositing large amounts of money on a short-term basis, at times on overnight terms, in the shadow banks, accepting as collateral various forms of bonds, including securitized products such as MBSs. Those institutions in turn used these short term funds to finance the sale and repurchase ("repo") operations of the shadow banks.

Such bonds were originally meant to be "informationally insensitive" liabilities – much like retail bank deposits that are widely accepted and exchanged without any need to assess the creditworthiness of individual depositors at any particular moment. Once housing prices crashed, however, and MBSs were found to be riskier than expected, "shadow bank" depositors began to lose confidence and rushed to redeem their collateral. Since shadow banking, much like retail banking, relies on the confidence that not all depositors will redeem at once, the run quickly unwound the system and forced depositing firms to accept substantial "haircuts" on the value of their collateral, translating into correspondingly significant losses on their balance sheet assets.

A few economists issued warnings as early as 2005 that the bubble was nearly at the breaking point. As Paul Krugman put it in August 2005, "Now we're starting to hear a hissing sound, as the air begins to leak out of the bubble."[16]

The warnings from Krugman and other experts were largely ignored until the crisis exploded some three years later. The most visible signs were the declining values of mortgage-related instruments that impacted a number of financial firms throughout 2008, crippling some of them. One leading investment bank, Bear Stearns, suffered substantial losses due to its heavy participation in the mortgage securitization business and was acquired by J.P. Morgan in a March 2008 marriage brokered by federal regulators. Perhaps the single event that pushed panic from falling home

---

[15] Gary Gorton, Slapped in the Face by the Invisible Hand: Banking and the Panic of 2007 (2009) (unpublished manuscript), *available at* http://papers.ssrn.com/sol3/papers.cfm?abstract_id=1401882 (prepared for the Federal Reserve Bank of Atlanta's 2009 Financial Markets Conference: Financial Innovation and Crisis (May 11-13, 2009)).

[16] Krugman, *supra* note 7.

and investment values into a full-blown crash was the collapse of the major investment bank Lehman Brothers in September 2008.

The fall of Lehman raised the level of system-wide alarm as various markets and actors that had been intertwined with Lehman, including major money-market funds that had been thought to be insulated from the MBS troubles, experienced run-like behavior. At the same time, global insurance giant American International Group (AIG) also faced the brink of collapse, as significant MBS-related (credit-swap) losses forced it to draw down its last lines of credit to pay its ongoing obligations. With close to a $40 billion shortfall looming, bankruptcy appeared the likely next step, averted only because of a massive investment by the U.S. Federal Reserve.[17]

III. Crises are Inevitable, the Particulars Are Unforeseeable

The historical perspectives from Kindleberger and from Reinhart and Rogoff are above all humbling. While the events of the past several years feel extraordinary, they are actually seen to be remarkably common when we take the longer view. Although no banking sector panic of these proportions had occurred in the United States since the Great Depression, several asset and stock bubbles have come and gone, and financial crises of various forms have been pervasive in both emerging and developed countries for hundreds of years.

Virtually every crisis in the recent financial history of the United States has been met with extensive legislative and regulatory responses advertised by their political sponsors as certain to avoid a recurrence. As all are well aware, these assurances proved illusory. New days yielded new ways of increasing financial leverage, debt, and asset prices beyond sustainable levels. These innovations, reinforced by human euphoria, eventually overcame, and defeated, the regulatory effort.

The first big-picture lesson to take away, therefore, is that financial crises will continue to happen, regardless of what particular regulatory actions are taken in response to the current one. Furthermore, while the general arc of financial crises has become familiar, the specifics are never quite the same. Even recognizing that bubbles tend to emerge in real

---

[17] *See* Eric Dash & Andrew Ross Sorkin, *Throwing a Lifeline to a Troubled Giant*, N.Y. TIMES, Sept. 18, 2008, at C1. *See generally* BAIRD WEBEL, CONG. RESEARCH SERV., R 40438, ONGOING GOVERNMENT ASSISTANCE FOR AMERICAN INTERNATIONAL GROUP (AIG) (2009).

estate, securities, and commodities, it remains difficult to separate real value increases from speculative mania while the increases are occurring. It is not surprising that "this time is different" rationalizations emerge and are often accepted, even though they have repeatedly been proven wrong in the past. Even if bubbles are recognized while they are happening, they may be difficult to "deflate" – the mania can be strong and contagious, policy options lacking, and the political will to interfere weak.

This is not to say that reform is hopeless, only that a broader perspective should shape both the type and degree of our policy goals. To the extent that we merely aim to avoid the particulars of the last crisis, we will be unsuccessful in preventing the next one. And to the extent that we try to avoid financial pain entirely, we are sure to be wasting time and resources, while foregoing opportunities for real economic growth. Reforms should therefore target generalized problems in the financial sector, and should focus on limiting damage from the inevitable swings, rather than naively seeking to eliminate them completely.

IV. Whether Government Actions Caused or Facilitated the Crash of 2008-2009

It is established beyond any reasonable dispute that debt – enormous amounts of debt – fueled the real estate bubble that turned into the 2008-2009 financial collapse. Nor is there any room to dispute that the collapse involved debt that entailed high leverage – large amounts of debt supported by little capital to provide a cushion against loss of value.

A broad consensus supports the discussion to this point. Few would dispute that highly leveraged investment in MBSs by the shadow banking system was a significant feature of the collapse. Nor would many dispute that significant amounts of high-risk, "sub-prime" mortgage loans were an important factor in fueling what proved to be the riskiest of large quantities of MBSs. Nor should it be doubted that significant holdings of long-term MBSs were financed by short-term borrowings. Much rested on the willingness of short-term lenders to renew their loans to the holders of MBSs.

Although a great deal of attention has been focused on the sub-prime loans and the production of MBSs that led to the bubble, less scrutiny has been focused on the source of the leverage that played a significant role in the growth of the bubble. For that reason, the remainder of this paper examines possible sources of that leverage and considers some policy decisions of U.S. authorities that may have facilitated the leverage.

Three government decisions are worthy candidates for thoughtful consideration:

First: Through 2003 the U.S. Federal Reserve eased credit to combat the recessionary forces that followed the March 2000 collapse of the dot-com bubble and the impact of the terrorist attacks of September 2001. In mid-2004, however, the Federal Reserve began to increase interest rates, resulting in a significant increase in those rates that lasted until the third quarter of 2007. The lower interest rates of the early part of the decade may have been a factor in the initial growth of debt that led to the real estate bubble. The increase in Federal Reserve rates in 2004-2006 suggests, however, that Federal Reserve policy likely was not a crucial factor in the expansion of debt over the entire period.

Second: In 2003, the U.S. Congress rejected a request for regulatory authority over the capital requirements applicable to Fannie Mae and Freddie Mac, two privately owned government sponsored enterprises (GSEs) charged with enlarging the supply of home mortgages.

Fannie Mae, or the Federal National Mortgage Association, was chartered in 1938[18] and converted into government owned corporation in 1954.[19] Its assignment was to conduct a wholesale mortgage business by buying mortgages in the secondary market and issuing MBSs derived from the mortgages it purchased.

Fannie Mae was converted in 1968 to a privately owned GSE, with certain tax advantages.[20] It was authorized in 1984 to deal in subordinate lien mortgages.[21] During the prelude to the crisis, it borrowed heavily to finance its operations. Because market participants deemed Fannie Mae to have an implied federal guarantee of its debt, it was able to borrow at

---

[18] *See* National Housing Act Amendments of 1938, ch. 13, § 1, 52 Stat. 8.

[19] Housing Act of 1954, Pub. L. No. 560, § 201, 68 Stat. 590, 612,

[20] Housing and Urban Development Act of 1968, Pub. L. No. 90-448, §§ 801-802, 82 Stat. 476, 536-42.

[21] Secondary Mortgage Enhancement Act of 1984, Pub. L. No. 98-440, § 203, 98 Stat. 1689, 1693.

interest rates close to those on U.S. Treasury debt and significantly below those charged other, entirely private borrowers.

Freddie Mac, or the Federal National Mortgage Corporation, was chartered in 1970 as a government owned corporation within the then federal savings and loan regulatory agency, the Federal Home Loan Bank Board.[22] Its function was similar to that of Fannie Mae; that is, it would buy mortgages from lenders, package the mortgages into securities, and then sell the securities to investors with a guaranteed principal value.

Freddie Mac was converted to a privately owned GSE in 1989.[23] Like Fannie Mae, it was able to borrow large amounts at lower interest rates than were available to other companies issuing debt of similar quality.

The question here is how to evaluate the congressional decision in 2003 to deny greater regulatory authority over the capital required of and thereby the leverage available to these two mortgage wholesalers. Neither the Republican majority nor the Democratic minority of the time displayed a taste for this medicine. Congressman Barney Frank – although a Democrat – most likely articulated the views of a bipartisan majority when he said at a committee hearing of September 25, 2003:

> I do not want the same kind of focus on safety and soundness [in regulating Fannie Mae and Freddie Mac] that we have [for national banks and savings institutions]. *I want to roll the dice a little bit more in this situation towards subsidized housing. . . .*"[24] [emphasis supplied]

Others took the same position, emphasizing what they considered the prime mission of these two GSEs – promoting, and indirectly subsidizing, inexpensive home mortgages. For example, Congresswoman Maxine Waters said: "[I]f it ain't broke, why do you want to fix it? Have the GSEs ever missed their housing goals?"[25]

---

[22] Emergency Home Finance Act of 1970, Pub. L. No. 91-351, § 303, 84 Stat. 450, 452.

[23] Financial Institutions Reform, Recovery, and Enforcement Act of 1989, Pub. L. No. 101-73, § 731, 103 Stat. 183, 429.

[24] *H.R. 22575 – The Secondary Mortgage Market Enterprises Regulatory Improvement Act: Hearing Before the H. Comm. on Fin. Services*, 108th Cong. 98 (2003) (statement of Rep. Barney Frank).

[25] *The Treasury Department's Views on the Regulation of Government Sponsored Enterprises: Hearing Before the H. Comm. on Fin. Services*, 108th Cong. 31 (2003) (statement of Rep. Maxine Waters).

Third: A year later, in 2004, the U.S. Securities & Exchange Commission (SEC) adopted a modified version of the Basel II capital standards to govern the capital of broker dealers.[26] This decision – perhaps unwittingly – enabled investment banks to enlarge their financial leverage greatly.

No less an authority than Harvard Law School Professor Hal Scott has summarized the impact of the SEC's action this way:

> In June 2004, the Commission . . . . permitted investment banks that would not otherwise be subject to Basel . . . to use Basel rules (subject to some SEC modifications). The five largest U.S. investment banks – Bear Stearns, Goldman Sachs, Lehman Brothers, Merrill Lynch, and Morgan Stanley – adopted this option both to reduce capital and to ensure that they escaped being regulated by the E.U. . . . . *This was ultimately a recipe for disaster.*[27]

These determinations by the Congress and the SEC did much to facilitate the growth of debt in the prelude to our crisis. The low capital required of, and the resulting high leverage available to Fannie Mae and Freddie Mac and the largest investment banks, were significant keys to the vast amount of debt incurred as a housing bubble grew.

The refusal of the Congress to increase capital requirements for Fannie Mae and Freddie Mac merits scrutiny. No doubt the Congress knew what it was doing. It was making a choice between two competing policies. The members no doubt understood that increasing the capital requirements for Fannie Mae and Freddie Mac would limit their capacity to purchase mortgages. They surely should have understood that imposing bank-like regulations on the capital of Fannie Mae and Freddie Mac would decrease the ability of those enterprises to take on, and securitize, the more risky mortgage loans. By opting in favor of maximizing the mortgage funds available to home buyers, the Congress signaled a readiness to take the risks associated with loosened credit underwriting standards and high leverage. This decision, despite the colorful language used in Congress, appeared to be a considered action intended to support the long-stand-

---

[26] *See* Alternative Net Capital Requirements for Broker-Dealers That Are Part of Consolidated Supervised Entities, 69 Fed. Reg. 34428 (June 21, 2004) (codified as amended at 17 C.F.R. pts. 200, 240).

[27] HAL S. SCOTT, THE GLOBAL FINANCIAL CRISIS 81 (2009) (emphasis supplied).

ing American policy of promoting and subsidizing home ownership. The question was whether to err on the side of constraining mortgage lending or to maintain the policy of easy mortgage money. The congressional majority of the time chose easy money.

One result was to encourage home ownership by down-playing safety and soundness and maximizing the lending capacity of Fannie Mae and Freddie Mac. The initial results were what the Congress sought – more Americans than ever before owned their own homes as the decade progressed.[28] Real estate values grew quickly. A non-trivial part of this growth came from sub-prime mortgages to borrowers who could not qualify under conventional standards of creditworthiness. Although Fannie Mae and Freddie Mac did not originate the loans, their ability to purchase the loans facilitated looser lending standards in the private sector. Ultimately the number of defaults on these mortgages caused significant losses in the value of the derivative instruments manufactured from the loans, derivatives that had been thought – mistakenly – to eliminate most of the risk of this debt.

The results were dire for Fannie Mae and Freddie Mac, the shareholders of the two companies, and the purchasers of MBSs. By mid-summer 2008, the two companies held or had guaranteed over $1 trillion in mortgages and had over $5 trillion in debt outstanding.[29] Both companies were severely overextended. Their limited capital was inadequate to absorb their losses. By September of that year, the two companies were on the verge of collapse. The federal government placed them in conservatorship and took control of their funding and operations.[30]

This brings us to the SEC's questionable application of Basel II standards to institutions that were central players in the "shadow banking" system. This term refers to financial institutions that are not depository institutions and that provide many important financial intermediation functions, but at the time were not subject to the regulatory regimes the United States applies to conventional commercial and savings banks.

---

[28] *Homeownership Rate for the United States*, FED. RESERVE BANK OF ST. LOUIS, (Mar. 4, 2015, 11:06 AM), http://research.stlouisfed.org/fred2/series/USHOWN (last visited Mar. 9, 2015).
[29] MARK JICKLING, CONG. RESEARCH SERV., RS 22950, FANNIE MAE AND FREDDIE MAC IN CONSERVATORSHIP 4 (2008).
[30] *See* David Ellis, *U.S. Seizes Fannie and Freddie*, CNNMONEY (Sept. 7, 2008, 8:28 PM), http://money.cnn.com/2008/09/07/news/companies/fannie_freddie/.

These SEC-regulated institutions included enterprises that sold and bought many of the mortgage based derivatives. Those derivatives and the underlying mortgages lost value to an extent that devastated the balance sheets of three of the five major SEC-regulated investment banks.[31]

Disaster thus followed the SEC's 2004 revision of its capital rules. That disaster affected each of the five large U.S.-based investment banks. Only two of the five survive today as independent businesses – a death rate of 60 percent. Bear Stearns and Merrill Lynch were subjected to government-forced and government-assisted mergers with J. P. Morgan and Bank of America, respectively. Goldman Sachs and Morgan Stanley survived, but used government financial assistance to overcome the market disruptions of 2008-2009. Lehman Brothers became bankrupt in a failure that precipitated one of the deepest and most rapid market collapses in modern times.

It is doubtful that the SEC can say anything persuasive in defending against Professor Scott's indictment. Perhaps the most hopeful thought is that the SEC's ability to repeat the error has been limited by the 2008 action of the Federal Reserve, which required Goldman and Morgan Stanley to become financial holding companies when they accepted government aid. Under U.S. banking regulatory law, that status brought the two companies under Federal Reserve regulation in important ways and may curtail the SEC's ability to repeat its mistake.[32]

Conclusion

The financial crisis of 2008-2009 was in significant measure rooted in conflicts inherent in public policies designed to promote economic growth and particularly home ownership. These conflicts may be inescapable in democracies like ours. Nonetheless, the U.S. Congress refused to act in 2003 when the seeds of the crisis were beginning to sprout and the following year the SEC enabled investment bankers – who are at the heart of the so-called "shadow banking system" – to increase the leverage their capital permitted.

It thus appears that the Congress must share at least part of the fault for the lack of effective control of the leverage available to Fannie Mae and

[31] *See* Financial Crisis Inquiry Commission, The Financial Crisis Inquiry Report 154 (2011) (written and submitted to Congress pursuant to Pub. L. No. 111-21).
[32] *See id.*

Freddie Mac. Absent a convincing defense that is yet to be mounted, the SEC must assume much of the blame for the absence of effective regulatory controls on the leverage available to investment banks. That failure of regulation facilitated the debt that mushroomed into the bubble that matured into our crisis.

How then should we assess the 2003 refusal of the Congress to permit regulation of the capital and thereby limit the borrowing power of the two GSEs, and the indefensible decision of the SEC to adopt capital rules that increased the leverage the investment banks could exercise in holding the mortgage backed securities?

One answer is to look at the outcome and call the decisions irresponsible and dangerous. By no means, however, was the outcome of the congressional decisions inevitable – without the subsequent action of the SEC, the disaster might have been avoided.

The line between too little financing and too much risk is never clear. Hindsight may tell us which policy was best at any time in the past. It was far more difficult to fault the congressional position in 2003 than it is now, after events have proved that 2003 was not the time to "roll the dice" with the capitalization of Freddie and Fannie. The dice nonetheless were rolled, and the U.S. economy ultimately showed the consequences.

The Financial Meltdown Crisis – Does the Nature of the Regulatory Failure Presage the Unlikelihood of Effective Solution?

DAVID LIPTON[*]

Preface

This article is a summary of a talk presented on March 8, 2010, at the University of Lisbon, Portugal, for The Ninth Conference on Portuguese and American Law. The timing of this talk was post financial meltdown but ante restructuring of our financial regulatory system. The question that the talk focused upon is whether the nature of the financial meltdown suggests regulatory misfeasance or malfeasance. In hindsight, we now know that, in America, a massive package of new financial oversight reforms was indeed adopted in the summer of 2010. This legislation incorporated many of the proposals for legislation that were being discussed at the time that the talk was presented. One might ask whether the adoption of this legislation negates the importance of the talk itself. This article argues that recent legislative initiatives augment the importance of the previous discussion. Part of the thesis of the talk and of the article is that the financial world is too creative and moves too fast for any regulation to keep pace with it. Does that mean that we should not bother regulating the financial markets? Absolutely not. If nothing else, the newly adopted legislation indeed will *hopefully* serve to lessen the possibility of a repeat of a similarly caused financial meltdown. But, as we see from the last financial meltdown, we did not have in place the kind of regulation to respond to the precise nature of the crises through which we passed. In all likelihood, we will again be saying that when the next financial crises befalls our economy.

* Professor of Law, Columbus School of Law, Catholic University of America.

DIREITO COMPARADO / COMPARATIVE LAW

The initial question this paper poses is reminiscent of the unfortunate response of one of the more articulate American presidents of the second half of the twentieth century who, when asked whether he was having sex with a White House aide, responded, under oath, "[i]t depends on what the meaning of the word 'is' is."[1] Similarly, to answer the question, "Does the Nature of the Regulatory Failure Presage the Unlikelihood of Effective Solution?" requires us to define what we mean by "regulatory failure."

Without trying to be comprehensive, a simple dichotomous definition can be devised. By "regulatory failure," we can mean that there were regulations in place, which should have prevented the financial meltdown but, due to either misfeasance or malfeasance of application, they failed to do so. This type of failure would be a failure to *effectively apply existing regulations*. Alternatively, regulatory failure might equally mean that there just were not the regulations in place to prevent the financial crises no matter how aptly these regulations might have been enforced. In other words, this second failure would be a failure to *put appropriate regulations in place*.

Finally, we want to recognize a subtle subset of this second definition of regulatory failure. It is possible that no regulations could have prevented the meltdown. In other words, perhaps there *was* a failure to put regulations in place. But, it might also be argued that there really was no failure, because no amount of regulations could have prevented the crisis we experienced.

To avoid excessive suspense, let us disclose up front that the analysis of the meltdown that is developed below defies the proposition that there was a failure to effectively apply regulations actually in place immediately preceding the crises. The paper will conclude that there was an absence of appropriate regulations. At the same time, the paper will raise the pros-

---

[1] Timothy Noah, *Bill Clinton and the Meaning of "Is"*, SLATE, (Sept. 13, 1998, 9:14 PM), http://www.slate.com/id/1000162/. In this article, the author notes that "[y]ears from now, when we look back on Bill Clinton's presidency, its defining moment may well be Clinton's rationalization to the grand jury about why he wasn't lying when he said to his top aides that, with respect to Monica Lewinsky, 'there's nothing going on between us.'" The author cited footnote 1,128 in the report of Kenneth Starr, independent counsel:
It depends on what the meaning of the word "is" is. If the – if he – if "is" means is and never has been, that is not – that is one thing. If it means there is none, that was a completely true statement.... Now, if someone had asked me on that day, are you having any kind of sexual relations with Ms. Lewinsky, that is, asked me a question in the present tense, I would have said no. And it would have been completely true. *Id.*

pect that no regulatory system could have prevented the meltdown. Further, it is possible that this remains the case today and that no regulations will prevent comparable meltdowns in the future.

Before continuing, it is important to emphasize that the author of this paper is a student of securities regulation. When the paper discusses regulatory failure, it is specifically focusing upon regulatory failure that applies primarily (but not exclusively) to securities regulation.

With the above definitions in mind and with the quick glance at how the discussion will conclude and with the caveat about the type of regulations, upon which the paper will focus, let us explore a fairly simplified view of what caused the financial meltdown.

The financial crisis of 2007 and 2008 was indeed the "perfect storm." It was an uncanny confluence of dangerous practices and events, any one of which might have somewhat harmed the national and world economies, but, which collectively wrecked havoc on banks, pension funds, credit markets, home ownership, and production and employment figures in the United States and around the world. Central to this crisis was a housing market bubble that grew dramatically in size in the last part of the 20th and the beginning of the 21st centuries. Fueled by low borrowing cost and easy credit, homeowners and investors significantly boosted both home prices and sale turnover rates.[2]

The ability of mortgage lenders to extend loans was placed on steroids by the tweaking of a previous practice of aggregating mortgages and reselling them. Collecting mortgages and selling pieces of them to investors in order to refill the coffers of the lender was not a new practice. But starting in the 1990s, investment bankers began to package a group of mortgages and then slice and dice sections (or "tranches" of these mortgages) on the basis of maturity or risk or interest or principal. They would then sell these tranches separately as securities. The notion was that the risk of any one mortgage would be balanced by the security of pieces of

---

[2] *See* John V. Duca, Fed. Reserve Bank of Dallas, *Making Sense of Inflated Housing Prices*, S.W. Econ. (Sept./Oct. 2005), *available at* http://www.dallasfed.org/assets/documents/research/swe/2005/swe0505b.pdf. The Federal Reserve Bank of Dallas indicated that high demand stemming from low interest rates caused a 60 percent increase in U.S. home prices between 1999 and 2005. Additionally, statistics and analysis provided by the bank detail a significant surge in home turnover. That is, between 2000 and 2005 housing turnover increased from around three to four percent to approximately twelve percent. *Id.*

other mortgages in the tranche. The more risky tranches would be sold with the highest interest rate for the investor. These collateralized mortgage obligations, or CMOs,[3] were supposed to eliminate or greatly lessen the risk of investment and to insure that the front-line lenders would have the funds to continue in their money making role of conducting mortgage lending.[4] In time, CMOs were even created by investing in pieces of other CMOs. These instruments, referred to as CMOs squared and, at times, cubed, were intended to even further lessen the risk of a poor investment.[5] All of this risk spreading might have made sense if the financial model upon which it was built reflected current reality. That reality was a fragile inflated housing price bubble that was soon to burst. The last time there was such a financial scenario with its attendant consequences was the Great Depression. The actual modeling used to calculate risk was

---

[3] A CMO consists of a bond backed by a pool of mortgages that is divided into multiple classes or "tranches." The cash flows to investors generated by the underlying pool represent payments from homeowners whose loans are in a given pool. These monthly payments are distributed or "passed through" to investors and include interest and principal payments. Logically, the monthly distributions are sensitive to interest rate shifts, loan defaults, and unscheduled prepayments as they relate to the underlying loans. THE DEPOSITORY TRUST & CLEARING CORP., EXAMINING THE GROWTH OF THE COLLATERALIZED MORTGAGE OBLIGATION MARKET 2 (Jan. 2003). *See also* U.S. Securities Exchange Commission, Collateralized Mortgage Obligations, http://www.sec.gov/answers/tcmos.htm (last visited Feb. 28, 2015).

[4] MICHAEL LEWIS, THE BIG SHORT: INSIDE THE DOOMSDAY MACHINE 23-24 (2010). The author explained that "[t]hirty billion dollars was a big year for subprime lending in the mid-1990s. In 2000, there had been $130 billion in subprime loans, and 55 billion dollars' worth of those loans had been repackaged as mortgage bonds. In 2005, there would be $605 billion in subprime mortgage lending, $507 billion of which found its way into mortgage bonds." This practice, as Lewis indicated, enabled the mortgage lenders to originate loans at such a feverish pace. Companies in the business of subprime lending learned not to make loans to people that could not repay them and, instead, to keep on making these loans and not keep them on their books. That is, they would "[m]ake the loans, then sell them of to the fixed income departments of Wall Street investment banks, which [would] in turn package them into bonds and sell them to investors." *Id.*

[5] By 2001, the original structure of securitized subprime mortgage loans had evolved. The newly developed synthetic collateralized debt obligation became a popular variation of its predecessor. Originally constructed of a single tranche, "insatiable investors quickly began demanding even better ways to juice up returns, so the banks produced a new twist on the CDO idea called a 'CDO squared.'" In this case, the instrument essentially represented a "CDO of CDOs" where the shell company "would purchase pieces of debt issued by *other* CDOs and then issue new CDO notes" that usually included the riskiest notes from the other CDOs. GILLIAN TETT, FOOL'S GOLD 93 (2009).

based upon far more recent markets.[6] Normally, financial models based on more current markets would make sense. This, however, was not the case in a situation in which current market models failed to include long-past market disasters. Indeed, these long-past market disturbances were far closer in nature to the events of the period from 2007 through 2009 than the housing market that existed in the two decades immediately preceding the crisis. In more recent markets, we saw ever rising prices with only small, occasional downturns.[7]

For many decades, most original mortgages were resold to re-lenders. The profit realized by the originator of the loan no longer came from the spread between his rate and his borrowing rate. Rather, the profit came from originating the loan. The more funds to which the originator had access, the more loans it could make, and the more profitable was its business. So originators were happy to sell their loans to an entity that would repackage them in a CMO. In fact, the loan originator was so eager to extend mortgages that originators began to offer "sub-prime" loans.[8]

---

[6] *Id.* at 32-34. More specifically, the 1980s witnessed the development of systems designed to measure risk not on the basis of vague hunches, as was the historical norm in this regard, but precise quantitative data and techniques. Formerly, banks relied on ad hoc methods for performing those calculations. While the emerging system represented an improvement to risk calculating and monitoring, banks premised the techniques on data taken from the immediately preceding three years. These banks assumed that the future markets would operate in a manner similar to that of the past markets – in hindsight, this reflected a fundamental structural flaw. *Id.*

[7] James A. Kahn, *Productivity Swings and Housing Prices*, 15 CURRENT ISSUES IN ECON. & FIN. 1 (2009), *available at* http://www.newyorkfed.org/research/current_issues/ci15-3.pdf. This article details trends in the booms in real estate prices, first in the 1970s and then in the 1990s, which lasted until the bubble burst in 2007. Overall, the article reflects the underlying statistics that represent a sustained appreciation in housing prices with intermittent downward trends occurring over a 40-year period in the U.S. housing market.

[8] Souphala Chomsisengphet & Anthony Pennington-Cross, *The Evolution of the Subprime Mortgage Market*, 88 FED. RESERVE BANK OF ST. LOUIS REV. 31, 37-38 (2006). This report, published by the Federal Reserve Bank of St. Louis, detailed the emergence of the subprime mortgage loan market. The authors' research indicated that the subprime mortgage market experienced significant growth between 1995 and 2003, a period in which the annual amount of such loans increased from $65 billion to $332 billion. The authors attributed this extreme growth to an increase in interest rates experienced in the mid-1990s which, as a consequence, caused the volume of mortgage originations to drop. Accordingly, the authors explained that "[m]ortgage brokers and mortgage companies responded by looking to the subprime market to maintain volume." *Id.* at 38.

Subprime mortgages are loans to borrowers who really do not have the means to support the payments, particularly not with adjustable rate mortgages.[9] At times, the originators relied upon a knowing misstatement of assets or income by the borrower. In fact, these were called "liar loans."[10] The advent of subprime loans and liar loans as well as the general loosening of lending standards increased the risk of the CMOs that were otherwise considered risk free. These CMOs were typically sold to institutional investors such as pension funds, banks, mutual funds, and insurance companies. Needless to say, the purchasers were never exclusively U.S. institutions.

One might suspect that institutional investors would know how to evaluate for themselves the risks of these CMOs that they were purchasing. To the contrary, not infrequently the concepts and algorithms upon which they depended were too complicated for even sophisticated investors to analyze. Then, we also have to remember that there were no models for

---

[9] The Federal Reserve published findings related to the rise in mortgage defaults that occurred in the U.S. housing market in the period preceding and during the financial crisis. The Fed's research found exceptionally high default rates of subprime adjustable-rate mortgages. The Fed attributed these defaults, in part, to the relatively poor risk attributes of these loans. CHRISTOPHER J. MAYER ET AL., THE RISE IN MORTGAGE DEFAULTS 8 (Nov. 2008), *available at* http://www.federalreserve.gov/PUBS/FEDS/2008/200859/200859pap.pdf. Previously, subprime borrowers with adjustable rate mortgages could cope with payment increases via refinancing (which was more possible because of the appreciation of home prices). However, rising interests rates coincided with other market forces to reduce the availability of refinancing options. Thus, delinquencies and defaults became prevalent. *Possible Responses to Rising Mortgage Foreclosures: Hearing Before the H. Comm. on Fin. Servs.*, 110th Cong. 24 (2007) (testimony of Richard F. Syron, Chairman & Chief Executive Officer, Freddie Mac).

[10] Alternative-A or "alt-A" loans originally targeted "financially savvy borrowers with strong credit scores who were self-employed or whose income fluctuated, who could not document their income or assets, or otherwise posed a high probability of default. As time passed, underwriting standards for alt-A loans began to relax." These "relaxed" loans, predicated upon little to no documentation and a lack of income verification in which the lender took the borrower's word as to earnings, became known as "liar loans." TALCOTT J. FRANKLIN & THOMAS F. NEALON III, MORTGAGE AND ASSET BACKED SECURITIES LITIGATION HANDBOOK § 7:49 (2010); *see also* ALVIN L. ARNOLD, REAL ESTATE TRANSACTIONS: STRUCTURE AND ANALYSIS WITH FORMS § 8:11 (2010). In 2006, an estimated 80% of subprime loans included below-market "teaser" rates, and nearly 80% of Alt-A loans (those to borrowers a cut above subprime) were liar loans. The "[l]oan-to-value ratios for these loans often exceeded 90%, and frequently the resources of the borrowers were further strained by second mortgages added to the mix. These subprime and Alt-A mortgages suffered default at record rates." MICHAEL T. MADISON ET AL., LAW OF REAL ESTATE FINANCING § 3:5 (2009).

an ultimate disaster of housing prices. The models, upon which the risk of these CMOs was based, were inherently unrealistic. Perhaps, most significantly, the one player in this perfect storm upon whom institutional investors could otherwise depend, the credit rating agencies (CRAs), had their own motivation for ignoring or not educating themselves about the risk of the CMOs. There were but a handful of credit rating agencies that controlled the rating market – Moody's, Standard and Poor's, and Fitch. They developed their own models to evaluate the risk of the CMOs and some were even published on the Internet.[11] Banks, producing the CMOs, would run their instruments through these models to see what rating they would get and, if necessary, would tweak their CMO to raise their rates.[12] Most importantly, the rating agencies were eager to get the business for rating the CMOs. A single rating could earn an agency $100,000 or more.[13] It would not take a financial wizard to recognize that low-grade ratings, given by rating agencies, would not encourage further business from that particular investment bank.

Near the end of the list of evil instruments and practices that were influential in creating this sad tale of financial doom and ruin are the credit default swaps (CDSs).[14] As with CMOs, there is not a uniform definition of what constitutes these instruments nor a uniform understand-

---

[11] TETT, *supra* note 5, at 100. In an effort to allay concerns and provide transparency with respect to the modeling the risks of CDOs and related products, rating agencies, such as Moody's, posted details of their models on the Internet. Tett explained that the ratings agencies attempted to be "very transparent" in everything that they did. *Id* (citing an unpublished interview of Paul Mazataud, a senior official at Moody's, Financial Times May 2005).

[12] *Id.* The publication of rating models by Moody's and other rating agencies enabled bankers to review exactly how the models worked. As a consequence, "[w]hen a banker had an idea for a new innovation, it would be run through the agency models to see what rating the product was likely to earn." *Id.*

[13] *Id.* at 101. While the ratings agencies commanded large fees, the banks "constantly threatened to boycott the agencies if they failed to produce the wished-for ratings." *Id.*

[14] The International Swaps and Derivatives Association (ISDA) defines a CDS as "a credit derivative contract," which is an instrument to shift credit risk from one party to another, "in which one party (the protection buyer) pays a periodic fee to another party (the protection seller) in return for compensation for default by a reference entity." ISDA further explains that the reference entity is not a party to the CDS and it is not necessary for the protection buyer to suffer an actual loss to be eligible for compensation if a credit event occurs. *Product Descriptions and Frequently Asked Questions*, INT'L SWAPS & DERIVATIVES ASS'N, http://isda.org/educat/faqs.html (last visited Feb. 28, 2015).

ing as to when they were first employed in relation to CMOs. For our purposes, it is sufficient to say that interest and currency swaps were first introduced in the early 1980s[15] and CDSs were first applied to CMOs in the mid-1990s.[16] A swap is much like an insurance policy. In the instance of the CDSs involved in the financial meltdown, the insurance policy was applied to absorb the risk of the underlying financial instrument, which was the CMO. The holder of the CMO, recognizing that there is some risk in the CMO instrument, contracted with an insurer to protect the holder against the risk of default on the CMO. In return, the insurer received a regular premium. If the CMO defaulted, the insurer was to pay the holder for its loss. If it does not default, the insurer got to keep the premiums. The purpose of the swap was to make the CMO a more attractive instrument for an issuer to sell. It allowed the investment bank, which created the CMO, to sell more CMOs.

In essence, the investor in the CMO trades its risk for a series of premium payments. The problem with the CDSs, again, was that they were not created with the belief that the entire housing market would suffer an apocalyptic decline. Rather, they were based upon a non-existent natural law of permanently appreciating real estate values. Accordingly, the model for both pricing the CDS and for evaluating the amount of capital that the issuer of the CDS would need to hold to cover its bets underestimated the risk that was insured. Until this risk is discovered, however, more CMOs were issued and more mortgage loans were extended. This was more than what the actual economy could afford. Even this set of facts and circumstances does not sound as terribly threatening to the economy as what it turned out to be. In order to place this summary of events in

---

[15] TETT, *supra* note 5, at 11-12 (citing author interviews). Tett detailed a currency swap transaction between IBM and the World Bank. As one of the first transactions that truly realized the potential of derivative swaps. Further, Tett explained that this new form of trade (CDSs) spread quickly and became an element of extremely complex transactions. Essentially, banks and investors realized that CDSs "help[ed] investors *reduce* risk or create a good deal *more* risk" depending on how the instruments were used. *Id.*

[16] *Id.* at 19 (explaining that, during a retreat in 1994, the derivatives group at J.P. Morgan first crafted the idea of insuring banks and other lenders against default risk in order to unleash a wave of capital into the economy); *see also id.* at 51-56 (noting that by the mid-1990s, the J.P. Morgan group focused on an idea to "turbo-charge" the market by bundling mortgages together, pooling the underlying risk, and then creating derivatives based on the whole pool rather than by individual loans).

perspective, it is necessary to realize that immediately prior to the financial meltdown, the total dollar value of CMOs that had been domestically issued was somewhere north of $10 trillion.[17] The total notional amount of CDSs that existed in 2007 was approximately $62 trillion.[18] These instruments all relied upon the belief that the housing market would continue to appreciate.

Like all bubbles, the one underlying the housing market collapsed.[19] This collapse, as we know, occurred halfway into the first decade of this century. As of late this past February, fully 24 percent of American homes are underwater (i.e., their appraised value is less than their outstanding mortgage).[20] Subprime mortgages provided subprime defaults. The unprecedented default rate had a cascading effect leading to defaults of the CMOs, thereby cutting off capital to the mortgage lenders, which put further downward pressure on the housing market prices. The default of the CMOs, in turn, triggered the call of the payment of the insured value (notional value) of the CDSs. Collectively, these events placed enormous financial pressure on mortgage lenders, banks, insurance companies, investment banking houses, and government mortgage security agencies.

---

[17] *See* 2 The Oxford Companion to American Politics 137 (David Coates ed., 2012).

[18] *ISDA Market Survey: Notional amounts outstanding at year-end, all surveyed contracts, 1987-present*, Int'l Swaps & Derivatives Ass'n, http://isda.org/statistics/pdf/ISDA-Market-Survey-annual-data.pdf.

[19] William Kristol, *Admit We Don't Know*, N.Y. Times, Nov. 24, 2008, at A25 (arguing that the origins of the economic crisis seem to be in the collapse of the housing bubble). The pronounced decline in the U.S. home price values provides an indication that the housing bubble, represented by high loan to volume ratios and home turnover, collapsed. That is, in the period from July 2006 to April 2009, the average home price declined greater than 33 percent. *See* Standard & Poor's Fin. Servs., LLC, S&P/Case-Shiller Home Price Index (July 2010), http://www.standardandpoors.com/indices/sp-case-shiller-home-price-indices/en/us/?indexId=spusa-cashpidff--p-us---- ("U.S. Home Price Values May 2010").

[20] Stephanie Armour, *Underwater, and With Few Options: Falling Home Values Sap Equity – and Safety Nets*, USA Today, Mar. 25, 2010, at 1A. The article noted that, according to a study of 10 major metro areas by First American CoreLogic for USA Today, "a typical borrower who is 'underwater' won't see positive gains in equity until 2015 to 2020, depending on the market." Based on this same study, USA Today determined that about 24% of all residential properties with mortgages had negative equity at the end of 2009, which is up from 10.7 million and 23% at the end of the third quarter of 2009.

DIREITO COMPARADO / COMPARATIVE LAW

We saw the liquidation of Countrywide,[21] the nation's largest mortgage lender, the financial failure of Bear Stearns and its federally assisted takeover by J.P. Morgan,[22] the government takeover of the two largest securitizers of mortgages, Fannie Mae and Freddie Mac,[23] the failure of the investment banking firm of Lehman Brothers,[24] the sale of the investment and brokerage house of Merrill Lynch to Bank of America,[25] the government's bailout and gain of equity control of the nation's largest insurance company, A.I.G.,[26] the failure of the largest depository institution in U.S. history, Washington Mutual,[27] as well as the conversion of most of the big

[21] David Mildenberg & Ari Levy, *Bank of America to Acquire Countrywide for 37% Less*, BLOOM-BERG, (July 1, 2008, 1:54 EDT), http://www.bloomberg.com/apps/news?pid=newsarchive& sid=af9EoP0ySH6c&refer=home (updating original plans indicating that Bank of America Corp. agreed to buy Countrywide Financial Corp., the home lender battered by the collapse of the subprime mortgage market, for about $4.1 billion, with a sale price of $2.5 billion or about 37 percent less than originally planned).

[22] Serena Ng & Carrick Mollenkamp, *Foreclosed On – By the U.S.*, WALL ST. J., Aug. 4, 2010, at C1, C16 (explaining that in the bailout, "J.P. Morgan Chase & Co. bought Bear Stearns but didn't want to take $30 billion of its assets, its portfolio of real-estate loans and securities," which the New York Fed absorbed in order to facilitate the bailout).

[23] Zachary A. Goldfarb & David Cho, *U.S. Considers Remaking Mortgage Giants*, WASH. POST, Aug. 6, 2009, at A1, A13. The U.S. Government effectively nationalized the mortgage leviathans Fannie Mae and Freddie Mac, after the companies grew far larger than sustainable. That is, the mortgage giants are now majority owned by the U.S. Government, which pledged more than $1.5 trillion to keep the companies functioning and provided $85 billion in direct aid while also buying mortgage securities and debt from Fannie Mae and Freddie Mac. *Id.*

[24] David Wessel, *Government's Trial and Error Helped Stem Financial Panic*, WALL ST. J., Sept. 14, 2009, at A1, A2 (noting that Lehman Brothers "was so battered it hadn't any collateral to secure a Fed loan" and, thus, the Government could not prevent its collapse). *See also* Andrew Ross Sorkin, *Bids to Halt Financial Crisis Reshape Landscape of Wall St.*, N.Y. TIMES, Sept. 15, 2008, at A1 (confirming that, after days of speculation, Lehman Brothers filed for bankruptcy protection and moved toward liquidation after the company failed to find a buyer).

[25] Louise Story, *Stunning Fall for Main Street's Brokerage Firm*, N.Y. TIMES, Sept. 15, 2008, at A1. "It's the end of an era for Merrill Lynch," which previously held the place at the top of America's brokerage firms. Merrill Lynch, after losing $45 million on mortgage-related investments, agreed to sell itself to Bank of America for roughly $50 billion. *Id.*

[26] Matthew Karnitschnig et al., *U.S. to Take Over AIG in $85 Billion Bailout; Central Banks Inject Cash as Credit Dries Up*, WALL ST. J., Sept. 16, 2008, at A1 (describing the U.S. Government bailout of AIG, under which the Federal Reserve Bank will lend up to $85 billion to AIG, and the U.S. government will, in return, get a 79.9% equity stake in the company).

[27] Eric Dash & Andrew Ross Sorkin, *In Largest Bank Failures, U.S. Seizes, Then Sells*, N.Y. TIMES, Sept. 26, 2008, at A1 (noting that Washington Mutual symbolized the excesses of the mortgage boom and, in the end, also represented the largest bank failure in U.S. history).

investment houses, such as Morgan Stanley and Goldman Sachs,[28] into bank holding companies so that they could receive funds from the Troubled Asset Relief Program,[29] or TARP.

Well, it would seem fair to ask, if that is not regulatory failure than what is? But again, we have to refer back to the definition we created for regulatory failure.[30] Was this financial meltdown the result of misapplication or non-application of regulations that were in place precisely to prevent events like this from occurring? The answer would appear to be that the meltdown was largely not the result of a failure to apply rules that were in place and that were designed to prevent such a meltdown. How can this conclusion be reached in light of the numerous regulatory systems that were in place? Again, the analysis to be applied focuses upon securities regulation.

For starters, the aggressive issuance of mortgages to those who could not really afford them, has historically not, for the most past, been the province of federal regulation. Often these were state matters and even in instances where the federal regulation might have played a role, there was a strong bias toward making home ownership a virtual birthright of U.S.

---

[28] Joe Nocera, *Short Memories at Goldman*, N.Y. TIMES, Oct. 24, 2009, at B1. The author explained that, early in the financial crisis, Goldman took advantage of government programs aimed to address bank vulnerabilities. At the moment of maximum vulnerability, the U.S. Government "let Morgan Stanley and Goldman Sachs become bank holding companies -- something it had earlier refused to allow Lehman Brothers to do." *Id.* This conversion enabled the companies to receive TARP funds and calmed the storm.

[29] The Emergency Economic Stabilization Act of 2008, adopted on October 3, 2008 in response to the severe financial crisis in America's economy, authorized the Department of the Treasury, through the TARP, "to purchase, and to make and fund commitments to purchase, troubled assets from any financial institution." Emergency Economic Stabilization Act of 2008, Pub. L. No. 110-343, § 101, 122 Stat. 3765, 3767. In order to carry out its mandate, Treasury developed a number of programs under TARP to stabilize our financial system and housing market including an outline for a strategy that "balances the capacity to respond to threats to the financial system that could undermine economic recovery with the need to exercise fiscal discipline and reduce the burden on taxpayers." U.S. DEPARTMENT OF THE TREASURY, TARP MONTHLY 105(A) REPORT – MAY 2010 (2010), *available at* http://www.treasury.gov/initiatives/financial-stability/reports/Documents/May%202010%20105(a)%20Report_final. pdf. Treasury designed TARP to include measures to stabilize the financial system as well as aid homeowners and small businesses by deploying the $560 billion Congress authorized to Treasury for insuring bad assets, purchasing toxic assets, and providing bailout funding to failing banks, among other recovery measures. *How Treasury Spent Its Bailout Funds,* WASH. POST, Nov. 28, 2009, at A13.

[30] *See supra* pp. 124-25.

DIREITO COMPARADO / COMPARATIVE LAW

citizens. Most subprime lenders began as independent consumer finance companies beyond the oversight of banking regulators.[31] In an interview in 2009, Federal Reserve Chairman Alan Greenspan explained that he did not think the Federal Reserve was suited to policing these lending abuses because of its focus on broader economic issues rather than those of the individual borrower.[32]

Well, what about the CMOs. These sliced and diced interests in a bundle of mortgages indeed are securities. We know that the U.S. Securities and Exchange Commission (SEC) regulates the issuance of securities. While that is true, the primary regulatory device, the completion and filing of an extensive registration statement applies only to the public issuance of securities, not to their "private placement."[33] Although the term private placement is a technical term, in almost all instances, sales of securities, regardless of their complexity, to institutional investors will not be considered publicly offered and their issuance will not require a registration statement. So most, though not all, of the CMO issuances were structured as private placements and, thus, were not registered offerings.

Even though private placements are not registered public offerings, there are anti-fraud provisions that apply even to private placements. Although these anti-fraud provisions apply, it is still necessary to demonstrate a material misstatement or omission and it is not clear that most of the CMOs were sold by means of such misstatements or omissions. One can verify that few investors are resorting to anti-fraud challenges to the

---

[31] Benjamin Applebaum, *As Subprime Lending Crisis Unfolded, Watchdog Fed Didn't Bother Barking*, WASH. POST, Sept. 27, 2009, at A1, A18. This article discussed the development of the subprime lending industry and explained that initially, these "firms made loans to people whose credit was not good enough to borrow from banks, generally at high interest rates, often just a few thousand dollars for new furniture or medical bills. But by the 1990s, thanks to big changes in laws, markets and lending technology, the companies increasingly were focused on the much more lucrative business of mortgage lending." *Id.* at A18.

[32] *Id.*

[33] Private placements are "transactions by an issuer not involving any public offering." 15 U.S.C. § 77d(2) (2008). That is, a private placement of securities represents an offering of securities in a private rather in a public context. This term presents a rather amorphous concept and there is no further statutory guidance in this regard. However, factors relevant to a judicial determination of whether an offering constitutes a public or private offering include: (i) the sophistication of the investor; (ii) information provided the investor; (iii) pressures placed on the investor. *See, e.g.*, Sec. & Exchange Comm'n v. Ralston Purina Co., 346 U.S. 119 (1953).

issuance of the CMOs by reviewing the material litigations in which the major creators of the CMO are named as defendants. In the most recently filed annual report on Form 10-K, filed by Goldman Sachs in 2009,[34] under the mandated section disclosing legal proceedings, there are 20 matters listed. Merely one of those matters relates to the issuance of CMOs. Under risk of making a fraudulent prediction, management suggests that none of these matters will be materially harmful to Goldman. The Goldman Sachs annual report describes this matter relating to the suit regarding CMOs as follows:

> GS&Co., along with numerous other financial institutions, is a defendant in an action brought by the City of Cleveland alleging that the defendants' activities in connection with securitizations of subprime mortgages created a "public nuisance" in Cleveland. The action is pending in the U.S. District Court for the Northern District of Ohio, and the complaint seeks, among other things, unspecified compensatory damages. Defendants moved to dismiss on November 24, 2008.[35]

In the subsequent year's Form 10-K filing, Goldman Sachs expanded its discussion of its litigation matters relating to the company's CMO and CDS activities but, again, Goldman did not appear to express much concern regarding pending litigation claiming anti-fraud violations and its impact upon the bottom line of this financial institution. In regard to potential investigations regarding its dealings in credit derivatives, the company reported that Goldman and its affiliates:

> have received inquiries from various governmental agencies and self-regulatory organizations regarding credit derivative instruments. The firm is cooperating with the requests.[36]

Shortly after Goldman filed its 2009 Form 10-K, the SEC did indeed bring a civil action against Goldman with respect to its CMO and CDS

---

[34] Goldman Sachs Grp., Inc., Annual Report (Form 10-K), at 51 (Jan. 26, 2009).

[35] *Id.*

[36] Goldman Sachs Grp., Inc., Annual Report (Form 10-K), at 49 (Feb. 26, 2010).

activities.[37] This civil action did indeed allege fraud. One might argue that the fact pattern was quite unique and not generic. It is interesting to note that when the SEC and Goldman settled this matter with a consent degree in which Goldman neither admitted nor denied its wrongdoing,[38] the settlement amounted to less than two weeks of profit for Goldman.[39]

There is little evidence that anti-fraud litigation, by private parties or regulatory bodies, regarding CMO issuances has been a successful route for punishing the excesses of such issuances. Seemingly none of the litigation has been initiated on the theory that the issuance of CMOs themselves, without accompanying false language, was fraudulent.

Can we not challenge the self-serving work done by the issuers of the CMOs in selling instruments that were not as fool proof as they were held out to be? Many of these issuers were investment bankers and brokerage houses. Does not the SEC have partial regulatory authority over these entities? Well, yes, as brokers, the SEC has full oversight authority regarding matters such as net capital and record keeping and sales practices. But, the SEC does not have authority to regulate the instruments they are selling to the public, unless the language used regarding the sale of these instruments is fraudulent.[40] It would have been difficult to say, except in hindsight, that generic disclosure information regarding CMOs was fraudulent.[41]

---

[37] SEC Litigation Release No. 21,489, *Goldman Sachs & Co. & Fabrice Tourre* (S.D.N.Y. Apr. 16, 2010), http://www.sec.gov/litigation/litreleases/2010/lr21489.htm.

[38] SEC Litigation Release No. 21,592, *Goldman Sachs & Co. & Fabrice Tourre* (S.D.N.Y. July 15, 2010), http://www.sec.gov/litigation/litreleases/2010/lr21592.htm.

[39] Zachary A. Goldfarb, *In Devising Punishments, SEC Faced with Competing Interests*, WASH. POST, Aug. 3, 2010, at A11.

[40] *See supra* note 33 and accompanying text.

[41] Logically, investors relied on the ratings issued by the CRAs and included in mandatory disclosure provisions to provide a basis for investment decisions with respect to transactions in mortgage-backed securities. However, the CRAs, and the corresponding disclosures pertaining to risks and other exposures of the mortgages underlying the CMOs, based the ratings models on information from a limited time span. Thus, the CRAs and issuers failed to effectively disclose information that, in fact, remained fundamental to an understanding of the associated risks. The predominate model used to determine the substance of the disclosures "did not appear to be well suited to cope with a situation where all the boats may capsize, en mass." TETT, *supra* note 5, at 102. In effect, the models failed to effectively address risks that one default would trigger another and, therefore, in no way accounted for the

The SEC did have the ability to challenge whether, with all the leverage involved in the CMO and CDS transactions, the investment banks were too highly leveraged to meet their net capital requirements. But, in fact, in 2004, the Commission allowed investment bank net capital restrictions to be controlled by a comprehensive net capital rule that was consistent with U.S. and international bank holding company and which came out of the Basel Accord.[42] The Commission staff believed that it was expanding its oversight of investment banks by applying a universal net capital rule (known as the Universal Rule).[43] This Universal Rule had a more comprehensive, less arbitrary method for calculating net capital. There are those who argue that this amendment allowed some investment banks to increase their debt from 12:1 to as high as 33:1.[44] But, even in hindsight, there is no agreement that this change constituted misfeasance or malfeasance in the enforcement of an existing rule.

What of the CRAs? If they were rating the investment worthiness of securities, certainly the SEC must have had significant authority over how they operated and perhaps how they would be compensated for the ratings they produced? But, as it turns out, the Commission historically wanted to avoid advising CRAs on the methodology used to determine credit ratings. The Commission specifically noted its concern that by regulating the CRAs, it would appear to be giving its "official seal of approval" on the ratings issued by the CRAs.[45] In 2006, Congress passed a Credit Rating Agency Reform Act, which provided the Commission with some

---

massive contraction in the U.S. housing sector, and broader economy, the presaged the financial crisis.

[42] Erik R. Sirri, Director, Division or Trading and Markets, U.S. Securities and Exchange Commission, Remarks at the National Economists Club: Securities Markets and Regulatory Reform (Apr. 9, 2009), *available at* http://sec.gov/news/speech/2009/spch040909ers.htm.

[43] *Id.*

[44] In an April 2009 speech on securities markets and regulatory reform at the National Economists Club, Erik Sirri (Director, Division or Trading and Markets, SEC) challenged such assertions. Mr. Sirri noted that although such arguments are a theme generally adopted by the press, they "lack foundation in fact." *Id.*

[45] References to Ratings of Nationally Recognized Statistical Rating Organizations, Exchange Act Release No. 34-58,070 (July 1, 2008). In this 2008 release, the Commission expressed concerns that investors interpret the term Nationally Recognized Statistical Rating Organizations (NRSROs) as an endorsement by the SEC regarding the quality of the credit ratings issued by NRSROs and, thus, consider such ratings credible. *Id.*

more limited additional regulatory authority.[46] The Commission adopted rules pursuant to this legislation over a period between 2007 and 2009.[47] The adopted rules were designed to address concerns about the integrity of credit rating procedures.[48] The rules basically rely upon public disclosure by the CRA of their procedures and methodologies. Even if these rules ultimately prove effective, they were not in place in time to impact upon on the financial crises.

Last, but certainly not least, were those fast growing, largely unregistered, broadly invasive financial instruments, designed to reduce risk, the CDSs. Of all of the instruments that might have been regulated, these perhaps demand central attention. And yet, fascinatingly, CDSs were specifically written out of the jurisdiction of the SEC as well as the Commodity Futures Trading Commission.[49] The President's Working Group,

[46] Credit Ratings Agency Reform Act of 2006, Pub. L. No. 109-291, 120 Stat. 1327. Congress passed this Act with the twin goals of improving ratings quality and protecting investors and the overall public interest. The Act, designed to foster accountability, transparency, and competition in the credit ratings agency industry, required NRSROs to register with the SEC, prohibited unfair, coercive, or abusive acts or practices, and provided certain rulemaking powers to the Commission with respect to oversight of credit ratings agencies.

[47] Oversight of Credit Ratings Agencies Registered as Nationally Recognized Statistical Rating Organizations, Exchange Act Release No. 34-55,857 (June 5, 2007). This release explained the rules adopted by the Commission with respect to implementing the Credit Ratings Agency Reform Act of 2006. The new rules, as detailed in the release, pertain to the definition of NRSRO and the Commission's authority to implement registration, recordkeeping and other rules regarding CRAs. Additionally, the release provided the rule and form prescribing the process for a CRA to apply for registration. This registration process, in effect, replaced the no-action letter process previously used in this regard.

[48] Amendments to Rules for Nationally Recognized Statistical Rating Organizations, Exchange Act Release No. 34-59,342 (Feb. 2, 2009). In this 2009 release, the Commission imposed additional requirements on NRSROs in order to alleviate concerns with respect to the integrity of CRA procedures and methodologies regarding structured finance products, particularly those related to mortgage backed securities. The SEC indicated that the amendments provided in the release were the result of examinations of the three largest NRSROs and require, among other things, increased transparency, prevention of conflicts of interests, and enhanced recordkeeping and reporting.

[49] See Commodity Futures Modernization Act of 2000, Pub. L. No. 106-554 app. E, 114 Stat. 2763A-365. Title I of the Commodity Futures Modernization Act of 2000 (CFMA) adopted the recommendations included in the Report of the President's Working Group (PWC or Group) by broadly excluding transactions in financial derivatives (i.e., "excluded commodities" such as currencies, interest rates, or other macro-economic indices or measures) between "eligible contract participants" from regulations under the Commodity Exchange Act (CEA).

a consortium of all federal agencies concerned with financial markets, reasoned that financial derivatives are not subject to manipulation as might be derivatives relating to physical commodities because the latter are in limited supply and can be squeezed or cornered.[50] The counter argument is since CDSs cannot be cornered they cannot be manipulated. Since the issue of manipulation was not central to the damaging role played by the CDS in the financial meltdown, this reasoning by the Working Group was of little relevance in justifying the non-regulation of these instruments.

We have discussed the areas in which the SEC might have had some regulatory responsibilities. Yet, we find limited authority of the SEC to regulate the instruments and practices central to the meltdown. In those instances in which the Commission did have authority, it often exercised

---

The definition of "eligible contract participants" covered the same types of "sophisticated" parties as the existing "swaps exemption." The definition of "eligible market participant" and "eligible swaps participant" both expressly enumerate categories of market participants such as, among others, regulated entities and investors with assets exceeding $10 million that the CEA permits to engage in complex financial transactions otherwise not available to retail customers. 7 U.S.C. § 1a(12) (2008); 17 C.F.R. § 35.1(b)(2). But, the CFMA expanded the scope of eligibility in its definition of "eligible market participants" by including individuals with assets in excess of only $5 million (rather than requiring $10 million) if the transaction related to managing risk associated with an asset or liability. 7 U.S.C. § 1a(12)(xi)(II). The PWC reviewed the causes of the market issues that confronted the U.S. economy during the financial crisis. The Group consisted of the Treasury Department, the Federal Reserve, the SEC, and the CFTC. After reviewing the underlying causes, the PWC issued a report that recommended certain measures designed to reduce the re-occurrence of the events leading up to the financial crisis by strengthening market discipline, enhancing risk management, and improving the efficiency of our nation's capital markets. *See* Press Release, U.S. Department of the Treasury, *President's Working Group Issues Policy Statement to Improve Future State of Financial Markets* (Mar. 13, 2008), *available* at http://www.treasury.gov/press-center/press-releases/Pages/hp871.aspx.

[50] REPORT OF THE PRESIDENT'S WORKING GROUP ON FINANCIAL MARKETS, OVER-THE-COUNTER DERIVATIVES MARKETS AND THE COMMODITY EXCHANGE ACT 16 (Nov. 1999), *available at* http://www.treasury.gov/resource-center/fin-mkts/Documents/otcact.pdf. That is, the Working Group, in 1999, unanimously recommending that exclusions from the Commodity Exchange Act with respect to OTC derivatives not be extended to agreements involving physical commodities. The Working Group based this recommendation on the characteristics of markets for non-financial commodities with finite supplies. For example, its Report noted that "in the case of agricultural commodities, production is seasonal and volatile, and the underlying commodity is perishable, factors that make the markets for these products susceptible to supply and pricing distortions and to manipulation." *Id.*

its authority. Only in retrospect, could we perhaps reason that the exercise by the Commission was inadequate.

Another way to explore whether appropriate regulatory authority to oversee our financial system existed prior to the meltdown is to review what has been done to alter the financial regulatory system since the meltdown. For, if we are now attempting to put in place rules to prevent what happened from reoccurring, then it is fair to conclude that there is a belief that adequate authority did not exist prior to the meltdown to prevent the financial crises from materializing. If there was not adequate regulatory authority prior to the meltdown, then, it again becomes difficult to argue misfeasance or malfeasance of applying regulatory authority in place at that time. And indeed, since the meltdown, there has been a massive attempt to restructure our financial oversight rules. These attempts led to the adoption of an array of financial oversight alterations that Congress signed into effect in the summer of 2010.[51] The effort to adopt this new regulatory system post meltdown further suggests that an appropriate oversight system did not exist prior to the meltdown.

Many of the provisions that found their way into the Dodd-Frank Wall Street Reform and Consumer Protection Act (Dodd-Frank Act)[52] were originally proposed in a Treasury Department white paper, produced in June 2009, concerning financial regulatory reform.[53] Some of the proposals that the Treasury Department presented in the white paper were quite generic. Other proposals in the white paper were more specific but still needed refinement before being crafted into legislation. The Treasury Report was 88 pages long and contained a nine-page summary of its recommendations. Those nine pages included summaries of approximately 93 recommendations on how to avoid a future financial meltdown. In some respects these proposals are no longer relevant. However, in another regard, they are quite relevant because they reflect the sum of the analysis conducted in order to develop a new financial regulatory regime. Without any attempt to order these proposals in terms of importance, some of the

---

[51] Dodd–Frank Wall Street Reform and Consumer Protection Act of 2010, Pub. L. No. 111-203, 124 Stat. 1376.

[52] *Id.*

[53] U.S. DEP'T OF THE TREASURY, FINANCIAL REGULATORY REFORM: A NEW FOUNDATION (2009), *available at* http://www.treasury.gov/initiatives/Documents/FinalReport_web.pdf.

highlights of these proposals that directly relate to the events described in this paper are:

- The creation of a financial services oversight council that, among other matters, would monitor systemic risk. Everyone seems to have their own definition of systemic risk. A working definition might be the risk that arises out of a confluence of financial activities and products the oversight of which is not limited to only one agency. Such an oversight body might have been able to connect the dots between the growth of subprime mortgages, the availability of capital through questionably safe CMOs, and the risk placed on the issuer of the CDSs that guaranteed the CMOs.
- The creation of a regulatory regime that would supervise the resolution of the failure of the large bank holding companies. This regime was intended to allow the orderly and hopefully reasoned dismantlement or reorganization of financial institutions that might otherwise be too big to fail.
- The creation of a Treasury working group to assess the capital strength and other prudential standards for all banks and bank holding companies.
- The creation of a new consumer financial protection agency, which would protect consumers from risky mortgage, credit card, and banking practices.
- Tightening the oversight of CRAs.
- The creation of comprehensive regulation of OTC Derivatives, including CDSs.

Many of these proposals proved to be controversial for reasons that were external to the specific needs for regulation. For example, while many thought there was a need for further consumer protection, challenges arose as to whether there should be a new agency with an existence distinct from other previously existing agencies.[54] The fact that the Treasury Depart-

---

[54] Brady Dennis & Benjamin Appelbaum, *Consumer Agency May Be Out; Dodd Mulls Compromise Passage of Financial Reform Is the Objective*, WASH. POST, Jan. 16, 2010, at A11 (noting that Senator Dodd discussed jettisoning plans for a standalone consumer financial protection agency as a compromise to secure passage of the broader financial reform legislation).

ment proposals met resistance and the history of the actual congressional debates provides another insight into the question of whether there was indeed regulatory failure leading up to the financial meltdown. Had the proposals not met with controversy, had the congressional debates been unified in the direction which they ultimately took, perhaps one could argue that there was a regulatory resolution that was available at the time of the financial meltdown. That resolution, however, was just not applied. But recent history suggests anything but uniformity of belief regarding how to respond to the financial meltdown. This absence of certainty on how to appropriately address the events leading to the crisis of 2007-2008, suggests that there was not a failure to apply a readily available and effective regulatory scheme. Rather, it seems that no such scheme existed.

In following the congressional debates leading up to the passage of the Dodd-Frank Act, one recognizes that even as late as two years after the financial meltdown, thinking on what would constitute an appropriate response to the financial regulatory confusion leading to the meltdown remained far from unanimous. That uncertainty suggests that even after the worst financial crisis in 80 years, there was no certainty as to what constituted appropriate safeguards against a reoccurrence of such a meltdown. As late as the last evening before the passage of the Dodd-Frank Act, many a night-long negotiation session resulted in significant compromises being made. These last minute compromises reflected deep divisions with respect to what represented the wisest course for preventing future crises.[55] The continued uncertainty as to the cure suggests that there was not, prior to the meltdown, a system in place to respond to such problems. This uncertainty also casts some reservations as to whether the

---

[55] *See* David Cho, *Lawmakers Guide Wall Street Reform into Homestretch*, WASH. POST, June 26, 2010, at A1. In order to render the bill eligible for passage, a number of Senators made significant concessions. For instance, Sen. Blanche Lincoln agreed to scale back a rather controversial provision that would require banks spin off all derivatives businesses into separately capitalized entities. In the final legislation, such action is required only for the riskiest instruments. *Id.; see also* Jim Puzzanghera, *Financial Overhaul Work Done: The Legislation to Dramatically Expand U.S. Oversight Is Expected to Get Final Approval Next Week*, L.A. TIMES, June 26, 2010, at A1 (noting that during the late hours of the night that Congress passed the bill, Members reached an agreement on the Volcker rule). The article describe that the Volcker rule, after accepting a proposal by Sen. Dodd, "would limit so-called proprietary trading – investments of the bank's funds for its own profit instead of its clients' – as well as investments in hedge funds and private equity funds." Puzzanghera, *supra*..

regulatory system adopted by Congress is indeed the appropriate system as we go forward.

It is reasonable to conclude that regulations were not in place to respond to newly created instruments and financing policies. We also know that the new instruments and the entire financing strategy grew extremely fast and generated considerable profits. Undoubtedly, this suggests regulatory failure in the sense that nothing was done to review the instruments, to advise as to their risk, or to check on the impact of their growth on our financial service sector. Thus, is it fair to say that this was an instance of a failure to create regulations? Undoubtedly, the answer is "yes." But, equally undoubtedly, the answer has to be that no regulatory system could have prevented this meltdown from occurring. Changes in financial products and strategies simply developed too quickly for the regulatory system to keep pace. Shortly after the financial meltdown, we discovered that the collateralizing of financial instruments had artificially inflated the financial stability of both Greece and Spain and, consequently, the economies of these two countries became volatile and potentially unstable.[56] This financial creativity came close to bringing down the governments of these countries.[57] While appropriate regulatory systems can be developed to prevent identical financial practices from creating similar financial crises in the future, it is uncertain whether regulatory imagination is sufficiently creative to anticipate problems created by newly devised financial products that might be developed in the future. Regulators are not fortunetellers. They are not divinely prescient. They do not react quickly to change. It is indeed perhaps beneficial that regulators do not react promptly. At

---

[56] *See* Landon Thomas, Jr., *Cost of Debt Adds to Fear About Spain*, N.Y TIMES, June 16, 2010, at B1 (discussing the financial uncertainties that resulted from "fears that Spain's financing costs could soon become too high for the economy to bear"); Jack Ewing, *Debtors' Prism: Who Has Europe's Loans?*, N.Y. TIMES, June 6, 2010, at B1 (noting the $2.6 trillion in debt collectively owed by Greece, Spain and Portugal – "three countries so mired in economic troubles that analysts and investors assume that a significant portion of that mountain of debt may never be repaid").

[57] *See* Michael Phillips et al., *Geithner Urges G-20 to Step Up Consumption*, WALL ST. J., June 5, 2010, at A9 (noting that the European Union and the International Monetary Fund created support funds "as Greece teetered near default and . . . Portugal's financial stability slipped"); Suzanne Daley, *Safety Nets Fray in Spain, As Elsewhere in Europe*, N.Y TIMES, June 28, 2010, at A4 (noting that "across Europe," economic instability has "fuel[ed] protests and strikes that have tied up airports, blocked highways and, in Greece, even turned deadly").

times, it takes a period of time to discern whether new products or practices are helpful or harmful.

Well, what does that say about the future? Don't bother regulating? Ignore the problems we discover? No, not at all. All regulation is in response to prior flaws. Sometimes, if we are very lucky, we can correctly anticipate future problems. Whether we can anticipate future problems, there is little doubt that we must do the best we can to reform extant regulatory systems to respond to problems we have discovered in the past. If catching future financial system flaws is uncertain, why do we bother attempting to respond to future problems? We certainly cannot catch all of the flaws; however, we can catch some of the weaknesses of financial regulation. It seems self apparent that catching some regulatory soft spots is far better than catching none. It remains important, however, to remember that any system that is put into place to regulate financial markets will not be foolproof.

Prologue

As mentioned in the Preface, Congress adopted the Dodd-Frank Wall Street Reform and Consumer Protection Act[58] in the summer of 2010 and President Obama signed the Act into law on July 21, 2010.[59] Most of the major issues that Congress tackled mirrored the issues addressed in the Treasury Report. The actual bill adopted by Congress included more than 2,000 pages of legislation. Although it would certainly be difficult to summarize this massive legislation, some of the more important changes should be noted. The financial reform act included:

- The establishment of a Financial Stability Oversight Council, which functions to identify risks to the financial stability of the United States that could arise from interconnected financial activities or institutions;
- Establishes a new resolution process for large financial companies which approach failure;

---

[58] Dodd–Frank Wall Street Reform and Consumer Protection Act of 2010, Pub. L. No. 111-203, 124 Stat. 1376.

[59] *See* Jim Puzzanghera, *Eyes on Wall Street with New Oversight; President Signs Broadest Overhaul of Financial Rules Since the 1930s*, CHI. TRI., July 22, 2010, at C25.

- Creates a new consumer financial protection agency, the Consumer Financial Protection Bureau;
- Applies similar leverage and capital requirements that apply to insured depository institutions to most bank holding companies, savings and loan holding companies, and other important non-bank financial companies;
- Directs federal bank regulators to create capital requirements for holding companies and depository institution which requirements will address activities that pose threats to the financial system through high-risk financial activities;
- Imposes comprehensive regulation of the derivatives market and effectively prohibits insured depository institutions from conducting certain derivatives business in the institution itself;
- Requires persons offering asset-backed securities to retain some of the risk associated with the offered securities; and,
- Reforms the regulation of CRAs and increases liability standards on these institutions.

It is instructive to note that many of the provisions of the Dodd-Frank Act require further rulemaking by administrative agencies before the impact of the legislation will be felt.[60] The significance of this additional rulemaking is that, even after adopting 2,000 pages of legislation, it is not precisely clear what avenue should be taken to resolve certain financial problems. It is also instructive to note that in solving some problems, it became immediately apparent that the Dodd-Frank Act was creating new

---

[60] *See* Dodd–Frank Wall Street Reform and Consumer Protection Act of 2010 Pub. L. No. 111-203, § 913, 124 Stat. 1376, 1824 (directing the Commission to conduct a study and draft a report regarding the effectiveness of legal and regulatory standards for broker-dealers and investment advisers); *id.* at § 921, 124 Stat. at 1841 (providing the Commission with rulemaking authority to restrict mandatory pre-dispute arbitration). Pursuant to the Dodd-Frank Act, the Commission and the Commodity Futures Trading Commission are tasked with promulgating at least 160 rules (with the SEC responsible for about 100 and the CFTC's burden at around 60) in addition to conducting numerous studies and drafting a number of reports. *See* Damian Paletta & Victoria McGrane, *Fighting Flares on New Rules For Street*, WALL ST. J., Aug. 21, 2010, at B1. Overall, "federal agencies are writing the more than 200 new rules required by the regulatory overhaul." Michael Casey, *Geithner Addresses Overhaul*, WALL ST. J., Aug. 3, 2010, at A5.

problems that had to be remedied.[61] This creation of additional problems again suggests that the achievement of a working financial reform system is not a certain task.

Finally, it is instructive to note how many of the provisions of the Dodd-Frank Act are actually responding to the specifics of the last meltdown, regulation of derivatives, regulation of CRAs, and limitation on the risk that the banking industry may absorb. Not unpredictably, the legislation is primarily designed to prevent a reoccurrence of the last meltdown. There are provisions that specifically speak to the next crises, such as the Financial Stability Oversight Council. But it might prove to be vainglorious to believe that regulators will be able to see next crises a priori. It would be fair to conclude that while the Dodd-Frank Act might be a good attempt to fix the last problem, it remains unclear whether it can prevent future problems.

---

[61] For example, the Dodd-Frank Act regards bond-ratings firms as "experts" and holds them liable for the quality of their ratings within the context of liability with respect to registration statements under Section 11. This aspect of the financial overhaul caused ratings firms to refuse to allow their credit ratings to be used in deal documents and created turmoil in the bond markets. As a consequence, on July 22, 2010, the Commission decided "it would temporarily allow bond sales to go ahead without credit ratings in bond offering documents, a move that would end a stalemate between ratings agencies and issuers." Anusha Shrivastava & Fawn Johnson, *SEC Breaks Impasse With Rating Firms The Wall Street Journal*, WALL ST. J., July 23, 2010, at C1. On a separate note, the Division of Corporate Finance issued a no-action letter with respect to the Dodd-Frank Act's requirement that, in disclosing a rating in a registration statement, the rating agency consent to be named an expert. In light of rating agencies' unwillingness to provide their consent, the no-action letter allows issuers to omit credit ratings from registration statements filed under Regulation AB until January 24, 2011. *See* Letter from SEC to Ford Motor Credit Company LLC & Ford Credit Auto Receivables Two LLC, (Nov. 23, 2011) (SEC No-Action Letter), *available at* https://www.sec.gov/divisions/corpfin/cf-noaction/2010/ford072210-1120.htm. A statement in this regard also issued by the Division of Corporate Finance, indicated this action is expected to provide issuers, rating agencies and other market participants with a transition period to implement changes to comply with the new statutory requirement while still conducting registered ABS offerings. Meredith Cross, Dir., Div. of Corp. Fin., U.S. Securities and Exchange Commission, Statement Regarding the Registered Asset-Backed Securities Market (July 22, 2010), *available at* http://www.sec.gov/news/speech/2010/spch072210mc.htm.

Cooking Up a Crisis: The Capital-Valuation Connection in U.S. Real Estate Markets

ANDREA BOYACK[*]

If this was a cooking show, and we were preparing to demonstrate how to create a complex dish that I'll call "The 2008 Financial Crisis," we would start out by assembling our various ingredients. In this case, our ingredients would include sophisticated financial products,[1] rating agency discretion,[2] investor rating mandates,[3] borrower credit

---

[*] Visiting Professor at George Washington University Law School. This paper was presented at the 9th Annual Conference on Portuguese and American Law, "The Financial Crisis: How We Got Here and How We Get Out" held on March 8, 2010 in Lisbon, Portugal as a joint initiative of the Catholic University of America, Columbus School of Law and Faculdade de Direito da Universidade de Lisboa.

[1] *E.g.,* Collateralized debt obligations (CDOs) are asset-backed securities deriving value from an underlying portfolio of assets. Bethany McLean, *The Dangers of Investing in Subprime Debt*, FORTUNE, Mar. 19, 2007. Collateralized mortgage obligations (CMOs) are asset-backed securities backed by mortgages. *See also infra* notes 17, 73 and accompanying text. In addition to trading in mortgage-backed securities themselves, a substantial market developed for insurance type derivatives, called credit default swaps, that guaranteed re-payment of mortgage in case of default and were independently traded as investment products (and subject to great speculation). *See* Randolph C. Thompson, *Mortgage Backed Securities, Wall Street, and the Making of a Global Financial Crisis*, 5 BUS. L. BRIEF (AM. U.) 51, 53 (2008).

[2] *See, e.g.,* John Patrick Hunt, *Credit Rating Agencies and the Worldwide Credit Crisis: The Limits of Reputation, the Insufficiency of Reform, and a Proposal for Improvement*, 1 COLUM. BUS. L. REV. 2009; Carol Ann Frost, *Credit Rating Agencies in Capital Markets: A Review of Research Evidence on Selected Criticisms of the Agencies*, J. ACCT., AUDITING, & FIN., 2010 (forthcoming; *available at* http://ssrn.com/abstract=941861).

[3] Primarily pursuant to 12 C.F.R. § 362.11 (prohibiting state and local entities and fiduciary investors from investing in "corporate debt securities not of investment grade"). This

DIREITO COMPARADO / COMPARATIVE LAW

assessments,[4] bank regulations,[5] and opaque accounting practices.[6] Many reformers today focus on one or more of these ingredients, calling for greater government oversight and regulatory reform,[7] and governments have attempted to respond.[8] But related in one way or another to each such

essentially gave the ratings from credit rating agencies the force of law. The impact of agency ratings was further increased by barriers to entry into the credit rating business created by the Securities and Exchange Commission in 1975. *See* Lawrence J. White, *The Credit Rating Agencies: Understanding their Central Role in the Subprime Debacle of 2007-2008*, CRITICAL REVIEW, 2010 (forthcoming; *available at* http://ssrn.com/abstract=1434483). Note that, in spite of 12 C.F.R. § 362.11, and in spite of standard practice of relying on agency ratings, Standard & Poor's credit rating contains the following disclaimer: "any user of the information contained herein should not rely on any credit rating or other opinion contained herein in making any investment decision." Other rating agencies include similar disclaimers on their ratings.

[4] *See, e.g.*, Creola Johnson, *Fight Blight: Cities Sue to Hold Lenders Responsible for the Rise in Foreclosures and Abandoned Properties*, 2008 UTAH L. REV. 1169 (2008).

[5] For discussion of Basel II's capital requirements, *see* Eric Y. Wu, *Basel II: A Revised Framework*, 24 ANN. REV. BANKING & FIN. L. 150 (2005).

[6] *See* Robert H. Herz & Linda A. MacDonald, *Understanding the Issues: Some Facts about Fair Value*, FASB.org, May 2008, http://www.fasb.org/articles&reports/uti_fair_value_may_2008. pdf; *see also* Jana Shearer, *Mark to Market: Delivering the Financial Crisis to Your Front Door*, 36 OHIO N.U. L. REV. 239 (2010) (arguing that accounting practices were more of a delivery mechanism for the crisis than its cause).

[7] *See, e.g.*, Steven L. Schwarz, *Too Big to Fail?: Recasting the Financial Safety Net*, Duke Law School Public Law and Legal Theory Research Paper Series No. 235, March 2009, *available at* http://papers.ssrn.com/sol3/papers.cfm? abstract_id=1352563; Bernard Shull, *Too Big to Fail in Financial Crisis: Motives, Countermeasures, and Prospects*, Levy Economics Institute of Bard College, Working Paper No. 601, June 2010, *available at* http://papers.ssrn.com/sol3/papers. cfm?abstract_id=1621909; Alison Hashmall, *After the Fall: A New Framework to Regulate "Too Big to Fail" Non-Bank Financial Institutions*, 85 N.Y.U. L. REV. 829 (2010).

[8] In response to the financial crisis, the U.S. Congress passed a series of laws, including the Economic Stimulus Act of 2008 (Pub. L. 110-185, providing for various types of economic stimuli, including tax rebates, intended to boost the U.S. economy, with a total taxpayer cost of an estimated $152 billion. *See* Budget Report: H.R. 5140: Economic Stimulus Act of 2008); the Emergency Economic Stabilization Act of 2008 which created the Troubled Asset Relief Program (TARP) (the American Recovery and Reinvestment Act of 2009) (Pub. L. 111-5). Also called "the Stimulus Act" or "the Recovery Act," this legislation made supplemental fiscal year government appropriations to be used in job creation, investment promotion and stimulation of consumer spending). These laws reflect the Keynesian economic concept that a government should spend to pull a country out of recession. *See* JOHN MAYNARD KEYNES, THE GENERAL THEORY OF EMPLOYMENT, INTEREST AND MONEY (1935); John Maynard Keynes, *The Maintenance of Prosperity is Extremely Difficult*, NEW DEAL THOUGHT, ED. OWARD ZINN, 403-09 (Bobbs-Merrill, 1966). Since this paper was presented, Congress enacted the Dodd-Frank Wall Street Reform and Consumer Protection Act (the Dodd-Frank Act), clearly the

factor is the volatile collateral pricing, which supported these extensions of credit in the first place. In assessing the repayment risk associated with making a mortgage loan, lenders evaluate two factors: credit and collateral. These factors are related. Although lenders look primarily to a borrower's ability and willingness to pay in order to assess the likelihood of loan repayment, sufficient collateral values can offset the risk of lending to lower-credit borrowers. When supported by valuable collateral, loans to riskier borrowers become less risky. When borrower credit fails, market evaluation of risk hinges on accurate real estate valuations. The "sharp corrections in housing markets" caused by over-estimation of property values provided a "trigger" for the financial crisis.[9] No analysis of proposed legal solutions is complete without considering the ingredient of values and value perceptions.

At its most basic level, the story of real estate finance starts with land valuation. Since mortgage finance frees trapped asset values, the price of land depends on the availability of capital. The more funds available to finance mortgages, the more liquid the collateral asset, and the higher its market value. Finance opportunities grow real estate values. Real estate price history over the past decade supports this conclusion: as money flooded real estate loans, real estate prices increased dramatically.[10] These

---

most comprehensive package of financial reform legislation in the U.S. since the crisis and possibly the most wide-reaching financial regulatory legislation ever.

[9] Deutsche Bank Research, *Commercial Real Estate Loans Facing Refinancing Risks: CMBS Only Part of a Growing Problem*, July 6. 2010, www.dbresearch.com [hereinafter DEUTSCHE BANK RESEARCH REPORT].

[10] From 1996 to 2006, U.S. national average house prices rose between 93% and 137%. *See* Office of Federal Housing Enterprise Oversight (OFHEO) House Price Index, http://www.fhfa.gov/Default.aspx?Page=195; STANDARD & POOR'S, S&P/CASE-SHILLER HOME PRICE INDICES 2009, A YEAR IN REVIEW 3 (Jan. 2010), *available at* http://www.standardand poors.com/indicies/sp-case-shiller-home-price-indicies/en/us/?indexId=spusa-cashpidff--p-us---- (illustrating that real estate prices dramatically rose between 1991 and 2005) [hereinafter S&P/CASE-SHILLER]. From 2001 to 2006, real estate values in seven metropolitan areas (Tampa, Miami, San Diego, Los Angeles, Las Vegas, Phoenix and Washington, DC) increased more than 80%. *Id.*; *see also* ROBERT SHILLER, IRRATIONAL EXUBERANCE (2d ed. 2005) [hereinafter SHILLER, IRRATIONAL EXUBERANCE]; Robert Shiller, *The Bubble's New Home*, BARRON'S (June 20, 2005), http://online.barrons.com/ article/SB111905372884363176.html. In the Barron's article, Shiller wrote that "the home-price bubble" had the "feel" of "the stock-market mania in the fall of 1999, just before the stock bubble burst in early 2000, with all the hype, herd investing and absolute confidence in the inevitability of continuing price appreciation. My

DIREITO COMPARADO / COMPARATIVE LAW

inflated prices were unrealistic and unsustainable.[11] The rather apocalyptic decline in U.S. real estate prices seems to have caught the entire market off-guard.[12] The structure of the modern U.S. mortgage finance system itself – rated securitization products sold to investors worldwide – enlarged the effect of real property price downturn this decade,[13] but these market changes do not explain *why* those real estate values changed to begin with. Since that is the key spark to both this latest financial boom and its bust, let's start our analysis there.

Real estate values are tricky ingredients, easily inflated by mortgage capital. Let me draw an analogy between capital and real estate values and the live cultures of yeast in baking. Yeast is a naturally occurring, ubiquitous microorganism, used by ancient Egyptians to make bread lighter and tastier. When left alone, yeast does nothing, but when fed with the right combination of sugar and starch, say in bread dough, yeast produces carbon dioxide which enlarges gluten proteins in flour. As Louis Pasteur demonstrated in 1859, it is the proper feeding of the cultures in yeast that causes the dough to expand and rise.[14]

Real property values have the same potential effect in our capital markets. Real property is inherently valuable because of its permanence

blood ran slightly cold at a cocktail party the other night when a recent Yale Medical School graduate told me that she was buying a condo to live in Boston during her year-long internship, so that she could flip it for a profit next year. Tulipmania reigns." Shiller, *supra*.

[11] *See, e.g.*, Graham Searjeant, *US Heading for House Price Crash, Greenspan Tells Buyers*, THE TIMES, Aug. 27, 2005, *available at* http://business.timesonline.co.uk/tol/business/economics/article559641.ece; *see also Greenspan Alert on US House Prices*, FINANCIAL TIMES. Sept. 17, 2002; *The bubble question*, CNNMONEY.COM, http://money. cnn.com/2004/07/13/real_estate/buying_selling/risingrates/; JUNE FLETCHER, HOUSE POOR: PUMPED UP PRICES, RISING RATES, AND MORTGAGES ON STEROID – HOW TO SURVIVE THE COMING HOUSING CRISIS (2005).

[12] *See, e.g.*, JONATHAN NORBERG, FINANCIAL FIASCO: HOW AMERICA'S INFATUATION WITH HOMEOWNERSHIP AND EASY MONEY CREATED THE ECONOMIC CRISIS (Cato Institute, 2009). A popularly distributed ("viral") PowerPoint called the "Subprime Primer" mocks the now discredited but previously relied-upon mantra that "real estate values will always go up." A copy of this PowerPoint can be viewed at http://www.slideshare.net/guesta9d12e/subprime-primer-277484.

[13] By 1990, capital finance was a global market. Rated securitization products backed by real assets were sold to investors worldwide. This enlarged the effect of real property price downturn. *See* ANDREW DAVIDSON, ANTHONY B. SANDERS, LAN-LING WOLFF, SECURITIZATION: STRUCTURING AND INVESTMENT ANALYSIS (Wiley 2003) (discussing securitization in detail).

[14] *See* JAMES J. WALSH, CATH. ENCYCLOPEDIA, *Louis Pasteur* (1913) (proving that fermentation is caused by living organisms, namely yeast).

and productivity, though such value has no direct economic effect when trapped by illiquidity or inalienability.[15] Like feeding yeast with sugars, however, "feeding" real estate value with readily-available capital can allow that trapped value to become liquid – creating usable wealth. The resulting mixture of land plus money causes real estate values to expand and grow, creating a real estate capital market which has a tendency to self-inflate. Policies and financial structures of the United States have fed a steady stream of capital into the real estate market mixture for years. Decades ago, the U.S. government fashioned secondary market entities whose mission was to provide the incentive and the ability for origination of more mortgage loans.[16] More recently, Wall Street master chefs designed scrumptious new products – packaging, rating, and selling asset-backed securities and their derivatives.[17] The robust secondary mortgage market in the United States increased the supply of mortgage capital which – like simple sugars added to yeast – fed real asset value.[18]

Increasing asset values created a wealth effect which in turn fueled demand for funds. Owners wanted to "cash out" the new value trapped in

---

[15] *See* Jon Christensen, *Land Rich, but Cash Poor, in the West*, N.Y. TIMES, Nov. 23, 1997; *Property Rich, Cash Poor*, TIME, Oct. 19, 1981, http://www.time.com/time/magazine/article/0,9171,924967,00.html.

[16] *See infra* notes 63-93 and accompanying text.

[17] For example, in 1983, Salomon Brothers and First Boston pioneered a financial debt vehicle called a collateralized mortgage obligation (CMO). First, a separate, special purpose entity (SPE) was created for the sole purpose of holding a pool (set) of mortgages. This SPE would issue bonds to investors who would receive payments according to prescribed priority levels (classes or tranches). The tranching of the CMOs could be done in a nearly infinite variety of ways (for example, sequence, parallel tranching, schedule bonds, defined maturity, non-accelerating, coupon tranching, or some combination of these), and the risks of such instruments could be further mitigated through various credit enhancement tools. *See generally* BRIAN P. LANCASTER, GLENN M. SCHULTZ & FRANK J. FABOZZI, STRUCTURED PRODUCTS AND RELATED CREDIT DERIVATIVES: A COMPREHENSIVE GUIDE FOR INVESTORS (2008); *see also* Hunt, *supra* note 2, at 7-9 (discussing rating of securitization products). For additional information regarding securitization of mortgages, see *infra* notes 69-74 and accompanying text. For a historic/literary account of securitization and debt markets, *see generally* MICHAEL LEWIS, LIAR'S POKER (1990).

[18] *See, e.g.*, Anthony Sanders, *The Subprime Crisis and its Role in the Financial Crisis*, 17 J. HOUSING ECON. 254 (2008); Richard Freeman, *'Fannie and Freddie Were Lenders': U.S. Real Estate Bubble Nears Its End*, EXECUTIVE INTELLIGENCE REV., June 21, 2002 ("Since 1995, the housing bubble has required between $400 to $600 billion per year in new mortgages to finance homeowners' purchase of new and existing homes at inflated prices.").

illiquid real property so that this value could be put to work in other investments – or be spent.[19] This wealth effect was intensified by government policies promoting home ownership for everyone.[20] When the anchors for real estate prices – namely risk assessments and leverage limits – fell away, real estate prices and the demand for real estate capital really took off.[21] The cycle perpetuated itself: increase in demand for mortgage funds led to banks increasing capital supply, and the increase in mortgage capital availability "fed" real estate values, raising prices. This in turn fueled even further demand for mortgage financing.

As these ingredients mixed, were allowed to rise, and were baked in the general boom years of the early twenty-first century,[22] we created a puffy concoction of flavor, and it was hard to determine how much of our masterpiece *was* flour and how much was really just air. But our marvelous soufflé has imploded,[23] and we are now left sorting out that very question.

Real Estate Capital Market Crash: Recipe Deconstruction

To facilitate analysis of this "recipe for disaster," I will discuss four intersecting factors that created the fragile over-inflated real estate capital market: (1) the nature of real property, (2) market changes which increased capital availability, (3) a widespread and unrestrained wealth effect, and (4) pervasive over-leverage combined with under appreciation of risk.

---

[19] *See infra* 75-76 and accompanying text.

[20] *Id.*

[21] *See infra* 114-130 and accompanying text.

[22] *See generally* ALAN S. BLINDER & JANET L. YELLEN, THE FABULOUS DECADE: MACROECONOMIC LESSONS FROM THE 1990s (2001); JOSEPH E. STIGLITZ, THE ROARING NINETIES: A NEW HISTORY OF THE WORLD'S MOST PROSPEROUS DECADE (2004).

[23] S&P/CASE-SHILLER, *supra* note 10, at 3 (real estate prices tumbled after 2005, reaching a record low in real estate price decline at -19% through the first quarter of 2009). Heather Landy & Renae Merle, *A Record Fall on Wall Street: Stocks Dive as Bailout Bill Fails to Pass*, WASH. POST, Sept. 30, 2008 (noting that the Dow Jones industrial average tumbled 7 percent, or 777.68 points, eclipsing the record point drop after the Sept. 11, 2001 terrorist attacks, to close at 10,365.45. The technology-heavy Nasdaq composite index slid 9.14 percent, or 199.61, to 1983.73, and the broader Standard & Poor's 500-stock index lost 8.79 percent, or 106.62, to close at 1106.39."); *see also* ROBERT J. SHILLER, THE SUBPRIME SOLUTION: HOW TODAY'S GLOBAL FINANCIAL CRISIS HAPPENED, AND WHAT TO DO ABOUT IT, 29-38, 87-113 (2008) (attributing the financial crisis to un-tempered increases in home prices); Ruth Mantell, *Home Prices Off Record 18% in Past Year, Case-Shiller Says*, MARKETWATCH, Dec. 30, 2008, http://www.marketwatch.com/story/home-prices-off-record-18-in-past-year-case-shiller-says.

I will then assess current proposals for solving the U.S. real estate crisis and worldwide credit crunch, from the perspective of how likely such proposals are to (a) solve mis-pricing trends and (b) temper the boom/bust cycle in real estate finance.

1. The nature of real property makes it particularly difficult to price

The intrinsic value of real property is indubitable, but assigning precise dollar figures to such value presents one of the great conundrums of secured finance. In some ways, land *is* the ultimate source of wealth: it is required for residence, it is required for all traditional means of production, it can never be truly replaced, and it lasts forever. In other words, real property is priceless.

And that is just the problem: because each piece of real property is unique, market pricing of land is always a bad fit.[24] But to capitalize real assets, we must arrive at a reliable price. We may look to comparative sales,[25] but land is the ultimate non-fungible good. We may measure the cost-to-replace,[26] but there is no replacing land – each piece is different and there is a finite supply. We may measure the stream of income a property produces,[27] but this valuation is vulnerable to wide swings in rental and occupancy rates and is arguably only relevant for income-producing property in any case.[28]

Land is not like other market goods. Real estate parcels are situate – they cannot be moved to fill shortages where they occur.[29] Because of the immobility of real property, price fluctuations caused by over-supply in one locality and over-demand in another will not balance out.[30] Although real

---

[24] An economist might put it this way: real estate *prices* are inherently "noisy" – imperfect measures of *valuation*.

[25] For a description of comparable sales methodology, *see* http://realestate.about.com/od/appraisalandvaluation/p/ compare_method.htm.

[26] The cost-to-replace methodology applies the concept of substitution. For a description of this pricing method, *see* http://www.propex.com/C_g_cost.htm.

[27] For a description of how to derive present value from stream of property income, *see* http://realestate.about.com/ od/appraisalandvaluation/p/income_method.htm.

[28] *See id.*

[29] It is people who must move, not real estate, should an imbalance between supply and demand of, say, housing occur – witness outlying suburb growth/population changes.

[30] *See* Dina ElBoghdady, *Foreclosure Activity Rises in Most Metropolitan Areas*, WASH. POST, July 30, 2010, at A14, http://www.washingtonpost.com/wpdyn/content/article2010/07/29/

estate capital markets today speak in terms of the *aggregate* and operate on a national – or even global – level, at bottom, the land assets are inherently and unchangeably local.

American law recognizes the difficulty in accurately pricing real estate. Although contracts for exchange of goods are *typically* enforced only in economic terms (by granting damages for breach),[31] courts routinely order specific performance of the actual real estate transaction rather than resort to money damages.[32] In the U.S. Supreme Court case of *B.F.P. v. Resolution Trust*, Justice Scalia refused to review the adequacy of a foreclosure sale price, recognizing that there is no benchmark for true value of real estate.[33]

Because market pricing is, at best, a good guess-timate, the values attached to real estate necessarily remain fragile, broadly susceptible to misapprehensions or changed expectations. Expected values of real estate necessarily rely on some prediction about changes over time. The longer the time horizon, the hazier such predictions. In the United States, where real estate transactions are measured in months or years and real estate financing spans decades, temporal risk is substantial. Changes in the applicable legal system regarding entitlements and liabilities can have drastic

---

AR2010072906271.html ("The 20 regions with the worst foreclosure rates were in the four states – Florida, California, Nevada and Arizona...."); Brad Heath, *Mortgage Collapse Started in Few Areas*, USA TODAY, Mar. 6 2009, at 01A (properties concentrated in a mere thirty-five counties accounted for half of country's foreclosure actions and "eight counties in Arizona, California, Florida, and Nevada were the source of about a quarter of the nation's foreclosures" in 2008). As of July 2010, 1 in 200 households in California are in foreclosure; 1 in 171 in Florida are in foreclosure; 1 in 167 households in Arizona are in foreclosure; and 1 in 82 households in Nevada are in foreclosure. *States with the Highest Foreclosure Rates*, CNBC.COM, http://www.cnbc.com/id/29655038/States_with_the_Highes_Foreclosure_Rates (last visited Aug. 12, 2010) (on file with author) (citing data from RealtyTrac's U.S. Foreclosure Market Report).

[31] *See, e.g.*, George T. Washington, *Damages in Contract at Common Law*, 47 LAW Q. REV. 345, pt. 1 (1931).

[32] At common law, land was subject to particular laws "simply because it was land – a favorite and favored subject in England." Kitchen v. Herring, 42 N.C. (7 Ired.) 137, 138 (1851). For an economic argument in support of special treatment of land, see William Bishop, *The Choice of Remedy for Breach of Contract*, 14 J. LEGAL STUD. 299, 305 (1985).

[33] 511 U.S. 531, 545 (1994) ("We deem, as the law has always deemed, that a fair and proper price, or a 'reasonably equivalent value,' for foreclosed property, is the price in fact received at the foreclosure sale, so long as all the requirements of the State's foreclosure law have been complied with.").

effects on a property's ultimate value as well.[34] The starting point for any transaction is the adage that contracts freely entered into will be enforced according to their terms. But the contractual "private law" of real estate finance operates in the context of numerous public laws, and many varied legal areas and authorities each potentially impact property values. *Federal* law impacts even local real estate deals, setting parameters for bankruptcy,[35] environmental liability,[36] securities regulation,[37] and tax consequences.[38] *State* laws establish the baseline property rights for all land in a particular state – meaning that in the United States, real property is subject to one of fifty distinct and complex state legal regimes, each with its own version of mortgage,[39] foreclosure,[40] liability,[41] ownership

---

[34] *See, e.g.*, Tahoe-Sierra Pres. Council, Inc. v. Tahoe Reg'l Planning Agency, 535 U.S. 302 (2002); Palazzolo v. Rhode Island, 533 U.S. 606 (2001).

[35] Under 11 U.S.C. § 362(a) (2006), all foreclosure proceedings are automatically stayed by the filing of any of the three types of bankruptcy proceedings. *See, e.g., In re* Ward, 837 F.2d 124 (3d Cir. 1988). Bankruptcy trustee may also avoid pre-bankruptcy dispositions of real assets if such dispositions are found to be preferential or fraudulent. 11 U.S.C. §§ 544, 548 (2006).

[36] *E.g.*, 42 U.S.C. §§ 9601-75 (commonly known as "CERCLA"); 42 U.S.C. §§ 6901-92 (known as "RCRA"). State laws also create environmental-based liabilities under various acts, sometimes called "baby CERCLA" acts. *See, e.g.*, CAL. HEALTH & SAFETY CODE §§25230(a)(2), 25359.7 (West 2010); 35 PA. CONS. STAT. ANN. § 6018.405 (West 2010).

[37] Although the SEC has been charged with sales of securitized products, certain asset-backed products fell outside of SEC oversight because of private placement, safe harbors, etc.

[38] For example, IRS regulations permit homeowners to deduct state property taxes, mortgage interest, and expenses allocable to a home office. *See* Tax Reform Act of 1976, 26 U.S.C. § 280A (2006). There are numerous other tax statutes that permit like kind exchanges, deferring gain on residence, etc. *See e.g.*, 26 U.S.C. §§ 1031, 1033, 1034 (§1034 repealed 1997).

[39] *See* RESTATEMENT (THIRD) OF PROPERTY: MORTGAGES § 4.1, cmt. a (1996) (discussing the differences between "lien theory" and "title theory" and the intermediate theory of mortgages among different states). States also differ in terms of lender liability and lender and seller disclosure requirements in real estate transactions.

[40] In Vermont and Connecticut, strict foreclosure still exists. 12 V.S.A. § 4531; CONN. GEN. STAT. ANN. § 49-15 (West 2010). In many other states, some variation of judicial foreclosure is method for disposition of the borrower's equity of redemption. *See* GRANT S. NELSON & DALE A. WHITMAN, REAL ESTATE FINANCE LAW 558-59 (4th ed. 2001). In about 60% of the states, lenders may include a power of sale in their mortgage instruments, permitting non-judicial foreclosure. NELSON & WHITMAN (4th ed. 2001), *supra*, at 581-85; *see, e.g.*, N.Y. REAL PROP. ACTS. LAW §§ 1301-91 (Consol. 2010). While the 2002 Uniform Nonjudicial Foreclosure Act promulgated by the National Conference of Commissioners on Uniform States Law has the potential of bringing state foreclosure laws into greater conformity, states have not yet

privileges,[42] and so forth. In addition, nowhere do local *municipalities* play a larger role than with respect to real property: investors ignore local regulations on land use and tenant rights at their peril.[43]

To further complicate the legal landscape, the concept of "equity" looms large in American real property law.[44] Mortgage financing operates almost completely in the realm of equitable interests, which grants courts the freedom to resolve disputes by fashioning whatever result it considers "just" and "fair."[45] The flexible approach of equity arguably leads to better individual solutions, but at the cost of predictability. And, as mentioned, market pricing relies on prediction.

Accuracy in real estate valuation is directly connected to information. While certain negative impacts on value may be discovered and accounted for in market pricing, it is not possible to foresee and manage all negative impacts *ex ante*.[46] And since values in real estate are at the mercy of so many changeable market and legal factors, an information gap or faulty prediction can lead to disastrous results.

---

adopted such measures. *See* Grant S. Nelson & Dale A. Whitman, *Reforming Foreclosure: the Uniform Nonjudicial Foreclosure Act*, 53 DUKE L.J. 1399 (2004).

[41] For example, nuisance law application to owners varies widely among (and within) jurisdictions. *See* Matthew Saunig, Comment, *Rebranding Public Nuisance:* City of Cleveland v. Ameriquest Mortgage Securities, Inc. *as a Failed Response to Economic Crisis*, 59 CATH. U. L. REV. 911, 916-25 (2010).

[42] For example, the public's right to access (and an owner's ability to exclude from) beachfront property varies widely based on geographic region within the United States. *See, e.g.,* Leydon v. Town of Greenwich, 750 A.2d 1122 (Conn. App. Ct. 2000), *aff'd on other grounds*, 777 A.2d 552 (Conn. 2001); Glass v. Goeckel, 703 N.W.2d 58 (Mich. 2005); Raleigh Ave. Beach Ass'n v. Atlantis Beach Club, Inc., 879 A.2d 112 (N.J. 2005); Greater Providence Chamber of Commerce v. Rhode Island, 657 A.2d 1038 (R.I. 1995).

[43] Localities govern land use extensively and have the primary taxing authority over real property. Local regulations on zoning and use restrictions have sizeable impacts on property valuation. *Compare* Prince George's Cnty. v. Sunrise Dev. Ltd. P'ship, 623 A.2d 1296, 1304 (Md. 1993), *with* VA. CODE ANN. § 15.2-2307 (2010). *See generally* JULIAN CONRAD JUERGENSMEYER & THOMAS E. ROBERTS, LAND USE PLANNING AND CONTROL LAW §5.28 (1998).

[44] *See, e.g., Anglo-American Land Law: Diverging Developments from A Shared History*, 34 REAL PROP. PROB. & TR. J. 443, 454 (1999); EDMUND H. T. SNELL, THE PRINCIPLES OF EQUITY (1916); John C. Murray, *Clogging Revisited*, 33 REAL PROP. PROB. & TR. J. 279 (1998).

[45] *See* David A. Super, *A New New Property*, 113 COLUM. L. REV. 1773, 1850 (2013).

[46] *E.g.,* Rosique v. Windley Cove, Ltd., 542 So. 2d 1014 (Fla. Dist. Ct. App. 1989) (denying rescission even though property was down-zoned between contract and closing); Sanford v. Breidenbach, 173 N.E.2d 702 (Ohio Ct. App. 1960) (denying specific performance sought by seller when home on property was destroyed by fire prior to closing).

Let's take a recent noteworthy example of precisely this problem: the purchase and finance of Stuyvesant Town, in New York City at the end of 2006.[47] By all rights and logic, if *any* real estate transaction should have been correctly priced, it should have been this deal. The buyer/borrower was a joint venture of Tishman Speyer and BlackRock – two of the *most* sophisticated and pre-eminent New York real estate investment companies, with top-dollar pricing analysts and decades of experience.[48] This was a commercial venture on a grand scale – the largest real estate deal *ever* – with a purchase price of $5.4 billion dollars at stake,[49] 80% financed by two capital market giants, Wachovia and Merrill Lynch.[50] Furthermore, valuation was based on expected stream of income, a methodology that typically yields more realistic results.[51] This was a case where everything suggested the most accurate possible price.

But... they were *off* – a margin of error to the tune of $3.5 billion (possibly more).[52] How could these pre-eminent market experts have so materially mis-priced a real estate asset? Hindsight reveals that these real estate pricing gurus mis-predicted the market, mis-apprehended the legal context, and misunderstood the asset itself.

The Stuyvesant Town purchase was for an 80-acre, 110-building piece of property on the lower east side of Manhattan – a huge parcel in a prime location.[53] But since this property was originally developed as a low-income

---

[47] Charles V. Bagli, *Megadeal: Inside a New York Real Estate Coup*, N.Y. TIMES, Dec. 31, 2006, http://www.nytimes.com/2006/12/31/business/yourmoney/31speyer.html (last visited Apr. 17, 2011).

[48] *See* Tishman Speyer/BlackRock, *Peter Cooper Village and Stuyvesant Town: Term Sheet for Investor Equity* (2006) (unpublished manuscript) (on file with author). *See generally* Megan McArdle, *Capitalist Fools*, ATLANTIC, Jan./Feb. 2010, *available at* http://www.theatlantic.com/magizine/archive/2010/01/capitalist-fools/7824/.

[49] *See generally* Raymond H. Brescia, *Line in the Sand: Progressive Lawyering, "Master Communities," and a Battle for Affordable Housing in New York City*, 73 ALB. L. REV. 715 (2010).

[50] *See* Charles V. Bagli, *MetLife Completes Sale of Stuyvesant Town*, N.Y. TIMES, Nov. 17, 2006, http://www.nytimes.com/2006/11/17/nyregion/17cnd-stuy.html?_r=0.

[51] *See* EILEEN APPELBAUM, ROSEMARY BATT & IAN CLARK, CTR. FOR ECON. & POLICY RESEARCH, FINANCIAL CAPITALISM, BREACH OF TRUST AND COLLATERAL DAMAGE 11 (Dec. 2011), *available at* http://cepr.net/documents/financial-capitalism-2011-11.pdf.

[52] Dawn Wotapka, *Tishman, BlackRock Default on Stuyvesant Town*, WALL ST. J., Jan. 8, 2010, http://online.wsj.com/article/SB10001424052748703535104574646611615302076.html. *See generally* DANIEL GROSS, DUMB MONEY: HOW OUR GREATEST FINANCIAL MINDS BANKRUPTED THE NATION 25-33 (2009).

[53] *See* Bagli, *supra* note 50.

DIREITO COMPARADO / COMPARATIVE LAW

housing project,[54] it is not only dated construction but, as Lewis Mumford quipped, it has "the architecture of the Police State."[55] While initially rent controlled, many of the units in Stuyvesant Town had been decontrolled,[56] a trend that Tishman and BlackRock anticipated would continue.[57] Sadly for them, a New York court in October 2009 not only prohibited further rent decontrol, but ordered thousands of the units previously freed to market forces returned to their prior rental status.[58]

It turns out that these real estate pricing gurus were wrong about the continued, robust growth of demand for New York residential real estate. In addition to missteps in pricing the legal risk, the market risk seems to have been virtually ignored. Although capital requirements for gaining control of Stuyvesant Town were massive, Tishman, BlackRock, Wachovia, Merrill and all of their many smart and sophisticated investors anticipated that it was well worth it to "unlock" the future profits that market rental pricing would generate.

In early 2010, Tishman and BlackRock defaulted on their mortgage loan, walking away from the deal and turning ownership over to their lenders (or what was left of those lenders).[59] The Stuyvesant Town deal was not only the highest priced real estate purchase ever, but also the largest mortgage default in history.[60] The property is considered to be worth about $1.8 billion dollars today – roughly $2.4 billion *less* than the principal amount of the mortgage loan, $3.4 billion *less* than Tishman and BlackRock had paid for it, and clearly several billions of dollars lower than these pricing experts had anticipated just three years before.[61] Quite a cautionary tale of how difficult, fragile, and finicky measurements of real property values can be!

---

[54] *See generally* SAMUEL ZIPP, MANHATTAN PROJECTS: THE RISE AND FALL OF URBAN RENEWAL IN COLD WAR NEW YORK 73-156 (2010).

[55] *Id.* at 148.

[56] *See* Brescia, *supra* note 49, at 719-24.

[57] *Id.* at 738-48.

[58] *Id.*; *see* Wotapka, *supra* note 52.

[59] Alan Rappeport, *Tishman and BlackRock default*, FIN. TIMES, Jan. 9, 2010, http://www.ft.com/cms/s/0/d2af81d2-fcbf-11de-bc51-00144feab49a.html#axzz3tWMSyPBB;*see* Charles V. Bagli & Christine Haughney, *Wide Fallout in Failed Deal for Stuyvesant Town*, N.Y. TIMES, Jan. 25, 2010, http://www.nytimes.com/2010/01/26/nyregion/26stuy.html.

[60] *See* Brent T. White, *The Morality of Strategic Default*, 58 UCLA L. REV. DISC. 155, 163 (2010).

[61] Hui-yong Yu et al., *Tishman Nears Restructuring, Sale of Stuyvesant Town (Update1)*, BLOOMBERG, Nov. 9, 2009, http://www.bloomberg.com/apps/news?pid=newsarchive&sid=aASVPDH5t7ZI.

You've probably heard it said that the three most important things in real estate are "location, location, and location."[62] Though oft-repeated, this formula has *never* really been true. The "location, location, location" mantra vastly oversimplifies the factors that impact the value of real estate. In a market context, the three most important impacts on real estate value are better summed up as: price, price, and price. Pricing drives transactions, creates nominal wealth and allocates risk. As this crisis shows, real estate pricing is important but fragile.

2. Changes in capital markets increased money flow to real estate
Real estate's price fragility makes it particularly vulnerable to changes in capital availability and finance structures. Over the past decades, three major changes to real estate capital markets increased the flow of funds and simultaneously increased demand for real estate capital. Ample supply of capital plus rising demand for asset liquidity pushed real estate prices up.

A. *The secondary mortgage market*
During the Great Depression in the 1930s, the U.S. government established the Federal National Mortgage Association (Fannie Mae).[63] Fannie Mae and its later-established "sister" entity – Federal Home Loan Mortgage Corporation (Freddie Mac) – are government sponsored enterprises, or GSEs, chartered by Congress and regulated by federal agencies, but owned by private shareholders.[64] Fannie and Freddie's mandate is to purchase

---

[62] The late Lord Harold Samuel popularized the expression: "There are three things that matter in property: location, location, location." The 1987 obituaries of Lord Samuel in Britain's *Sunday Times* and *Financial Times* and a 2007 issue of *The Daily Telegraph* all identify Lord Samuel as the coiner of this expression, though William Safire of *The New York Times* disputes his authorship. William Safire, *On Language: Location, Location, Location*, N.Y. TIMES, June 26, 2009 (Magazine), *available at* http://www.nytimes.com/2009/06/28/magazine/28FOB-onlanguage-t.html.

[63] National Housing Act of 1934, 12 U.S.C. § 1716 (2006).

[64] Emergency Home Finance Act of 1970, 12 U.S.C. §§ 1451-1459 (2006). For details on the structure and purposes of Fannie Mae and Freddie Mac, see Robert Van Order, *Understanding Fannie and Freddie*, RICHARD'S REAL ESTATE & URBAN ECONS. BLOG, (July 31, 2008), http://real-estate-and-urban.blogspot.com/2008/07/robert-van-order-on-fannie-and-freddie.html. Previously, in 1968, Fannie Mae had been split into a "private" corporation (Fannie Mae) and a publicly financed institution with explicit government guaranty of repayment of securities (Government National Mortgage Association or Ginnie Mae). In addition to Fannie and Freddie, there are twelve Federal Home Loan Banks (sometimes called the "mini-GSEs").

qualifying residential loans from mortgage originators.[65] This encourages the flow of capital directly by replenishing the capital stores of primary lenders.[66] Instead of waiting for up to 30 years for repayment of mortgage funds by borrowers, the secondary mortgage market allowed lenders to renew their lending funds almost immediately. The GSEs also encourage real estate capital indirectly by (a) inducing more long-term mortgages to be made (protecting and encouraging home buying/borrowing) and (b) giving originators of mortgage loans security against default risk (protecting and encouraging home lending).[67]

Fannie and Freddie purchased, and continue to purchase, qualifying residential loans from mortgage originators. To qualify for purchase by the GSEs, a loan must meet certain standards: for example, a loan could not be too big or too risky.[68]

In the 1980s, Fannie and Freddie began raising capital to purchase these qualifying mortgages by pooling hundreds and thousands of those qualifying mortgages and selling shares to private investors.[69] Mortgaged-backed securitization allows broader participation in the "lender" side of the real estate finance market.[70] It also spreads the risk of default among many people and many properties, hedging against risk of economic downturn for an individual borrower or a certain locality.[71] Holding a share of

These banks perform similar functions as Fannie and Freddie (providing funds to originating lending institutions).

[65] GRANT S. NELSON & DALE A. WHITMAN, REAL ESTATE FINANCE LAW 932-41 (5th ed. 2007).

[66] *See* NELSON & WHITMAN, *supra* note 65.

[67] *See About Fannie Mae: Loan Limits,* FANNIE MAE, http://www.fanniemae.com/aboutfm/loanlimits.jhtml (last revised Jan. 24, 2011) [hereinafter About Fannie Mae]; *see also* Gail Cohen, *How to Qualify for a Fannie Mae Loan,* EHOW, http://www.ehow.com/how_5107817_qualify-fannie-mae-loan.html (last visited Jan. 24, 2011).

[68] *See About Fannie Mae, supra* note 67; Cohen, *supra* note 67.

[69] *See* FRANK J. FABOZZI & FRANCO MODIGLIANI, MORTGAGE AND MORTGAGE-BACKED SECURITIES MARKETS 19-20 (1992). Fannie and Freddie only securitized a portion of their loans, however, much of their mortgage purchases were financed with debt.

[70] *See* DAVIDSON ET AL., *supra* note 13. Investor risk arises from various sources, including risk of loan default and non-repayment as well as risk of interest rate change and prepayment of mortgages. It is important to remember that even if risk was appropriately included in pricing, these debt securities represent a future stream of income rather than a currently available liquid – or even liquidatable – asset.

[71] Securitization eliminates risk through splitting a group (pool) of mortgage loans into multiple classes (tranches) with a hierarchy of repayment rights (the top tranche has the

an asset-backed obligation pool was considered a safe investment, not just because debt obligations were collateralized, but because the process of pooling and securitizing the obligations minimized each investor's risk of loss.[72] Investor risk was further lessened by GSE guarantied returns, and the ability of the GSEs to make good on their commitments was implicitly supported by the federal government.[73] Unsurprisingly, these debt securities were rated AAA or AAA+.[74]

The GSE secondary market and securitization system significantly sped up the flow of mortgage finance capital, making real estate values more liquid and keeping interest rates low.[75] More capital flowing to the loan originators increased homeowner access to funding. Increasing the *supply*

---

least risky position in terms of credit and prepayment risk). The tranching of the pool will reduce risks for investors holding the top positions who are buffered by lower-positioned investors bearing the first loss. Theoretically, that is true even if the entire pool is made up of risky mortgage loans: the lower tranches act as a risk shock absorber. Wall Street opined that pooling and tranching can be done successively, reducing the top-tiered securities risk with each re-tranching. This theory, widely accepted in the dawn of the 21st century, seems to work less well under real market stress. Ultimately, valuation models for securitized products proved more problematic than securitization itself. For an overview comparison of securitization and traditional bank lending, see Gerald Hanweck, Anthony B. Sanders & Robert Van Order, *Securitization Versus Traditional Banks: An Agnostic View of the Future of Fannie Mae, Freddie Mac and Banks*, FinReg21 (Sept. 28, 2009), http://www.finreg21.com/lombard-street/securitization-versus-traditional-banks-an-agnostic-view-future-fannie-mae-freddie-ma. A concise description of the development of mortgage-backed securitization can be found at Kurt Eggert, *Held Up in Due Course: Predatory Lending, Securitization, and the Holder in Due Course Doctrine*, 35 Creighton L. Rev. 503, 535-50 (2002).

[72] *See* Davidson et al., *supra* note 13; *see also* Eggert, *supra* note 71 (describing the benefits of securitization to investors and lenders).

[73] *See* Robert Van Order, *The U.S. Mortgage Market: A Model of Dueling Charters*, 11 J. Housing Res. 233, 233-39 (2000) [hereinafter Van Order, *Dueling Charters*].

[74] *Debt Securities: Understanding Fannie Mae Debt: Fannie Mae Credit Ratings, Fannie Mae* (July 27, 2006), http://www.fanniemae.com/markets/debt/understanding_fm_debt/credit_ratings. jhtml?p=Debt (last revised Jan. 15, 2009) (describing Fannie's senior debt as Aaa/AAA from each of the major ratings agencies: Moody's, S&P, and Fitch). Although Freddie's preferred stock was downgraded to Baa3 (the lowest investment grade rating) in August 2008, Freddie's senior debt credit rating remains Aaa/AAA from the ratings agencies. *See Freddie Mac Courts Investors, Buffett Passes*, Taipei Times, Aug 24, 2008, at 11, *available at* http://www.taipeitimes. com/News/biz/print/2008/08/24/2003421257.

[75] *See* Robert Van Order, *Understand Fannie and Freddie*, Richard's Real Estate & Urban Econs. Blog, (July 31, 2008), http://real-estate-and-urban.blogspot.com/2008/07/Robert-van-order-on-fannie-and-freddie.html; Van Order, *Dueling Charters*, *supra* note 73, at 233-39.

of real estate capital also made financing cheaper, spurring lenders to creatively increase borrower *demand* by offering a broad spectrum of mortgage products, many promising little or no equity investment and small interest-only monthly payments.[76] Ample supply of funds and rising demand for liquidity put upward pressure on real estate prices. As real properties appreciated, individual and aggregate asset wealth grew.

The majority of all U.S. residential mortgage loans today are components of these huge securitized pools of debt;[77] about 40 to 50% of total residential mortgage debt being serviced through Fannie and Freddie investment structures and 10 to 15% through similar "private label" systems.[78] In terms of both market share and actual dollars, GSE securitized debt is huge. In terms of market share and in actual dollars, GSE securitized debt is huge: when Fannie Mae and Freddie Mac were put into conservatorship in September 2008, they had $5.4 trillion of guaranteed mortgage-backed securities debt between them.[79]

Because of government's implicit (and later explicit) underwriting of Fannie and Freddie, the losses accruing to those pools of securitized debt are socialized (ultimately paid for by the government), while the profits are privatized. Incidentally, the same situation exists with commercial banks: federal deposit insurance prevents banks from "going under," thus spreading the risks/costs over the entire public. The Wall Street bailout

---

[76] In the first half of 2005 for example, the market for would-be borrowers was "ultra-competitive" and interest-only loans made up 28.5% of all mortgage loans, according to the mortgage data company Loan Performance. Suzanne Stewart & Ike Brannon, *A Collapsing Housing Bubble?*, REG., Spring 2006, at 16.

[77] *See* David Ellis, *U.S. Seizes Fannie and Freddie*, CNNMONEY.COM (Sept. 7, 2008, 8:28 PM), http://money.cnn.com/2008/09/07/news/companies/fannie_freddie/index.htm (indicating that "half the mortgage debt in the country" was owned by Fannie and Freddie as of September 2008).

[78] *Id.*; Van Order, *Dueling Charters, supra* note 73, at 237; *see also* STAFF OF H. COMM. ON OVERSIGHT & GOV'T REFORM, 111TH CONG., THE ROLE OF GOVERNMENT AFFORDABLE HOUSING POLICY IN CREATING THE GLOBAL FINANCIAL CRISIS OF 2008 12 (Comm. Print 2009).

[79] *See* Press Release, James B. Lockhart, Dir., Fed. Hous. Fin. Agency, Statement on Behalf of Federal Housing Finance Agency, 1 (Sept. 7, 2008), *available at* http://www.fhfa.gov/webfiles/23/FHFAStatement9708final.pdf; *see also Hearing Before the H. Comm. on Fin. Servs.* (March 23, 2010) (statement of Anthony B. Sanders, Member, Mercatus Center's Financial Markets Working Group), *available at* http://mercatus.org/video/housing-finance-reform ("[T]he combined debt load for Fannie Mae, Freddie Mac, and the Federal Home Loan Bank [currently] stands at $8 trillion.").

has been criticized for retroactively creating this same system, on a huge scale, to failed investment banks.[80] Socializing losses while privatizing profits incentivizes risk-taking, and since risk is separated from reward, price calculations reflect possible "upside" returns untempered by accurate considerations of any "downside" risks. Supposedly, such systemic mis-incentives can be corrected through regulation.

The GSE charters recognized the risk-taking potential and attempted to mitigate it through regulation.[81] Yet loan purchase criteria and other regulation restraints failed to insulate the GSEs from inordinate risk.[82] First, the sheer size of Fannie and Freddie's market share increased their vulnerability to economic downturns.[83] Also, while purchases of overly risky loans were theoretically limited, creative loan structuring allowed riskier loans to sneak into GSE loan pools through the back door.[84] Lax requirements regarding reservation of capital for purchased loans made Fannie and Freddie's position that much more precarious – only 2.5% of the value of securitized loans was kept as capital reserves.[85]

---

[80] For a discussion of the Wall Street bailout, see VERN McKINLEY & GARY GEGENHEIMER, CATO INST., BRIGHT LINES AND BAILOUTS: TO BAIL OR NOT TO BAIL, THAT IS THE QUESTION (April 21, 2009), *available at* http://object.cato.org/sites/cato.org/files/pubs/pdf/pa-637.pdf.

[81] *See* David Reiss, *Fannie Mae and Freddie Mac and the Future of Federal Housing Finance Policy: A Study of Regulatory Privilege*, 61 ALA. L. REV. 907 (2010); Michael J. Lea, *Sources of Funds for Mortgage Finance*, 1 J. HOUSING RES. 139 (1990).

[82] *See* Reiss, *supra* note 81; David J. Reiss, *Ratings Failure: The Need for A Consumer Protection Agenda in Rating Agency Regulation*, Banking & Fin. Services Pol'y Rep., November 2009.

[83] Julia Patterson Forrester, *Fannie Mae/Freddie Mac Uniform Mortgage Instruments: The Forgotten Benefit to Homeowners*, 72 MO. L. REV. 1077 (2007). For a systemic critique of Fannie Mae and Freddie Mac's role, see David J. Reiss, *First Principles for an Effective Federal Housing Policy*, 35 BROOK. J. INT'L L. 795 (2010).

[84] *See* Reiss, *Ratings Failure*, *supra* note 82; Van Order, *Dueling Charters*, *supra* note 73. Economists at Fannie Mae and Freddie Mac also reasoned that the market provided a mechanism for accurate subprime mortgage risk pricing. *See* Amy Crews Cutts & Robert Van Order, *On the Economics of Subprime Lending* (Freddie Mac, Working Paper No. 04-01, 2004), *available at* http:// www.freddiemac.com/news/pdf/subprime_012704.pdf.

[85] *The Future of the Federal Housing Administration's Capital Reserves: Assumptions, Predictions, and Implications for Homebuyers: Hearing Before Subcomm. on the Hous. and Cmty. Opportunity of the H. Comm. on Fin. Servs.*, 111th Cong. 8 (2009) (statement of Edward Pinto, Real Estate Financial Services Consultant); Dale Arthur Oesterle, *The Collapse of Fannie Mae and Freddie Mac: Victims or Villains?*, 5 ENTREPRENEURIAL BUS. L.J. 733 (2010); David Reiss, *The Federal Government's Implied Guarantee of Fannie Mae and Freddie Mac's Obligations: Uncle Sam Will Pick Up the Tab*, 42 GA. L. REV. 1019, 1022 (2008). For example, on Sept. 25, 2003 at the House Financial Services

In July 2008, the U.S. Treasury indicated that the government would bail out Fannie and Freddie if necessary.[86] In September 2008, the Treasury placed Fannie and Freddie into conservatorship, reorganizing the enterprises and infusing them with new capital.[87] At the time, this was the largest state rescue in history, to the tune of $100 billion (though just a fraction of the later Wall Street bailout plan).[88] Rescuing Fannie and Freddie was

Committee hearing, in a debate about whether the GSE's capital reserve requirements should be increased from a mere 2.5%, Representative Barney Frank in a now-infamous quote, said: "I do think I do want the same kind of focus on safety and soundness that we have in OCC [Office of the Comptroller of the Currency] and OTS [Office of Thrift Supervision]. I want to roll the dice a little bit more in this situation towards subsidized housing...." *See* Op-Ed, *What They Said about Fan and Fred*, WALL ST. J., Oct. 2, 2008, at A19 (quoting Rep. Barney Frank). This was a conscious policy choice to take on more governmental risk in order to promote broader homeownership. On the other hand, the Congressional Budget Office's 1996 report, expressing frustration over the inability of government to limit GSE scope, concluded by saying: "Once one agrees to share a canoe with a bear, it is hard to get him out without obtaining his agreement or getting wet." Binyamin Applebaum, Carol D. Leonning & David S. Hilzenrath, *How Washington Failed to Rein in Fannie, Freddie*, WASH. POST, Sept. 14, 2008, at A1 (quoting the Congressional Budget Office Report).

[86] Stephen Labaton, *Treasury Acts to Shore Up Fannie Mae and Freddie Mac*, N.Y. TIMES, July 14, 2008, http://www.nytimes.com/2008/07/14/washington/14fannie.html?_r=0&pagewanted=all.

[87] *See* David Ellis, *U.S. Seizes Fannie and Freddie*, CNNMONEY.COM (Sept. 7, 2008, 8:28 PM), http://money.cnn.com/2008/09/07/news/companies/fannie_freddie/index.htm; *see also* Krugman, Op-Ed, *Fannie, Freddie, and You*, N.Y. TIMES, July 14, 2008, at A17; Press Release, James B. Lockhart, Dir., Fed. Hous. Fin. Agency, Statement on Behalf of Federal Housing Finance Agency, 1 (Sept. 7, 2008), *available at* http://www.fhfa.gov/webfiles/23/FHFAStatement-9708final.pdf; FEDERAL HOUSING FINANCE AGENCY, FACT SHEET, QUESTIONS AND ANSWERS ON CONSERVATORSHIP, *available at* http://www.fhfa.gov/wefiles/35/FHFACONSERVQA.pdf; *Oversight Hearing to Examine Recent Treasury and FHFA Actions Regarding the GSEs: Hearing Before the H. Comm. on Fin. Servs.*, 110th Cong. (Sept. 25, 2008) (statement of Herbert M. Allison, Jr., President and Chief Executive Officer, Fannie Mae) [hereinafter Allison Testimony], *available at* http://www.fanniemae.com/media/speeches/2008/index.jhtml?p=Media&s=E xecutive+Speeches&t=2008+Executive+Speeches. For information on GSE investigations conducted during conservatorship activities, see Press Release, Federal Housing Finance Agency, FHFA Issues Subpoenas for PLS Documents (July 12, 2010), *available at* http://www.fhfa.gov/webfiles/15935/PLS_subpoena_final__7_12_10.pdf.

[88] *See* Allison Testimony, *supra* note 87 (addressing how Freddie Mac pursued its mission to support the mortgage market, provide liquidity, and prevent foreclosures since the conservatorship began); James Lockhardt, Acting Dir., Office of Fed. Hous. Enter. Oversight (OFHEO), Testimony Before the Financial Crisis Inquiry Commission (Apr. 9, 2010), *available at* http://fcic-static.law.stanford.edu/cdn_media/fcic-testimony/2010-0409-Lockhart.pdf (explaining the Freddie Mac remediation process). *See generally* Press Release, Fed. Hous. Fin. Agency,

necessary to keep the residential mortgage market machinery from completely grinding to a halt and mitigated the impact of the crash on homeowners and homebuyers.[89] The only way to keep the residential mortgage market from completely freezing up was to enable Fannie and Freddie to keep buying loans.[90] The impact of Fannie and Freddie's market presence – and the effect of their bailouts – can be understood by comparing GSE securities with securitizations of those market segments where Fannie and Freddie did *not* have a significant presence: namely, unqualified mortgage loans. Loans that were too big ("jumbo loans") or too risky ("subprime loans") were privately securitized.[91] The subprime mortgage market was the first real estate crash "heard 'round the world,"[92] and the jumbo market, representing loans

Questions and Answers on Conservatorship, http://www.fhfa.gov/webfiles/35/ FHFACON-SERVQA.pdf (explaining conservatorship and how it will affect the Federal Housing Finance Agency). The initial 2008 Wall Street bailout plan announced just weeks later was much larger – $700 billion. Some later estimates suggest that the true cost of the private label bailout may be hundreds of billions more. *See* Deborah Solomon et al., *New Bank Bailout Could Cost $2 Trillion*, WALL ST. J. (Jan. 29, 2009), http://online.wsj.com/article/SB123319689681827391.html.

[89] *See* Allison Testimony, *supra* note 87; *see also* Robert Van Order, *Privatization Won't Reduce Risk*, N.Y. TIMES, Mar. 8, 2011 ("That is the paradox of guarantees. They produce incentives to take on too much risk, as they did with Fannie and Freddie after 2004 and with the savings and loans in the 1980s, but they also limit systemic risk and panic. It's hard to have one without the other.").

[90] U.S. DEP'T OF TREASURY & U.S. DEP'T OF HOUS. & URBAN DEV., REFORMING AMERICA'S HOUSING FINANCE MARKET: A REPORT TO CONGRESS (2011); Van Order, *Dueling Charters*, *supra* note 73; *A Responsible Market for Housing Finance: A Progressive Plan to Reform to Reform the U.S. Secondary Market for Residential Mortgages*, CTR. FOR AM. PROGRESS (Jan. 2010) [hereinafter Secondary Market Report], http://www.americanprogress.org/issues/2011/01/pdf/responsiblemarketforhousingfinance.pdf; Rick Newman, *Kill Fannie and Freddie? Not Likely*, U.S. NEWS & WORLD REP. (Feb. 21, 2011), http://money.msn.com/investing/kill-fannie-and-freddie-not-likely- usnews.aspx.

[91] In 2006 alone, nearly 3 million subprime loans were originated and funded with an aggregate of over $1 trillion. *State of the U.S. Economy and Implications for the Federal Budget: Hearing Before the H. Comm. on the Budget*, 110th Cong. 10 (2007); *see also* Yulia Demyanyk & Otto Van Hemert, *Understanding the Subprime Mortgage Crisis* 32 (Dec. 5, 2008), http://ssrn.com/abstract=1020396.

[92] From July 2007 to August 2009, 1.8 million homes were lost to foreclosure and 502 million more residential foreclosures were begun. *See* CONGRESSIONAL OVERSIGHT PANEL, MAY OVERSIGHT REPORT, REVIVING LENDING TO SMALL BUSINESSES AND FAMILIES AND THE IMPACT OF THE TALF 1-3 (2009). Nationally, between 10% and 13% of mortgage borrowers have defaulted and face foreclosure, according to the Lender Processing Services figures, as reported at PR Newswire, *LPS September 'First Look' Mortgage Report: August Month-End Data Shows More Delinquent Loans Entering Foreclosure Process*, REUTERS (Sept. 15, 2010, 6:47 PM),

DIREITO COMPARADO / COMPARATIVE LAW

for larger, more expensive homes, remains in peril, particularly with respect to real estate in California, Arizona, Nevada, and Florida.[93]

B. *Globalization of the U.S. real estate capital markets*

The transformation of local U.S. real estate markets into global finance opportunities increased available capital by widening the scope of potential investors.[94] Before the U.S. savings and loan crisis in 1980, *local* lending and saving institutions dominated residential home finance in the United States.[95] Deposits by local residents into savings accounts formed

---

http://www.reuters.com/article/idUS224331+15-Sep-2010+PRN20100915. Another article reporting these figures calculates that this rate indicates more than 7.2 million mortgage loans are behind on their payments. Carrie Bay, *Residential Mortgage Delinquency Rate Surpasses 10%: LPS*, DSNews.com (Feb. 4, 2010), http://www.dsnews.com/articles/mortgage-delinquency-rate-surpasses-10-lps-2010- 02-04. The foreclosure rate is ten times pre-crisis levels, and the aggregate number of foreclosure sales in one month (around 100,000 nationwide) is now similar to the number of pre-crisis foreclosure sales for an entire year. Alex Viega, *Foreclosure Rate: Americans on Pace for 1 Million Foreclosures in 2010*, Huffington Post (Aug. 15, 2010, 5:07 PM), http://www.huffingtonpost.com/2010/07/15/foreclosure-rate- American_n_647130.html.
[93] *See* Shayna M. Olesiuk & Kathy R. Kalser, *The 2009 Economic Landscape, The Sand States: Anatomy of a Perfect Housing-Market Storm*, 3 FDIC Q., no. 3, 2009 at 26, *available at* http://www.fdic.gov/bank/analytical/quarterly/2009_vol3_1/Quarterly_Vol3No1_entire_issue_FINAL.pdf (discussing the acute nature of the housing downturn in Arizona, California, Nevada, and Florida); *see also* ElBoghdady, *supra* note 30, at A14 ("The 20 regions with the worst foreclosure rates were in the four states – Florida, California, Nevada and Arizona."); Brad Heath, *Most Foreclosures Pack into Few Counties*, USA Today (Mar. 6, 2009, 7:13 PM), http://www.usatoday.com/ money/economy/housing/2009-03-05-foreclosure_N.htm (explaining that properties concentrated in a mere thirty-five counties accounted for half of the country's foreclosure actions, and eight counties in Arizona, California, Florida, and Nevada were the source of a quarter of the nation's foreclosures in 2008). As of July 2010, 1 in 200 households in California were in foreclosure; 1 in 171 households in Florida were in foreclosure; 1 in 167 households in Arizona were in foreclosure; and 1 in 82 households in Nevada were in foreclosure. *States with Highest Foreclosure Rates*, CNBC.com, http://www.cnbc.com/id/29655038/States_with_the_Highest _Foreclosure_Rates (last visited Aug. 16, 2011) (citing data from RealtyTrac's U.S. Foreclosure Market Report).
[94] *See This American Life: Giant Pool of Money Wins Peabody*, (Public Radio International radio broadcast Apr. 5, 2009), *available at* www.pri.org/business/giant-pool-of-money.html (broadcast transcript on file with author) [hereinafter *This American Life Broadcast*] (describing the growth in the "global pool of money," namely fixed income securities that from 2000 to 2006 grew from $36 trillion to $70 trillion).
[95] Before the savings & loan crisis in 1980, local thrifts (saving/lending institutions) dominated residential home finance in the United States. During the decades prior to 1980, deposits by local residents into savings accounts formed the source of primary mortgage capital. Because of the

the source of primary mortgage capital prior to 1980.[96] Because of the narrow geographic focus of these home lenders, funding decisions were made in the familiar context of the applicable locality

This symmetrically local finance system – funds in and funds out within the same community – has been replaced now by global sources of capital.[97] This has increased potential volume but has decreased lender locality expertise. The trend toward global capital sources started in the 1970s when skyrocketing global oil prices and double-digit inflation eroded traditional investment returns.[98] By not keeping pace with inflation, savings effectively *lost* value. So investors took their money and ran to the newly-created, higher-return money market funds. When savings and loans were unable to continue traditional home lending, commercial banks, including national lenders, stepped in to fill the gap.[99]

The shift of home financing to national banks standardized structures, legal forms, and insurance throughout the country.[100] While this lowered costs for the national lenders and ultimately made pooling and securitizing residential mortgages easier,[101] uniform instruments did not reflect identical state laws.[102]

narrow geographic focus of these home lenders, funding decisions were made in the context of the applicable locality. For a concise description of how the primary mortgage market dominated home lending prior to the 1970s and securitization, see Thompson, *supra* note 1, at 51-52.

[96] *See* Van Order, *Dueling Charters, supra* note 73; *see also The Downturn in Fact and Figures*, BBC NEWS (Nov. 21, 2007), http://news.bbc.co.uk/2/hi/business/7073131.stm [hereinafter BBC NEWS REPORT].

[97] *See* Van Order, *Dueling Charters, supra* note 73; Thompson, *supra* note 1, at 52 ("As mortgage backed securities performed outstandingly and generated profits, Wall Street, and almost every other international player became euphoric about these new debt instruments. Believing them to be reliable and safe investments, an array of world renowned financial institutions flocked to invest."). In addition to foreign investment in U.S. real estate, "[m]any foreign markets copied the United States model by creating similar debt instruments based on their housing markets." Thompson, *supra* note 1, at 52; *see also* Pelma Jacinth Rajapakse, *Issuance of Residential Mortgaged-Backed Securities in Australia – Legal and Regulatory Aspects*, 29 U. NEW S. WALES L.J. 173 (2006) (describing similar securities in Australia).

[98] Thompson, *supra* note 1, at 51-53.

[99] *Id.*

[100] Michael H. Schill, *The Impact of the Capital Markets on Real Estate Law and Practice*, 32 J. MARSHALL L. REV. 269, 269-79 (1999).

[101] It is by far easier to securitize loans represented by uniform mortgage instruments. This is one reason that commercial mortgage-backed securitization has lagged so significantly behind residential MBS.

The *commercial* real estate market, has lagged residential both in terms of securitization volume and source of lending capital.[103] The lack of GSE participation in commercial lending and the fact that individual commercial loans are larger, more complex and diverse than their residential counterparts increases securitization costs and lessens the ability to spread risk.[104] Even so, the commercial mortgage-backed security (CMBS) market has recently experienced significant growth.[105]

C. The unbundling of finance functions in real estate lending

Before 1980, all the major real estate finance functions were performed by the entity making the loan, but today, loan origination, funding, servicing, and allocation of credit risk are performed by different market actors.[106] Mortgage brokers originate loans, and because origination fees create the brokers' profits, brokers are inclined to encourage bigger and more loans to be made.[107] Brokers then sell loans to mortgage banks which fund the

---

[102] Typically, multi-state lenders and purchasers use standardized forms with state-specific riders prepared by local counsel. Unlike credit card debt (which is also securitized), there is no ability to use contractual choice of law provisions to opt out of the jurisdiction in which the real estate is located, at least with respect to the underlying mortgage or deed of trust and assignment of rents. Fannie and Freddie have also had a profound influence on the document standardization trend. *See* Andrew Lance, Note, *Balancing Private and Public Initiatives in the Mortgage-Backed Security Market*, 18 REAL PROP. PROB. & TR. J. 426, 438.

[103] DEUTSCHE BANK RESEARCH REPORT, *supra* note 9, 7-9. The report also notes that housing markets in Europe "follow developments in the U.S. markets with a time lag. *Id.* at 3.

[104] *See* Schill, *supra* note 100, at 273-74.

[105] Global CMBS issuance hit its highest point ever in 2007 at a volume of $324 billion – five times the volume of 2000. Then the CMBS market plummeted the following year to $25 billion in 2008 – only about 10% of its value just the year before. DEUTSCHE BANK RESEARCH REPORT, *supra* note 9, at 8; *see also* John B. Levy, *CMBS Volume Hits Record High*, NAT'L REAL ESTATE INVESTOR (Aug. 1, 2005), http://nreionline.com/commentary/finance/real-estate_cmbs_volumehits/. In 2008, CMBS volume fell dramatically and has yet to recover. *See, e.g.*, Al Yoon, *CMBS Volume Now Seen Plunging to Six-Year Low*, REUTERS (Apr. 3, 2008), http://www.reuters.com/article/2008/04/03/mortgages-commercial-volume-idUSN0342726520080403; Jim Clayton, *P&Ls: Pricing, Liquidity and Leverage*, PREA QUARTERLY, Winter 2009, at 46-52. The decline has been so dramatic that pricing for CMBS products is now unreliable due to lack of comparables.

[106] *See* Van Order, *Dueling Charters*, *supra* note 73, at 233.

[107] As mortgages became more commoditized, attorneys became more marginalized in the home finance transaction context. Brokers have assumed the de facto role of borrower advisor, with owing legal duties to borrowers.

loans.[108] After closing, the borrower will interact with the loan servicer,[109] but credit risk is assumed by the purchaser of the loans, the secondary market institution,[110] often with insurance companies providing credit enhancement to the mortgage pool.[111] Investors in the pool provide the actual funds through purchase of mortgage-backed securities.[112] Unbundling the various finance elements effectively divorced risk assessment and default risk from funding decisions and money sources. This makes risk both harder to measure and easier to ignore.

3. Rising real estate values created a wealth effect that accelerated market expansion

My young children have a book called *Alexander, Who Used to be Rich Last Sunday* in which the five-year-old title character, through a series of risky moves and poor expectations, manages to quickly lose his entire fortune – of $1.[113] This has happened to us – except our case is worse because we never actually *had* that dollar "last Sunday," we just borrowed the sum, anticipating that we would *get* the dollar "next Sunday."

The precipitous rise in property values in the early few years of the twenty-Firts century created what *The Economist* called the "biggest bubble in history."[114] Total value of residential property in developed countries rose by more than $30 trillion over those five years, equivalent to 100% of those countries' combined GDPs.[115] Ponder the magnitude of that increase. By way of comparison, the United States' stock market bubble of the late 1920s – which lead to the Great Depression – was equivalent to 55% of GDP.[116] The increase in perceived property values leading up to our current financial crisis was enormous, in both real and relative terms.

---

[108] *See* NELSON ET AL., REAL ESTATE TRANSFER, FINANCE, AND DEVELOPMENT: CASS AND MATERIALS 916-1011 (8th ed. 2009).

[109] *See generally* Van Order, *Dueling Charters, supra* note 73.

[110] *Id.*

[111] Thompson, *supra* note 1, at 53.

[112] Karen Yourish & Laura Stanton, *Anatomy of the Housing Collapse*, WASH. POST, June 15, 2008, at A11; Alec Klien & Zachary Goldfarb, *The Bubble, Part 1: Boom*, WASH. POST, June 15, 2008, at A1.

[113] JUDITH VIORST, ALEXANDER, WHO USED TO BE RICH LAST SUNDAY (1987).

[114] *In Come the Waves: The Global Housing Boom*, ECONOMIST (June 16, 2005), http://www.economist.com/node/4079027 [hereinafter ECONOMIST ARTICLE].

[115] *Id.*

[116] *Id.*

DIREITO COMPARADO / COMPARATIVE LAW

While financial crises historically have been presaged by real estate appreciation and manifested in erosion of home prices, 2008 was different: real estate values were a cause as well as an indicator. Because the real estate capital markets were working so well and money was flowing freely, it was easy to use secured financing to extract increases in real estate value in the form of capital. The ease of liquidating real estate values promotes market transactions – in fact, secured financing has been called a cornerstone of capitalism. The problem here wasn't that people could extract money out of increased property valuations *per se*, rather, it was problematic that (1) these values may not have been realistic, and (2) there was no anchor in terms of accurate risk assessments or equity requirements (a.k.a. – leverage limits).

With the economic upswing, increasingly available mortgage funds were fed to the organic concept of real estate values. With values up, demand for real estate investments rose,[117] which tautologically supported rising prices. Growth in asset values created a perceived increase in wealth, and homeowners and investors responded to this "windfall" by going on an asset value liquidation and consumer spending spree.[118]

During the "boom," real estate markets were hyperactive. Through the mechanism of secured finance, homeowners "traded up" for bigger and more expensive houses and/or "cashed out" the asset value increase.[119] Others sought to share in this property appreciation by purchasing residential property as short-term investments, hoping to resell – or "flip" – them after a matter of months.[120] Loan originations increased with funding capital from the now-global real estate capital market.[121] Everyone saw real estate

---

[117] *See, e.g.,* Steven Pearlstein, *With Bubbles Popping Worldwide, No Wonder the Economy's Gone Flat*, WASH. POST, Oct. 7, 2008, at D1. From 2001 to 2006, the volume of subprime and Alt-A loans quintupled, from $0.2 trillion in 2001 to $1.0 trillion in 2006. By 2008, volume had contracted to only $0.1 trillion.

[118] Thompson, *supra* note 1, at 54-55. (calling the mortgage-backed securitization craze an "unchecked feeding frenzy.")

[119] *See* S&P/CASE-SHILLER, *supra* note 10; *Breaking New Ground in U.S. Mortgage Lending*, FDIC, http://www.fdic.gov/bank/analytical/regional/ro20062q/na/2006_summer04html (last visited Jan. 14, 2011) [hereinafter *Breaking New Ground*].

[120] For a description of the popularity of television "reality" show with respect to speculative real estate, see NORBERG, *supra* note 12, at 8-9; *see also* Buck Hartzell, *Real Estate Bubble? You Bet!*, FOOL.COM (Oct. 26, 2005), http://www.fool.com/personal-finance/retirement/2005/10/26/real-estate-bubble-you-bet.aspx [hereinafter MOTLEY FOOL BUBBLE ARTICLE].

[121] *See supra* note 97.

as a safe bet.[122] Ironically, this changed the market's characterization of real property, which started viewing the inherently illiquid and non-fungible asset as a liquid, market good.[123]

The investment and finance website, *Motley Fool*, cautioned of the real estate "bubble" in 2005 and catalogued evidence of a runaway wealth effect:[124]

- Compensation in the residential housing development sector had gone through the roof – Bob Toll, CEO of Toll Brothers (a national builder of luxury homes), earned $50 million that year, making him the thirteenth most highly compensated CEO in the world.[125]
- "Flipping" properties (buying as a short-term investment) had become so popular that a multiple reality television shows documented the trend, starting with the aptly named *Property Ladder*.[126]
- Mortgages had become riskier. Federal Reserve Chairman Alan Greenspan admitted that "home prices seem to have risen to unsustainable levels,"[127] and an *Economist* article disclosed that in 2005, "42% of all first-time buyers and 25% of all buyers made no down payment on their home purchase."[128]
- Consumer spending accounts had risen above the 75-year average of 65.5% to a high of 70% of U.S. GDP – 80% of which was mortgage debt.[129] Household debt in the United States in 2007 was at 130% of income, up from 60% in 1982.[130]

---

[122] *See* SHILLER, IRRATIONAL EXUBERANCE, *supra* note 10, at 57-60 (arguing that increase in press coverage of, and advertisements for, investment opportunities grew real estate investment).

[123] *See, e.g.*, Schill, *supra* note 100, at 271-74.

[124] MOTLEY FOOL BUBBLE ARTICLE, *supra* note 120; *see also* ECONOMIST ARTICLE, *supra* note 114.

[125] *Forbes List of Executive Pay*, FORBES.COM, http://www.forbes.com/static/execpay2005/rank. html (last visited Jan. 26, 2011).

[126] The first show was *Property Ladder*, which aired June 23, 2005. A month later, no less than three shows on house "flipping" were on the air, including *Flip This House* and *Flip That House*. *See* NORBERG, *supra* note 12, at 8-9.

[127] *The Economic Outlook: Hearing Before the Joint Econ. Comm.*, 109th Cong. 5 (2005) (statement of Hon. Alan Greenspan, Chairman, Board of Governors, Federal Reserve System), *available at* http://www.federalreserve.gov/BOARDDOCS/TESTIMONY/2005/200506092/default.htm.

[128] ECONOMIST ARTICLE, *supra* note 114.

[129] *The Value Investor*, CENTURY MGMT. NEWSL. (Dec. 31, 2004), at 17, 20, http://www.centman. com/PDF/ValueInvDec2004.pdf.

[130] *See* REUVEN GLICK & KEVIN J. LANSING, FED. RESERVE BANK OF SAN FRANCISCO, CONSUMERS AND THE ECONOMY, PART I: HOUSEHOLD CREDIT AND PERSONAL SAVING, Figure 2 (Jan. 10, 2011).

The dramatically increasing prices of real property in the years leading up to the crisis led both owners and investors to pursue more real estate financing opportunities: owners sought to capture their equity bump and investors sought to share in the wealth created by increased asset values. Secured financing made liquidating asset appreciation value easy, and government policies and market systems encouraged the flow of capital into home loans. The owners and investors alike relied on their expectation of increasing appreciations to justify their value liquidation and extensions of credit, but by 2008, the appreciation trend of U.S. real estate had halted and started going in reverse. Where margins were thin and leverage was high, depreciations led to increasing numbers of defaults, foreclosures, and write-offs. The previously frenzied pace of real estate transactions and the torrents of capital flowing from financial markets simultaneously "froze up" – making it harder to sell or finance properties.

Since 2008, U.S. real estate values have fallen by $4.2 trillion,[131] the largest decline in history; and an amount equal to the GDP of France, Spain and Portugal combined. Although the vanished value doesn't represent mass destruction of assets (it is not as if $4 trillion worth of real estate has been wiped off the planet), this is no mere "paper loss." The dollars representing this lost value have already been spent. It was our reaction to the wealth increase during the boom that hamstrings our ability to bounce back from the bust.

Just as increased capital availability pumped up the market, the lack of capital for refinancing has been driving prices down. All that "wealth" which was translated from paper to cash will eventually need to be repaid. But without robust finance markets and without untapped real estate equity holdings, there is no value to fill the void.

My 94-year-old grandmother frequently chides: *"The rich stay rich by acting poor, and the poor stay poor by acting rich."*[132] In the years precipitating the crisis, we certainly were acting rich. But since our fortune was in *perceived* asset values, spending on reliance of this wealth led us to the financial brink.

---

[131] *See* S&P/CASE-SHILLER, *supra* note 10; *see also* INT'L MONETARY FUND, EXECUTIVE SUMMARY, *available at* http://www.imf.org/external/pubs/ft/weo/2009/01/pdf/exesum.pdf (last visited Feb. 11, 2011).

[132] Gladys B. Wise, herself a veteran of the Great Depression.

4. Well-meaning policies and risk assessments caused a runaway leverage epidemic

A final – and crucial – factor that inflated real estate prices was the removal of the "anchor" of required equity reserves at the same time as policies and attitudes were driving demand for real estate ownership and real estate investments higher and higher.

The aggressively pro-homeownership stance of the U.S. government "fed" real estate demand.[133] Promotion of home ownership is politically popular, crosses party lines, and gets votes. Helping people *buy* homes when they may not otherwise be able to and helping people *keep* homes when they would otherwise face foreclosure are seen as legitimate policy and social welfare goals.[134] Through tax incentives, homeowner legal protections, and public housing programs, the U.S. government not only creates opportunities to buy a home, but encourages universal home ownership as good for society and as the fulfillment of every individual's "American Dream."[135]

An ownership society will arguably increase individual wealth, civic participation, and political freedom.[136] Since owners might spend less for housing than renters, disposable income and consumer spending increases. Building equity in a home grows wealth and incentivizes saving.[137] In addi-

[133] *See, e.g.*, Applebaum, Leonnig & Hilzenrath, *supra* note 85 (quoting HUD Secretary Henry Cisneros' statement that Fannie and Freddie were "part of [the] equation" for the policy that "stress[ed] homeownership as an explicit goal for this period of American history").

[134] Senator John Sununu explained that part of the housing boom was caused by a political problem since no one wanted to appear to be anti-housing. FINANCIAL FIASCO: HOW AMERICA'S INFATUATION WITH HOME OWNERSHIP AND EASY MONEY CREATED THE ECONOMIC CRISIS, CATO INSTITUTE (Sept. 1, 2009), http:www.cato.org/event.php?eventid=6419 (featuring event video and a downloadable MP3).

[135] The federal government has state that "[o]wning a home is part of the American dream." Bd. Of Governors of the Fed. Reserve Sys., Interest-Only Mortgage Payments and Payment-Option ARMs – Are They for You? 1 (2006), *available at* http://www.federalreserve.gov/pubs/mortgage _interestonly/mortgage_interestonly.pdf; *see also* NORBERG, *supra* note 12, at 5 ("The U.S. political establishment had actually paved the way for a real-estate boom.... Homeownership is viewed as part of the American dream, as a route from poverty and social exclusion to independence and responsibility.").

[136] *See, e.g.*, JB McCombs, *Refining the Itemized Deduction for Home Property Tax Payments*, 44 VAND. L. REV. 317, 325-26 (1991).

[137] *See, e.g.*, George McCarthy, Ford Foundation, Remarks at A New Way Forward: Center for American Progress (Feb. 4, 2010), *available at* http://www.americanprogress.org/is-

tion, ownership of real property is strongly linked to individual autonomy. Professor Richard Pipes went so far as to say that legal structures supporting real property ownership are a prerequisite to true political freedom.[138]

Some systemic pro-home-ownership legal developments are unobjectionable. For example, in the 1970s, every state in the nation passed laws allowing multi-family housing units to be individually owned.[139] Because of the statutory innovation of the condominium, apartments could be sold – not just leased – and urban dwellers could join the ranks of homeowners.[140]

The protective stance of U.S. courts and legislation toward mortgagors represents another aspect of home ownership promotion. In acquiring financing, the law mandates various disclosures in making home loans,[141] and in foreclosing on defaulted mortgage debt, the law mandates specific protective procedures, increasing lender costs but guarding against unfair borrower victimization.[142]

---

sues/2010/02/sustainable_homeownership_event.html (click "full event video"); *cf.* SHILLER, IRRATIONAL EXUBERANCE, *supra* note 10, at 37 (calling saving through real estate appreciation an "illusion").

[138] *See generally* RICHARD PIPES, PROPERTY AND FREEDOM (1999).

[139] Condominium ownership structure became popular in the United States after the 1961 amendment to the National Housing Act permitting FHA-insured mortgages on condominium units. The FHA promulgated a model statute that was adopted or adapted by every state by 1969. *See* GERALD KORNGOLD & PAUL GOLDSTEIN, REAL ESTATE TRANSACTIONS: CASES AND MATERIALS ON LAND TRANSFER, DEVELOPMENT AND FINANCE 589 (5th ed. 2009).

[140] *See* Stephen D. Teaford, *Homeownership for Low-Income Families: The Condominium*, 21 HASTINGS L.J. 243 (1970); Comment, *Condominiums and the 1968 Housing and Urban Development Act: Putting the Poor in Their Place*, 43 S. CAL. L. REV.309 (1970); *cf.* Michael Diamond, *Rehabilitation of Low-Income Housing Through Cooperative Conversion by Tenants*, 25 AM. U. L. REV. 285 (1976).

[141] Lenders must make disclosures to the government under the Fair Housing Act, the Civil Rights Act of 1968, 42 U.S.C. § 3605 (2006), the Equal Credit Opportunity Act (ECOA), 15 U.S.C. § 1691f (2006), the Home Mortgage Disclosure Act, 12 U.S.C. § 2803 (2006), and the Community Reinvestment Act of 1977 (CRA), 12 U.S.C. § 2904 (2006), in order to ensure non-discriminatory lending practies. Under the Home Ownership and Equity Protection Act and the Truth in Lenidng Act of 1994, 15 U.S.C. §§ 1601-1677f (2006), and under the Real Estate Settlement Procedures Act (RESPA), 12 U.S.C. §§ 2601-2617 (2006), lenders must make explicit disclosures to borrowers regarding all costs of finance (fees, charges, interest) and risk of loss. State laws usually mandate additional mortgage lender disclosures.

[142] *See* NELSON & WHITMAN, *supra* note 65, at 600-95. Since foreclosure is a creature of equity, judicial treatments and statutory requirements with respect to such proceedings focus on fairness to the borrower. During the Great Depression, additional statutory protections for

Some market-intrusive promotions of home ownership have been criticized, as either too costly (typically measured in terms of lost tax income) or unfair allocation of government resources away from the truly needy.[143] By granting homeowners tax relief, for example, the U.S. government effectively subsidizes the costs of home ownership. Owner occupants can deduct mortgage interest from owed federal income tax,[144] and there are numerous ways to decrease and defer capital gains tax liability.[145] Currently, in an effort to lure buyers back to the market, the government is offering an $8,000 reward for buying your first home.[146]

Fannie and Freddie's mandate to promote "housing affordability" and government guaranties of mortgage debt for certain populations translates into another sort of "subsidy" of home-buying. There are numerous government policies and programs making it easier for people to qualify to purchase homes – particularly targeting lower income and first-time would-be homebuyers.[147] Some of these programs, such as the Community Reinvestment Act (CRA),[148] have been blamed for the subprime

---

borrowers facing foreclosure became common. *See id.* at 568-850 (discussing foreclosure law development and judicial and statutory limits on foreclosure proceedings).

[143] *See* McCombs, *supra* note 136; Mark Andrew Snider, *The Suburban Advantage: Are the Tax Benefits of Homeownership defensible?*, 32 N. Ky. L. Rev. 157 (2005); Roberta F. Mann, *The (Not So) Little House on the Prairie: The Hidden Costs of the Home Mortgage Interest Deduction*, 32 Ariz. St. L.J. 1347 (2000).

[144] I.R.C. § 163(h) (2006). Interest deductions are not allowed for consumer loans (credit cards, car loans, etc.). In 1994, however, 68% of home loans were actually used to pay down consumer debt. *See* Kenneth Temkin et al., U.S. Dep't Hous. & Urban Dev., Subprime Markets, the Role of GSEs, and Risk-Based Pricing (2002), *available at* http://www.huduser.org/publications/pdf/subprime.pdf.

[145] I.R.C. § 27. For example, if investment real estate is "exchanged" for a like-kind property under section 1031 of the tax code, gain from the sale. *See* Treas. Reg. § 1.1031(a)-1(b) (2009).

[146] American Recovery and Reinvestment Act of 2009 (Pub. L. 111-5) (2009). Although legislators argued this tax credit would stimulate the real estate market, the statistics show just the contrary. *Falling Again*, Economist (June 23, 2010), http://www.economist.com/blogs/freeexchange/2010/06/housing_markets_2; *see, e.g.*, Martin Hutchinson, *Don't Be Fooled by the Housing Market's False Bottom*, Money Morning, Dec. 31, 2009, http://www.moneymorning.com/2009/12/31/housing-market-false-bottom (boosting housing "by just about every artificial means you can imagine," keeps housing prices unrealistically high and skews housing indicators from representing actual market fundamentals).

[147] For example, the federal government provides mortgage insurance to qualifying homebuyers.

[148] 12 U.S.C. §§ 2901-2908 (2006). The CRA was strengthened by FIRREA in 1989 and the Housing and Community Development Act in 1992. A 1995 resolution promulgated tests to

crisis[149] (although the CRA did not cover most subprime lending).[150] Not only can borrowers who lack income support potentially qualify for a home loan under these programs, but government home-buying assistance indirectly promotes an entitlement culture with respect to property ownership.[151]

The costs of such subsidies are substantial. Such tax breaks and home-buying programs have been criticized as unfair preferences of a lower-middle class over the truly needy segments of the population.[152] Furthermore, these government subsidies may create windfalls as well as buying incentives, since many would-be buyers would have purchased with or without the governmental policies. Still, the government subsidies of homeownership might be worth it, if they are effective.

So do all these efforts work? Has homeownership increased? In 1940, 40% of Americans owned their own homes.[153] This figure was up to 62% by 1960.[154] By 2006, homeownership hit a record level of 69%,[155] but home-

---

ensure that home mortgage lenders were meeting the needs of low and moderate income neighborhoods. Community Reinvestment Act Regulations, 60 Fed. Reg. 22156 (May 4, 1995); *see* David Schon, *The Community Reinvestment Act in Today's Markets*, 7 J. AFFORDABLE HOUS. & COMMUNITY DEV. L. 270, 271-73 (1998). The CRA is a regulatory agency instruction and provides no private right of action. *See* Lee v. Bd. of Governors of the Fed. Reserve Sys., 118 F.3d 905 (2d Cir. 1997).

[149] *See, e.g.*, CONGRESSIONAL OVERSIGHT PANEL, FORECLOSURE CRISIS: WORKING TOWARD A SOLUTION 73 (2009) [hereinafter CONGRESSIONAL OVERSIGHT REPORT] (statement of Rep. Jeb Hensarling: "[M]andates like the CRA ended up becoming a significant contributor to the number of foreclosures that are occurring because they required lending institutions to abandon their traditional underwriting standards in favor of more subjective models to meet their government-mandated CRA objectives."); *see also* Raymond H. Brescia, *Part of the Disease or Part of the Cure: The Financial Crisis and the Community Reinvestment Act*, 60 S.C. L. REV. 617 (2009).

[150] Brescia, *supra* note 149, at 642; *see* CONGRESSIONAL OVERSIGHT REPORT, *supra* note 149, at 83 (statement of Richard Neiman, Damon Silvers, and Elizabeth Warren: "[M]ost disturbing is the suggestion that CRA has been a factor in the current financial meltdown, when the facts demonstrate just the opposite.").

[151] *See generally* NORBERG, *supra* note 12.

[152] Nicholas J. Brunick & Patrick O'B. Maier, *Renewing the Land of Opportunity*, 19 J. AFFORDABLE HOUS. & CMTY. DEV. L. 161, 189 (2010).

[153] *Historical Census of Housing Tables: Homeownership*, U.S. CENSUS BUREAU, http://www.census.gov/hhes/www/housing/census/historic/owner.html (last revised Dec. 2, 2004) [hereinafter *Census of Housing*].

[154] *Id.*

[155] Touting the rising homeownership rate and the role of Fannie and Freddie, Leland Brendsel told Congress that "America enjoys the wold's best housing finance system.... In fact, our nation's

ownership rapidly fell back as the market cooled. At the end of 2009, home ownership had declined to 67.2% – the same level as in early 2000.[156] This decline is particularly discouraging because it is concurrent with demographic factors predicting an *increase* of American home ownership – namely the baby boomer population moving into their prime home-owning years.[157] It appears that despite the real estate heyday pre-2008 and in spite of all the government programs, policies, incentives for home ownership, the end-result of the past decade on home ownership has been a net zero impact. All the ownership gains during the housing boom have already been washed away by the housing bust.

Although a would-be buyer can take advantage of tax incentives and freer flowing funding (through GSE secondary financing), the biggest hurdle typically faced by low-income would-be home buyers is not tight capital markets but rather their own lack of income to sufficiently cover debt obligations, in terms of saving for a "down payment" and making monthly mortgage payments.[158] Traditionally, buyers had to pay at least 20% of a home's price at closing.[159] But new mortgage products over the past several years and more aggressive combinations of senior and jun-

mortgage finance system works so well that most Americans take for granted a reliable supply of low-cost mortgage credit in communites across the nation, every day." *The Housing Finance Regulatory Improvement Act-Part I: Hearing on H.R. 3703 Before the Subcomm. On Capital Mkts., Sec. & Gov't Sponsored Enters. And the H. Comm. on Banking & Fin. Servs.*, 106th Cong. 267 (2000) (statement of Leland C. Brendsel, Chairman and Chief Executive Officer, Freddie Mac).

[156] *Housing Vacancies and Homeownership*, U.S. CENSUS BUREAU, http://www.census.gov/hhes/www/housing/hvs/annual06/ann06t20.html (last revised Feb. 12, 2007); *see also* Haya El Nasser, *Drop in Homeownership Likely to Continue*, USA TODAY, Aug. 6, 2009, http://www.usatoday.com/news/nation/2009-08-05-rental_N.htm.

[157] Chris Isidore, *Home Ownership in Record Plunge*, CNNMoney.com, Jan. 29, 2008, http://money.cnn.com/2008/01/29/news/economy/home_ownership_vacancies/?postversion=2008012913. Of course, one could argue that without government subsidies and other homeownership promoting policies, the decline in ownership rates would have been even more precipitous.

[158] Lack of income can both reduce a borrower's FICO score and lessen a borrower's ability to save enough money to make a substantial down payment.

[159] For borrowers unable to put 20% of the purchase price down on a home, lenders typically demanded that borrowers pay insurance over the increase of depreciation risk that the lower equity percentage created. Some mortgage insurance offered by the government and other insurance was offered by private mortgage insurance companies (PMIs). Mortgage bankers who ultimately sold their loans to the GSEs were traditionally strong participants in the government-insured markets. Saving associations have generally relied on PMI. In more

ior debt enabled more and more borrowers to increase their leverage.[160] High leverage solved the first problem as, in anticipation of eternal asset value appreciation, banks began to offer 100% loan-to-value ratio home financing. And interest-only loans and "teaser-rate" loans solved the second problem – at least in the short run.[161]

Reminiscent of new car purchase promotions, homes became "no money down and low monthly payment" products. When borrowers start with no equity cushion, and continue to avoid establishing any equity cushion, the collateralized debt is *completely* at the mercy of asset depreciation. Any value decrease puts the loan "underwater."[162] Ironically, over-leverage and low monthly payments hurt – rather than helped – vulnerable populations. In addition, a homeowner with an interest-only loan builds up no equity by making his monthly mortgage payments and effectively stripped lenders of their collateral support.[163] Exuberant buyers of mortgage-backed securities suffer the same fate.[164]

recent years, all lenders shifted toward PMI and uninsured loans. *See* NELSON & WHITMAN, *supra* note 65, at 927.

[160] Although popularly termed "new mortgage products," most of the products popularized in the past decade were not truly new. Negatively amortizing loans, variable interest rate loans, loans with balloon payments, and so-called hybrid ARMs (fixed interest rates followed by a period of variable interest rates) have all existed since the 1980s. However, these more exotic products became more and more the norm during the era of escalating housing prices as a way for people to afford mortgages on higher and higher priced homes with stagnant salary levels. *See* Sanders, *supra* note 18 (discussing the changing market for home loan products).

[161] *See* Kimberly Blanton, *Adjustable-Rate Loans Come Home to Roost*, BOSTON GLOBE, Jan. 11, 2006, at D1. Greenspan endorsed the adoption and expansion of adjustable–rate mortgage products in 2004 when short-term rates were near historic lows Greenspan also lulled investors, asserting that "securitization by Fannie and Freddie allows mortgage originators to separate themselves from almost all aspects of risk associated with mortgage lending." Bill Mann, et al., *The People Responsible for Fannie Mae and Freddie Mac*, MOTLEY FOOL (Sept. 10, 2008), http://www.fool.com/invessting/dividends-income/2008/09/10/the-people-responsible-for-fannie -mae-and-freddie-.aspx (quoting Alan Greenspan).

[162] Thompson, *supra* note 1, at 55 ("Some estimate that now millions upon millions of homes in the United States have negative equity."); *see also* Karen Blumenthal, *'Underwater' Need Not Mean Foreclosure: Why Most People Who Owe More Than a Property's Worth Will Still Keep Their Homes*, WALL ST. J., Nov. 5, 2008, at D1.

[163] Borrowers who owe more to a lender than a home is worth are vastly more likely to abandon both home and mortgage, particularly if the debt obligation is non-recourse (the lender cannot seek recovery from the borrower personally).

[164] *See, e.g.*, Andrew Frye, *Insurer Losses Trigger Most Regulator Intervention in a Decade*, BLOOMBERG (July 19, 2010), http://www.bloomberg.com/news/2010-07-19/insurer-loses-in-

But the leverage problem spread far beyond low-income homebuyers. Economically speaking, higher leverage means greater rates of return when appreciation is held constant – if you put down less money, the percentage gain *on* that money is far greater. All market participants were lured by the higher return rate in higher-leveraged financings.[165]

The high degree of permitted leverage also increased property prices, based both on higher anticipated rates of return and the "other people's money" effect.[166] Although in theory the capital structure of a real estate investment should *not* much affect the value of the underlying asset, people acted as though it did. In addition, it was far easier for buyers to "pay" greater prices when such increases did not impact their own out-of-pocket costs. It is far easier to spend someone else's money than your own.

Although high leverage *leavens* higher prices through expected greater returns, greater potential for *risk* theoretically should temper price inflation. But since modern market structures had split risk off from the investor return calculation, there was no anchor to property appreciations. By definition, present value is mis-priced if rewards are analyzed and risks are ignored.

As Richard Bookstaber warned in his book, *A Demon of Our Own Design*, "the externalities to high leverage are greater than they appear ... in instances where it really matters, the liquidity that is supposed to justify the leverage will disappear with a resulting spiral into crisis."[167] Recent

---

u-s-trigger-most-regulator-intervention-in-a-decade.html (explaining that the two biggest life insurance companies reported billions of dollars in quarterly losses form mortgage-backed securities investments).

[165] Although 260,000 subprime mortgages defaulted in 2004, the number of seriously delinquent conventional mortgages increased more than 143% between 2004 and 2007. JOINT CTR. FOR HOUS. STUDIES AT HARVARD UNIV., *America's Rental Housing: The Key to a Balanced National Policy* 1 (2008). Taking greater risk in the face of greater reward reflects basic economic theory. *See* RICHARD A. POSNER, A FAILURE OF CAPITALISM: THE CRISIS OF '08 AND THE DESCENT INTO DEPRESSION 78-79 (2009).

[166] *See generally* RICHARD A. POSNER, THE CRISIS OF CAPITALIST DEMOCRACY (2010) (discussing how the profit motive causes companies to take undue risks when the money they gamble is no their own); Russell Roberts, *Gambling With Other People's Money: How Perverted Incentives Caused the Financial Crisis*, MERCATUS CENTER, GEORGE MASON UNIV. (May 2010), http://mercatus.org/publication/gambling-other-peoples-money (last visited Apr. 22, 2011). The 1991 movie "Other People's Money" by Alvin Sargent, based on the play by Jerry Steiner of this same title illustrates this concept.

[167] RICHARD BOOKSTABER, A DEMON OF OUR OWN DESIGN 258-260 (2008).

events have proven this statement true. Leveraging to the hilt is like Icarus flying too close to the sun – exhilarating but perilous.[168] High leverage real estate financing is particularly dangerous because it is coupled with an inherently illiquid asset whose pricing is always in flux.

Commercial Real Estate: Market Crisis Redoux

Although the past couple years have been traumatic, there may be more "unpleasantness" shortly to come. The U.S. *commercial* real estate market, which lags behind residential in terms of price reactions and operates on a shorter lending cycle, is poised to come crashing down on this already-imploded market mess. Some reports estimate that commercial real estate asset values *have* already fallen by 43% over their boom-cycle peak – an even greater drop than that which crippled the U.S. residential housing market.[169] While delinquency rates in commercial loans have continue to rise since 2008, the true test of market viability will come this year and the next as $1.4 trillion in commercial loan balloon payments come due.[170]

Typically, commercial owners refinance at maturity to fund balloon payments; but the loans about to come due are *vintage 2005* and thereabouts – and it was a *"very bad year"* for mortgage loan quality.[171] Not only is

---

[168] *See id.* (see front cover of Bookstaber, *A Demon of our Own Design*).

[169] Matt Hudgins, *Property Valuations Improve in Primary Markets, but Other Areas Struggle*, NAT'L REAL ESTATE INVESTOR (Apr. 7, 2011), *available at* http://nreionline.com/finance-amp-investment/property-valuations-improve-primary-markets-other-regions-struggle

[170] *See* Standard & Poor's, *Industry Outlook: The Worst May Still Be Yet To Come For U.S. Commercial Real Estate Loans*, Feb.1, 2010, *available at* www.standardandpoors.com/ratingsdirect.

[171] In August 2006, Steven Krystofiak, president of the Mortgage Brokers Association for Responsible Lending, in a statement at a Federal Reserve hearing on mortgage regulation, reported that his organization had compared a sample of 100 stated income mortgage applications to IRS records, and found almost 60% of the sampled loans had overstated their income by more than 50 percent. Steven Krystofiak, Statement at the Federal Reserve 4 (Aug. 1, 2006), *available at* http://www.federalreserve.gov/secrs/2006/august/20060801/op-1253/op- 1253_3_1.pdf; Mark Gimein, *Inside the Liar Loan: How the Mortgage Industry Nurtured Deceit*, SLATE (Apr. 24, 2008), http://www.slate.com/id/2189576. Speaking of "liar loans," *Slate* magazine opined that the "simplest aspect of the crisis to understand" is also the "most troubling, because it's not about complicated financial dealings and can't be fixed with bail-outs. It's about an astounding breakdown of social norms." *Id.* The GSEs also increased their loan size limits by nearly two-fold, but this increase was only truly significant in increasing volume after the housing meltdown began. Mark Calabria of the Cato Institute estimates that a quarter of all loans purchased by Fannie Mae in 2005, and 10% of all loans purchased by Freddie Mac in 2005, was from Countrywide. Kerri Panchuk, *GSEs Inflated Subprime Bal-*

capital generally *unavailable* to fill the refinancing gap, lenders are particularly *unwilling* (or even, based on tighter lending policies, *unable*) to lend on high-leverage, risky projects. Owners simply do not have the equity capital to pay down the leverage sufficiently. With capital markets still frozen and trillions of dollars coming due on these high-leverage products, we could see another wave of defaults, depreciations, and market destabilization.

Elizabeth Warren, chair of the Congressional Oversight Panel, which tracks the ongoing financial bailout by Congress, confirms that "there's been an enormous bubble in commercial real estate, and it has to come down."[172] Warren predicts that as commercial real estate debts become due, "[t]here will be significant bankruptcies among developers and significant failures among community banks."[173] Most community banks have – so far – fared somewhat better than larger banks in this crisis, but with all these commercial real estate loans coming due, that may quickly change. Although the largest American banks – those that were "too big to fail" – have relatively little exposure in commercial real estate finance, the correspondingly large exposure of small-to-medium sized commercial banking institutions may cripple such lenders.[174] We don't yet know how and to what extent the U.S. government will intervene. Congress is clearly worried and has encouraged banks to modify loan terms if borrowers cannot refinance when payment is due.[175] The banks may need no encouragement

---

loon Before it Popped, CATO INST. (March 15, 2011), http://www.housingwire.com/2011/03/15/gses-inflated-subprime-balloon-before-it-popped-cato-institute.

[172] V. Dion Haynes, *In D.C., More Evidence that Commercial Real Estate Headed for Foreclosure Crisis*, WASH. POST, Feb. 19, 2010, http://www.washingtonpost.com/wp-dyn/content/article/2010/02/18/AR2010021805904.html.

[173] *Id.*

[174] Compare Silla Brush, *Aid Boost Sought for Real Estate*, THE HILL, July 22, 2010 [hereinafter The Hill Article] ("Paul Merski, chief economist of the Independent Community Bankers of America, said that some of the statistics of possible losses are "sensationalized" but that there are risks to small banks"). Merski has said that the vast majority of small community banks are well capitalized and have put away loan loss reserves to handle any downturn in commercial real estate." Commercial Real Estate, *The Next Real Estate Bubble*, NEWS JUNKIE POST, Feb. 24, 2010, *available at* http://newsjunkiepost.com/2010/02/24/the-next-real-estate-bubble/. The large-scale failure of small-to-medium banks could fundamentally alter the banking industry, the market share of banking already being held more and more by the biggest four banks (Bank of America, JP Morgan Chase & Co., Citigroup and Wells Fargo & Company).

[175] On Feb. 22, 2010, Senate Banking Committee Chair Christopher Dodd wrote a letter to Federal Reserve Chair Ben Bernanke calling for efforts to encourage banks to modify com-

– the current trend for lenders faced with borrower inability to pay off at maturity is to "extend and pretend."[176]

As we brace ourselves for the meltdown to come in commercial real estate, we will likely see still more value evaporate. Although solving this crisis requires learning from our banking and securitization mistakes, we clearly must also consider the real property factor – the role of the "dirt."

Taking Prices (and "Solutions") With a Grain of Salt

Yeast, being a living organism, is among the least predictable of ingredients. The very property that makes it desirable to cook with – its ability to grow and rise – makes it challenging to use in producing a consistent product. So it is with real estate values: lack of market consistency and the ability for dramatic price inflation when mixed with mortgage capital can be an uncontrollable combination. Just as we use salt in bread-making to control the growth of yeast, we can use our understanding of risk to temper the effects of loose capital. We must recognize this natural cycle of cheap money, asset over-pricing, and increased "wealth" and use policies and planning to control it.

The initial governmental reaction to and effort to control the 2008 financial crisis was to add more money to the financial system.[177] This tact slowed the descent of the market otherwise in freefall, but does not actually create a market rebound, nor does it prevent the cyclical over-pricing from reoccurring in the future.[178] Policies funneling money into the market – from purchasing troubled assets[179] to short-term tax incentives for home

---

mercial real estate loans and asking for a report on actions taken by the Fed to contain the pending crisis. *See* http://dodd.senate.gov/?q=node/5474; *see also* David Ellis, *The commercial real estate dilemma*, CNNMONEY.COM, Feb. 4, 2010 (at money.cnn.com/2010/02/04/news/companies/banks_commercial_real_estate/)(discussion of potential responses, citing statements by Elizabeth Warren and Timothy Geithner) [hereinafter CNNMoney Article].

[176] *See* DEUTSCHE BANK RESEARCH REPORT, *supra* note 9. *See also* CNNMoney Article, *supra* note 176 (quoting statements regarding "extend and pretend" from Tanya Azarchs, credit analyst and managing director for Standard & Poor's).

[177] *See supra* notes 86-90 and accompanying text.

[178] *See generally* CARMEN M. REINHART & KENNETH S. ROGOFF, THIS TIME IS DIFFERENT: EIGHT CENTURIES OF FINANCIAL FOLLY (2009).

[179] Troubled Asset Relief Program (TARP) is a program permitting government purchase of "toxic" assets from financial institutions. When passed in 2008, TARP was anticipated to cost taxpayers $356 billion, but more recent estimates put its cost at $89 billion. Paritosh

buying[180] to subsidizing short sales of defaulted home loans[181] – might prime the pump of a frozen capital market. However, a simultaneous clamp down of new regulations in lending and higher scrutiny of loans likely counteracts such effects.

One goal of proposed new regulations and closer oversight is to force both primary lenders and the secondary mortgage market offerors to behave more circumspectly. In this way, regulation can mandate the use of risk (salt) to temper the effect of the funding (yeast) on the real property pricing (leavened dough).

Real estate finance has been called the basis of a capitalist economy because of its importance in translating captured value into liquidity. But market price of real property is fragile. Ignoring risks and failing to leave a margin for error is reckless. This isn't a new lesson – we've learned it before.[182] "With all the research input, the sophisticated economic analysis, the jolly conferences, the attention to decision making structures, and the increased understanding of risk and reward, how could so many have failed to see that all the known parameters were bursting apart?" said Peter Bernstein ... back in 1974.[183]

Today, we find ourselves lamenting a recipe that has gone horribly wrong: a spoiled and rancid product. But in our effort to renew the process, we should not chuck out all of our ingredients – we just need to learn the right lessons from this economic "cooking experiment" gone awry. Real estate finance capital, like yeast in baking, is tremendously useful but must be used judiciously. We do not need to restrict our diet to the "unleavened bread" of untapped and unliquidated real property values, but we should approach market assessments with a "grain of salt." Hopefully our analysis of what went wrong will lead to a better understanding of the chemical – well... the *economic* – properties of the real estate capital market.

Bansal, *US Bailout Cost Seen Lower at $89 Bln*, REUTERS (Apr. 11, 2010), http://mobile.reuters.com/article/governmentFilingsNews/idUSN1116401920100412?ca=moto. *See supra* note 8.

[180] *See* Luke Mullins, *The $8,000 First-Time Home Buyer Tax Credit Program Expands: 5 Things to Know*, U.S. NEWS & WORLD REPORT, May 29, 2009, http://money.usnews.com/money/blogs/the-home-front/2009/05/29/the-8000-first-time-home-buyer-tax-credit-program-expands-5-things-to-know.

[181] *See* David Streitfeld, *Program to Pay Homeowners to Sell at Loss*, N.Y. TIMES, Mar. 8, 2010, at A1.

[182] *See* REINHART & ROGOFF, *supra* note 178.

[183] Peter L. Bernstein, *What this Journal is about*, 1 J. PORTFOLIO MANAGEMENT 5, 5 (1974).

Balancing on One Leg: the International Standard Setting Response to the Global Financial Crisis

MICHAEL W. TAYLOR[*]

Ever since the Group of Twenty Summit on Financial Markets and the World Economy issued its Declaration in Washington, D.C. on 15th November 2008, the political leaders of the world's leading economies have insisted that any regulatory response to the Global Financial Crisis must itself be global in scope. As they announced in their Declaration:

> Regulation is first and foremost the responsibility of national regulators who constitute the first line of defense against market instability. However, our financial markets are global in scope, therefore, intensified international cooperation among regulators and strengthening of international standards, where necessary, and their consistent implementation is necessary to protect against adverse cross-border, regional and global developments affecting international financial stability.[1]

Since the Declaration the main international standard setting bodies – including the Basel Committee on Banking Supervision, the International

---

[*] Adviser to the Governor, Central Bank of Bahrain; formaly Head of Banking Policy, Hong Kong Monetary Authority; Senior Economist, InternationalMonetary Fund; Reader in Financial Regulation, ICMA Centre, University of Reading.

[1] G20 Summit on Financial Markets and the World Economy, Nov. 14-15, 2008, *Declaration*, (Nov. 15, 2008), *available at* https://g20.org/wp-content/uploads/2014/12/Washington_Declaration_0.pdf.

DIREITO COMPARADO / COMPARATIVE LAW

Organisation of Securities Commissions, and the International Accounting Standards Board – have been engaged in a major review of the relevant international standards for financial services following the agenda that the Washington Summit set out for them. This chapter concentrates on the activities of the Basel Committee on Banking Supervision, since problems of the banking sector were at the heart of the global financial crisis.

There are good reasons why the regulatory response to the financial crisis needs to be internationally coordinated. The crisis itself has demonstrated that the global financial system is closely interconnected with the result that defaults on mortgages in California or Michigan can have serious repercussions for financial institutions in Europe, the Middle East and Asia. The episode provides plenty of examples of the cross-border spillover effects which provide one of the main justifications for international regulatory standards.[2] A second major motivation behind the emphasis on international coordination was the fear that if some jurisdictions strengthened their regulatory standards but others did not, there would be a risk of damaging regulatory competition – a "race to the bottom" – in which financial services would migrate to the less tightly regulated jurisdictions. From one perspective, jurisdictions that had recently suffered a crisis might actually welcome the migration of financial services business elsewhere as the burden of future bailouts might thereby be reduced; but such a trend is generally regarded as politically undesirable given the consequent loss of employment and tax revenues. Moreover, as long as governments around the world maintain their commitment to a world of free capital flows, any financial business regulated in one part of the world still has the potential to engage in activities that could destabilize the financial systems of other jurisdictions. By contrast, uncoordinated regulatory action that resulted in wide variations of regulatory standards across the globe could seriously impede the free movement of capital. Ensuring a coordinated international regulatory response to the crisis can therefore be seen as underpinning a commitment to free capital markets.

The Basel Committee has made some progress in revising the international prudential standards for banks in the light of the lessons of the crisis. At the time of writing, its new proposals (colloquially known as "Basel

---

[2] *See* HEIDI MANDANIS SCHOONER & MICHAEL W. TAYLOR, GLOBAL BANK REGULATION: PRINCIPLES AND POLICIES (2009).

III") seem destined to be endorsed by the leaders of the G20 nations at the summit that is scheduled to be held in Seoul, Republic of Korea, in November 2010. Collectively, these proposals should result in internationally active banks being better capitalized, more liquid and less leveraged than they were in the years prior to the crisis. Nonetheless, as I shall argue in this chapter, the Basel III framework represents only one leg of the crisis response, which Bank of England Governor Mervyn King has described as a "three legged stool."[3]

Governor King has argued that the crisis response needs also to be based on two other legs: structural regulation and mechanisms to handle the orderly winding up of financial institutions that operate on a cross-border basis. The structural regulation leg concerns restrictions on "the activities which insured retail deposits are allowed to finance."[4] The 1933 Banking Act (the "Glass-Steagall Act") which institutionalized the separation of investment and commercial banking represents the most frequently cited example of structural regulation, the provisions of which were, of course, repealed in the years preceding the financial crisis. The leg, by contrast, concerns ensuring that banks are not "allowed to become so complex, so systemically crucial to the system that no one can contemplate their disappearing."[5] Both the second and third legs represent different but complementary responses to the "Too Big to Fail" (TBTF) problem which only came to be fully recognized after the crisis entered into its most serious phase after the failure of the investment bank, Lehman Brothers. This is the problem that some financial institutions may be too large (or too interconnected) for their failure to be a realistic option, and therefore they will always enjoy the implicit promise of support from the public authorities, whether in terms of capital or liquidity, in the event that they encounter difficulties. This implicit guarantee is undesirable both because it creates a competitive advantage for these firms vis-à-vis smaller ones and also because it creates moral hazard, i.e., it encourages greater risk-taking by the shareholders and managers of these institutions, secure in the knowledge that if the risks pay off they will stand to gain the

---

[3] Mervyn King, evidence to the House of Commons Treasury Select Committee, 26th January 2010, Q136.
[4] Mervyn King, evidence to the House of Lords Economic Affairs Committee, 24th November 2009, Q29.
[5] *Id.*

benefits, whereas if the risks go wrong the taxpayer will ultimately stand behind them.

Despite the urgent need for policy-makers to address the TBTF problem through the structural and resolution routes, the issue has not received the international attention that the financial crisis has clearly shown is necessary. Instead, since November 2008 there have been increasing indications that individual countries are seeking their own solutions to the TBTF problem. The adoption of the "Volcker Rule" in the United States, now written into the Dodd-Frank Wall Street Reform and Consumer Protection Act, is one example of this creeping re-nationalisation of regulatory policy. The Volcker Rule, which places a limit on bank's direct investments in hedge funds and private equity of capital and which places restrictions on their proprietary trading activities, has much to recommend it.[6] Nonetheless, it was introduced in the United States quite independently of a similar initiative in any other major economy. As far as the majority of countries in the European Union are concerned, there seems little prospect of a serious attempt to dismantle the universal banking model, although Britain may come closest to following the United States lead depending on the outcome of an Independent Commission established by the British government and that is due to report by September 2011.

The issue of cross-border resolution has received even less attention from senior policy-makers and legislators, notwithstanding an attempt by the Basel Committee to raise the profile of the issue in a March 2010 report.[7] Events during the financial crisis, especially the failure of Lehman Brothers, illustrated that the current nationally-based regimes for resolving failed financial institutions are not well adapted to a financial system in which firms increasingly operate on a cross-border basis. The current regime results in both the unequal treatment of creditors in different jurisdictions and, by virtue of its complexity, makes it difficult for any large cross-border financial institution to fail without causing systemic effects. The lack of an effective cross-border resolution framework is therefore an important factor in cementing the TBTF problem in place.

[6] *See* Michael Taylor, *The Volcker Rule: Wrong Answer or the Right Answer?*, CENTRAL BANKING J., Summer 2010.

[7] BASEL COMM. ON BANKING SUPERVISION, REPORT AND RECOMMENDATIONS OF THE CROSS-BORDER BANK RESOLUTION GROUP, (March 2010), *available at* http://www.bis.org/publ/bcbs169.pdf.

In this chapter, I will argue that as far as structural regulation is concerned the "re-nationalization" of regulatory policy should not be regarded as a cause for concern. The fact that the international standard setting process has been incapable of delivering agreements on structural regulation is, at worst, an inconvenience. In the past, the global financial system has managed perfectly well with universal banks (from Europe) existing side-by-side with a Glass-Steagall separation of investment and commercial banking (in the United States). There seems no reason why something resembling this state of affairs should not again exist in the future. More of a problem is the failure of the international standards setting process adequately to address the problem of handling the cross-border insolvency of a major financial firm. This leg of the stool unquestionably requires an international component; but so far it is an issue which has not attracted the attention it needs or deserves, and current mechanisms of international cooperation are not well-adapted to dealing with it. As a result, the international response to the global financial crisis has been left balancing precariously on one leg of a three legged stool.

Background on the international standard setting process

The primary international setting body for banking is the Basel Committee on Banking Supervision (Basel Committee or BCBS) which is hosted by the Bank for International Settlements in Basel, Switzerland. The BCBS was established by the central bank governors of the Group of 10 countries at the end of 1974 and meets regularly four times a year. It carries out a standard setting work through approximately 30 technical working groups and task forces. Countries are represented on the Committee by their central bank and also by an authority with formal responsibility for the prudential supervision of banking where this is not the central bank. Since the global financial crisis the Committee's membership has been expanded to incorporate representatives from all of the G20 countries, with the result that it now comprises 27 members.

The BCBS does not possess any formal supranational supervisory authority and its conclusions do not, and have never been intended to, have legal force. Instead, the Committee formulates broad supervisory standards and guidelines and recommends statements of best practice in the expectation that individual countries will take steps to implement them through detailed arrangements (including through statute law) in

DIREITO COMPARADO / COMPARATIVE LAW

a way that is best suited to their national system. In this way, the Committee "encourages convergence towards common approaches and common standards without attempting detailed harmonization of member countries' supervisory techniques."

In the 35 years or more of its existence, the Basel Committee has been responsible for a number of major initiatives. The first of these, in 1975, was the Basel Concordat which aimed to establish rules for the allocation of responsibilities for the supervision of cross-border banks between their home and host regulators.[8] The Concordat has been amended on several occasions, most notably following the insolvency of Banco Ambrosiano in 1982 and the Bank of Credit and Commerce International (BCCI) in 1991. However, the Basel Committee is best known for the capital adequacy framework commonly referred to as the Basel Capital Accord. This system provided for the implementation of a credit risk measurement framework with a minimum capital standard of 8% of risk-adjusted assets by the end of 1992. Since it was first agreed in 1988, this framework has been progressively introduced not only in member countries but in virtually all other countries with active international banks. In 1996 the Capital Accord was supplemented by rules for the measurement of market risk in respect of banks' portfolios of traded assets and in 1999 the Committee issued a proposal for a new Capital Adequacy Framework to replace the 1988 Accord. This new framework, colloquially known as Basel II, consists of three pillars: minimum capital requirements, which seek to refine the standardised rules set out in the 1988 Accord and which in their most advanced forms permit banks to use their own internal estimates of likely losses; supervisory review of an institution's internal assessment process in capital adequacy; and effective use of disclosure to strengthen market discipline as a complement to supervisory efforts. A final version of the document was issued in 2004 with an implementation date of 1st January 2007.

The Basel II capital framework has attracted a great deal of criticism since the global financial crisis first developed and it has been argued that it played a contributory role in the build-up to the crisis.[9] However,

---

[8] In this context, a "home" regulator is responsible for the licensing and prudential supervision of the parent company, whereas the "host" regulators are responsible for the licensing and prudential supervision of its branches or subsidiaries in their jurisdictions.

[9] On this point, see Andrea Resti & Andrea Sironi, *What Future for Basel II?*, 8 CESifo DICE Report 3 (2010).

many of these criticisms are misplaced, since the Basel II framework had not been adopted in most countries in the years immediately prior to the financial crisis.[10] Instead, banks' capital adequacy had been assessed using the earlier 1988 risk measurement framework (now known as "Basel I") which financial innovation had gradually made less effective. In particular, securitization had permitted banks to move assets off balance sheet thereby escaping Basel I's capital requirements, despite the fact that the banks nonetheless faced some significant residual risks. It was, however, true that neither Basel I nor Basel II contained any rules on liquidity risk, i.e., the risk that banks may lack sufficient liquid resources (such as cash or government bonds) to meet large and unexpected outflows of funds. Although many bank supervisors had regarded liquidity risk as the key risk to banks in the years before the 1980s, the Basel Committee had instead concentrated on developing increasingly more elaborate mechanisms for the assessment of credit risk. The Basel Committee had intended to supplement the Basel I framework with parallel rules on liquidity risk, but agreement among its members on how to measure this risk and on the types of financial instrument that could be considered to be high quality liquid assets. As a result, no international agreement on liquidity standards was achieved between 1988 and the outbreak of the financial crisis.

The work of the Basel Committee is a typical example of what some international relations theorists have referred to as a "policy network".[11] Policy networks are groups of experts drawn from a range of countries who meet to agree standards and common practices on matters of mutual concern. Throughout much of its history the Basel Committee has operated as a policy network of mainly technocratic specialists and has attracted comparatively little political or public attention as a result. This situation was changed by the global financial crisis, and in particular the instruction from the G20 leaders at the November 2008 Washington D.C. Summit that the Basel Committee revise its standards to guard against a repeat of the crisis. For the first time in its history the Committee was required to act in accordance with an externally imposed deadline and to be answerable to the political leaders of the G20 for the outcome of its negotiations.

---

[10] However, it is important to distinguish between the criticism that Basel II was in some sense a contributory *cause* of the crisis, and the valid observation that the crisis has raised legitimate questions about the principles underpinning the Basel II framework.

[11] *See* ANNE-MARIE SLAUGHTER, A NEW WORLD ORDER 230-33 (2004).

Response to the Crisis: Part I

The Basel Committee's work programme has been shaped in two distinct phases, before and after the most extreme phase of the financial crisis that followed the bankruptcy of Lehman Brothers in September 2008. A particularly important document in framing the Basel Committee's response pre-Lehman Brothers was a report produced in March 2008 by the Senior Supervisors Group (SSG) which comprised representatives of U.S. regulators (the Board of Governors of the Federal Reserve System, the Office of the Comptroller of the Currency, the Federal Reserve Bank of New York, and the Securities and Exchange Commission) as well as four leading European regulators (the Swiss Federal Banking Commission, the Bank of France, the German Federal Financial Regulator, and the UK's Financial Services Authority).[12]

The SSG considered the lessons to be drawn from the relative performance of a group of major financial institutions in handling the first phase of the financial crisis in which dislocation to the market for Asset-Backed Securities (ABS) had imposed significant mark-to-market losses on major banks and other financial institutions. Its primary focus was on the risk management practices at these major banks and it aimed to draw conclusions from those banks which had (at least at that point) managed the crisis relatively well. On the basis of its observations it defined an agenda for strengthening supervisory oversight, and in particular it noted the need for the Basel Committee to strengthen the efficacy and robustness of the Basel II capital framework by:

- Reviewing the framework to enhance the incentives for firms to develop more forward-looking approaches to risk measures (beyond capital measures) that fully incorporate expert judgement on exposures, limits, reserves, and capital; and
- Ensuring that the framework sets sufficiently high standards for what constitutes risk transfer, increases capital charges for certain securitized assets and asset-backed commercial paper (ABCP) liquidity facilities, and provides sufficient scope for addressing implicit support and reputational risks.

---

[12] SENIOR SUPERVISORS GROUP, OBSERVATIONS ON RISK MANAGEMENT PRACTICES DURING THE RECENT MARKET TURBULENCE, (2008), *available at* http://www.newyorkfed.org/newsevents/news/banking/2008/SSG_Risk_Mgt_doc_final.pdf.

In addition, the SSG observed that there was a need to strengthen the management of liquidity risk, and it also undertook that its individual members would review and strengthen their existing guidance on risk management practices, valuation practices, and the controls over both. Finally, the SSG also expressed its support for measures to improve the quality and timeliness of public disclosures, and in particular to consider whether improving disclosure practices would reduce uncertainty about the scale of potential losses associated with problematic exposures, and the appropriate accounting and disclosure treatment of exposures to off-balance sheet vehicles.

Although the report of the SSG was produced at a time when the financial crisis appeared to mainly an issue relating to valuation losses on securitized assets and to banks' obligation to provide liquidity support to off-balance sheet vehicles which they had sponsored, it nonetheless set much of the Basel Committee's subsequent work agenda. In consequence, when the Basel Committee published a consultation document in November 2009 outlining its proposals to strengthen the resilience of the banking system, a large part of the document reflected the observations and conclusions that the SSG had drawn in March 2008.[13] Among these issues were new rules for the treatment of securitized assets, and changes to the capital adequacy rules for assets held in the trading book of a bank to ensure their equivalent treatment with assets held in the banking book. Where banks had undertaken to provide liquidity support to an off-balance sheet vehicle that they had sponsored, the Basel Committee also proposed that such facilities would attract an appropriate capital charge, a situation which had not previously prevailed.

Response to the Crisis: Part II
Nonetheless, the evolution of the financial crisis during 2008 meant that bank supervisors have, of necessity, been required to consider some more fundamental issues than those relating to the relatively technical adjustments to the capital measurement framework that flowed from the SSG report. These issues include: the need for banks to maintain more, and

---

[13] BASEL COMM. ON BANKING SUPERVISION, CONSULTATIVE DOCUMENT: STRENGTHENING THE RESILIENCE OF THE BANKING SECTOR (December 2009), *available at* http://www.bis. org/publ/bcbs164.pdf.

DIREITO COMPARADO / COMPARATIVE LAW

higher quality, capital; the need to limit leverage in the system; the need to ensure that banks have adequate stocks of high quality liquid assets; and the need to moderate the impact of the credit cycle through adjustments in capital ratios.

(a) The quality and quantum of capital

As the financial crisis deepened during the course of 2008 it became apparent that banks had been holding too little capital in relation to their risks. Under both the Basel I and Basel II capital framework banks were permitted to meet the 8% minimum capital requirement through a combination of financial instruments that were categorized either as "Tier 1" or "Tier 2". The Tier 1 instruments are primarily paid up share capital and reserves, i.e., equity as determined by the difference between a bank's assets and liabilities. Tier 2 includes various forms of subordinated debt, both perpetual and term, plus general provisions and hybrid debt capital instruments up to a maximum of 50% of Tier 2. The amount of Tier 2 in a bank's capital base is not permitted to exceed the total of its Tier 1 capital. The Basel II capital framework did not change the definition of capital contained in Basel I. Nonetheless, over the years this apparently simple framework had become diluted as financial innovation resulted in the development of capital instruments that banks lobbied hard to have included in their Tier 1 capital structure. In addition, the definition also permitted various forms of non-cumulative perpetual preferred stock to be counted as part of Tier 1.

Although prior to the financial crisis all leading international banks appeared to be well capitalized on this measure, it soon became apparent that their levels of capital adequacy were not sufficient to maintain market confidence. Bank analysts in both the credit rating agencies and in counterparty banks began to concentrate not on the Basel measure of capital, but on a much narrower definition of capital represented by Tangible Common Equity (TCE). Tangible Common Equity essentially comprises a bank's shareholders' funds, i.e., common stock (not including preferred stock) and accumulated reserves. In the depths of the crisis the soundness of banks was being assessed by market participants against this relatively narrow measure, since only the capital included in this definition was capable of absorbing losses on a "going concern" basis. Other forms of capital instruments that Basel had recognised, such as subordinated debt, would only absorb losses in the event that the bank was placed into insolvent liquidation. Thus if market participants needed assurance about the ability of a bank to continue operating even in the most adverse economic conditions but without becoming insolvent, only a narrow definition of capital was capable of performing such a role.

In recognition of the clearly expressed market view in the depths of the crisis, in its November 2009 consultation paper the Basel Committee proposed sharply to curtail its current definition of capital instruments and to place greater emphasis on high quality Tier 1. Among other things, this would involve removing certain components of capital from Tier 1 entirely. These elements include deferred tax assets, which are assets on a company's balance sheet that may be used to reduce any subsequent periods income tax expense. For example, a deferred tax asset can arise due to the carryover of a net loss from one accounting period to another. Obviously, however, the value of a deferred tax asset can only be realized if a corporation continues to trade into the next accounting period and therefore it is of limited value in providing protection to bank depositors against catastrophic losses.

Although the case for a narrow definition of capital should be obvious, especially in the context of recent experience, it has nonetheless been difficult for the Basel Committee to achieve consensus on a narrower definition of capital. As is often the case in the Committee's deliberations, individual members are reluctant to agree to proposals which they see as resulting in a comparative disadvantage for their banks. Since continental European banks have traditionally relied on items such deferred tax assets as a component of their capital, their regulators have been reluctant to agree to a revised standard which would exclude these items completely. The effect of doing so would be to force these banks to raise substantial additional capital at a time when their ability to do so is compromised by global financial conditions. As a consequence, the final version of the Basel III proposals has watered down the original concept of a narrow definition of capital, with items such as deferred tax assets being permitted up to 15% of Tier 1.

(b) Leverage ratio

Work by the Bank of England's financial stability department has provided a very clear picture of the rise in banking leverage in the UK in the years prior to the crisis. In some cases leverage more than doubled in the period between 1997 and 2008. This was, of course, reflected in a much improved return on equity as much of the enhanced leverage was used to invest in high yielding assets such as collateralized debt obligations. The pattern in Britain was repeated in many other advanced economies.

Since the introduction of Basel I in 1988 bank regulators have not generally attempted to place direct limits on a bank leverage. Both Basel I, and its successor Basel II, use a risk adjusted measurement of banks' assets, with discount factors being applied to categories of assets to reflect their presumed risk. In the past, the alternative of a simple leverage ratio which measures capital-to-assets without adjusting for risk has been dismissed as too crude and too easily subject to manipulation. For example, it has been argued against a leverage ratio that two banks could both show the same amount of leverage, whereas one has invested entirely in government bonds (which therefore carry little or no credit risk) while the other has invested in high yielding junk bonds (which carry a relatively high risk of default). A simple leverage ratio would create an incentive for bank management to shift towards riskier assets since this would be a way of generating higher returns for the same amount of leverage.

The simple answer to this argument is that the financial crisis has shown that measures of risk are themselves at best crude and incomplete. Substantial losses were incurred on assets which were considered to be very low risk immediately prior to the financial crisis (e.g., the AAA-rated tranches of CDOs). Accordingly banks had been required to allocate relatively little capital to support these assets. As we now know, the estimates of the risk of loss (probability of default) produced by either the credit rating agencies or by banks' own internal measures of risk significantly underestimated these risks. Given that the measures of risk have proved to be so inaccurate, the relatively crude and simple leverage ratio framework has appeared to be rather more attractive than in the past. In fact, some regulatory agencies did not abandon the use of a leverage ratio even though they had also adopted the Basel risk-based framework. Both the U.S. and Canadian regulators have applied a leverage ratio in parallel to a risk-adjusted ratio, while it has been adopted in Switzerland following the financial crisis.

Nonetheless, proposals for a leverage ratio in parallel to the risk adjusted ratio have met with strong resistance from a number of major international banks and even from some regulators. Moreover, agreement within the

Basel Committee has been complicated by the fact that the definition of the leverage ratio is not quite as simple as it might appear. For example, it is possible to debate whether a bank's assets should include only those which appear on its balance sheet, or should be extended to also encompass off-balance sheet items as well. The latter are potentially a very significant part of a bank's overall asset as they include, for example, OTC derivatives.

If OTC derivatives are included then a further question is whether they should be included on a gross or a net basis. A bank that has a derivatives portfolio will have written multiple contracts with the same counterparty bank. At any given point in time, some of these contracts will have a positive value while others will have a negative value. Under counterparty netting arrangements encouraged by the standard industry documentation developed by the International Swaps and Derivatives Association (ISDA), counterparty netting of positive and negative positions is both permitted and encouraged. On a net basis a particular bank may have only a relatively small net-positive or net-negative position with a counterparty, whereas its gross derivatives portfolio will be many times larger.

(c) Liquidity
As noted above, liquidity standards have been relatively neglected by bank supervisors in recent years. Although at the start of the 1970s mandatory reserve requirements were central to the regulation of banks, by the end of the decade they had fallen out of fashion as central banks changed their approach to controlling money and credit growth by relying instead on their ability to manipulate short-term interest rates. In consequence supervisory attention shifted in the 1980s from liquidity to risk-based measures of capital, culminating in the first Basel Accord. Differences among members of the Basel Committee deriving from variations in the structure of their money markets and different central bank policies on acceptable collateral for re-discount operations also hindered the development of international liquidity standards. Prior to the crisis the Basel Committee's most recent foray into the subject had been in 2000. This resulted in a document that set out ten principles for liquidity risk management, but which failed to set out any detailed recommendations on how liquidity risk should be measured and controlled.

The global financial crisis has forced the international standard setters to take seriously the need for a set of agreed liquidity requirements.

DIREITO COMPARADO / COMPARATIVE LAW

It became obvious as the crisis deepened that not only had banks operated with too little capital and too high leverage but that they also had run large liquidity risks on the assumption that they would always be able to cover any shortfall in their funding needs by borrowing short-term in the interbank markets. When these markets froze following the failure of Lehman Brothers, many banks were unable to cover their funding gaps without assistance from the central banks. Ensuring stronger liquidity buffers to avoid the need for central banks to provide liquidity in such large amounts in future thus became a central focus of the international standard setting agenda.

The result was a paper published by the Basel Committee in parallel to its paper on *Strengthening the Resilience of the Banking Sector* in December 2009.[14] This proposed two broad methodologies for the identification and control of liquidity risk:

1. A Liquidity Coverage Ratio. This identifies the amount of unencumbered, high quality liquid assets an institution holds that can be used to offset the net cash outflows it would encounter under an acute short-term stress scenario specified by supervisors. The specified scenario entails both institution-specific and systemic shocks built upon actual circumstances experienced in the global financial crisis. The scenario entails:

- a significant downgrade of the institution's public credit rating;
- a partial loss of deposits;
- a loss of unsecured wholesale funding;
- a significant increase in secured funding haircuts; and
- increases in derivative collateral calls and substantial calls on contractual and non-contractual off-balance sheet exposures, including committed credit and liquidity facilities. As part of this metric, banks are also required to provide a list of contingent liabilities (both contractual and non-contractual) and their related triggers.

2. Net Stable Funding Ratio. The net stable funding (NSF) ratio measures the amount of longer-term, stable sources of funding employed by an institution relative to the liquidity profiles of the assets funded and the potential for

[14] *Id.*

contingent calls on funding liquidity arising from off-balance sheet commitments and obligations. The standard requires a minimum amount of funding that is expected to be stable over a one year time horizon based on liquidity risk factors assigned to assets and off-balance sheet liquidity exposures. The NSF ratio is intended to promote longer-term structural funding of banks' balance sheets, off-balance sheet exposures and capital markets activities.

Following the consultation period, the Basel Committee decided not to implement the NSF before 2018, following an "observation period" designed to assess its operation in practice. In industry submissions to the Committee it was argued that the NSF would require a fundamental reassessment of the business strategies of many banks which are founded on their ability to operate with maturity mismatches exceeding those found in other businesses, i.e., they fund long-term assets (such as loans) with short-term liabilities (such as demand deposits). Raising additional long-term funding to reduce the extent of maturity mismatching in banks' balance sheets was seen as particularly problematic given that capital markets remained disrupted following the financial crisis.

(d) Counter-cyclical capital requirements

The idea that bank capital requirements should be adjusted according to the state of the overall economy is theoretically attractive. Economic activity undergoes periodic cycles which can be magnified by the financial sector, resulting in asset price bubbles followed by an almost inevitable bust. As currently calibrated bank capital requirements do little to moderate these cycles and may even exaggerate them since they remain constant over time.[15] The Basel Committee's minimum 8% ratio applies both when the economy is in a deep recession and when euphoric conditions are producing asset price bubbles. By remaining constant over time the capital ratio can constrain banks from lending during a recession, when their capital base shrinks as the result of absorbing losses, and it also does nothing to discourage them from making excessive loans in boom conditions. It has been argued that the global financial crisis followed a long

---

[15] For a detailed explanation of these criticisms of the Basel framework, see BRUNNERMEIER ET AL., GENEVA REPORTS ON THE WORLD ECONOMY 11: THE FUNDAMENTAL PRINCIPLES OF FINANCIAL REGULATION (2009).

period of asset price inflation which neither monetary nor regulatory policies did anything to address. It would therefore be desirable to adjust capital ratios according to economic conditions and by doing so may have the effect of smoothing economic cycles, making both recessions less deep and booms less prolonged.

The November 2008 declaration by the G20 heads of government included a commitment to study the possibility of using adjustments in capital ratios to prevent excessive boom conditions from occurring. However, there are immense technical difficulties in the way of implementing such an approach in practice. Some of these difficulties concern identifying a suitable point in the credit cycle for capital requirements to be either lower or raised, while there also remain issues concerning how effective raising or lowering capital requirements will be in practice. For example, even if capital requirements are a binding constraint on domestic banks, raising capital requirements may not have the effect of moderating boom conditions as borrowers will be able to access loans from outside the domestic banking system, such as from banks located in other jurisdictions. Secondly, in boom conditions it will be relatively easy for those banks which are the most exposed to asset markets experiencing bubble conditions to raise new capital, since they will appear to be highly profitable and therefore a desirable investment. Finally, the application of counter-cyclical capital requirements will require regulators to "take away the punch bowl"[16] when asset markets are booming. This could be politically difficult given that rising asset prices, such as in real estate, are often highly popular with voters. Only a regulatory agency enjoying a high degree of independence is likely to have the discretion to adjust capital requirements in the way proposed.

Despite the technical difficulties involved in establishing counter-cyclical capital requirements, the Basel Committee published a Consultative Document in July 2010 setting out its proposals.[17] In essence this pro-

---

[16] A phrase first coined by the William McChesney Martin, Chairman of the Federal Reserve Board, 1951-1970, to describe the role of a central bank in constraining what one of his successors would describe as "irrational exuberance." *See* William McChesney Martin, Chairman, Bd. of Governors of the Fed. Reserve Sys., Address before the New York Group of the Investment Bankers Association of America (Oct. 19, 1955).

[17] BASEL COMM. ON BANKING SUPERVISION, CONSULTATIVE DOCUMENT: COUNTERCYCLICAL CAPITAL BUFFER PROPOSAL (July 2010), *available at* http://www.bis.org/publ/bcbs172.pdf.

poses that individual countries will be able, at their discretion, to require banks to hold an additional capital buffer in the form of an "add on" to their minimum required capital if aggregate private sector credit grows faster than its long-term trend rate relative to GDP growth. However, as the Basel Committee acknowledges, the aggregate private sector credit/GDP measure does not work well in all jurisdictions and at all times. Therefore, a large element of judgment and discretion will be inevitable in decisions to apply the capital buffer add ons.

Other initiatives to develop counter-cyclical requirements have made little progress. One concept that attracted initial interest was a measure adopted by the Bank of Spain in 2000 that requires banks to make a "statistical" provision at the time that a loan is originated.[18] This contrasts with the current practice under international financial reporting standards (IFRS) which requires a provision to be made only when a loss has been incurred. The statistical provisioning approach resulted in the Spanish banks building up an additional buffer against losses representing approximately 1% of their total assets. Although the statistical provision provided Spanish banks with an additional cushion against losses, initially allowing them to write off bad loans without depleting their capital reserves, nonetheless as Spain's economic problems deepened during the course of 2009 it became apparent that the statistical provision had not solved the problem of pro-cyclicality. In particular, the statistical provisioning approach had failed to prevent the accumulation of imbalances in the Spanish economy, and in particular the high levels of exposure of the Spanish banks to the real estate sector which experienced a classic boom and a bust cycle.

The two other legs of the stool

The issues being considered by the Basel Committee attempt to respond to serious deficiencies in the regulatory framework that were identified as a result of the financial crisis. It is clear that banks held too little liquidity in the years before the crisis, that the quality and quantum of capital was inadequate to provide assurance to counterparties in conditions of

---

[18] Santiago Fernández de Lis & Alicia García Herrero, *The Spanish Approach: Dynamic Provisioning and Other Tools*, *in* TOWARDS A NEW FRAMEWORK FOR FINANCIAL STABILITY (David Mayes, Robert Pringle & Michael Taylor eds., 2009).

market stress, that regulatory requirements did little to prevent the build up of excessive leverage, and that capital requirements did not constrain the asset price boom that preceded the crisis. The contribution of the international standards setters to filling these clear gaps in the international framework is essential for the avoidance of a repeat of the financial crisis.

Nonetheless, the Basel Committee's agenda covers only a portion of the issues that the financial crisis has thrown into relief. To use the analogy employed by Bank of England Governor Mervyn King to which I referred earlier, the Basel Committee's response is only one leg of a three legged stool. The other two legs, as described by Governor King, are structural regulation and resolution mechanisms. In the remainder of this chapter I will discuss these major issues which so far have remained outside the Basel Committee's remit and work programme. I will argue that although some degree of national variation in approaches to structural regulation can be tolerated, a successful international resolution regime is needed to address the problem of cross-border financial institutions. Unfortunately, however, progress on developing an international consensus on the last issue is proving to be elusive.

(a) Structural regulation

Structural regulation – i.e., the legislatively imposed separation of certain financial activities – was largely abandoned in the years preceding the crisis. The most high-profile example was the repeal of the provisions of the 1933 Banking Act in the United States (colloquially known as the Glass-Steagall Act) which had mandated a separation between commercial and investment banking. This was repealed by the Gramm-Leach-Bliley Act of 1999, which had been preceded by a steady erosion of the legislative administration boundary by the decisions of regulators. However, the United States was not unique in dismantling structural regulation, and in the United Kingdom a similar process had occurred in the mid-1980s, albeit as the result of administrative action rather than legislation. In continental Europe structural barriers were rare, since the dominant model of finance was that of the universal bank in which both commercial and investment banking activities were conducted on the same balance sheet. To the extent that individual continental European countries retained some elements of structural regulation, many of these requirements were removed in the wake of the implementation of Europe's single market programme, which also assumed that universal banking would be the appropriate model.

After the financial crisis entered its most extreme phase following the events of September 2008, there was a reawakening of interest in the potential of structural regulation to mitigate the risks to the financial system and to the tax payers who ultimately stand guarantee for the financial system. This revival of interest became most obviously apparent in the form of the Volcker Rule, named for former chairman of the Federal Reserve Board, Paul Volcker, who was its leading champion. As originally proposed by Volcker, the Rule involved two separate, and apparently unrelated requirements. The first is an extension of the cap on market share contained in the 1994 Riegle-Neal Act which permitted interstate bank branching. As a condition of this, Riegle-Neal imposed a 10% cap on the share of national deposits of any American bank. The first part of Volcker's proposal is to prohibit banks from exceeding the same 10% market share, but with a wider definition of size that takes account of the riskiness of assets, as well as the total level of liabilities, both from deposits and other funding sources. The second part of the Volcker Rule involves a restriction of proprietary trading activities which, in the words of a report from the Group of Thirty that Volcker chaired "present particularly high risks and serious conflicts of interest" for large systemically important banking institutions. The report went on to recommend that "sponsorship and management of co-mingled private pools of capital (that is hedge and private equity funds in which banking institutions' own capital is co-mingled with client funds) should ordinarily be prohibited and large proprietary trading should be limited by strict capital and liquidity requirements."

Volcker justified both elements of his proposals on the grounds that both were necessary to address the "Too Big to Fail" (TBTF) problem. Volcker argued that breaking up TBTF institutions was not a viable policy option, and therefore the next best solution was to prevent banks from engaging in activities which were unrelated to their core functions and which were better undertaken by non-bank financial intermediaries. As he remarked in a column written for the *New York Times* to justify his proposals "the point of departure is that adding further layers of risk to the inherent risks of essential commercial bank functions doesn't make sense, not when those risks arise from more speculative activities far better suited for other areas of the financial markets."

DIREITO COMPARADO / COMPARATIVE LAW

The Volcker Rule has now been incorporated in the Dodd-Frank Act which leaves regulators with wide discretion in implementing it. However, there have been few signs that other jurisdictions are prepared to consider a similar approach to that of the Volcker Rule. Despite repeated statements of support for the concept of structural regulation by Governor King and by other senior staff at the Bank of England, there have been few indications of political support for these initiatives in the United Kingdom. The British government has, instead, appointed an Independent Commission to study this issue with a deadline for issuing its report of September 2011. Among the terms of reference of the Independent Commission are to make recommendations concerning "structural measures to reform the banking system and promote stability and competition, including the complex issue of separating retail and investment banking functions."[19] The United Kingdom's willingness to consider the case for some form of structural regulation is not, however, replicated elsewhere in the European Union where universal banks that combine both commercial and investment banking activities are typical of financial system structure. Nor has the concept of structural regulation attracted much support in Asia or in the Americas outside the United States. For example, Julie Dickson, the Canadian Superintendent of Financial Institutions argues that size limitations of the kind envisaged by the Volcker Rule could produce unintended consequences: "some note that the rule in the U.S. which limits a bank's share of the deposit market led to undue reliance on wholesale funding, which then created other risks. So imposing a rule on size is not something that is ready for prime time just yet."[20]

In the absence of international consensus on the possible shape of future structural regulation, or even of the need for structural regulation, it is not surprising that this issue has not been adopted as part of the Basel Committee's work programme. In any case, the Committee is not well adapted to addressing issues of this type which would require the member countries to amend the legal framework that they apply to banks

---

[19] Press Release, HM Treasury, Sir John Vickers to Chair Independent Commission on Banking (June 16, 2010), *available at* https://www.gov.uk/government/news/sir-john-vickers-to-chair-the-independent-commission-on-banking..

[20] Julie Dickson, Superintendent, Office of the Superintendent of Fin. Institutions Canada, Remarks to Fin. Servs. Invitational Forum, Too Big to Fail and Embedded Contingent Capital (May 6, 2010), *available at* http://www.osfi-bsif.gc.ca/eng/docs/jdlh20100506.pdf.

(as in the Dodd-Frank Act) rather than merely developing new regulations within an existing legal structure. As long as the Basel Committee's membership comprises regulatory agencies and central banks it is not in a position to develop new structural regulations as these require new primary legislation. To put the point in terms of the distinction between primary and secondary legislation or between law-making and rule-making: the Basel Committee can discuss changes that would involve new secondary legislation (which the regulators can introduce in the form of new rules) but it lacks the remit to discuss new primary legislation which would be required if structural regulation is to be reintroduced. By their very nature, regulators whose responsibility it is to apply existing law cannot make new laws, although they may of course propose them. In consequence, even if there was a clear policy consensus in favour of structural solutions to the TBTF problem, the Basel Committee would not be the right body to agree these changes at an international level.

(b) Resolution regimes for cross-border banking groups

A second issue on which primary legislation is required concerns bank resolution regimes and the need for an effective legal framework for managing the orderly wind down of a failed bank. The objective of these resolution regimes is to be able to allow banks to fail while permitting the essential economic functions that they provide (principally the payments system function) to continue to operate; in other words the depositors of a failed bank should be able to continue to make payments, such as writing cheques or using debit cards, and to withdraw cash from their accounts notwithstanding the liquidation of the institution with which those accounts are held. In addition, the resolution regime should minimize the risk that the failure of a bank will have significant knock-on effects on the rest of the financial system, for example by disrupting the complex web of contractual obligations that form part of modern capital markets, especially in the over-the-counter derivatives markets. It was this complex web of contractual relationships that ultimately made the collapse of the investment bank Lehman Brothers so disruptive to the wider financial system.

The global financial crisis clearly illustrated the absence of effective bank resolution regimes in several countries, most notably the United Kingdom. The failure of the mortgage bank Northern Rock in September

2007 occurred against the background of a UK regulatory regime which only had the option of applying general insolvency law to a failed financial institution. This gave the authorities few options for trying to organize an orderly resolution of Northern Rock, such as the U.S. concept of conservatorship, under which a bank's management is replaced by management appointed by the regulator and where a stay on the execution of creditors' claims is imposed until a financial restructuring of the firm can be carried out. The Banking Act 2009, enacted in the United Kingdom following the Northern Rock experience, has now gone a considerable way towards remedying this deficiency by providing the Bank of England, as the resolution authority, with a range of options including the formation of a "bridge bank" to permit essential functions to be preserved notwithstanding a bank's failure.

In the United States the bank resolution regime was significantly more flexible than that previously in place in the United Kingdom. Nonetheless, the powers of regulators to impose an orderly restructuring on the liabilities of non-bank financial institutions were very limited. As a result, U.S. regulators lacked the power and authority to undertake a bank-like resolution of institutions such as Bear Stearns, Lehman Brothers, and AIG. Had such authority existed, it can be argued that the failure of Lehman Brothers would have been far less disruptive to the global financial system than was actually the case. This legislative deficiency has been remedied by provisions of the Dodd-Frank Act, which creates resolution authority for non-bank financial intermediaries to parallel the powers that the Federal Deposit Insurance Corporation (FDIC) has previously exercised over banks.

While these legislative developments have been important in closing some clear gaps in the authorities' ability to handle failing financial institutions, there remains a major issue which so far the international standard setting process has not adequately addressed. This is the problem of how to deal with the failure of a large financial institution that is operating on a cross-border basis. Commenting on the collapse of Lehman Brothers, Lord Adair Turner, the current chairman of the UK's Financial Services Authority, has remarked:

> The failure of Lehman Brothers demonstrated ... that decisions about fiscal and central bank support for the rescue of a major bank are ultimately by

home country national authorities focusing on national rather than global considerations. It also illustrated that separate legal entities and nationally--specific bankruptcy procedures have major implications for creditors.

A Basel Committee working group on cross-border bank resolution, which reported in March 2010, described the current arrangements for dealing with cross-border bank failures as predominately a "territorial approach" in which each jurisdiction "resolves the individual parts of the cross-border financial institution located within its national borders."[21] The reasons for the predominance of this approach are not hard to fathom: "National authorities tend to seek to ensure that their constituents, whether taxpayers or member institutions underwriting a deposit insurance or other fund, bear only those financial burdens that are necessary to mitigate the risks to their constituents."[22] In other words, although banks and other financial institutions are international in life they are national in death.

The Basel Committee working group from which the above quotations have been taken also produced a set of ten recommendations. These cover such matters as the need for effective national resolution powers, the convergence of national resolution methods, contingency planning, cross-border cooperation and information-sharing, and the reduction of the complexity and interconnectedness of group structures. However, many of the recommendations of the working group cannot be implemented by supervisory action alone, and the report acknowledges that many of its recommendations will require new statute law if they are to be introduced.

However, the Basel Committee working group also noted that "crisis resolution frameworks are largely designed to deal with domestic failures and to minimize the losses incurred by domestic stakeholders. As such, the frameworks are not well suited to dealing with serious cross-border problems."[23] The working group expounded two possible approaches to develop a more effective framework for handling the failure of a cross-border bank.

---

[21] BASEL COMM. ON BANKING SUPERVISION, *supra* note 7, ¶ 7.
[22] *Id.* ¶ 8.
[23] *Id.* ¶ 6.

The first approach – which might be described as "territorial plus" – would be to encourage individual countries to adopt broadly similar resolution regimes and to supplement these arrangements with informal arrangements to ensure greater information sharing and cooperation among the national authorities. Although the powers of the relevant national authorities would become broadly similar (as happened when the Banking Act 2009 in Britain gave the Bank of England a similar range of resolution tools to those historically employed by the FDIC in the United States), the responsibility for the resolution of a large cross-border financial institution would still remain diffused, with each of the countries in which the institution has operations applying their own resolution regimes to those national operations. However, the territorial approach to handling cross-border bank failures might also be made more effective through the implementation of "recovery and resolution plans" (also known as "living wills" or "funeral plans") which require cross-border financial institutions to have put in place procedures to facilitate their orderly winding up. In some cases, these plans might also require financial conglomerate groups to simplify their legal and organizational structures so that, in the event of their insolvency, it would be possible for separate national subsidiaries to be resolved under national resolution regimes with only limited implications for the position of creditors in other jurisdictions.

The second approach would be to establish a universal, comprehensive framework for the resolution of cross-border financial groups. This arrangement would accord primacy to the resolution of all domestic and cross-border activities of a failing financial group by the jurisdiction in which the institution is headquartered or possibly by a supranational entity. Such a framework would need to be set out in a binding legal instrument, possibly an international treaty, and would need prior agreement on several difficult issues. For example, it would be necessary to agree in advance on rules for burden sharing if the institution's assets are insufficient to satisfy the claims of all of its creditors. There would also need to be rules on deciding which was the competent authority to conduct resolution proceedings for each part of the group, and rules governing the exchange of information between these authorities. There would also need to be a process to ensure the equal treatment of creditors, depositors, counterparties and shareholders regardless of the jurisdiction in which they are located. Underpinning these arrangements would be harmonization of national rules governing cross-border crisis management and resolution, including common definitions of bank insolvency, avoidance powers, minimum rights and obligations of creditors, the ranking of claims and rights to set-off.

While still holding out the possibility of a treaty-based structure, the Basel Committee working group seems to have concluded that this approach would appear to be beyond the realm of practical politics. Even in the European Union, where something closer to the treaty-based approach prevails, the evidence of the crisis was that cross-border financial groups were resolved on a primarily territorial basis. However, the "territorial plus" approach on which the working group could find greater consensus cannot be implemented by supervisory action alone. It is noteworthy that several of the working group's recommendations would require statutory change to become effective, for example with individual countries changing their bank resolution laws to conform to some international standard along the lines of the UNCITRAL model insolvency law. Missing from the international process at present is a mechanism to connect the recommendations of the bank supervisors with the drafters of a model law, let alone with the national legislatures that are alone capable of making the necessary legislative enactments. While the Dodd-Frank Act in the United States contains provisions that require regulators to ensure that systemically important firms put in place resolution and recovery plans, there has been little evidence otherwise of a deliberate convergence of resolution regimes. Given that an effective resolution regime is one of the primary tools for addressing the "Too Big To Fail" problem, this missing link in the international standard setting process is a major deficiency.

Conclusion

This chapter has reviewed the international regulatory response to the financial crisis, with particular reference to the agenda being pursued by the Basel Committee, the main international standard setting body for the banking industry. It has argued that, although the coordination of prudential regulation is important, an adequate response to the financial crisis requires measures which go beyond relatively limited remit of the Basel Committee. The need to deal with the "Too Big To Fail" problem in particular stands out. Although there has been no significant international consensus on structural re-regulation, the failure to address the need for a more coordinated

DIREITO COMPARADO / COMPARATIVE LAW

response to the resolution of large complex cross-border banking groups is a much more serious deficiency of the international standard setting process.

Unlike prudential regulation, which can be adjusted by regulatory authorities using their delegated rule-making authority, the other two legs of Governor King's stool will require new legislation to complete, and therefore require the involvement of different experts, and ultimately a political commitment from national leaders. As presently constituted, however, the international framework for standard setting does not provide a mechanism to secure the needed level of legislative coordination and cooperation. In effect, the remaining two legs of the stool can only be international coordinated if there is agreement to align statute law according to some common principles and approaches. There is thus a need to bring together experts from finance ministries, and perhaps also justice ministries, who have the responsibility for drafting legislation, and for involving their minister in what is essentially a political decision. In theory, the Financial Stability Board might provide one mechanism for achieving this outcome. Nonetheless, as presently constituted it does not involve the requisite mix of political and expert input, while its work agenda does not extend to the structural leg of the stool. Although it has been undertaking some work on the resolution of cross-border banks, this is mainly in the area of contingency planning and information sharing rather than the alignment of national statutes which is the key to the whole process.

Finally, it is worth emphasizing that it would be mistaken to focus exclusively on regulatory solutions to the financial crisis. This is to misunderstand and misidentify its causes. It is as fundamentally foolish to attempt to identify one single cause of the global financial crisis – whether regulatory failure, the greed of bankers, or a misguided policy of encouraging home ownership in the United States through sub-prime lending – as it is to seek a single cause of a complex historical event like the French Revolution. Many other factors were at work, including macroeconomic imbalances on a global scale (excess savings in the emerging world, particularly East Asia, and excess borrowing in the developed world, particularly the United States), the distortions that result from treating interest payments as a tax-deductible item, and a system of flawed incentives that flowed from banks ceasing to hold loans to maturity and instead packaging them for sale to investors (the so-called "originate-to-distribute" model of finance). Regulatory failures there were, but besides some of these other elements it is doubtful that they were one of the prime factors in causing the financial crisis.

Because there were so many diverse factors at work in causing the global financial crisis, inevitably the policy response must be multi-faceted and must involve the use of a number of different policy instruments, including monetary policy, fiscal policy and taxation. Inevitably, regulatory reform, even if internationally coordinated, can only form a small part of the overall solution. In the first phase of the financial crisis it had appeared that some relatively minor adjustments to the established framework of international prudential standards would be sufficient to guard against a repeat. By the time that the crisis had reached its most acute phase in the final quarter of 2008 it was obvious that more radical regulatory change was needed. It was at this point that the need for the other two legs of the regulatory stool began to be recognized by senior policy-makers. Nonetheless, even if the international response to the financial crisis eventually succeeds in fitting all three legs to the stool, it is worth remembering that the primary causes of the crisis were not regulatory and a recurrence will not be prevented by regulation alone.

Antitrust in Distress: Causes and Consequences of the Financial Crisis[1]

MIGUEL MOURA E SILVA[*]

1. Introduction

Taking a step back to the end of the twentieth century, we can recognize the harbingers of the financial crisis in episodes of localized financial meltdowns such as the Enron scandal (in particular regarding the unsupervised use of Structured Investment Vehicles to leverage capital and engage in risky transactions)[2] and the earlier Long Term Capital Management Fund debacle with the ensuing rescue by large Wall Street banks under the Federal Reserve's leadership.[3] In the recent financial crisis the telltale signs of greed, overconfidence in upward trends, the vulnerability of the financial sector to highly counterpart-dependent trades are also to be found. However, they were compounded by years of lax monetary policy, poor corporate governance (particularly visible in the fall of Lehman Brothers[4]) and also government failures in regulation. In short, hubris,

---

[*] Professor, University of Lisbon Law School.

[1] This paper is based on the remarks presented at the Ninth Conference on Portuguese and American Law, *The Financial "Crisis": How We Got Here How We Get Out"*, University of Lisbon Law School, March 8, 2010.

[2] For an overall account, see Bethany MCLEAN; Peter ELKIND, *The Smartest Guys in the Room*, New York: Penguin, 2004.

[3] Excellently described in Roger LOWENSTEIN, *When Genius Failed*, New York: Random House, 2000.

[4] For an account of the final days of Lehmann Brothers, see Andrew Ross SORKIN, *Too Big to Fail*, London: Allen Lane, 2009.

DIREITO COMPARADO / COMPARATIVE LAW

plain and simple, unchecked by appropriate institutional mechanisms and government supervision and regulation seems to have contributed to the (almost) perfect financial storm.

A general analysis of the causes of the 2007-2010 financial crisis is beyond the scope of this paper. What I propose to do is to evaluate the role of antitrust in the causes and consequences of the crisis. If market turmoil and financial upheaval can shatter the groundwork of competitive markets that antitrust seeks to protect, the shockwaves are sure to be felt in the intellectual foundations of competition policy. In section 2, I consider whether antitrust contributed to the financial crisis and briefly describe the pre-crisis role of competition policy on both sides of the Atlantic with regard to the transformations that the banking sector underwent in recent decades. Section 3 analyses the crisis response on the antitrust front. Of particular importance are the two areas where the bailouts tend to collide with antitrust: mergers and, in the European context, State aid. Section 4 then looks at the challenges that economic crises have placed on antitrust enforcers. Section 5 ends with some final remarks.

2. Antitrust and the Causes of the Financial Crisis

The debate on the causes of the 2007-2010 financial crisis will no doubt continue for years to come.[5] What seems to be a fairly consensual point is that, as then Deputy Assistant Attorney General for Economics, Carl Shapiro stated:

> [I]t seems clear to me that the crisis in the financial sector primarily reflects a failure of government *regulation*, not any underlying failure in the ability of well-regulated competitive markets to serve consumers and promote economic growth.[6]

---

[5] "The current global economic crisis had its roots in slack economic policy and huge strategic errors by the banks. Permitted by weak regulation and driven by biased incentives, the banks borrowed (and lent) far too much given their low capital bases, and were caught out when the housing price bubble began to burst, heralding large-scale defaults. The global reach of this behavior was compounded by the sale and purchase of opaque mortgage-backed securities and their derivatives between financial institutions." Bruce LYONS, "Competition Policy, Bailouts, and the Economic Crisis", 5 *Competition Policy International* 25 (2009), at 26.

[6] Carl SHAPIRO, "Competition Policy in Distressed Industries", *in* ABA Section of Antitrust Law, *Competition as Public Policy* Chicago: ABA Publishing, 2010, p. 17.

If there are many culprits for the crisis, antitrust enforcement does not seem to be one of them.[7] As to the question of how to respond to the crisis, one obvious solution would have been to see it as another episode of the perpetual gale of creative destruction of the market system at work. The problem is that whereas antitrust (or competition law and policy, as it is known in Europe) is currently primarily concerned with the efficient working of markets, and this requires free entry and free exit from the markets, banking does not fit well with free exit. Thus, a focus on efficiency in markets at large may conflict with central concerns regarding the banking sector.

It is simple enough to say that inefficient firms should leave the market and that markets punish managerial mistakes. However, when the firm at issue is a large bank it is to be expected that a special case will be argued on its behalf.[8] This is due to the contagion risks that plague the financial sector.[9] The specific regulatory question that arises is how to align incentives so that firms are deterred from incurring excessive risks (the moral hazard problem).

The way antitrust has been applied to financial firms has depended, to a significant extent, on the governing regulatory framework. Traditional

---

[7] See Howard A. SHELANSKI, "Enforcing Competition During an Economic Crisis", 77 *Antitrust L.J.* 229 (2010) at 230: "there is no evidence that antitrust law has ever so affected investment incentives that it caused or contributed to an economic crisis". According to Jenny, p. 451: "Is not the banking crisis evidence of a failure of competition on the banking sector? The answer to this second question is clearly no. The crisis arose and grew, on the one hand, because prudential regulation did not prevent some banks from taking excessive risks and, on the other hand, because the asset valuation method had magnifying effects which weakened the banking sector in a period of rapid decline in the value of financial assets, the result of which was to worse the systemic risk that the sector was facing." Frédéric JENNY, "The Economic and Financial Crisis, Regulation and Competition", 32 *World Competition* 449 (2009) at 451. However, others criticize lax antitrust enforcement in the U.S., particularly regarding mergers in the banking sector. See Darren BUSH, "Too Big to Bail: The Role of Antitrust in Distressed Industries", 77 *Antitrust L.J.* 277 (2010).

[8] See JENNY, "The Economic and Financial Crisis, Regulation and Competition", at 449: "Thus, unlike what happens in most goods and service markets, where a firm's failure represents an opportunity for its competitors, the failure of a firm in the banking and financial sector is liable to have systemic effects".

[9] See LYONS, "Competition Policy, Bailouts, and the Economic Crisis", at 27-28: "It is an unfortunate truth that banking is different to other industries due to a unique combination of two essential characteristics that create the potential for systemic economic collapse: contagion within the banking sector and contagion from banks to the entire real economy."

DIREITO COMPARADO / COMPARATIVE LAW

analytical tools such as market definition have been adjusted to the specific characteristics of these sectors, as exemplified by the concept of "cluster markets", confirmed by the 1963 judgment of the U.S. Supreme Court in *Philadelphia National Bank*.[10]

In the U.S. jurisdiction over banking mergers is concurrently assigned to the Department of Justice[11] and federal regulatory authorities: the Federal Reserve Board and the Office of the Comptroller of the Currency.[12] It appears that in recent decades the Federal Reserve Board has been conscious of the need to take antitrust concerns seriously in its review, thus lowering the risk of conflict with the Department of Justice, and a workable cooperative approach has been followed by these agencies.[13] In such an institutional setting, a natural division of tasks would be for the Department of Justice to focus on purely competitive concerns and the regulators to address specific issues, such as financial stability.[14] On the all important issue of remedies, that are likely to include divestments in horizontal merger cases, the system encompasses a regulatory approach, with the Federal Reserve Board assuming a major role, in exchange for an exemption from the normal litigation that arises in other areas of merger control.

---

[10] *U.S. v. Philadelphia National Bank*, 374 U.S. 321 (1963). On market definition in the banking sector, see Dean F. AMEL; Timothy H. HANNAN, "Defining Banking Markets According to Principles Recommended in the Merger Guidelines", 45 *Antitrust Bull.* 615 (2000); Dean F. AMEL; STARR-MCCLUER, "Market Definition in Banking: Recent Evidence", 47 *Antitrust Bull.* 63 (2002); Andrew R. BIEHL, "The Extent of the Market in Retail Banking Deposits", 47 *Antitrust Bull.* 91 (2002); Anthony W. CYRNAK; Timothy H. HANNAN, "Is the Cluster Still Valid in Defining Banking Markets? Evidence from a New Data Source", 44 *Antitrust Bull.* 313 (1999); Erik A. HEITFIELD, "What do Interest Rate Data Say About the Geography of retail Banking Markets?", 44 *Antitrust Bull.* 333 (1999). For an European perspective of the issue, see Cento VELJANOVSKI, "Banking Mergers: Transaction Costs and Market Definition", 21 *E.C.L.R.* 195 (2000).

[11] The Federal Trade Commission has no jurisdiction over banking.

[12] For an overview, see J. Robert KRAMER, "Antitrust Review in Banking and Defense", 11 *Geo. Mason L. Rev.* 111 (2002).

[13] *Ibid.* at 116-117.

[14] Maurice Stucke seems to argue in favor of the Department of Justice broadening its analytical focus to compensate for a possible policy failure on the part of the Federal Reserve Board. See Maurice E. STUCKE, "Lessons from the Financial Crisis", 77 *Antitrust L.J.* 313 (2010), at 323: "Thus, competition authorities face the current dilemma. On the one hand, merger policy currently does not offer the tools to intelligibly make this risk assessment. On the other hand, to be effective competition advocates, the FTC and DOJ cannot ignore the systemwide risks from a merger."

On balance, merger policy towards banking has been quite lenient in the United States in the last decades. As two commentators put it:

> Few mergers are denied on competitive grounds and, under current policy, there is little reason to believe that there will be any important barriers to future mergers among most of the largest banking organizations that now exist worldwide.[15]

And yet, this passive approach contrasts with their conclusion that:

> However, there is little evidence that, as a result, consumers and small businesses have gained from greater efficiency and competition. There is some evidence that mergers, even though carefully scrutinized for anticompetitive structural effects in local markets, have had anticompetitive consequences; and that the bank consolidation movement is producing new structural configurations that tend to restrain competition.[16]

It could be argued that the cooperative institutional framework tends to lend more relevance to alleged efficiency gains, particularly when these reinforce regulatory concerns over financial stability. Even discounting this sectorial bias, the increasing role of efficiencies together with a higher threshold of tolerance to market concentration in the general antitrust approach of federal agencies and courts seems to account for the relative absence of competitive issues in bank mergers.[17] This is to be contrasted,

---

[15] Gerald A. HANWECK; Bernard SHULL, "The Bank Merger Movement: Efficiency, Stability and Competitive Policy Concerns", 44 *Antitrust Bull.* 251 (1999).

[16] *Ibid.* at 252.

[17] Darren Bush partially blames antitrust enforcement for the financial crisis on account of this perceived bias. See Darren BUSH, "Too Big to Bail: The Role of Antitrust in Distressed Industries", at 279-280: "The view of this article is that antitrust has contributed to the economic crisis in several ways: First and foremost, the use of mainstream economic theory in the most recent decades of antitrust enforcement has served to focus analysis of conduct potentially harmful to consumers on issues of efficiency and welfare effects. Moreover, within the analytical framework of contemporary antitrust, efficiencies are king. It is with a skeptical eye that courts and often times particular enforcement regimes view anticompetitive harms arising from consolidation. Conversely, efficiencies are often considered with less skepticism than should be the case. At the same time, any discussion of other motivations for antitrust enforcement, including concern about concentration of political power into the hands of a

DIREITO COMPARADO / COMPARATIVE LAW

however, with the apparent lack of credible efficiency gains in most of the mega-merger deals of past decades.[18]

Overall, efficiency gains and risk-diversification arguments have dominated merger analysis by U.S. agencies and too-big-to-fail concerns have been disregarded in two ways.[19] Firstly, no reasonable analytical framework has been developed to take increased systemic risk into account, particularly in the mega-merger deals of the 1990s and early 2000s.[20] The business as usual approach has accepted increased concentration in banking as generally benign and a natural consequence of deregulation.[21] Secondly,

few large (multi-national) corporations, has been eliminated from antitrust discourse. While this legitimate concern has been expressed in political protests, antitrust law has largely ignored the notion that corporate political power may create significant economic effects that in turn may affect the structure and function of the market."

[18] According to Johan A. LYBECK, *A Global History of the Financial Crash of 2007-10*, Cambridge: Cambridge Univ. Press, 2011, at 325, scale economies are not a strong argument in favor of banking mega-mergers: "The optimal scale in banking is quite small; traditional banking is a labor-intensive activity. There would appear to be no or few economies of scale above total assets of $ 10 billion. At the end of 2009, Bank of America, JPMorgan Chase and Citigroup were probably 200 times larger than is needed to achieve efficient scale". Lybeck estimates that "[e]ven where economies of scale exist, they are unlikely to exceed 5 percent of total assets".

[19] As Maurice Stucke puts it "in focusing on the short-term static effects (such as whether the banks post-merger may raise rates for specific categories of borrowers), antitrust enforcers can fail to see or assess the long-term impact of major factors, such as the merger's impact on the efficiency, competitiveness, and stability of the overall financial system." See STUCKE, "Lessons from the Financial Crisis", at 317.

[20] According to Darren Bush, "[i]nstead, the proper focus of antitrust should be upon whether or not consolidations and other transactions create serious economic or political consequences for consumers. The economic consequences arise not only from anticompetitive harms, but from efficiencies that fail to appear and which potentially lead to further consolidation in industries poised to cause ripple effects throughout the economy in times of distress. A permissive antitrust policy based upon the notion that efficiencies are everywhere while anticompetitive effects are speculative not only does disservice to consumers but runs afoul of the very purpose of the Clayton Act." See BUSH, "Too Big to Bail: The Role of Antitrust in Distressed Industries", at 311. See also LYBECK, *A Global History of the Financial Crash of 2007-10*, at 321: "Not only were banks large to begin with, the crisis made the big banks even bigger, as a number of them swallowed weaker colleagues." Thus, Bank of America acquired Countrywide and Merril Lynch, going from total assets of 1.72 trillion USD in 2007 to 2.22 trillion in 2009. JP Morgan Chase takeover of Bear Sterns and Washington Mutual, increased total assets from 1.56 trillion USD in 2007 to 2.18 trillion in 2008.

[21] See STUCKE, "Lessons from the Financial Crisis", at 323. "Thus, in creating a financial institution too-big-to-fail, a merger can adversely affect consumers and other market participants by reducing the requisite degree of diversity for the financial network to remain stable.

the implicit subsidy in too-big-to-fail policy and the competitive advantage that larger banks derive from it has not been considered in the analysis of the competitive impact of reviewed transactions.[22] In fact, such gains from growing to become a too-big-to-fail bank may actually count as benefits as they lower their costs of equity capital.

In the current institutional setting, it is hard to conceive of antitrust analysis being made to incorporate such impacts. One of the issues that have been echoed by several commentators is whether the role of anti-trust agencies should be broadened to include systemic risks and other regulatory concerns.[23]

Whereas the establishment of a nationwide banking system is relatively recent in the United States and stems from the deregulation movement that started in the seventies, Europe has a deliberate policy of market inte-gration. Furthermore, integration has been enhanced by monetary inte-gration among the Eurozone economies.

Under the EU merger control system, the European Commission has exclusive jurisdiction over mergers of "Community dimension".[24] How-

---

Moreover, in being deemed too-big-to-fail, financial institutions can engage in risky behavior with the confidence of a government bailout, and thus enjoy a competitive advantage over smaller rivals that are permitted to fail."

[22] See HANWECK; SHULL, "The Bank Merger Movement: Efficiency, Stability and Competi-tive Policy Concerns", 275-276. BUSH, "Too Big to Bail: The Role of Antitrust in Distressed Industries", at 309: "The intertwining of large financial institutions and large insurance institutions made it impossible to allow proper market responses, including bankruptcy, to occur. Accordingly, by being 'too big to fail' and by bailout, many companies gain a com-petitive advantage over small state or regional banks by being propped up through crises, so that the cycle of consolidation and bailout continues without correction. The guarantee of a bailout could exacerbate the behavior that causes the crisis." LYBECK, *A Global History of the Financial Crash of 2007-10*, at 319 quotes a study by the Center for Economic and Policy Research (CEPR) that estimates the implicit subsidy provided to too-big-to-fail financial institutions in a staggering 34 trillion USD, thus creating costs for consumers and distorting competition vis-à-vis smaller banks.

[23] STUCKE, "Lessons from the Financial Crisis", at 323: "The issue, then, is to what extent is antitrust analysis inadequate when it ignores a merger's systemwide risks. The federal antitrust agencies cannot assume that the Council or their sister agencies will engage in this analysis adequately for the financial industry."

[24] Under article 1 (2) of Regulation no. 139/2004, a concentration is considered to have Community dimension where the combined aggregate worldwide turnover of all the undertakings involved is more than EUR 5000 million and he aggregate Community-wide turnover of each of at least two of the undertakings concerned is more than EUR 250 million.

ever, Community dimension is subject to the so-called "two-thirds rule", that is to say, a merger will not be under the European Commission's jurisdiction where the firms involved make more than two-thirds of turnover within a single Member State. Thus, bank mergers in Europe have generally fallen under national purview, where "national champion" arguments may play a role in gaining approval of proposed transactions (or in rejecting hostile bids against politically friendly management).

Where the two-thirds rule is not met, cross-border mergers that have Community dimension will fall under the exclusive jurisdiction of the European Commission. It should be noted that EU rules allow Member States to protect legitimate interests even where a merger has Community dimension. These legitimate interests may include relevant public interests regarding banking, such as preventing systemic risk.[25] Nevertheless, what has happened is that Member States seek to protect their domestic banks on nationalist grounds, by challenging mergers under banking and insurance law.[26] It is ironic that too-big-to-fail may be addressed as a national interest and that it has not happened due to the narrow protectionist focus that tends to prevail at national level, and yet no similar provision exists for the European Commission to take into account when reviewing mergers with an European dimension.

That is to say, where mergers are subject to the European Commission approval, regulatory concerns may only be voiced by Member States. This stands in stark contrast with the achievement of the Eurozone and the European Central Bank role. Should the latter be broadened to encompass Eurozone-wide banking supervision, some mechanism will have to be devised to allow for some input from the European Central Bank on cross-border mergers.

This may then be trumped by the so-called two-thirds rule; where each of the undertakings concerned achieves more than two-thirds of its aggregate Community-wide turnover within one and the same Member State, the concentration will not be considered as having a Community dimension. Article 1 (3) provides lower turnover thresholds of EUR 2500 million and EUR 100 million, respectively, where there are significant operations in three or more Member States, also subject to the two-thirds rule.

[25] Article 21 (4) of Regulation no. 139/2004.

[26] See, e.g., European Commission decision of October 20, 1999, Case IV/M.1616, *BSCH/A. Champalimaud.*

3. Antitrust and Crisis Response

If history is relevant to today's crisis, what it is most likely to suggest is that abandonment of antitrust is clearly the wrong response to financial crisis. In many respects this is also the lesson taught by the political reaction to the Great Depression in the international trade arena. Shielding domestic firms from competition, both from foreign and domestic competition, proved a recipe for disaster in the inter-war period.

Among these responses the inevitable parallel is with President Roosevelt's early New Deal initiatives. The National Industrial Recovery Act of 1933 pursued a return to cartels, now managed under the guidance of the federal government with dire economic consequences. The hardships of the recession were likely exacerbated by such efforts to undermine competition.[27] Even the long-established *per se* prohibition of horizontal price fixing was disregarded in *Appalachian Coals v. U.S.* (1933).

President Roosevelt subsequently abandoned this skepticism on the virtues of competition and there was a move to more rigorous antitrust enforcement, particularly following the appointment of Thurman Arnold as head of the Antitrust Division at the Justice Department.[28]

Dan Crane has expressed skepticism as to the existence of any historical lesson.[29] Although he considers that since the repeated response to situations of economic and war emergency has been to suspend antitrust enforcement, then riding out the storm may be the best approach. However, this has not been the dominant trend on both sides of the Atlantic. The first Assistant Attorney General nominated by President Obama has drawn two lessons from the New Deal experience:

> The lessons learned from this historical example are twofold. First, there is no adequate substitute for a competitive market, particularly during times

---

[27] See Harold L. Cole; Lee. E. Ohanian, "New Deal Policies and the Persistence of the Great Depression: A General Equilibrium Analysis", 112 *J. Pol. Econ.* 779 (2004). According to these authors, in that period, cartels led to higher prices and higher unemployment. See also Hawley, Ellis W., *The New Deal and the Problem of Monopoly: A Study in Economic Ambivalence*, 2nd ed., New York: Fordham University Press, 1995.

[28] Waller, Spencer Weber, *Thurman Arnold – A Biography*, New York: New York University Press, 2005.

[29] Daniel A. Crane, "Antitrust Enforcement During National Crises: An Unhappy History", 12 *Global Competition Policy* 2 (2008); Daniel A. Crane, "Did We Avoid Historical Failures of Antitrust Enforcement During the 2008-2009 Financial Crisis?", 77 *Antitrust L.J.* 219 (2010).

of economic distress. Second, vigorous antitrust enforcement must play a significant role in the Government's response to economic crises to ensure that markets remain competitive.[30]

In the United States, in face of a perceived lax antitrust policy under President George W. Bush, the Obama administration has put forward a new antitrust agenda, particularly in the area of unilateral conduct (monopolization).[31] Some signs of a more activist enforcement policy have been particularly visible in some merger cases such as the AT&T/T-Mobile and NASDAQ OMX/ NYSE Euronext deals as well as the ongoing United States v. Apple and others case (e-book publishing). The Obama antitrust agenda has also focused on so-called pocketbook issues, establishing a link between active antitrust enforcement and providing indirect relief for consumers.[32]

Similar concerns have been voiced in the European Union.[33] And yet, the Lisbon Treaty has clearly downplayed competition as a foundation of market integration, bowing to the pressure of France's president at the time, Nicholas Sarkozy. Whereas under the Treaty of Rome, one of the objectives set out in article 3 (g) was to establish "a system ensuring that competition in the internal market is not distorted," the Lisbon Treaty has

---

[30] Christine A. VARNEY, "Vigorous Antitrust Enforcement in this Challenging Era", Remarks as prepared for the United States Chamber of Commerce, May 12, 2009, available at http://www.justice.gov/atr/public/speeches/245777.htm.

[31] *Ibid.* See also Spencer Weber WALLER; Jennifer WOODS, "Antitrust Transitions", 32 *World Competition* 189 (2009). Some commentators have disputed the claim of lax antitrust enforcement during the Bush administration. See William E. KOVACIC, "Rating the Competition Agencies: What Constitutes Good Performance?", 16 *Geo. Mason L. Rev.* 903 (2009).

[32] See Sharis A. POZEN, "Promoting Competition and Innovation Through Vigorous Enforcement of the Antitrust Laws on Behalf of Consumers", Remarks as Prepared for the Brookings Institution, Washington, D.C., April 23, 2012, available at http://www.justice.gov/atr/public/speeches/282515.pdf.

[33] Philip LOWE, "Competition Policy and the Global Economic Crisis", 5 *Competition Policy International* 3 (2009), at 6: "competition policy should arguably focus on those sectors that either directly or indirectly affect household expenditure to the greatest extent in order to ease the burden on consumers, as well as on sectors that are the most important for productivity growth." See also JENNY, "The Economic and Financial Crisis, Regulation and Competition", at 461: "To the extent that competition authorities are independent institutions and that one of their objectives is to be perceived as fulfilling a useful function for society, it is also likely that in a period of economic crisis they will, more than in the past, choose to tailor their activities to markets which are particularly important for the economically and socially weakest groups."

confined this objective to a Protocol annexed to the Treaty on the Functioning of the European Union (Protocol No. 27).[34]

On the other hand, the financial nature of the crisis and the fact that massive bailouts have been necessary seems to have revived, at least nominally, state aid control. Early on pressure was put to the Commission to essentially forego any State aid analysis.[35] It should be noted that state aid control has little parallel in other jurisdictions, including the United States, the exception being the WTO subsidies rules. EU rules on State aid perform a crucial function within the legal framework of the single market. Were Member States free to subsidize their domestic firms, this could trigger similar responses from other Member States, leading to a subsidies war. If this is undesirable in international trade and subject to the WTO Subsidies Agreement, it could have devastating effects to European economic integration. Thus, although grounded on the concept of "distortion of competition", State aid control is not to be confused with antitrust proper as the latter addresses market failures arising from the exercise of market power, not the distortions brought about by the use of public resources.

In this regard there has been a strong policy response by the Commission, and the clear and immediate danger of the crisis led to shorter delays and more flexible procedures. At least on the face of it, it seems that the Commission approach was of flexing the rules and maintaining adherence to principle. It should be noted that, according to the European Commission, between October 1, 2008 and October 1, 2011, it approved aid to the financial sector Europe-wide of € 4.5 trillion or 36,7% of EU GDP.[36]

---

[34] See Alan RILEY, "The EU Reform Treaty and the Competition Protocol: Undermining EC Competition Law", 28 *E.C.L.R.* 703 (2007).

[35] As admitted by the then Director-General for Competition. See LOWE, "Competition Policy and the Global Economic Crisis", at 4 "At the outset of the crisis there was pressure on the Commission to set aside the competition rules on State aid, in order to allow EU Member States freedom to implement financial sector rescue measures as they saw fit." In exactly the same words, see Neelie KROES, "Competition policy and the crisis – the Commission's approach to banking and beyond", 55 *Antitrust Bull.* 715 (2010), at 717: "In other words, we wanted to stop a subsidy war."

[36] A full analysis of the Commission's State Aid framework would be beyond the scope of this paper. The subject has been amply commented. See Lorenzo COPPI; Jenny HAYDOCK, "The Approach to State Aid in the Restructuring of the Financial Sector", 5 *Competition Policy International* 77 (2009); Damien GERARD, "Managing the Financial Crisis in Europe: Why Competition Law is Part of the Solution, Not of the Problem", 12 *Global Competition Policy* 1

DIREITO COMPARADO / COMPARATIVE LAW

Competition framework for state aid introduced some measures that may help bring incentives more in line. The Recapitalization Communication's approach of distinguishing between fundamentally sound and distressed banks seems particularly useful. Yet, as the crisis broadens this distinction may become less clear. In any case, the Commission's framework is insufficient to eliminate the payoffs of too big to fail. Further steps in market integration may follow, particularly in view of discussions of a banking union in June 2012.

4. Consequences of the Financial Crisis: Antitrust in Distress?

The question that these developments raise and that I would like to address now is what are the consequences of the financial crisis regarding the level of antitrust enforcement in the United States and in Europe.

It is clear that unlike the New Deal's initial response to the Great Depression, there is no tolerance for crisis cartels or other such output reducing restrictive practices. Given the very high costs that such restraints impose on other businesses and on consumers, the mere fact that tough policies on cartels on both sides of the Atlantic have been maintained clearly sends a strong message that there will be no safe harbors for cartelists. One should however be weary of the fact that the crisis has led to pressure to take the economic situation into account in imposing fines on defendants. The European Commission has responded with caution to such requests and seems to consider that such considerations will play an exceptional role in its fining policy.[37]

(2008); KROES, "Competition policy and the crisis – the Commission's approach to banking and beyond"; Abel Moreira MATEUS, "The Current Financial Crisis and State Aid in the European Union: Has It Been Timely and Appropriate?", 12 *Global Competition Policy* 1 (2008); Abel Moreira MATEUS, "The Current Financial Crisis and State Aid in the EU", 5 *European Competition Journal* 1 (2009); Abel Moreira MATEUS, "Banking Regulatory Reform: "Too Big to Fail" and What Still Needs to be Done", 7 *Competition Policy International* 22 (2011); Phedon NICOLAIDES; Ioana Eleonora RUSU, "The financial crisis and state aid", 55 *Antitrust Bull.* 759 (2010); Charalambos SAVVIDES; Daniel ANTONIOU, "Ailing Financial Institutions: EC State Aid Policy Revisited", 32 *World Competition* 347 (2009); Ulrich SOLTESZ; Christian VON KOCKRITZ, "From State Aid Control to the Regulation of the European Banking System – DG COMP and the Restructuring of Banks", 6 *European Competition Journal* 285 (2010); Ulrich SOLTESZ; Christian VON KOCKRITZ, "The 'temporary framework' – the Commission's response to the crisis in the real economy", 31 *E.C.L.R.* 106 (2010).

[37] LOWE, "Competition Policy and the Global Economic Crisis", at 22: "The Commission does have the option of reducing the cartel fine it would impose if the company in question

With regard to unilateral practices, the fact that this area of antitrust has been the subject of a heated debate, particularly following the Microsoft cases in the 1990s, tends to obscure whether there is a slowdown due to a cautious approach adopted by antitrust authorities or whether there is a retrenchment due to the crisis and worries over political spillovers from prosecuting powerful firms. Only time will tell, although there are no signs that enforcement is significantly lower than in the past decade.

Another area where pressure has been felt is that of mergers, particularly regarding a possible relaxing of the requisites for the failing firm defense,[38] a more flexible approach to divestiture remedies[39] – where viable buyers may be quite scarce due to financial constraints – and arguments in favor of taking concerns about employment into account in the substantive analysis of mergers.[40] Given the high profile of the transactions that tend

---

is unable to pay. A reduction of this kind could only be granted if paying the fine would seriously endanger the economic viability of the company. While this situation might occur in the context of the crisis, the Commission would make an extremely careful assessment before granting any such reduction." One puzzling case is the Portuguese Competition Authority's Decision to take the economic crisis into consideration in determining fines on a bid-rigging cartel case, although the facts at issue took place at the latest two years before the beginning of the financial crisis and that cartelists were found to have made substantial profits, estimated at values well above the fines imposed in this case. On this case, the so-called Catering Services Cartel Case, see Miguel MOURA E SILVA, "Anti-cartel enforcement in Portugal: A short chronicle of an uphill struggle", 32 *E.C.L.R.* 37 (2011). In EU and Portuguese competition law there is a general principle that fines will take into account the ability to pay on behalf of the defendant. See the 2006 European Commission *Guidelines on the method of setting fines imposed pursuant to Article 23(2)(a) of Regulation No. 1/2003*, Official Journal C 210, Sept. 1st, 2006, p. 2, at paragraph 35: "In exceptional cases, the Commission may, upon request, take account of the undertaking's inability to pay in a specific social and economic context. It will not base any reduction granted for this reason in the fine on the mere finding of an adverse or loss-making financial situation. A reduction could be granted solely on the basis of objective evidence that imposition of the fine as provided for in these Guidelines would irretrievably jeopardise the economic viability of the undertaking concerned and cause its assets to lose all their value."

[38] SHELANSKI, "Enforcing Competition During an Economic Crisis", at 235-236.

[39] JENNY, "The Economic and Financial Crisis, Regulation and Competition", at 462-463. SHELANSKI, "Enforcing Competition During an Economic Crisis", at 237.

[40] LOWE, "Competition Policy and the Global Economic Crisis", at 19: "It is sometimes argued that in times of crisis, it would be appropriate for the Commission to be able to take into account other wider considerations, such as employment. However, experience has shown that a legal instrument such as the EC Merger Regulation is most effective when it is directed to one single objective. Employment concerns need to be addressed through other instruments. It is hard to see how it would be possible to agree on the wider objectives that

DIREITO COMPARADO / COMPARATIVE LAW

to raise concerns on both sides of the Atlantic, one would expect this to be the weak point of antitrust in the face of political pressure.

It is evident that at least procedurally antitrust agencies have had to act under very tight time constraints. We can find examples of such expedited merger approvals in the United States and in Europe in the aftermath of the near-meltdown of the financial sector. Wells Fargo acquisition of Wachovia was approved by the Federal Reserve Board in only nine days.[41] And the European Commission authorized the BPN Paribas/Fortis merger two weeks before the normal deadline.[42]

Whereas procedural efficiency is certainly important for businesses, one cannot help but feel at least some disquiet over such quick-look approvals of deals, particularly when one considers that, even with possible redeeming features, they may just add to the too-big-to-fail problem. Perhaps this outcome was inevitable in the "fog-of-war" that surrounded attempts to contain the financial crisis, but it is also clear that more thought ought to be given to providing effective (and not just expedient) antitrust scrutiny. As things stand, we may very well conclude that, at least in the financial sector, regulatory objectives such as stability trump maintaining open and competitive markets.[43]

Professor Darren Bush has highlighted another troubling sign in other industries, such as airlines. He notes the contrasting attitude towards the United/US Airways merger in 2002, where the merger was blocked in the United States, and the Delta/Northwest merger in 2008, approved by the Department of Justice.[44] One is hard-pressed to see why

should be taken into account in our assessment or, indeed, how it would be possible to agree on how these objectives should be implemented."

[41] SHELANSKI, "Enforcing Competition During an Economic Crisis", at 236.

[42] See KROES, "Competition policy and the crisis – the Commission's approach to banking and beyond", at 725: "The robustness and flexibility of the EC Merger Regulation are evidenced by the Commission's ability and willingness to adopt its authorization decision two weeks before the normal deadline in the BNP Paribas/Fortis merger case13 in December 2008."

[43] See Albert A. FOER, "Preserving Competition After the Banking Meltdown", 12 Global Competition Policy 1 (2008), at 7: "In normal times, the failing company defense is given much scrutiny and a heavy dose of skepticism, but these are not normal times. When decisions have to be made over the weekend, antitrust scrutiny is going to take a back seat to the immediacy of a crisis."

[44] See BUSH, "Too Big to Bail: The Role of Antitrust in Distressed Industries", at 300-301: "A possible example of the double standard of antitrust in economic difficulties appears in the airline industry. In particular, when comparing the proposed (and ultimately blocked) United/

the fundamentals of antitrust analysis should change in a crisis.[45] Given the recent opposition to high-profile mergers by the Department of Justice under the Obama administration, it seems that this case may simply be an anomaly or else justified by a very specific factual context (or another example of lax antitrust enforcement, according to critics of the Bush administration).

Overall, antitrust enforcement does not seem to be seriously weakened in the United States and at the EU level. Yet there are troubling signs that as the current sovereign debt crisis deepens, at least some Member States may want to put a lid on antitrust. Furthermore, not all EU Member States have reacted to the crisis with strict adherence to antitrust principles.

At national level, even in cases where a competition case can be made against a merger, recent developments present a bleak picture. In the United Kingdom the 2008 takeover of HBOS by Lloyds TSB was considered by the Office of Fair Trading to lead to a substantial lessening of competition in the markets of personal current accounts and in banking services to small and medium sized enterprises, especially in Scotland. On October 31, the Secretary of State for Business, Enterprise and Regulatory Reform approved the merger on public interest grounds.[46] This is troubling since banking markets are still mainly of national dimension and merger activity in the banking sector has been essentially domestic, even following the financial crisis.[47]

US Airways merger in 2002 and the 2008 Delta/Northwest merger, which DOJ approved, the limited evidence available could be read to suggest that Delta and Northwest might have benefited from a more lenient review in light of the particularly difficult economic situation of the airline industry during the review of the transaction."

[45] See Ken HEYER; Sheldon SIMMEL, "Merger Review of Firms in Financial Distress", 5 *Competition Policy International* 103 (2009), at 116: "Severe economic downturns may lead to more proposed mergers between financially distressed firms, but it does not imply that looser standards ought to be applied when evaluating them."

[46] VICKERS, John Stuart, "Financial Crisis and Competition Policy: Some Economics", 12 *Global Competition Policy* 1 (2008). As Vickers highlights, the Secretary of State made a public statement on September 18, 2008 according to which he would clear the merger on public interest grounds. However, financial stability was only legally established as a relevant public interest ground for approval of a merger on October 24, 2008. The Competition Appeal Tribunal upheld the decision.

[47] LOWE, "Competition Policy and the Global Economic Crisis", at 16: "The picture under the EC merger control rules is quite different. In contrast with the wholesale government interventions providing financial support to the banking and insurance sectors, there has

In Portugal, crisis response involved the nationalization of the ailing bank BPN in November 2008. The nationalization was justified by the Government on the ground of a systemic risk – despite its relatively low market share – and effective control was handed to Portugal's largest and State-owned bank, CGD. The fact that this amounted to a horizontal merger does not seem to have troubled the Government and the Portuguese Competition Authority appears to have been sidelined. In fact, it was only called to approve a transaction regarding the BPN's privatization in late 2011.

At the time, the Portuguese Government presented a bill, approved by Parliament, providing for financial intervention by the State in private banks while granting a temporary exemption from merger notification. In accordance with Law 63A/2008 the Government could overrule prohibition decisions on grounds of urgency, risk circumstances and the protection of the Portuguese financial sector stability.

Since national governments, unlike the European Commission, are elected and politically responsible before national parliaments, they are also more likely to heed to calls for a relaxation of antitrust enforcement. This creates tension with competition policy as the latter is legally grounded in the founding treaties that will prevail over national law. Furthermore, the European Commission safeguards the enforcement of treaty rules not just with regard to firms and competition rules, but also vis-à-vis Member States with respect to the legal framework of the single market.

As the crisis deepens and recovery fails to take hold, the risks to antitrust are far more dangerous and less visible today. A global economic slowdown will tend to make it easier for those claiming a less aggressive antitrust policy is necessary to foster growth. As Vickers has put it, "[i]t is a familiar pattern that when the going gets tough, some of the not-so-tough seek exemptions from competition law."[48] This is exactly the opposite of what should be pursued, for very much the same reasons that a return to protectionism would have led us to a crisis like the Great Depression.[49]

---

been relatively little merger activity directly related to banking rescue or restructuring (or other financial firms) that has been subject to review by the Commission. Some cases – such as the Lloyds/HBOS merger in the United Kingdom and the Commerzbank/Dresdner merger in Germany – have been dealt with by National Competition Authorities in the relevant EU Member States."

[48] VICKERS, "Financial Crisis and Competition Policy: Some Economics".

[49] See LOWE, "Competition Policy and the Global Economic Crisis", at 5: "The link between effective competition and economic growth is particularly important in times of economic

5. Concluding Remarks

I will now conclude with some remarks on the (trillion) dollar question: what can antitrust do to prevent further crises? Given the acknowledged origins of the crisis, it would seem that the main issue to address is whether merger policy should incorporate systemic risk into efficiency considerations. In other words, if too-big-to-fail is the problem, at least when "too-big" is caused by merger of previously independent banks, antitrust seems to be at hand to prevent such growth.[50] The problem is that, firstly, there seems to be no ground, under competitive analysis, to prohibit a merger merely on the ground that the resulting firm will be too-big-to-fail. Secondly, the reasons in favor of using antitrust to pursue a sectorial goal are, in essence, the result of admitting a regulatory failure. Solutions to the too-big-to-fail problem must therefore be found chiefly within the regulatory context.[51] After all, since competition authorities are viewed as more independent from any particular sector, they could be relied upon to impose measures that regulators, particularly those that tend to identify market stability with absence of competition, do not have the will to adopt.[52] The role that antitrust may play in this regard is thus a very limited one, confined as it is by a growing focus on efficiency gains as a defense

recession. As markets characterized by effective competition make companies innovate more, they drive economic growth through the improvement of total factor productivity. Total factor productivity growth can be several percentage points higher in sectors where the intensity of competition is higher. This can make the difference when markets cannot rely on large amounts of capital to stimulate growth."

[50] This does not address organic growth, much as the Dodd-Frank legislation. See LYBECK, *A Global History of the Financial Crash of 2007-10*, at 319.

[51] For a description of some proposals to address too-big-to-fail, see LYBECK, *A Global History of the Financial Crash of 2007-10*, at 332. Gary H. STERN; Ron J. FELDMAN, *Too Big To Fail – The Hazards of Bank Bailouts (With a New Preface)*, Washington, D.C.: Brookings Institution Press, 2009.

[52] This seems to be the point of view of Elena CARLETTI; Giancarlo SPAHNOLO; Stefano CAIAZZA; Caterina GIANNETTI, "Banking Competition in Europe: Antitrust Authorities at Work in the Wake of the Financial Crisis", 33 World Competition 615 (2010), at 641: "Should competition authorities simply look at competition issues or should they also consider stability concerns? And if so, in what way? Despite having the task of promoting competition, it is not clear that having the competition authorities solely focusing on this task is the right approach. In addition, the consequences of competition policy on bank stability are anything but clear. For instance, when allowing a merger, should competition authorities take the costs of the creation of banks that are 'too big to fail' into account?" The authors do not attempt to answer these questions.

for large horizontal mergers, on the one hand, and an institutional setting that defers to financial regulators. Proposals for the break-up of banks on grounds of bigness and systemic risk may only be justified by regulatory concerns and can hardly find justification in discredited deconcentration theories in vogue in the 1960s.[53]

The financial crisis may increase the bias toward accepting ever-larger firms as the result of efficiency gains. Since the large banks were not allowed to go under and not only survived the crisis but actually grew larger, this may lead to thinking that it is bigness itself that accounts for survival – not the bailouts and taxpayers' money. In a next round of industry consolidation, the crisis may actually be used to legitimate purported efficiency gains in growth by acquisition, at least where there are no limits to such growth. Even in the United States, it seems a bold proposition to expect that the three groups that already exceed the 10% mark (Bank of America, JP Morgan Chase and Citigroup) will not be looked upon – in a future crisis – to further digest any of their smaller competitors or indeed to merge themselves.[54] After all, if an orderly takeover is needed, to whom will central banks look to? The recent crisis showed who the usual suspects are.

[53] LYBECK, *A Global History of the Financial Crash of 2007-10*, at 367: "Even if both competition aspects and the lack of economies of scale indicate the need for a break-up of megabanks, as most recently proposed by John Kay, it cannot be done by individual countries, but only by worldwide agreements, which appear highly unlikely. It seems much better to achieve limitations on size by higher capital standards à la Switzerland (and perhaps in the UK?)."

[54] See BUSH, "Too Big to Bail: The Role of Antitrust in Distressed Industries", at 278: "At least with respect to the latest crisis in the financial industry, it could be said that a crisis begets bailout which begets consolidation, which in turn makes it more likely that a future crisis will beget bailout."

III Parte / Part III

DESENVOLVIMENTOS DO DIREITA DA ENERGIA
DEVELOPMENTS IN ENERGY LAW

(10ª conferência, Washington, 2011
10th conference, Washington, 2011)

Scope of Energy Law

ANTONIO DE LECEA[*]

Introduction

Greetings and congratulatory remarks for the Organizers and Law School. Welcome to distinguished guests and participants.

A quick glance at the program of this Conference reveals the great scope of Energy law. It reflects how intertwined Energy law is with the spheres of both economics and politics. It shows the national, regional, and international dimensions of Energy law.

Energy law is indeed the point of convergence of several disciplines of private law like company law or civil law. Energy law has also followed the significant expansion of administrative law in particular as regards the legal and regulatory framework. It has continued to expand as societies considered that new regulatory criteria like consumer or environmental protection had to be added to the traditional ones of fair competition, security of supply, or affordable access to service for the less advantaged sectors of the population. And this evolution of regulation: deregulation.

Energy law has also gained in complexity as sources of energy have diversified. The traditional legal disciplines relevant for fossil or hydro-based energy have been complemented with those addressing the specificities and challenges of new sources of energy, like nuclear or biofuels.

[*] Deputy Chief of Mission, European Union Delegation to the United States of America.

The development of financial derivatives linked to energy have led energy law to encroach in the also vast realm of financial law.

In the European Union the national layer of legislation is complemented with a supranational framework that prevails over national laws, even over national constitutional norms in those areas where the Union has been empowered to legislate.

The interaction between National Law and EU Law
Supremacy of EU law
The principle:

EU law is superior to national laws, which means that EU law takes precedence where a conflict arises between EU law and the law of a Member State, the EU law overrules national law.

The supremacy of EU law doctrine emerged from the EU Court of Justice in case 6/64; Costa vs. ENEL, where it ruled that EU law would not be effective if Mr. Costa could not challenge national law on the basis of its alleged incompatibility with EU law.

Case 6/64; Costa vs. ENEL

The case was a landmark decision of the European Court of Justice which established the supremacy of EU law over the national laws of its Member States.

> *"It follows from all these observations that the law stemming from the treaty, an independent source of law, could not, because of its special and original nature, be overridden by domestic legal provisions, however framed, without being deprived of its character as community law and without the legal basis of the community itself being called into question."*

Direct Effect
The principle:

Direct effect is the principle of EU law according to which provisions of Union law may, if appropriately framed, confer rights and impose obligations on individuals which the courts of European Union Member States are bound to recognize and enforce.

The principle of direct effect was first established in the case Van Gend en Loos, where the EU Court of Justice established that treaty articles were capable of creating personal rights for Van Gend en Loos – meaning; that provisions of the Treaty Establishing the European Economic Community were capable of creating legal rights which could be enforced by both natural and legal persons before the courts of the Community's Member States.

The principle direct effect has subsequently expanded, so that it is capable of applying to virtually all of the possible forms of EU legislation: treaty articles, regulations, decisions, directives – where the most important of which are regulations and in certain circumstances to directives.

Direct effect is applicable when the particular provision relied on fulfils the Van Gend en Loos criteria.

Case; Van Gend en Loos

"The Community constitutes a new legal order of international law for the benefit of which the states have limited their sovereign rights, albeit within limited fields and the subjects of which comprise not only member states but also their nationals. Independently of the legislation of member states, community law therefore not only imposes obligations on individuals but is also intended to confer upon them rights which become part of their legal heritage. These rights arise not only where they are expressly granted by the treaty, but also by reason of obligations which the treaty imposes in a clearly defined way upon individuals as well as upon the member states and upon the institutions of the community." – Judgment of the Court of 5 February 1963.

The Van Gend en Loos criteria
The provision must:

- be sufficiently clear and precisely stated,
- be unconditional or non-dependent, and
- confer a specific right for the citizen to base his or her claim on.

If these criteria are satisfied, then the right or rights in question can be enforced before national courts. Of course whether or not any particular measure satisfies the criteria is a matter of EU law to be determined by the EU Courts.

Varieties of direct effect:

In Van Gend en Loos it was decided that a citizen was able to enforce a right granted by European Community legislation against the state – the question of whether rights could be enforced against another citizen was not addressed. In Defrenne v. SABENA, the European Court of Justice decided that there were two varieties of direct effect: vertical direct effect and horizontal direct effect, the distinction drawn being based on against whom the right is to be enforced.

- *Vertical direct effect* concerns the relationship between EU law and national law – specifically, the state's obligation to ensure its observance and its compatibility with EU law, thereby enabling citizens to rely on it in actions against the state (or against an "emanation of the state" as defined in Foster v. British Gas plc).
- *Horizontal direct effect* concerns the relationship between individuals (including companies). If a certain provision of EU law is horizontally directly effective, then citizens are able to rely on it in actions against each other. Directives are usually incapable of being horizontally directly effective due to the fact that they are only enforceable against the state. Certain provisions of the treaties and legislative acts such as regulations are capable of being directly enforced horizontally.

External Energy Relations and International Law
Energy Charter Treaty

Over the years the changes in the world of energy have intensified, posing new challenges before national and regional economies.

In view of this, the European Union is looking to:

- Improve the efficiency of its energy markets.
- Increase their stability by encouraging further network interconnections and diversity of reliable energy supply.
- Achieve maximum possible sustainability through the promotion of greener energy sources.

These goals can only be reached by taking into account major evolutions on the energy scene beyond the EU borders.

Common challenges for Energy Security in Wider Europe

Energy security challenges facing countries in Europe and beyond, and on the more efficient ways of managing the interdependence between energy producers and consumers to the mutual benefit of all parties along the energy value chain.

Challenges for energy security are global; we are all facing rapid changes in the energy environment:

- Energy price environment is volatile.
- Producing countries seek stronger participation downstream.
- Global energy demand is more and more driven by the rapidly growing economies outside the traditional OECD area.
- We see greater state involvement in the global energy markets.
- Environmental protection, which used to focus on prevention of pollution, is now increasingly focusing on reducing global greenhouse gas emissions and mitigating their climate change impact.

The problem is not that sources of energy are unavailable. But there is a real risk that our use of these resources, which has been the engine for so many improvements in human welfare, could ultimately propel us towards environmental degradation and conflict.

Putting the global energy economy on a secure path of development will require renewed and joint efforts from governments and international organisations.

Meeting policy goals in relation to energy security requires a recognition of our interdependence in matters of energy, and an understanding that genuine security and stability need to be based on mutual benefits and advantages – as well as strong communication – all along the energy value chain. It would be a mistake if current challenges led to the emergence of new barriers to international trade and cooperation, under the banner of energy independence.

The questions are: how to manage interdependence most effectively and how to create functioning and balanced international frameworks that can mitigate the associated risks.

- A starting point is to find common principles that can underpin international cooperation.

o For the Energy Charter these are expressed in a political declaration from 1991, signed by almost 60 countries across the world. These countries include major energy producers as well as transit countries and net energy importers, all of whom have subscribed to certain core principles:
  – national sovereignty over energy resources, respect for contract and property;
  – stable and open frameworks for flows of energy, capital, technology and investment;
  – an orientation towards market solutions;
  – non-discrimination;
  – transparency; and,
  – energy efficiency and sustainable development.

The first point is to underline that the main mechanism for managing interdependence is through the operation of an international energy market.

The main task for governments must be to ensure the operation of international market mechanisms. And this by putting in place predictable, transparent and non-discriminatory conditions for trade and investment. In this way, they can help to ensure that flows across borders of capital investment, of technology, and, ultimately, of energy itself are directed in the most efficient way.

More broadly, governments along the energy value chain have to create an environment that will allow the right mix of new energy technologies to emerge for use of fossil fuels and alternative energy sources.

While some interests are shared by all countries, each player along the energy value chain has interests that need to be taken into account.

The reality demonstrates that there is a mismatch between security of supply and security of demand. Within existing technology limits a resource-owning state can secure physical supply. Security of supply implies that an exporting state keeps its promises linked to supply deals and backs them. And does not misuse its sovereign position to interfere with supply deals.

Looking at the other end of the energy chain, an energy importing state cannot guarantee physical demand, which is ultimately the result of individual consumer decisions. However, exporting states will at least ask for predictability of the market framework and the rules under which energy is imported into a country. Long-term contracts with a minimum pay provision were and still are a successful model of a fair balance between security of supply and security of demand.

In addition to the efforts of national governments, an interdependent energy world needs institutions to promote coordination and to provide a stable framework for cooperation. This is precisely why the Energy Charter Treaty occupies such a valuable and distinctive place in the international legal architecture. It demonstrates that it is possible to bring a large, diverse group of countries together within a legally binding framework on the basis of common principles and mutual interest.

The Treaty is a unique, legally binding multilateral mechanism for cooperation in the energy sector, which brings together producers, transit countries and consumers of energy. Its key strength is in protecting investment and encouraging flows of energy, investment capital and technology across member countries, to mutual benefit. It provides a serious foundation for harmonising the interests of all participants, gives us – so to say – universal alphabet for energy cooperation. I would like to take a moment to present the Charter's distinctive contribution to international energy security.

The need for massive investment to meet future energy demand is well documented. But in time of global financial crisis and of extreme volatility of energy prices this represents an extremely difficult and dangerous challenge. Uncertainty about future return of investment is a very bad thing for investors, certainly when investments, as it is the case in energy, are huge and made on a long term basis. This will in no doubt scare not only the traditional actors of the energy sector, but also the financial community which in the past was positive and is now disconcerted.

Low prices, if permanent, will jeopardise some existing investments, can put a halt to planned major investments.

Those investments are nevertheless absolutely necessary for the decades to come. Their cancellation or even postponement will endanger the security of supply and in consequence the economy as a whole. In this gloomy context, long-term decisions in the energy sector need assurances that contracts and property will be respected. The Energy Charter Treaty's original binding mechanisms for investor protection, including the tested option of investor-state arbitration, are designed to provide this legal security.

The promotion of reliable transit is a key component of the Charter's work. The Charter has become a leading inter-governmental forum for exchanging information on issues such as access to transit pipelines, tariff-setting, congestion management and investment in new transit infrastructure. This is complemented by work on non-binding instruments that can facilitate new cross-border infrastructure projects, such as the Charter's Model Agreements for Cross-border Pipelines.

The Charter's work on energy efficiency is based on a special Protocol. This protocol requires its signatories to formulate strategies and policy aims, to establish appropriate legal frameworks, and to develop specific programmes for the promotion of efficient energy use and the reduction of harmful environmental practices.

Mutual benefit, recognition of and respect to each other's interests, will secure not temporary, but long-term and stable solutions.

The Energy Charter Treaty as part of International Law

The ECT is an international agreement in the meaning of the Vienna Convention on the Law of Treaties 1969. It establishes rights and obligations of CPs in a legally binding manner.

In contrast to most international treaties, article 45 expressly provides for its provisional application prior to ratification by a CP, provided that such application is not inconsistent with its internal legal order. However, according to article 45 (2), any signatory has the right, when signing the agreement, to declare that it is not able to accept provisional application. Even in the case of exclusion of provisional application, the institutional provisions of the ECT (e.g. on participation in the Charter Conference, voting rights, budget) shall remain applicable, provided that this is not inconsistent with the laws and regulations of the respective signatory.

According to article 45 (2) (b), a signatory that does not apply the ECT provisionally – and investors of this signatory – may not claim the benefits of provisional application by other signatories (principle of reciprocity).

Pursuant to article 46, no reservations may be made to this Treaty. According to article 47, each CP has the right to withdraw from the agreement at any time after five years from the date on which the ECT has entered into force for this CP. Such withdrawal shall become effective one year after the date of the receipt of the notification of withdrawal by the Depositary. However, the Treaty protects existing investments of foreign investors in the territory of the withdrawing CP for an additional period of twenty years.

Energy Security
Diversification is key to increased competition and enhanced security of supply. It is imperative that the structure of the energy sector is resilient to shocks through interconnection and diversification. This way the energy sector avoids being vulnerable to geopolitical crisis. Although there are no major problems in Europe at the moment, the turmoil in Libya shows us that it is important to rely on several partners and cooperation.

On the EU level, gas supplies are diversified along three corridors:

1. Northern Corridor from Norway.
2. Eastern Corridor from Russia.
3. Mediterranean Corridor from Africa.

But in some regions a single source dependency still prevails. The goal is an implementation of infrastructure allowing physical access to at least two different sources. The EU has identified priority corridors to achieve this objective:

1. The Southern corridor linking the EU gas market to the largest deposit of gas in the world in the Caspian/Middle East basin.
2. Linking the Baltic, Black, Adriatic and Aegean Seas.
3. North/South Corridor to remove internal bottlenecks and increase short-term deliverability.

The aim of this priority is to ensure uninterrupted crude oil supplies to land-locked EU countries in Central-Eastern Europe, currently dependent on limited supply routes. Diversification of oil supplies and interconnected pipeline networks would also help not to increase further oil transport by vessels, thus reducing the risk of environmental hazards in the particularly sensitive and busy Baltic Sea and Turkish Straits.

With both energy consumption and dependency on oil and gas imports growing and supplies becoming scarcer, the risk of supply failure is rising. Securing European energy supplies is therefore high on the EU's agenda. Besides promoting energy efficiency, the European Union promotes a broad mix of energy sources. Moreover, it aims for diversity in suppliers, transport routes and transport mechanisms. Several safeguard mechanisms shall secure energy supply for European citizens and industries: building reliable partnerships with supplier, transit and consumer countries reduces the risks of Europe's energy dependency. Member countries have to keep emergency stocks of gas and oil and ensure investments in electricity networks. A coordination mechanism has been set up so that Member States can react uniformly and immediately in emergency cases.

EU Energy Policy
The energy challenge is one of the greatest tests faced by Europe today. Rising energy prices and increasing dependence on energy imports jeopardize both security and competitiveness. Our main goal is safe, secure, sustainable and affordable energy supply for the 500 million EU citizens. Our main challenges remain: completion of internal energy market, energy investment and development and energy security.

We are committed to ensuring developments in the single market that address the energy sector, remove borders, enables the connected flow of energy and avoid segmentation.

Internal market: What do we want to achieve?
The existence of a competitive internal energy market is a strategic instrument in terms both of giving European consumers a choice between different companies supplying gas and electricity at reasonable prices, and of making the market accessible for all suppliers, especially the smallest and those investing in renewable forms of energy. Making the internal energy market a reality will depend above all on having a reliable and coherent energy network in Europe and therefore on infrastructure investment. A truly integrated market will contribute to diversification and thus to security of supply.

By opening up European energy markets to competition – a process which started ten years ago – Europe's citizens and industries have gained many benefits: more choice, more competition to keep prices down, better service and improved security of supply. Since July 2004, small-business costumers in all EU countries have been free to switch their supplier for gas and electricity; in July 2007 all consumers gained the same freedom. They are also entitled to transparent conditions in contracts and be protected from misleading practices and misinformation by suppliers.

Independent national regulatory authorities have been established in each EU country to ensure that suppliers and network companies operate correctly and actually provide the services promised to their customers. Based on yearly reports by the national regulators, the European Commission is monitoring the market closely, identifying obstacles and shortcomings. Since 2003, heads of the national energy regulatory authorities meet in the European Regulators Group for electricity and gas. It acts as an advisory group, assisting the Commission in consolidating the Internal Market for electricity and gas.

As a number of shortcomings still exist in progress towards a truly open gas market, a third legislative package was adopted by the Commission in September 2007. This recommends, among other things, the effective separation of supply and production activities, harmonisation of the powers of national regulators, better cross-border regulation and effective transparency.

The European Union is also working to improve the infrastructure required to transport energy as efficiently as possible to where it is needed. EU legislation aims to make the market accessible for all suppliers and eliminate barriers to cross-border trade. Further challenges include the harmonization of market rules, as well as the creation of an environment for new investments.

Regulation is a necessary tool to protect innovation and enforce competition. Regulations that are transparent, dynamic and fair encourage growth and progess.

The 3rd Energy Package

The "3rd energy package", an ambitious EU energy law adopted in 2009, brings more choice, investment and security of supply to the EU energy sector. A series of wide ranging rules for Europe's electricity and gas markets, the proposed measures aim to benefit every single EU citizen by giving consumers greater choice, fairer prices, cleaner energy and regional solidarity in term of security of supply. With this piece of legislation the European Union aims to make the energy market fully effective and to create a single EU gas and electricity market.

What new aims does this "package" have? The 3rd Energy package promotes effective unbundling of energy production and supply interests from the network, increases the transparency of retail markets and promotes

DIREITO COMPARADO / COMPARATIVE LAW

better cross-border collaboration and investment. More effective regulatory oversight is enforced by the establishment of the Agency for Cooperation of Energy Regulators (ACER) which will ensure cooperation between national regulatory authorities and take decisions on cross border issues.

Liberalisation of the Energy Sector

The 3rd Energy package is a step toward the liberalization of the energy sector within the European Union. The liberalization of the internal market in energy has been addressed as a means to promote growth. The European Union has identified that constraints to liberalization and open internal markets hinder growth. To achieve a higher level of liberalization we will need continued regulation of access and pricing of the natural monopoly areas and promotion of competition. In order to move forward we must identify what the main barriers to competition are, improve the functioning of energy markets and increase cross border integration. Robust efforts must be made to create a more integrated, interconnected and competitive market.

As the President of the European Commission José Manuel Barroso has stated "We need a common European response to combat climate change, the achieve greater energy security and to provide abundant energy at fair prices for citizens... This is only possible of we have a competitive and free gas and electric market."

Development of the EU energy sector mirrors the founding principals of the European Union – elimination of barriers, free flow of people and products and a free internal market.

Regulation of the Energy Sector in the United States

JOSEPH T. KELLIHER[*]

Introduction

Issues relating to energy regulation in the United States and European Union are a matter of both personal and professional interest. I am a former regulator, a former chairman of the U.S. Federal Energy Regulatory Commission (FERC or Commission); now a recovering regulator. I am now a senior officer of NextEra, one of the largest electricity companies in the United States, subject to a complex panoply of federal and state regulation.[1] Since NextEra is also one of the largest gas shippers in the United States, I remain interested in the quality and effectiveness of U.S. economic regulation of the electricity and natural gas industries.

---

[*] Executive Vice President, Federal Regulatory Affairs, NextEra Energy, Inc. (NextEra); Chairman, U.S. Federal Energy Regulatory Commission (2005-2009), Commissioner (2003-2005, 2009); B.S.F.S., Georgetown University School of Foreign Service; J.D., *magna cum laude*, American University, Washington College of Law. This Article represents the views of the author and not necessarily the views of NextEra.

[1] NextEra is a leading clean energy company with 2010 revenue of more than $15 billion, nearly 43,000 megawatts of generating capacity, and about 15,000 employees in 28 states and Canada. Headquartered in Juno Beach, Florida, NextEra's principal subsidiaries are NextEra Energy Resources, LLC, which together with its affiliated entities is the largest generator in North America of renewable energy from the wind and sun, and Florida Power & Light Company, which serves approximately 4.5 million customer accounts in Florida and is one of the largest rate-regulated electric utilities in the country. Through its subsidiaries, NextEra collectively operates the third largest U.S. nuclear power generation fleet.

I was once on the giving end of regulation and now find myself on the receiving end. It is a different perspective. I continue to read many FERC orders, and occasionally I read an order whose merits I strongly disagree with, only to notice that I voted for it. That should not be too much of a surprise. I voted for more than 7,000 orders during my tenure at FERC, and it would be height of arrogance to presume there was no possibility of error in that sea of votes.

As FERC chairman, I met frequently with European national energy regulators to discuss regulatory policy and regulatory structure. These discussions were very interesting. I was always impressed with the quality of European national regulators – they were highly qualified and dedicated public servants.

We openly discussed the U.S. regulatory experience. I frankly acknowledged which policies had worked, which had failed, and how we reacted to those failures. In our discussion of the U.S. experience, I was mindful of Winston Churchill's observation about Americans: "You can always count on the Americans to do the right thing – after they've tried everything else."[2] Much current U.S. regulatory policy could be characterized as a reaction to failed policies of the past, the product of trial and error. But it is certainly better to learn from mistakes than persist in error.[3]

EU national regulators were also open in their discussions. In particular, they raised questions such as whether there should be a "European FERC," a continental regulatory body. My former European colleagues also had many questions about the path the United States took in its journey towards competitive wholesale power markets. A frequent topic a few years ago was the California and Western power crisis. European national regulators wanted to understand both the causes of the crisis and which policies were best tailored to avoid a recurrence. I explained that the California and Western power crisis should properly be seen as a failure of regulation rather than a failure of competition.

European regulators were also very interested in the U.S. success – and lack of success – in developing a robust energy infrastructure. There was a particular interest in development of liquefied natural gas (LNG) import

---

[2] *Available at* http://brainyquote.com/quotes/quotes/w/winstonchu135259.html.
[3] NICCOLO MACHIAVELLI, THE PRINCE 124 (George Bull trans., Penguin Books 1979) (stating that an intellect that neither comprehends by itself or learns from mistakes is "useless").

projects, since Europe anticipated that it would be competing with the United States for LNG imports, a competition that now appears to have dissipated. Another area of infrastructure development of interest to European regulators was the electric transmission grid.

A common topic was the question of U.S. electric transmission open-access policy and whether the United States should have gone beyond "functional unbundling" and required ownership separation of generation and transmission. Functional unbundling involved requiring vertically integrated utilities subject to FERC's plenary jurisdiction to provide open access to their transmission network to competing wholesale power suppliers in exchange for access fees. By contrast, ownership separation requires complete vertical disaggregation such that utilities are required to divest either their generation or transmission assets. The United States elected functional unbundling rather than ownership separation.

The merits of functional unbundling versus ownership separation were clearly an issue that divided European national regulators. Some seemed to politely view the FERC functional unbundling policy as a timid half measure; others suggested the U.S. approach got it about right, while still others seemed to view it as a radical step.

We also discussed how our respective countries were trying to develop climate change policies that achieved a balance between energy and environmental policy. U.S. and EU energy regulators recognized that climate change policy is equal parts energy and environmental policy. From the point of view of U.S. and EU energy regulators, climate change policy was recognized as too important to be left to the tender mercies of environmental regulators.

I also had interesting discussions with EU regulators and market participants about European gas markets. A few years ago, I spoke at the Flame conference in Amsterdam. There was a lot of discussion about sources of gas imports to Europe, and the question was posed to the audience about which import source was more reliable – pipeline gas from Russia, imports from North Africa, or LNG imports from the Middle East. I was very surprised that the audience by lopsided margin preferred Russian gas imports, especially since the conference occurred during one of the periods where Russia had cut-off gas shipments through the Ukraine to Europe.

The reason U.S. and EU energy regulators were interested in exchanging views was that they were grappling with the same basic challenges –

how to assure security of energy supply at a reasonable cost over a period of time, while meeting environmental policy objectives. For that reason, the European experience is of as much interest to U.S. energy regulators as the U.S. experience is to Europe.

Structure of the U.S. Energy Industry
General
Although the structure of the U.S. energy industry does not dictate regulatory structure, the nature of regulation must reflect industry structure to some extent. Different regulatory structures will work better or worse depending on the structure of the industry subject to regulation.

Claiming that the regulatory regime must "reflect" industry structure does not necessarily mean that it must be designed to accommodate or preserve industry structure, only that it must be developed with some appreciation of that structure. Indeed, a regulatory regime may be expressly designed to change industry structure, such as the Public Utility Holding Company Act of 1935, which was intended to break up the large utility holding companies and restructure the U.S. electricity industry.[4] Depending on industry structure, a particular regulatory policy may have a greater or lesser chance of success.

The focus of this article is economic regulation of the energy sector in the United States. It will focus on those sectors of the U.S. energy sector subject to the greatest level of economic regulation, namely the electricity and natural gas industries, not the petroleum industry. This article will also not discuss nuclear energy regulation, which is more properly characterized as safety regulation rather than economic regulation.

Some differences in energy regulation between the United States and the European Union are to be expected, given the differences in industry structure.

Electricity Industry Structure
The U.S. electricity industry has a very complex structure – it is very heterogeneous in composition, much more so than other countries. The electricity sector is heavily vertically integrated, but vertical integration has never

---

[4] Public Utility Holding Company Act of 1935, Pub. L. No. 74-333, 49 Stat. 803 (codified at 15 U.S.C. §§ 79-79z-6) (repealed 2005).

been the absolute rule as it has been in many other countries, and still is in some countries, such as Japan. For example, for decades many distribution utilities in the United States owned no generation and little or no transmission, including most municipal utilities and rural electric cooperatives.

However, while not all utilities were vertically integrated in the sense that they owned generation as well as distribution and transmission, until 1978, electric generation was controlled almost entirely by vertically integrated enterprises. In 1978, vertically integrated utilities controlled 97% of generation, with self-generation by industrial enterprises accounting for the remainder.[5]

But competition policy, authored largely by FERC with a supporting role by the U.S. Congress, promoted development of the independent power producer sector. Since the mid-1980s, most U.S. electricity supply additions have been accounted for by independents, not vertically integrated utilities.[6]

Currently, the United States has about 1,500 generators of all types – vertically integrated utilities, independent power producers, affiliated power producers. Some generators are government utilities – federal government utilities such as the Bonneville Power Administration and Tennessee Valley Authority, state government utilities such as New York Power Authority and Lower River Colorado Authority, and municipal government utilities such as Los Angeles Department of Water and Power, and a host of smaller municipal utilities.[7] Other generators are nonprofit corporations such as rural electric generation and transmission cooperatives. Cooperatives are legally nonprofit corporations, not government agencies.[8]

In short, the U.S. generation markets has four different classes of generators: 1) independent power producers; 2) affiliated power producers, competitive companies affiliated with a vertically integrated utility; 3) for-profit vertically integrated utilities; and, 4) nonprofit utilities, both the government utilities and cooperatives.

---

[5] U.S. Dep't of Energy, The Changing Structure of the Electric Power Industry 2000: An Update 117 (2000).

[6] See Fed. Energy Regulatory Comm'n, PL04-9-000, Minutes of Technical Conference on Public Utilities' Acquisition and Disposition of Merchant Generating Assets 5 (June 10, 2004).

[7] See, e.g., Electric Power Industry Overview 2007, U.S. Energy Info. Admin., http://www.eia.gov/cneaf/electricity/page/prim2/toc2.html (last visited Mar. 14, 2015).

[8] See id.

DIREITO COMPARADO / COMPARATIVE LAW

From a national perspective, the U.S. generation sector is highly disaggregated, which provides a sound foundation for competition policy. It would be much more difficult to rely on competition to control market power exercise if control of generation were concentrated. However, the United States does not have a national electricity market, markets are regional in nature, and generation market power in some regions is more concentrated. As a general rule, generation market power is more concentrated in the European Union than the United States, which has implications for competition policy.

As a byproduct of federal competition policy, many vertically integrated utilities spun their generation out into non-utility generation affiliates.[9] That changed the nature of vertical integration in the U.S. electricity industry, but did not eliminate it. A corporate entity that owns a utility that controls both distribution and transmission, and a non-utility affiliate than owns generation is still vertically integrated.

With respect to transmission, the U.S. high-voltage power grid is relatively large – more than 200,000 miles or 321,868.8 kilometers – much more developed than the European network.[10] But the U.S. grid is highly constrained in many areas. The U.S. grid was developed largely by individual utilities to serve their retail customers, not to serve the interstate or regional market. The interconnection of local systems after the 1965 Blackout in the Eastern United States sped establishment of the interstate grid.

Although large, the U.S. power grid is not adequate to meet needs of twenty-first century. The U.S. grid is owned largely by vertically integrated utilities – 97% of grid is owned by vertically integrated utilities, 3% by independent transmission companies or transcos. That is a similarity with the European Union, where vertical integration of transmission is mostly the norm. However, there are increased efforts by new entrants to build transmission in the United States. Federal policy has long promoted independent transmission, and new policy initiatives may further promote that end.[11]

---

[9] *See* Report of the National Council on Electricity Policy: State Policies for Financing Electricity Resources 4 (2007), *available at* http://www.ncouncil.org/Documents/FINALPayingPowerPlants.pdf.

[10] U.S. DEP'T OF ENERGY, POWER ELECTRONICS RESEARCH & DEVELOPMENT: PROGRAM PLAN 3 (April 2011).

[11] *See* Promoting Transmission Investment through Pricing Reform, 71 Fed. Reg. 43,339 (July 31, 2006) (codified as amended at 18 C.F.R. § 35.35); Transmission Planning and Cost

Most countries have a handful of grid owners – the United Kingdom has a single for-profit transco, National Grid. The United States has roughly 500 owners of the interstate transmission grid. Fractured ownership of the interstate grid is perhaps the greatest weakness of the U.S. electricity industry structure. I believe we have too many grid owners, and many grid owners do not control networks of sufficient size and regional scope. Some recent U.S. electric utility mergers would create larger networks, but the rationale for these mergers was not consolidation of grid ownership and it cannot be said there is a movement to consolidate grid ownership. If anything, the United States may go in the opposite direction if there is significant new entry.

The nature of grid ownership in the United States is also important. Roughly two-thirds of the grid is owned by corporations subject to plenary FERC transmission regulation. The remaining third is owned by unregulated transmitting utilities, namely government utilities and non-profit cooperatives.[12] In some regions, such as the Western United States, unregulated utilities own 50% of the interstate power grid.

In many regions, the United States has established regional transmission organizations (RTOs) and independent system operators (ISOs) to operate the regional transmission grid and, in some cases, run day-ahead and real-time power markets. These RTOs and ISOs are typically structured as non-profit corporations.

With respect to local distribution, the United States has more than 3,000 entities that perform local distribution and make retail sales. Vertically integrated utilities account for most retail sales. For-profit, investor-owned utilities account for most retail sales, but there are a large number of state and municipal utilities and retail service (2,000) and cooperatives (900) that provide local distribution.

Competitive retail sales have developed unevenly in the United States. Not all states are open to retail competition, but retail competition is highly developed and competitive in certain states, such as Texas.

With respect to market structure, the United States does not have a national electricity market, but a series of regional markets. At the same

---

Allocation by Transmission Owning and Operating Public Utilities, 76 Fed. Reg. 49842, 49963 (Aug. 11, 2011) (codified as amended at 18 C.F.R. Pt. 35).

[12] Federal Power Act § 211A(a), 16 U.S.C. § 824j-1(a) (2010).

time, many of these regional markets are also international or North American. With political boundaries removed, a map of the North American transmission system would look as if the United States and Canada were part of the same country. The western United States is part of a regional market that encompasses western Canadian provinces and part of Mexico. New England is part of a regional market that includes eastern Canadian provinces, Quebec, and six U.S. states. New York is part of a regional market that includes Quebec and Ontario. The Midwest Independent Transmission System Operator is part of a regional market that includes Manitoba and Ontario as well as all or part of twelve U.S. states.

There are significant differences in these regional markets that go far beyond geography. Most U.S. regions have competitive wholesale power markets, but the nature of the competitive markets varies. In New England, most generation is supplied by independent power producers. There is not much vertical integration left in New England, at least in its most pure form. Independent power producers rely on the capacity market, rather than long-term contracts. The New England market is highly competitive. The New York market is similar to the New England market, with a high level of divestiture and reliance on independent power producers for its electricity supply.

In the West, generation market participants include independent power producers, for-profit utilities and non-profit utilities. The competitive wholesale market revolves largely around bilateral contracts, with good price transparency at hubs.

Other RTO regions, such as PJM, have a similar mixture of generation market participants, with a smaller role for non-profit utilities, and are competitive markets that rely on both capacity markets and long term bilateral contracts. In the Southeast, the wholesale market is relatively small and illiquid, with poor transparency, mostly long-term contracts, and surplus sales.

Wholesale power markets are workably competitive in most regions of the United States. There is relative ease of entry for many kinds of generation, particularly renewables and natural gas generation. To varying degrees, regional wholesale power markets have the characteristics of perfect competition.

Gas Industry Structure

A few things stand out about the structure of U.S. natural gas industry, especially in contrast with power industry. There is much less vertical integration in the natural gas industry than power industry.

There is a separation among natural gas producers, interstate pipelines, and local distribution companies, at least at the corporate level. Affiliation between pipelines and local distribution companies or producers is not uncommon, but vertical integration is achieved only at the holding company level. The same company does not control production, transportation, and local distribution; there are separate affiliated companies, with each company pursuing its own interest. It is not unusual for local distribution companies to contest rate increases filed by affiliated interstate natural gas pipelines. Vertical integration in the natural gas industry is not the same as in the power industry, where many utilities are vertically integrated in the classic sense, with generation, transmission, and local distribution provided by the same company.

The role of government as a market participant is much smaller in the natural gas industry than the power industry. The role of government utilities is basically limited to local distribution – there are many municipal gas utilities that provide local distribution service, but no government pipeline companies or government gas producers, by contrast with electric generation, transmission, and local distribution, where the role of government as a market participant is significant.

There are thousands of natural gas producers in the United States. Natural gas production is highly unconcentrated, and there is great ease of entry. Natural gas production in the United States has all the hallmarks of perfect competition, which is why gas production is no longer subject to economic regulation. That was not always the case. As a result of the U.S. Supreme Court decision in *Phillips*,[13] the United States attempted to regulate natural gas prices for nearly 40 years, an effort that can only charitably be described as unsuccessful.

The U.S. experience with natural gas price controls showed how economic regulation can discourage investment, retard competition, and create supply shortages. Price controls led to declining natural gas production in the United States in the 1970s. Fortunately, Congress decontrolled nat-

---

[13] Phillips Petroleum Co. v. Wisconsin, 347 U.S. 672 (1954).

ural gas prices and resolved to rely on competition to both assure security of supply and control natural gas prices.[14] Natural gas price decontrol revived domestic gas production and made the shale gas revolution in the United States possible.

The U.S. natural gas pipeline network is very robust, much more robust than the U.S. electric transmission system, spanning more than 300,000 miles, or nearly 5000,000 kilometers.[15] Likewise, the U.S. network is more robust and integrated than the European network. As was the case with the electric transmission network, the natural gas pipeline network is more properly considered a North American network rather than a U.S. network, and the United States and Canada share a highly interconnected pipeline network.

Natural gas pipelines in the United States are very large regional networks, much larger than the grid systems owned by electric utilities. There is much more ownership concentration in natural gas pipelines than in U.S. electric transmission. While the United States has 500 grid owners spanning three different classes, mostly vertically integrated, both for-profit and non-profit, and a small transco share, 30 pipelines own nearly 80% of the interstate pipeline network. All of these pipelines are for-profit corporations.

U.S. natural gas markets are regional in nature, as is the case with wholesale power markets. However, the regional natural gas markets are larger in size, more homogeneous in nature, and every regional natural gas market is workably competitive.

The development of tremendous domestic shale gas reserves is having a fundamental impact on U.S. natural gas markets. In a few short years, the United States went from being "short" of natural gas,[16] urgently developing LNG import projects, to authorizing LNG exports.[17] Shale gas production is different from traditional natural gas production, more similar

---

[14] *See* Natural Gas Policy Act of 1978, Pub. L. No. 95-621, § 121, 92 Stat. 3350, 3369 (repealed 1989); Natural Gas Wellhead Decontrol Act of 1989, Pub. L. No. 101-60, § 2, 103 Stat. 157, 157.
[15] *See About U.S. Natural Gas Pipelines*, U.S. ENERGY INFO. ADMIN., http://www.eia.gov/pub/oil_gas/natural_gas/analysis_publications/ngpipeline/index.html (last visited Mar. 14, 2015).
[16] FED. ENERGY REGULATORY COMM'N, 2006 STATE OF THE MARKETS REPORT 34 (2007) ("Global LNG supplies are crucial to the energy future of the United States.").
[17] The U.S. has long authorized LNG exports from Alaska to foreign markets. *See* U.S. ENERGY INFO. ADMIN., U.S. LNG MARKETS AND USES 3 (Jan. 2003), *available at* http://www.eia.gov/pub/oil_gas/natural_gas/feature_articles/2003/lng/lng2003.pdf.

to mining or manufacturing. Natural gas pricing, both overall price and volatility, may be affected.

One aspect of U.S. natural gas markets that is very different from Europe is the nature of the markets and natural gas pricing. The most striking difference is that in the United States the price of natural gas reflects the relative supply and demand for natural gas, while in most parts of Europe the price of natural gas is tied to oil prices, which seems an anachronism from a U.S. perspective. The United States has many liquid hubs where natural gas is traded, and there is very good price transparency in U.S. natural gas markets. Most U.S. natural gas sales are short term in nature, relying on prices set on hubs or exchanges. By contrast, Europe has few hubs, there is much less transparency in gas markets, and gas sales tend to be longer in nature.

Natural gas storage is highly developed in the United States, far more developed than gas storage capacity than Europe. FERC policy initiatives have promoted further development of U.S. gas storage capacity in recent years.[18]

Structure of U.S. Energy Regulation
Federalist Scheme of U.S. Energy Regulation
The United States has a federalist regulatory scheme for regulation of the electricity and natural gas industries. The federal government has an important role, and states also have important roles. At the inception of U.S. energy regulation more than 100 years ago, there was no federal energy regulation; regulation was limited to state and municipal governments. The first step toward federal energy regulation occurred in 1906, when the Hepburn Act amended the 1887 Interstate Commerce Act, the first federal regulatory statute in the United States.[19]

The Hepburn Act was one of the accomplishments of the great reformer President, Theodore Roosevelt.[20] The original Interstate Commerce Act

---

[18] Rate Regulation of Certain Natural Gas Storage Facilities, 71 Fed. Reg. 36,612, 36,636 (June 27, 2006) (codified as amended at 18 C.F.R. Pt. 284) (allowing market based pricing for storage projects to facilitate the development of new gas storage capacity).

[19] Hepburn Act, ch. 3591, 34 Stat. 584 (1906) (codified as amended in scattered sections of 49 U.S.C.).

[20] LEWIS L. GOULD, THE PRESIDENCY OF THEODORE ROOSEVELT 164-5 (1st ed. 1991); H.W. BRANDS, TR: THE LAST ROMANTIC 546-48 (1997). The bulk of U.S. energy regulatory law

DIREITO COMPARADO / COMPARATIVE LAW

was designed to control the abuses of the railroads. The original law proved largely ineffective, and the Hepburn Act gave it teeth and expanded the scope of the Act beyond railroads to include oil pipelines. This was part of the federal government's attempts at the turn of the last century to regulate the large U.S. oil monopolies. Subsequent energy regulatory laws were modeled on the Interstate Commerce Act, as amended by the Hepburn Act.

But the real impetus for federal energy regulation was a U.S. Supreme Court decision that blocked state attempts to regulate interstate commerce, namely the *Attleboro* decision.[21] The *Attleboro* decision held that states could not regulate interstate commerce in electricity.[22] By properly barring state attempts to regulate interstate commerce, a field reserved to Congress and the federal government by the U.S. Constitution, a regulatory gap ensued. The Supreme Court barred state regulation of interstate commerce in natural gas on the same constitutional grounds.[23]

Congress filled that gap with two New Deal laws, the Federal Power Act of 1935 and its fraternal twin, the Natural Gas Act of 1938. Importantly, those laws did more than fill the "*Attleboro* gap." They established new federal powers not implicated in *Attleboro*. These New Deal laws laid down the jurisdictional split between federal and state regulators. In the area of electric regulation, the federal government was made responsible for wholesale power sales and the transmission of electric power in interstate commerce,[24] and granted other authorities.[25] States were responsible for retail sales and local distribution.[26] In the area of natural gas regula-

---

as it relates to the electricity and natural gas industries can be traced to two presidential families, the Roosevelts and the Bushes. The Hepburn Act and federal hydropower law were largely shaped by President Theodore Roosevelt, the Federal Power Act and Natural Gas Act were enacted by President Franklin D. Roosevelt, while the Energy Policy Act of 1992 and Energy Policy Act of 2005 were enacted by President George H.W. Bush and President George W. Bush.

[21] Pub. Utilities Comm'n v. Attleboro Steam Co., 273 U.S. 83 (1927).

[22] *Id.* at 90.

[23] Missouri v. Kansas Gas Co., 265 U.S. 298 (1924).

[24] Federal Power Act § 201(a), 16 U.S.C. § 824 (2010).

[25] These additional authorities include the authority to review mergers and asset sales, Federal Power Act § 203, 16 U.S.C. § 824b (2010), and approve security issuances, Federal Power Act § 204, 16 U.S.C. § 824c (2010).

[26] Federal Power Act § 201(b)(1), 16 U.S.C. § 824(b)(1) (2010).

tion, the federal government was made responsible for wholesale natural gas sales and interstate transportation of natural gas.[27] Consistent with the jurisdictional divide in electric regulation, states were responsible for retail sales and local distribution.[28] By and large, those remain the jurisdictional boundaries between federal and state energy regulation in the United States today.

To be clear, there is no constitutional limitation on federal regulatory authority in this area. The federal government could completely displace state energy regulation. The state regulatory role exists more for practical and political reasons than legal reasons; the federal government has never seen any reason to seek to wholly displace state regulation of the electricity and natural gas sectors.

However, the jurisdictional boundaries between federal and state governments are pressured by a number of factors, including market changes, structural change within the industry, as well as technological developments. Currently, the traditional jurisdictional boundaries are tested by smart grid deployment, demand response and energy efficiency, and distributed generation.

While jurisdictional boundaries remain largely where they were placed in the 1930s, the relative importance of the state and federal regulatory role has shifted over time, largely due to market changes. Simply put, as wholesale power sales became a relatively larger part of the total electricity market over time, FERC regulation became relatively more important. This is not to say that there have not been some adjustments to the jurisdictional boundaries laid down 75 years ago that expanded federal authority, just that most of the growth in the federal regulatory role compared to the state regulatory role resulted from changes in markets rather than changes in law.

Ongoing market and technological developments threaten to continue that trend. In some cases legislation has been enacted or proposed to expand the federal role to accommodate these developments. For example, smart grid devices will likely be deployed across the jurisdictional boundaries that have long demarcated federal and state responsibility. For that reason, the Energy Independence and Security Act of 2007 granted

---

[27] Natural Gas Act § 1(b), 15 U.S.C. § 717(b) (2010).
[28] *Id.* § 1(c).

DIREITO COMPARADO / COMPARATIVE LAW

FERC authority to set smart grid standards, even for smart grid devices that would be attached to otherwise nonjurisdictional facilities such as local distribution facilities, otherwise subject to state jurisdiction, or home appliances, not otherwise subject to economic regulation.[29]

Demand response is another development that tests jurisdictional boundaries. Some demand response advocates believe the greatest value for demand response would likely be achieved by reducing consumption during peak periods in response to high wholesale prices. However, many states do not allow market pricing for retail electricity, preferring to set regulated rates that do not vary based on time of day or demand level. Energy efficiency advocates have pushed for a larger federal role in order to accelerate progress towards improved energy efficiency. As a result, Congress has considered legislation to expand the authority of the federal government in this area at the expense of states.[30]

The growth of distributed resources raise questions about jurisdiction over the local distribution system. For 75 years, FERC has had jurisdiction over transmission, while states have retained jurisdiction over local distribution. However, the distinction between these two categories of facilities has never been entirely clear and the same facilities can be used for both transmission and local distribution. To some extent, local distribution is defined by point of reference to transmission and generation; local distribution takes power from the interstate grid and delivers it to retail customers. That distinction is threatened by distributed resources, which can turn a retail consumer into a wholesale seller. If local distribution is usually considered the delivery network between the wholesale network and retail customers, the expansion of distributed resources and use of local distribution to make wholesale sales by retail customers, could invite FERC regulation of network access.[31]

Federal and state jurisdictional boundaries do vary in some important respects between the electricity and natural gas regulation. One important difference relates to siting. FERC has exclusive jurisdiction over the

---

[29] Energy Independence and Security Act of 2007, Pub. L. No. 110-140, § 1305(d), 121 Stat. 1492, 1787 (codified as amended at 42 U.S.C. § 17385).

[30] American Clean Energy and Security Act of 2009, H.R. 2454, 111th Cong. §§ 101, 201 (2009).

[31] Nat'l Ass'n of Regulatory Utility Comm'rs v. FERC, 475 F.3d 1277, 1282 (D.C. Cir. 2007).

siting of interstate pipelines, and has had that authority since 1947.[32] That process works very efficiently, and has produced a very robust network.[33] As a case in point, the largest natural gas pipeline built in the United States in recent years was the REX West pipeline. That project was 713 miles or 1,148 kilometers long and crossed five states.[34] Yet, FERC was able to site the project in 11 months.[35] Another large gas pipeline was the MidContinent Express project, which was more than 500 miles and 800 kilometers long and crossed five states.[36] FERC sited that project in nine months.[37] By contrast, it took 13 years to site a 90 mile or 144 kilometer high-voltage electric transmission project between two states under state siting.[38]

The United States relies principally on state and local siting for electric transmission facilities. In those states that lack a state siting body, siting decisions for interstate transmission projects are made by local governments. In my view, exclusive reliance on state and local siting of interstate electric transmission facilities does not work and will never succeed. It takes too long, the outcome is too uncertain, and the process tends to be highly politicized, with decisions rooted in politics rather than merit. Differences in the siting process help explain why the U.S. natural gas pipeline network is so much more robust than our interstate power grid. I believe there is a need to reform electric transmission siting to establish effective federal siting.

---

[32] Natural Gas Amendments of 1947, Act of July 25, 1947, ch. 333, 61 Stat. 459 (codified as amended at 15 U.S.C. § 717f(h)).

[33] Between 1997 and 2002, FERC sited 9,316 miles of interstate natural gas pipelines. *Approved Pipeline Projects (1997-2002)*, FED. ENERGY REGULATORY COMM'N, http://www.ferc.gov/industries/gas/indus-act/pipelines/approvedprojects.asp (last visited Mar. 14, 2015) [hereinafter *FERC Pipeline Siting Review*]. By contrast, between 2000 and 2007, states sited 668 miles of cross-border lines 230 kV and higher. Fed. Energy Regulatory Comm'n, Electric Transmission Siting, presentation (2007), slide 2, *available at* http://www.ferc.gov/industries/electric/indus-act/siting/transsiting-present.pdf.

[34] *See FERC Pipeline Siting Review, supra* note 33.

[35] *Id.*

[36] *Id.*

[37] *Id.*

[38] *See* Wyoming-Jackson Ferry 765-kV Project, *available at* http://www.aep.com/about/transmission/Wyoming-Jacksons_Ferry.aspx; *see also* Presentation, Rockies Express Pipeline: REX-West Project, Item No. C-2 (Sept. 21, 2006), *available at* http://www.ferc.gov/EventCalendar/Files/20060921112558-C-2.pdf.

While the exclusive siting regime for interstate natural gas pipelines has been a proven success, it may not be necessary to establish an exclusive federal process for siting electric transmission. States are relatively efficient at siting electric transmission facilities needed by a state regulated utility to serve regulated customers in that state. However, there is a class of transmission projects that is not efficiently sited by state and local governments, namely backbone transmission projects designed to serve a region, rather than just the customers of the local utility. The benefits of these projects typically extend to multiple states, yet the broader the region that benefits the more difficult it is to secure approval in the siting state or states.

Other differences in the character of electricity and natural gas regulation result more from differences in industry structure than differences in statutory authority. As noted above, there is much less vertical integration in the natural gas industry than the electricity industry. The natural gas industry structure aligns neatly along jurisdictional lines. Even where an enterprise is vertically integrated, there is corporate separation among gas production, transportation, and distribution that makes regulation more effective.

Natural gas producers have been deregulated, at least with respect to economic regulation. Interstate natural gas pipelines are regulated by FERC. Local distribution companies are either regulated by the states or unregulated. In the case of municipal governmental natural gas utilities, such local distribution companies are self-regulated. This tidy alignment of industry structure with jurisdictional boundaries reduces the prospect of conflict between federal and state energy regulators. As a result, there is much less tension in federal and state regulation when it comes to natural gas regulation than electric regulation.

The foundation for federal energy regulation in the United States is the Commerce Clause of the U.S. Constitution.[39] For that reason, federal electric and natural gas regulation does not extend to those states and island territories where there is no interstate commerce in electricity or natural gas, namely Hawaii, Alaska, Guam American Samoa, the Virgin Islands, and Puerto Rico. Conflict between federal and state energy regulation is usually resolved by application of the Supremacy Clause,

---

[39] *See* U.S. CONST. art. I, § 8, cl. 3.

resulting in state preemption.[40] Even though the jurisdictional boundaries were laid down 75 years ago, legal tests of federal and state jurisdiction continue.[41]

There is a peculiar limitation on federal electricity regulatory authority in Texas, which is interconnected with the lower 48 and does engage in interstate commerce in electricity. There is a provision in U.S. electricity law that limits the ability of the federal government to regulate interstate commerce in electricity in Texas.[42] The origins of this provision are the "midnight wiring" in Texas in the late 1970s.[43] Since Texas did not want to be subject to federal electricity regulation, a political deal in 1978 created a legal fiction that Texas does not engage in interstate commerce in electricity, and is thereby not subject to plenary electricity regulation by FERC.[44] Texas was an independent nation for nine years between 1836 and 1845, and that experience is seared into the Texas consciousness. Texas later entered the Union by treaty, the only state to do so, and I have always suspected that Texas considered this treaty to be a merger of equals.[45] This aspect of federal electricity law seems to bear that out.

Federal energy regulation in the United States is entrusted to FERC, a relatively old agency that was originally established in 1920 as the Federal Water Power Commission. The original mission of the agency was a pure infrastructure role, licensing hydropower projects as fast as it pos-

---

[40] *See id.* art. VI, cl. 2. Section 204 of the Federal Power Act is a rare instance of "reverse preemption," where federal law provides that state law preempts federal law with respect to review of utility security issuances. Federal Power Act § 204(f), 16 U.S.C. § 824c(f) (2010).

[41] *Nat'l Ass'n of Regulatory Utility Comm'rs*, 475 F.3d at 1282; New York v. FERC, 535 U.S. 1, 4-5 (2002).

[42] Federal Power Act § 201(e), 16 U.S.C. § 824(e) (2010). The parenthetical "(other than facilities subject to such jurisdiction solely by reason of section 210, 211, or 212)" was inserted into section 201(e) by PURPA. Public Utility Regulatory Policies Act of 1978, Pub. L. No. 95–617, § 204(b)(2), 92 Stat. 3117, 3140. Section 201(e) defines "public utility," which is the principal entity subject to FERC jurisdiction under the Act. This change had the effect of exempting Texas from FERC regulation when its interconnection with the rest of the United States was required by interconnection and wheeling orders. In essence, Texas does engage in interstate commerce, but only under compulsion of FERC orders, however nominal.

[43] Richard D. Cudahy, *The Second Battle of the Alamo: The Midnight Connection*, 10 Nat. Resources & Env't 56, 85 (1995).

[44] *Id.*

[45] Joint Resolution for the Admission of Texas into the Union, H.R.J. Res. 1, 29th Cong., 9 Stat. 108, 108 (1845).

261

sibly could. That mission has steadily expanded over time. Congress has expanded the infrastructure mission to include a broader range of facilities and added new missions such as economic regulation, safety, enforcement, and electric reliability. FERC is the primary energy policymaker in the federal government, at least with respect to electricity and natural gas markets.

In the 1930s, the Federal Power Act and Natural Gas Act expanded the FERC mission, establishing an economic regulatory role for the first time.[46] Economic regulation of oil pipelines was not entrusted to FERC until 1978, with enactment of the Department of Energy Organization Act of 1977, which transferred this function from the Interstate Commerce Commission.[47]

As mentioned, the scope of the FERC infrastructure role has been expanded over time. The siting of natural gas pipelines and storage projects was added in 1949,[48] and a limited role in siting electric transmission projects was added in 2005.[49] Over time, FERC has been entrusted with additional authority and new missions. A safety mission with respect to hydropower projects was established by the agency in the 1960s. In 2005, Congress entrusted FERC with enforcement powers and a new electricity reliability role in the Energy Policy Act of 2005.[50]

This article only addresses FERC's economic regulatory mission, not the other missions. The principal object of FERC's economic regulatory mission is well settled, namely to "guard the consumer from exploitation."[51] That mission has not changed over the past 75 years. What has changed dramatically, as discussed below, is the manner in which FERC discharges this duty.

---

[46] *See* Federal Power Act, ch. 687, 49 Stat. 863 (1935) (codified as amended at 16 U.S.C. § 791a et seq.); Natural Gas Act, ch. 556, 52 Stat. 821 (1938).

[47] Department of Energy Organization Act, Pub. L. No. 95-91, § 402(b), 91 Stat. 565, 584 (1977) (codified as amended at 42 U.S.C. § 7173(b)).

[48] *See supra* note 32 and accompanying text.

[49] Energy Policy Act of 2005, Pub. L. No. 109-58, § 1221, 119 Stat. 594, 946 (codified as amended at 16 U.S.C. § 824p(b) (2005)).

[50] *Id.* §§ 1284(e), 1211, 16 U.S.C. §§ 316A, 824o (2010).

[51] NAACP v. Federal Power Comm'n, 520 F.2d 432, 438 (D.C. Cir. 1975) ("[o]f the Commission's primary task there is no doubt, however, and that is to guard the consumer from exploitation").

Notwithstanding its name, the U.S. Department of Energy (DOE) has virtually no energy regulatory authority. Historically, the primary function of the DOE was the design, testing, and manufacture of nuclear weapons. Now, the DOE is focused on its important science mission, as well as on environmental mitigation and remediation of the sites where it used to manufacture nuclear weapons. The DOE's primary energy function is energy research and development, which could be considered an aspect of its broader science mission. The DOE is charged with development of national energy policy, but has little ability to implement such policy.[52]

The federalist scheme of energy regulation in the United States does not have a parallel in the European Union. However, as the European Union seeks to establish continental energy markets it may find that it needs a continental regulator to accompany those markets. If so, the U.S. experience with federalist regulatory schemes may be relevant to Europe as it considers how to promote and effectively regulate continental energy markets while retaining national regulators.

Competition Policy

Competition policy has been the foundation of federal electricity and natural gas regulatory policy for nearly 30 years. Competition policy is not only long-standing, it has deep roots. Three federal laws that establish or ratify competition policy with respect to wholesale power markets, the Public Utility Regulatory Policies Act of 1978 (PURPA),[53] the Energy Policy Act of 1992,[54] and the Energy Policy Act of 2005.[55] Two federal laws enacted during this period established competition in natural gas markets, the Natural Gas Policy Act of 1978 and the Natural Gas Wellhead Decontrol Act of 1989.[56] Competition policy is bipartisan, supported by both Republicans and Democrats. Every FERC chair during this period

---

[52] 42 U.S.C. § 7112 (2010).

[53] Pub. L. No. 95-617, 92 Stat. 3117 (1978) (codified as amended at 16 U.S.C. §§ 824a-1 to a-3, 824i-k, 2601-2645, and scattered sections of 16 and 42 U.S.C.).

[54] Pub. L. No. 102-486, §§ 711, 721, 106 Stat. 2776, 2906, 2915 (1992) (codified at 15 U.S.C. § 79z-5a (repealed 2005) and amending 16 U.S.C. § 824j).

[55] Pub. L. No. 109-58, §§ 1221, 1231, 1241, 1253, 1281, 1283, 1284(e), 119 Stat. 946, 955, 961, 967, 978-980 (2005) (codified as amended at 16 U.S.C. § 824p(b), 824j-1, 824s, 824a-3, 824u, 824v, 825o-1).

[56] *See supra* note 14.

has supported competition policy, and every U.S. president since Jimmy Carter has either embraced or accepted competition policy as the foundation for energy regulation of the electricity and natural gas industries in the United States.

At its core, competition policy is directed at assuring adequate electricity and natural gas supply at a reasonable price by reliance on competitive forces. It pursues this end by adopting regulatory means to prevent exercise of market power and promote effective competition, such as requiring open access to the interstate electric and natural gas networks. This reliance on regulatory means contrasts with the approach of antitrust and competition authorities, which favor structural remedies such as divestiture. Competition policy restrains market power exercise through regulation so that competition is effective, and then relies largely on competitive forces to assure just and reasonable wholesale power and natural gas prices.

The great regulatory economist, the late Alfred Kahn, put it well when he described all markets as being governed by a mixture of regulation and competition.[57] Competition policy relies on a mixture of competition and regulation, and that mixture changes as markets change. The challenge of regulatory policy is to find the best possible mixture of the two.[58]

However, other than natural gas production, competition policy in the power and gas sectors does not rely exclusively on competition, and regulation is essential to police market power. For that reason, under competition policy regulation of the electricity and natural gas sectors has certainly changed, but it has not disappeared. In short, competition policy relies on both competition and regulation. Despite widespread perceptions to the contrary, "deregulation" has never been the policy of the U.S. government with respect to electricity and natural gas markets. The United States has never relied solely on competition to produce just and reasonable rates.

Literally, "deregulation" means the absence of regulation. The best proof that the United States never deregulated is a review of mountain of evidence that FERC never stopped regulating wholesale power markets. The FERC regulatory role has certainly changed over time. Thirty years ago, FERC wholesale power regulation largely consisted of setting whole-

---

[57] 2 ALFRED E. KAHN, THE ECONOMICS OF REGULATION: PRINCIPLES AND INSTITUTIONS iii (MIT Press 1988) (1971).
[58] *Id.* at iii, 113-14.

sale power rates for individual sellers through cost-of-service regulation, more properly seen as profit-level regulation, since classic-rate regulation is much more effective in controlling profit levels than cost of service.[59] Market power exercise was prevented by setting rates for each seller that were not "unjust and unreasonable."[60]

Now, FERC approves market rules, prevents market power exercise through market based rate authorization and regional market rules. FERC polices market behavior through a market manipulation rule,[61] and enforces its rules with enforcement authority that allows it to impose civil penalties of $1 million per day per violation.[62] By no means can this panoply of regulation be considered "deregulation." The FERC regulatory role is certainly different than it was thirty years ago – but not smaller. In many respects, wholesale power sales are subject to greater regulation than in the distant past when there were no regional market rules, no reporting requirements relating to market-based rate authorization, no market manipulation rule, and no civil penalty authority in the event of violations.

Competition policy was produced through a collaboration of FERC and the Congress. There was a synergism between the two branches of the federal government, each pursuing the same end and taking steps at different points in time, frequently alternating from one to the other. But when Congress acted, it acted in a manner that showed it viewed FERC as its partner in this enterprise, convinced that FERC had the same objective in mind, since congressional action generally granted FERC discretionary power to promote competition, authorizing FERC to act rather than requiring FERC to do so.

FERC established competition in wholesale power sales by authorizing public utilities to charge market-based rates rather than cost-based rates determined through classic cost-of-service ratemaking, once a seller proved it lacked market power and agreed to certain conditions. Competi-

---

[59] *Id.* at 26-31.

[60] Federal Power Act §§ 205-206, 16 U.S.C. §§ 824d-824e (2010); Natural Gas Act §§ 4-5, 15 U.S.C. §§ 717c-717d (2010); Joseph T. Kelliher, *Market Manipulation, Market Power, and the Authority of the Federal Energy Regulatory Commission*, 26 ENERGY L.J. 1, 4 (2005).

[61] Prohibition of Energy Market Manipulation, 71 Fed. Reg. 4244, 4258 (Jan. 26, 2006) (codified as amended at 18 C.F.R. Pt. 1c).

[62] Federal Power Act § 316A, 16 U.S.C. § 825o-1 (2010); Natural Gas Act § 21, 15 U.S.C. § 717t (2010); Natural Gas Policy Act of 1978 § 504(c), 15 U.S.C. § 3414(c) (2010).

DIREITO COMPARADO / COMPARATIVE LAW

tion policy led FERC to take steps to assure open grid access, since whole-sale competition could not succeed if the vertically integrated utilities that owned most of the grid could exercise vertical market power against potential competitors.[63] It also led FERC to approve a host of market rules[64] and, ultimately, adopt rules to prevent market manipulation.[65]

Competition in wholesale natural gas markets was sparked by natural gas price decontrol legislation enacted by Congress.[66] FERC acted to make this competition effective competition by requiring interstate natural gas pipelines to unbundle transportation from wholesale gas sales and offer transportation to nonaffiliates on a nondiscriminatory basis.[67] With that step, FERC could rely on intense competition among natural gas producers to produce effective competition.

Congress took the first step in the development of competition policy, both with regard to wholesale power and natural gas markets. The Public Utility Regulatory Policies Act of 1978 (PURPA) promoted competition in wholesale power markets, but only by accident.[68] PURPA included provisions to promote non-utility generation through mandatory purchases of power produced by qualifying facilities.[69] However, the policy goal that was pursued was not the promotion of competition, but the promotion of renewable energy and energy efficiency.[70] Arguably, PURPA failed to meet its express objectives, but the law did create a new class of non-utility generators that was a necessary foundation for competitive markets. PURPA did include a provision that was manifestly intended to promote competition by allowing transmission customers to request wheeling

---

[63] *See* Joseph T. Kelliher, Comment, *Pushing the Envelope: Development of Federal Electric Transmission Access Policy*, 42 AM. U. L. REV. 543, 548-49 (1993).

[64] *See* Kelliher, *supra* note 60, at 11.

[65] *See supra* note 61.

[66] *See supra* note 14.

[67] *Restructuring of Interstate Natural Gas Pipeline Services*, 59 FERC ¶ 61,030 (Order No. 636) (codified at 18 C.F.R. Pt. 284) (1992), *order on reh'g*, 60 FERC ¶ 61,102 (Order No. 636-A), *order on reh'g*, 61 FERC ¶ 61,272 (Order No. 636-B), *reh'd denied*, 62 FERC ¶ 61,007 (1993), *aff'd in part and remanded in part sub. Nom, United Distrib. Cos. v. FERC*, 88 F.3d 1105 (D.C. Cir. 1996), *cert. denied, Associated Gas Distrib. v. FERC*, 520 U.S. 1224 (1997), *order on remand*, 78 FERC ¶ 61,186 (Order No 636-C), *order on reh'g*, 83 FERC ¶ 61,210 (Order No. 636-D)(1998).

[68] Public Utility Regulatory Policies Act of 1978, Pub. L. No. 95-617, 92 Stat. 3117.

[69] *Id.* § 210, 16 U.S.C. § 824a-3 (2010).

[70] *Id.* § 2, 16 U.S.C. § 2601 (2010).

across utility transmission systems.[71] However, the wheeling provisions of PURPA proved ineffective.[72] The first step towards promoting competition in wholesale natural gas markets was also taken by Congress, through enactment of partial natural gas price decontrol in the Natural Gas Policy Act of 1978.[73]

In the 1980s, FERC began authorizing market-based sales of wholesale power on an experimental basis, and imposing transmission open access conditions to mergers and market-based rate authorizations. FERC also developed open access policies with respect to natural gas transportation,[74] resulting in its landmark pipeline unbundling order.[75]

Congress acted again, including provisions in the Energy Policy Act of 1992 designed to promote competition in wholesale power markets, reforming the PURPA wheeling provisions and creating a new class of non-utility wholesale power competitors, exempt wholesale generators.[76] Encouraged by the policy support for competition policy, FERC issued its landmark transmission open access order.[77]

What is remarkable is that competition policy was not seriously threatened by the California and Western power crisis of 2000-2001. During the crisis, FERC was criticized for not acting to prevent market manipulation

---

[71] *Id.* § 203 (adding new section 211 to Federal Power Act, codified at 16 U.S.C. § 824j (2010)).

[72] Kelliher, *supra* note 63, at 550-52.

[73] *See* Pub. L. No. 95-621, § 121, 92 Stat. 3350, 3369 (repealed 1989).

[74] *Regulation of Natural Gas Pipelines After Partial Wellhead Decontrol*, 50 Fed. Reg. 42,408 (Order No. 436)(Oct. 18, 1985), FERC Stats. & Regs. ¶ 30,665 (1985), *vacated and remanded, Associated Gas Distrib. v. FERC*, 824 F.2d 981 (D.C. Cir. 1987), *cert. denied*, 485 U.S. 1006 (1988), *readopted on an interim basis*, Order No. 500, 52 Fed. Reg. 30,334 (Aug. 14, 1987), FERC Stats. & Regs. ¶ 30,761, *remanded, American Gas Ass'n v. FERC*, 888 F.2d 136 (D.C. Cir. 1989), *readopted*, Order No. 500-H, 54 Fed. Reg. 52,344 (Dec. 21, 1989), FERC Stats. & Regs. ¶ 30,867 (1989), *reh'g granted in part and denied in part*, Order No. 500-I, 55 Fed. Reg. 6605, FERC Stats. & Regs. ¶ 30,880 (1990), *aff'd in part and remanded in part, American Gas Ass'n v. FERC*, 912 F.2d 1496 (D.C. Cir. 1990), *cert. denied*, 498 U.S. 1084 (1991).

[75] *See supra* note 67 and accompanying text.

[76] Pub. L. No. 102-486, §§ 711, 721, 106 Stat. 2776, 2906, 2915 (1992) (codified at 15 U.S.C. § 79z-5a (repealed 2005) and amending 16 U.S.C. § 824j).

[77] *Promoting Wholesale Competition Through Open Access Nondiscriminatory Transmission Services by Public Utilities; Recovery of Stranded Costs by Public Utilities and Transmitting Utilities*, 61 Fed. Reg. 21540 (Order No. 888)(1996), FERC Stats. & Regs. ¶ 31,036 (1996), *aff'd in relevant part sub nom. Transmission Access Policy Study Group v. FERC*, 225 F.3d 667 (D.C. Cir. 2000), *aff'd sub nom. New York v. FERC*, 535 U.S. 1 (2002).

DIREITO COMPARADO / COMPARATIVE LAW

and not imposing civil penalties, generally without regard for the fact that market manipulation was not barred by federal electricity law and FERC lacked any effective civil penalty authority in this area. President George W. Bush was resolved to prevent another power crisis and proposed legislation to fill these gaps and provide FERC with authority to sanction market manipulation and impose civil penalties,[78] and Congress agreed, enacting the Energy Policy Act of 2005.[79]

As a matter of legislative draftsmanship it would have been a simple matter to abandon competition policy, a few words dropped in the Federal Power Act that limited "just and reasonable" rates to rates determined through cost-of-service ratemaking. But not only did that not happen, it was never even proposed. Instead, Congress focused on improving competition policy, perhaps because it had helped author competition policy over the years. In my view, if competition policy can survive the California and Western power crisis, it is likely to survive any other test that is likely to be presented in the future.

The history of the development of competition policy in the U.S. shows that sometimes the most significant and long-enduring changes in government policy can be achieved by a series of incremental reforms pursued on a bipartisan basis over time, rather than a single revolutionary and bold stroke that enjoys support from only one political party.

The true legal foundation for competition policy is not these relatively modern laws, but the original electricity and natural gas regulatory laws enacted in the 1930s, the Federal Power Act and Natural Gas Act.[80] FERC reinterpreted provisions in these laws decades after enactment and found new meaning that had previously escaped them, allowing the agency to authorize market-based rate sales of wholesale power and require nondiscriminatory access to pipeline networks and the interstate transmission grid.[81]

---

[78] Letter from the Hon. Dan Brouillette, Assistant Sec'y of Energy for Congressional and Inter-governmental Affairs, U.S. Dep't of Energy, to Senator Jeff Bingaman, Chairman, S. Comm. on Energy and Natural Resources 2 (Oct. 9, 2001).

[79] Pub. L. No. 109-58, §§ 1221, 1231, 1241, 1253, 1281, 1283, 1284(e), 119 Stat. 946, 955, 961, 967, 978-980 (2005) (codified as amended at 16 U.S.C. § 824p(b), 824j-1, 824s, 824a-3, 824u, 824v, 825o-1).

[80] *See supra* note 46.

[81] Federal Power Act §§ 205, 206, 15 U.S.C. §§ 824d, 824e (2010); Natural Gas Act § 5, 15 U.S.C. § 717d (2010).

The modern laws effectively ratified these reinterpretations of relatively old law, while granting new authority.

The question often arises as to whether competition policy has been a success in the United States. In the end, it may be difficult to answer the question to anyone's complete satisfaction because it involves a counter-factual – what would wholesale power and natural gas markets look like today if FERC had never authorized market-based rate wholesale power sales and opened up the power grid and pipeline network, and Congress had never decontrolled gas prices? The California and Western power crisis was seen by many as a failure of competition. To the contrary, the crisis was much more a failure of regulation than a failure of competition, mostly failed state regulation in California.

Competition policy in the United States has been a great success. At the most basic level, it has produced adequate supplies of electricity and natural gas at reasonable prices over a sustained period. It has given customers more choice, both of wholesale power sellers and natural gas sellers. Competition policy has strengthened the infrastructure, both the pipeline network and power grid. Competition puts much greater down-ward pressure on costs than classic cost-of-service ratemaking, which effec-tively polices profit margins rather than cost. Importantly, competition shifted risk from the consumer to market participants. Competition pol-icy is also a sounder foundation for the ongoing transition in the United States toward clean energy than classic rate regulation.

However, competition policy remains a work in progress. If competi-tion policy is a pursuit of the perfect balance between reliance on regu-lation and competitive forces, that balance must continue to change as markets develop. Competition policy cannot be static. There is also a need to defend competition policy from political interference designed to affect market outcomes, such as lowering wholesale prices through state-sanc-tioned exercise of buyer market power. The temptation to allow consum-ers to choose at will between the lower of market and regulated outcomes remains, but markets cannot succeed on that basis. FERC remains com-mitted to protecting the integrity of competition policy.[82]

---

[82] *See* PJM Interconnection, L.L.C., 135 FERC ¶ 61,022 (2011) (reforming Minimum Offer Price Rule to prevent downward price manipulation orchestrated by State of New Jersey).

Changes in U.S. Energy Regulatory Policy

It may be useful to examine how energy policy changes in the United States. There is a natural tendency to believe that there is only one path for such change – enactment of new law. But the discussion above of how competition policy developed in the United States shows that that assumption is not correct. In the United States, there are three paths for changes in regulatory policy – enactment of new law by Congress and the President, implementation and reinterpretation of new and existing law by regulatory agencies, and judicial review of agency decisions by federal courts.[83]

Congress has played a very significant role in the development of energy regulatory policy in the United States for decades. As noted earlier, the energy industry was one of the first sectors subject to federal regulation. Congress will likely continue to play a leadership role in the future in this area, although the prospects of enactment of major new laws in the near term are at best uncertain.

But implementation and administration of a law is not a "paint by numbers" exercise; it involves the exercise of discretion by a regulatory agency. When reading a statute, it may be clear what an agency is required to do and what it is barred from doing. What may be less clear is what it *may* do, depending on how well or badly the statute is written, how expansively the agency chooses to interpret statutory language, and the level of legal risk it is willing to assume, when considering the prospect of judicial challenge to that interpretation.

As a general rule, laws written during the New Deal grant a regulatory agency more discretion than more modern regulatory statutes. A review of the Federal Power Act[84] with the Telecommunications Act of 1996[85] and the Clean Air Act Amendments of 1990[86] would lead a reader to conclude that these laws were written by two entirely different legislative bodies. In a sense, they were. The 74th Congress that enacted the Federal Power Act displayed a much greater confidence and trust in regulatory agencies than the 101st and 104th Congresses that adopted the Clean Air Act Amend-

---

[83] *See generally* Joseph T. Kelliher & Maria Farinella, *The Changing Landscape of Federal Energy Law*, 61 ADMIN. L. REV. 611, 624-51 (2009).

[84] 16 U.S.C. §§ 824-824w (2010).

[85] Pub. L. No. 104-104, 110 Stat. 56 (1996).

[86] Pub. L. No. 101-549, 104 Stat. 2399 (1990).

ments and Telecommunications Act. These later laws manifest a level of distrust and suspicion of regulatory agencies.

Another general rule is that the more poorly a law is written, the more license it gives a regulatory agency to interpret that law creatively, since courts will generally only reverse an agency's interpretation of an ambiguous statute if that interpretation is unreasonable, the agency's interpretation does not have to be the most reasonable reading of the law.[87]

In fact, the biggest changes in U.S. energy regulatory policy with respect to the electricity industry over the past 30 years involved decisions by FERC, not Congress. In both cases, these changes resulted from FERC's reinterpretation of a statute adopted a half-century earlier or more to find an entirely new meaning. In the first case, in the 1980s, FERC found that a "just and reasonable" rate was not limited to rates set by classic cost-of-service ratemaking and that a rate set by market forces could be considered "just and reasonable," as required by the Federal Power Act, if the seller lacked market power.[88] In the second instance, in 1996, FERC found that its authority to prevent undue discrimination and preference in the provision of transmission service of electric energy in interstate commerce allowed it to require jurisdictional transmission owners to file open access tariffs and provide nondiscriminatory transmission service to their competitors.[89] These fulsome reinterpretations of relatively old laws have been examined by the federal courts and upheld.[90]

The courts play an active role in shaping U.S. energy regulatory policy as well. One might suspect that this role is characterized by restraint, that when courts act, they act to preserve the status quo and reprove agency reinterpretations of existing law. But that is not the case. Courts are as likely to expand U.S. regulatory agency power as restrain it.[91] Perhaps the best example of that is the decision by the Supreme Court in *Phillips* to grant FERC's predecessor agency the authority to regulate natural gas prices, a power the

---

[87] Am. Forest & Paper Ass'n v. FERC, 550 F.3d 1179, 1183 (D.C. Cir. 2008) (stating that when a statute is "not ... a masterpiece of legislative draftsmanship" an agency is not held to the best interpretation of the statutory language, only a reasonable one).

[88] Kelliher, *supra* note 60, at 2-11.

[89] *See supra* note 77.

[90] California *ex rel.* Lockyer v. FERC, 383 F.3d 1006, 1011-13 (9th Cir. 2004); La. Energy & Power Auth. v. FERC, 141 F.3d 364, 365 (D.C. Cir. 1998).

[91] Kelliher & Farinella, *supra* note 83, at 627-34.

agency was convinced it did not possess.[92] The courts have also affirmed the broadest FERC reinterpretations of its existing legal authority.[93]

The path for regulatory policy change in the European Union may be narrower than in the United States, with a more exclusive reliance on changes in law, particularly directives. The role of courts may be smaller than in the United States, and there is no continental sector regulator such as FERC with regulatory powers that could be reinterpreted over time.

Relationship of Energy and Environmental Regulation
One new development in U.S. energy regulation is the growing importance of environmental regulation over the energy sector, and how that influences energy policy. There is fiction in the United States that there are two separate universes, one known as "energy policy" and another known as "environmental policy."

These separate domains are governed by separate laws and charged to separate agencies. Historically, there has been virtually no communication between federal energy and environmental regulators in the United States; they operate as if in separate worlds.

I accepted that fiction for many years, focusing my attention on energy regulation, and studiously avoiding environmental regulation as if it would be improper if I were familiar with this separate universe. That lasted until one day out of curiosity I perused a climate change proposal and was shocked to realize that at the heart of climate change policy were questions such as how much electricity the United States should consume, how it should be generated, and how it should be priced. Like Saul of Tarsus on the road to Damascus, I had an epiphany and realized that climate change was as much energy policy as environmental policy. I have paid attention to climate change policy ever since. In retrospect, it is embarrassing it took as long as it did for me to have my epiphany and understand that the separation of energy and environmental policy is artificial in many respects.

I cannot speak from personal experience about the level of communication and coordination among U.S. state energy and environmental

---

[92] *See supra* note 90.
[93] Transmission Access Policy Study Group v. FERC, 225 F.3d 667 (D.C. Cir. 2000), *aff'd sub nom.* New York v. FERC, 535 U.S. 1 (2002); *Lockyer*, 383 F.3d at 1011-13; *La. Energy & Power*, 141 F.3d at 365.

regulators, but my discussions with state energy regulators suggest that there is no better coordination at the state level in the United States than at the federal level.

There is a need for more communication and more coordination between U.S. energy and environmental regulators at both the federal and state level. Credit is due to the Obama administration for recognizing this need at the federal level and establishing an agency working group that includes both FERC and U.S. Environmental Protection Agency. FERC chair Jon Wellinghoff should be applauded for his active participation in this working group.

There may be better coordination of energy and environmental policy in Europe than is the case in the United States. Perhaps this is an area where the United States can learn from Europe.

Independent Regulation
One hallmark of energy regulation in the United States is independent regulation. Energy regulatory bodies, both federal and state, are typically structured as multi-member commissions whose members are given fixed terms of office and can only be removed for cause. That is true for FERC, and the norm for most, but not all, state agencies. The hallmark of independence is limits on removal of federal and state regulators by the executive, the President or a governor. For example, the FERC chairman and commissioners "may be removed by the President only for inefficiency, neglect of duty, or malfeasance in office."[94]

As an independent agency, FERC is not subject to control by the President or the U.S. Congress. By contrast, the Department of Energy is an executive branch agency, not an independent agency, so the secretary of energy and other key agency officials are subject to the control of the President and serve at his pleasure and are removable at will. But as noted earlier, the Department of Energy has a lesser role in U.S. energy regulation.

Independent regulation was developed out of recognition that the decisions energy regulators must make are difficult, and typically involve balancing costs and quality of service over a period of time, frequently a long term basis. Independence was granted in part because regulatory decisions

---

[94] Department of Energy Organization Act § 401(b), 42 U.S.C. § 7171(b) (2010).

demand the trained judgment of a body of experts,[95] and also because the regulatory agencies are quasi-judicial in the way they make decisions.[96] It is difficult for politicians or officials who serve at the pleasure of politicians to give due weight to the long term over the short term, and politicized regulation tends to strive to deliver the lowest possible cost in the short term, sacrificing higher quality of service and even lower average costs over time.

Not all utility regulation in the United States is high quality, and the quality of utility regulation in the United States varies among the states. Sensible state regulation has produced good results in many jurisdictions. However, the decisions of some state regulatory bodies over the years are more politicized than others, and their decisions much less predictable, and more politically dictated. There have been threats to independent regulation in some states. In my view, an erosion of independent regulation may result in a short-term focus that does not recognize the need to make investments today to assure quality of service and reasonable prices over the horizon.

While independent regulation is more characteristic of energy regulatory bodies, that is not the case with regard to U.S. environmental regulators. Environmental regulators typically are not independent agencies, but instead are executive branch agencies subject to the political control of the President, in the case of federal environmental regulators, and governors, with respect to state environmental regulators. To the extent there is improved coordination between energy and environmental policy, that coordination entails reaching across the divide that otherwise demarcates independent energy regulatory agencies and executive branch environmental agencies.

Interestingly, some of the threats to independent regulation are related to state efforts to consolidate energy and environmental regulatory bodies.[97] While efforts at improved coordination in this area are to be applauded, most of these proposals subordinate formerly independ-

---

[95] Humphrey's Ex'r v. United States, 295 U.S. 602, 624 (1935).

[96] *Id*. at 628-29.

[97] *See, e.g.*, Act Reorganizing the Governor's Cabinet and Certain Agencies of the Executive Department, Mass. St. 2007, c. 19 § 22 (2007) (reorganizing the state public utility commission to merge it with executive branch agencies and make commissioners removable at will).

ent energy regulators, and make them executive branch agency officials, removable at will by a governor or lesser official.

Relationship of Antitrust Agencies and Sectoral Regulators

One clear difference between U.S. and European energy regulation is the relationship between antitrust agencies or competition authorities and regulatory bodies like FERC, known as sectoral regulators in EU parlance. In the United States, FERC has vastly more authority over the electricity and natural gas industry than U.S. antitrust agencies, the U.S. Department of Justice and U.S. Federal Trade Commission, which are limited mostly to merger review.[98]

By contrast, in Europe, competition authorities appear to be much more important than sectoral regulators like national energy regulators. In part, that may be due to the lack of a continental energy regulatory agency, the lack of a "European FERC" to use common shorthand used in discussions between U.S. and EU energy regulators.

The inverse relative importance of antitrust and sectoral regulators in the European Union was reflected in the significant network divestures by E.ON and RWE that resulted from investigations by the Directorate-General for Competition. E.ON agreed to divest its ultrahigh voltage transmission system in Germany and a substantial amount of generation, or 4,800 megawatts. Likewise, RWE agreed to divest its entire Western German high-pressure gas transmission network. Antitrust and competition authorities share an enthusiasm for structural remedies and a suspicion of regulatory remedies. If the U.S. antitrust agencies had the same relative authority as the Directorate-General for Competition has in the EU, there is little doubt they would follow the same course, seeking to restructure the electricity industry to reduce vertical integration.

Comparison of U.S. and EU Energy Regulation

Differences in regulatory structure are no doubt shaped by differences in industry structure, but there are other factors as well, such as history, political organization, and regulatory philosophy.

As discussed above, differences in industry and market structure influence regulatory structure. Interstate commerce in electricity and natural

---

[98] Verizon Commc'ns, Inc. v. Law Offices of Curtis V. Trinko, LLP, 540 U.S. 398, 412 (2004).

gas is more important to the U.S. market than supra-national trade has been in the European Union, and has been so for some time. As a result, the economic activity that was not subject to effective state regulation in the United States or national regulation in the European Union was larger in the United States going back much further in time. That distinction helped create the need for a regulatory body like FERC in 1935 with authority to regulate interstate commerce in electricity and natural gas, something that is only a topic of discussion in the European Union.

The United States adopted competition policy for electricity and natural gas markets well before the European Union. The fact that horizontal market power in both the electricity and natural gas industries is more disaggregated in the United States than the European Union and that the power grid and pipeline networks in the United States are relatively stronger provided a stronger foundation for competition policy in the United States. The United States has also taken steps to assure open access to the grid and pipeline networks.

With regard to regulatory structure, the United States has adopted a federalist approach, with both federal and state regulators playing important roles. The relative importance of federal and state regulators in the United States has shifted as a result of market changes over time. Disagreements between federal and state regulators are generally resolved in favor of federal regulators, through federal preemption. There are multiple paths for changes in U.S. regulatory policy – enactment of new law by Congress and the President, implementation and reinterpretation of existing and new laws by regulatory agencies, and court review and reinterpretation of laws. Independent regulation is characteristic of energy regulation in the United States.

By contrast, the European Union largely relies on national regulation by member states; there is no EU regulator of electricity and natural gas markets. There seems to be one path for regulatory policy change, enactment of directives by the European Commission. Disagreements between nations and the Commission regarding such directives would be resolved through litigation against the member country. Sectoral regulators in the European Union in most cases are not independent of political control.

But the European Union does not rely exclusively on national sectoral regulation. Sectoral regulation is bolstered by the larger role afforded competition authorities. The competition authority has demonstrated an active interest in energy markets, which has adopted measures to promote effective competition. Given the market power issues in the European Union, in the absence of a "European FERC" the competition authority may continue to be active in this area. The role of antitrust authorities in the United States with respect to energy markets is much smaller, in part due to the presence of FERC. As the EU market expands, it may need to either erect a "European FERC" or accept a large, continued presence of competition authorities.

While the U.S. and EU regulatory models are different, they may both enjoy the same level of success in the end. The central challenge in energy regulation today is assuring security of supply at a reasonable cost, while meeting environmental policy objectives. There is no reason to suppose that both regulatory models cannot meet this challenge with success. But it is probably prudent for both U.S. and EU regulators to peer over the Atlantic from time to time and observe the success and failure of the other model to see if there are any lessons to be learned.

The Past, Present, and Future of Energy Regulation

RICHARD J. PIERCE, JR.[*]

I view my role in this symposium as providing a brief overview of the history of energy regulation in the United States over the last half century, followed by alternative predictions of the future – one optimistic and one pessimistic. I will begin with a description of the history of energy regulation in the hope that we can learn lessons from it that will help us choose a promising approach for the future.

I. The Past
A. Oil – 1960 to 2011

The United States implemented poor fiscal and monetary policies in the 1960s that led to high and rising economy-wide inflation. President Nixon responded to that problem with economy-wide wage and price controls in 1971.[1] Wage and price controls had devastating effects on the economy that caused them to be the subject of near universal criticism by 1973. At that time, they were eliminated for all sectors of the economy except oil and petroleum products.[2]

---

[*] Lyle T. Alverson Professor of Law, George Washington University. I benefited greatly from comments I received on an earlier version of this Essay from Rob Glicksman and the participants in the George Washington University Works in Progress Group. This paper was originally published in the UNIVERSITY OF UTAH ENVIRONMENTAL LAW REVIEW.

[1] Exec. Order No. 11,615, 34 Fed. Reg. 15727 (Aug. 17, 1971).

[2] 38 Fed. Reg. 22,536 (Aug. 22, 1973) (to be codified at 6 C.F.R. pt. 150).

Several factors in addition to economy-wide inflation led to large increases in the price of oil and petroleum products.[3] First, air quality rules implemented in the 1960s induced many electric utilities and industrial consumers to switch from coal to oil or gas, thereby increasing demand for oil. Second, the U.S. position on the 1973 Arab-Israeli War led the Arab members of the Organization of Petroleum Exporting Countries (OPEC) to impose an embargo on exports of oil to the United States for several months. That embargo produced shortages and increases in the price of petroleum products in the United States. More important, the success of the embargo suggested to all members of OPEC that they could increase their wealth by withholding supplies from the market and thereby increasing the global price of oil. They began to do so, with a resulting four-fold increase in the price of oil.

The United States responded to this sequence of events by retaining price controls on oil and petroleum products when it eliminated economy-wide price controls in 1973. The United States imposed oil price controls continuously until 1981. Their effects included long lines at gas stations, implementation of a complicated rationing system, cross-subsidization of imports, increased dependence on imported oil, an increased global price of oil, and lots of work for lawyers.[4] In 1981, President Reagan deregulated the price of oil and petroleum products.[5] With cross-subsidies of imports eliminated, the price of oil declined significantly.[6] The oil market has performed well since, and OPEC has little power to increase prices artificially by withholding supplies today.

B. *Natural Gas – 1960 to 2011*
In 1954, a five-justice majority of the U.S. Supreme Court held that the Federal Power Commission (FPC) was required to regulate the wellhead price

---

[3] For detailed discussion of the history of regulation of crude oil and petroleum products, see PAUL W. MACAVOY, AM. ENTER. INST., FEDERAL ENERGY ADMINISTRATION REGULATION, REPORT OF THE PRESIDENTIAL TASK FORCE (1977).

[4] For detailed discussion of the effects of price controls on crude oil and petroleum products, see KENNETH ARROW & JOSEPH KALT, PETROLEUM PRICE REGULATION: SHOULD WE DECONTROL? (1979).

[5] Exec. Order No. 12,287, 3 C.F.R. 124 (1982).

[6] For a detailed description of the history of oil prices, see *Oil Price History and Analysis*, WRTG ECONOMICS, http://www.wtrg.com/prices.htm (last visited Apr. 11, 2011).

of natural gas.[7] FPC began to impose price controls in the 1960s.[8] By the late 1960s, air quality rules had increased demand for gas by encouraging switching from coal to oil or gas, and price controls had reduced the supply of gas. The result was a shortage that grew through the 1970s.[9] The effects of the price controls and the shortage included millions of people out of work due to factory closings, cross-subsidization of imports, an increased global price of gas, and implementation of a complicated rationing system.

Congress responded by enacting the Natural Gas Policy Act of 1978[10] (NGPA) – a statute that divided gas supplies into twenty-three categories, each subject to a different price ceiling. NGPA created a combination of conditions that most economists previously believed to be impossible – a surplus of gas combined with above market prices for many types of gas.[11] NGPA also created a situation in which the artificially low regulated price of "old" domestic gas cross-subsidized "high cost gas" and imported gas. Gas in those categories sold for prices two to four times the market price of gas.[12]

Beginning in 1985, the Federal Energy Regulatory Commission (FERC), FPC's successor, issued a series of orders in which it: (1) deintegrated the gas market vertically, separating the natural monopoly functions from the structurally competitive functions, (2) subjected the structurally competitive wholesale gas market to unregulated competition, and (3) imposed a common carrier form of regulation on the natural monopoly gas transportation function.[13] With competition in place and cross-subsidies eliminated, the price of gas declined significantly.[14] The gas market has performed well since.

---

[7] Phillips Petroleum v. Wisconsin, 347 U.S. 672 (1954).

[8] Richard J. Pierce, *Reconstituting the Natural Gas Industry from Wellhead to Burnertip*, 9 ENERGY L.J. 1 (1988).

[9] For detailed descriptions of the effects of controls on the wellhead price of gas, see Richard J. Pierce, *Reconsidering the Roles of Regulation and Competition on the Natural Gas Industry*, 97 HARV. L. REV. 345 (1983); Richard J. Pierce, *Natural Gas Regulation, Deregulation, and Contracts*, 68 VA. L. REV. 63 (1982) [hereinafter Pierce, *Natural Gas*].

[10] Natural Gas Policy Act of 1978, Pub. L. No. 95-621, 92 Stat. 3351 (1978).

[11] For a detailed description of the effects of NGPA, see Pierce, *supra* note 8, at 11–18.

[12] Pierce, *Natural Gas, supra* note 9, at 84–88.

[13] Federal Energy Regulatory Commission, 50 Fed. Reg. 42,408 (Oct. 18, 1985) (to be codified at 18 C.F.R. pt. 2); Federal Energy Regulatory Commission, 57 Fed. Reg. 13,267 (Apr. 16, 1992) (to be codified at 18 C.F.R. pt. 284).

[14] Richard J. Pierce, *The State of the Transition to Competitive Markets in Natural Gas and Electricity*, 15 ENERGY L.J. 323 (1994).

DIREITO COMPARADO / COMPARATIVE LAW

Over the period between 2007–2011, gas producers have combined two traditional practices – horizontal drilling and hydraulic fracturing of shale formations – with excellent results. The supply of gas has increased significantly, with a large resulting decrease in price.[15] Gas is now less than half the price of oil.[16] However, concern that some chemicals used in hydraulic fracturing are having adverse effects on water quality has resulted in pressure to increase regulation of hydraulic fracturing.[17] It seems clear that regulation will (and should) increase to some uncertain extent with some uncertain resulting increase in cost and, hence, in the price of gas.

C. *Electricity – 1960–2011*

Air quality rules implemented in the 1960s encouraged utilities to install expensive pollution control technologies, to switch from coal to gas, and to begin construction of 200 nuclear generating plants. Economy-wide inflation combined with fuel switching and pollution controls significantly increased the cost of generating electricity.[18]

The oil and gas shortages of the 1970s and a desire to achieve energy independence induced Congress to enact two statutes in 1978. The first statute was the Powerplant and Industrial Fuel Use Act (PIFUA)[19] which required utilities and industrial consumers to switch from oil and gas to coal. PIFUA prohibited electric utilities from constructing new generating plants that were designed to burn oil or gas.[20] Congress later repealed PIFUA in 1987.[21] By the late 1980s PIFUA was a counterproductive anachronism. The government-created shortages of oil and gas that had inspired

---

[15] Gideon Rachman, *Shale Gas Will Change the World*, FINANCIAL TIMES, May 24, 2010, *available at* http://www.ft.com/cms/s/0/d8c79266-6764-11df-a932-00144feab49a.html#axzz1JH2JKIvv.

[16] As of August 13, 2010, the price of gas in the U.S. was $4.49/MMBtu, while the price of crude oil in the U.S. was $13.66/MMBtu. *Comparative Fuel Prices*, NATURAL GAS WEEK, Aug. 16, 2010, at Weekly Tables & Graphs.

[17] David Biello, *What the Frack? Natural Gas from Subterranean Shale Promises U.S. Energy Independence – with Environmental Costs*, SCI. AM., Mar 30, 2010, *available at* http://www.scientificamerican.com/article.cfm?id=shale-gas-and-hydraulic-fracturing.

[18] *See generally* Paul L. Joskow, *Inflation and Environmental Concern: Structural Change in the Process of Public Utility Price Regulation*, 17 J.L. & ECON. 291 (1974).

[19] Powerplant and Industrial Fuel Use Act of 1978, Pub. L. No. 95-620, 92 Stat. 3289 (1978).

[20] For a description of PIFUA, see Richard J. Pierce, *Introduction: Symposium on the Powerplant and Industrial Fuel Use Act of 1978*, 29 U. KAN. L. REV. 297 (1981).

[21] U.S. ENERGY INFO. ADMIN (EIA), *Petroleum Chronology of Events 1970–2000* (May 2002).

enactment of the statute were long gone,[22] and it seemed silly to require utilities to rely exclusively on the dirtiest fuel, coal, when they had access to abundant, clean, and inexpensive natural gas.

The second statute Congress enacted in 1978 was the Public Utility Regulatory Policies Act (PURPA).[23] PURPA encouraged utilities to buy electricity from non-utility generators (NUGs) at above market prices if the NUGs used specified preferred technologies that included cogeneration and low head hydro.[24] It also encouraged utilities to use customer funds to make purchases, such as insulation, high efficiency light bulbs, and high efficiency appliances, which were designed to increase their customers' energy efficiency.[25] Some states, primarily California and the northeastern states, required utilities to enter into long-term contracts to purchase large quantities of electricity from NUGs at prices far above market, and rewarded utilities for using their customers' money to make large energy efficiency purchases on behalf of their customers.[26]

The unit price of electricity increased significantly as a result of: (1) economy-wide inflation, (2) higher costs of fuel and pollution controls, (3) higher than expected costs of constructing nuclear generating plants, (4) methods of regulation used to reflect the cost of new plants in prices that overstated the cost of those plants, and (5) a decline in demand caused partly by the increased price of electricity and partly by an economic downturn.[27] The price of electricity increased most in the states that required utilities to buy a lot of electricity from NUGs at above market prices and that rewarded utilities that used large quantities of their customers' money to make efficiency purchases on their behalf. The price of electricity was

---

[22] *See supra* notes 1–17 and accompanying text.

[23] Public Utility Regulatory Policy Act of 1978, Pub. L. No. 95-617, 92 Stat. 3117 (1978).

[24] For a description of PURPA, see John T. Miller Jr., *Conscripting State Regulatory Authorities in a Federal Electric Rate Regulatory Regime: A Goal of PURPA Partially Realized*, 4 ENERGY L.J. 77 (1983).

[25] *Id.*

[26] Bernard S. Black & Richard J. Pierce, *The Choice Between Markets and Central Planning in Regulating the U.S. Electricity Market*, 93 COLUM. L. REV. 1339, 1347–48, 1354–89 (1993); Paul L. Joskow & Donald B. Marron, *What Does Utility-Subsidized Energy Efficiency Really Cost?* SCIENCE, Apr. 16, 1993, at 281.

[27] Richard J. Pierce, *Public Utility Regulatory Takings: Should the Judiciary Attempt to Police the Political Institutions?* 77 GEO. L. J. 2031, 2047–52 (1989) [hereinafter Pierce, *Pubilc Utility*].

almost twice as high in those states as in the states that did not take those actions.[28]

The increased price of electricity produced a consumer backlash that was particularly strong in the states with the highest electricity prices. State regulators used a variety of regulatory doctrines to disallow billions of dollars in investments in cancelled or completed nuclear generating plants.[29] One hundred plants were completed, while another one hundred partially completed plants were cancelled.[30] No utility has been willing to invest in a new nuclear generating plant since the investment disallowances of the 1980s.

The large increases in the price of electricity also provided the impetus to attempt to restructure the electricity market in a manner similar to the successful restructuring of the gas market in the 1980s – vertical deintegration of structurally-competitive functions from monopoly functions, imposition of deregulated competition on the structurally-competitive wholesale market, and imposition of common carrier type regulation on the monopolistic transmission function.[31] FERC initiated such a restructuring effort in 1996.[32]

After years of halting progress, FERC abandoned its attempt to restructure the electricity market. The failure of that restructuring effort was attributable to many factors, including: (1) inadequate FERC jurisdiction, (2) the fragmented corporate structure of the utility industry, (3) resistance from some states that wanted to retain complete control over their utilities, and from some utilities that did not want to confront competition, (4) low short-term price elasticity of demand coupled with inability to store electricity, (5) serious errors made by FERC and by many states, (6)

---

[28] Thus, for instance, in 1993, the average price of electricity was 9.69 cents in California, 10.72 cents in New York, and 9.98 cents in Massachusetts, but it was only 5.22 cents in Tennessee, 4.32 cents in Kentucky, and 6.23 cents in Virginia. *See* U.S. ENERGY INFO. ADMIN., ELECTRIC POWER ANNUAL 2009, 1990 – BLES AVERAGE BY STATE BY PROVIDER (E/A-861) (2010), *available at* http://www.eia.doe.gov/cneaf/electricity/epa/average_price_state.xls.

[29] Richard J. Pierce, *The Regulatory Treatment of Mistakes in Retrospect: Cancelled Plants and Excess Capacity*, 132 U. PA. L. REV. 497–99, 519–21 (1984).

[30] Pierce, *Public Utility, supra* note 27, at 2048–53.

[31] Richard J. Pierce, *Using the Gas Industry as a Guide to Reconstituting the Electricity Industry*, 13 RES. L. & ECON. 7, 16–17 (1991).

[32] Federal Energy Regulatory Commission, 61 Fed. Reg. 21,540 (May 10, 1996) (to be codified at 18 C.F.R. pts. 35 & 385).

the combination of extraordinarily high prices and intermittent blackouts experienced in California in 2000–2001, and (7) the 2001 scandal involving the misconduct and ultimate demise of Enron, the largest participant in the nascent competitive electricity market.[33]

II. The Present and Future

At present, we focus primarily on the use of energy regulation to pursue two goals – energy independence and mitigation of global warming. We rely mainly on three tools to pursue those goals – subsidies for domestic carbon-free sources of energy, mandates to electric utilities to increase the percentage of total electricity they generate from carbon-free fuels, and novel uses of the Clean Air Act (CAA).

I see two potential future courses of action – continuation of the status quo or substitution of a large carbon tax for the tools we are now attempting to use. Continuation of the status quo will produce a lot of work for lawyers but poor results for the nation and the world. By contrast, we can maximize the efficacy and efficiency of our efforts if we drop one of our goals – energy independence – and substitute a large carbon tax for the expensive and ineffective tools we are now using in an effort to mitigate global warming.

A. We Should Pursue Only the Goal of Mitigation of Global Warming

It makes no sense to pursue energy independence as a goal.[34] Any effective effort to replace all foreign sources of energy with domestic sources would cost trillions of dollars, with little, if any beneficial effects. We are dependent on foreign sources for many important goods. There is no more reason to be concerned about our dependence on foreign sources of energy than to be concerned about our dependence on foreign sources for a myriad other important resources.

Lithium is a particularly good example of a resource that is critical to the nation's future and that is, or should be, of greater concern than ener-

---

[33] Richard J. Pierce, *Completing the Process of Restructuring the Electricity Market*, 40 WAKE FOREST L. REV. 451, 479–93 (2005).

[34] For detailed explanations of the expense and futility of pursuing the goal of energy independence, see Richard J. Pierce, *Energy Independence and Global Warming*, 37 ENVTL. L. 595 (2007); Richard J. Pierce, *Déjà Vu All Over Again – The Return of Project Independence and Rate-Payer Funded DSM*, 16 ELECTRICITY J. 77 (2003).

gy.[35] Lithium is critical to any effort to manufacture efficient batteries.[36] That, in turn, is critical to our ability to improve the efficiency with which we generate and consume electricity. The United States produces only a tiny fraction of the lithium we use.[37] Most of the world's lithium supply is in Bolivia[38] – a country with an unstable anti-American government and an economy based primarily on cocaine.[39] By contrast, the largest sources of U.S. energy imports by far are our neighbors, Canada and Mexico, and we are much less dependent on foreign sources of energy than on foreign sources of lithium.[40] Electric cars are being sold politically as a means of avoiding dependence on insecure foreign sources of oil, but a fleet of electric cars would render us dependent on far less secure foreign sources of lithium. I trust Canada far more than I trust Bolivia.

Some people maintain that we could reduce threats to our national security and/or our level of defense spending if we attained energy independence.[41] There is no evidence to support that widely held view, and it is inconsistent with a quick survey of the major threats that now concern us. We import no energy from any of the five countries that are of greatest concern to us today – North Korea, Afghanistan, Pakistan, Iran, and China. Indeed, four of the five are themselves dependent on foreign sources of energy, and even Iran must import large quantities of gasoline every year.[42] Reducing our dependence on Canada and Mexico as our primary suppliers of energy would have no effect whatsoever on the potential threats to our national security posed by North Korea, Afghanistan, Pakistan, Iran, or China or on our need to devote large sums to national defense.

---

[35] For a detailed analysis of the importance of lithium and its supply and demand, see DUNDEE CAPITAL MARKETS, LITHIUM – HYPE OR SUBSTANCE? (2009).

[36] *Id.* at 3-4.

[37] *Id.* at 17.

[38] *Id.*

[39] For a detailed description of Bolivia, see *Background Note: Bolivia*, U.S. DEP'T OF STATE (May 13, 2010), http://www.state.gov/r/pa/ei/bgn/35751.htm.

[40] *U.S. Imports by Country of Origin*, U.S. ENERGY INFO. ADMIN., http://www.eia.doe.gov/dnav/pet/pet_move_impcus_a2_nus_ep00_im0_mbbl_m.htm (last released Mar. 30, 2011).

[41] *E.g.*, Thomas L. Friedman, *Fighting Our Oil Addiction*, PITTSBURGH POST-GAZETTE, Dec. 21, 2010, *available at* http://www.post-gazette.com/pg/10355/1112241-109.stm.

[42] Iran Country Analysis Brief, U.S. ENERGY INFO. ADMIN., *Iran Country Analysis Brief*, http://www.eia.doe.gov/countries/cab.cfm?fips=IR (last updated Jan. 2010).

By contrast, there is overwhelming evidence that global warming will have catastrophic effects, including the death of millions of people and the displacement of hundreds of millions of people, primarily in impoverished areas like central Africa, central India, Bangladesh, and coastal Indonesia.[43] There is also persuasive evidence that global warming can be mitigated by reducing global emissions of green house gases (GHG), including carbon dioxide (CO_2), the most ubiquitous GHG.[44] We should continue to embrace mitigation of global warming as an important goal of energy policy.

We can greatly simplify our choice of means to pursue our goals if we drop pursuit of the ill-conceived goal of energy independence and pursue only the goal of mitigation of global warming. As long as we continue to attempt to pursue both goals simultaneously, we will be forced to make tradeoffs that sacrifice one goal to further the other. Thus, for instance, President Carter's expensive and ill-fated attempt to obtain energy independence relied heavily on maximum substitution of coal for oil and gas.[45] Such a policy would be terrible from a global warming perspective. Use of coal results in twice as much emissions of CO_2 as use of natural gas and about 50 percent more emissions than use of oil.[46] Our present policy of providing massive subsidies for use of corn-based ethanol to replace gasoline is even worse from a global warming perspective. Substitution of corn-based ethanol for gasoline induces increases in deforestation to create land that can be used to cultivate corn and other food crops.[47] When the effects of those land use changes are added to the CO_2 emissions that result from the process of growing corn and converting it into ethanol,[48] substitut-

---

[43] The United Nations has collected a large body of publications that analyze the causes and consequences of global warming on its website. See *Climate Change*, UNITED NATIONS ENVTL. PROGRAMME, http://www.unep.org/climatechange/ (last visited Apr. 11, 2010).

[44] IEA GREENHOUSE GAS R&D PROGRAMME, CO2 EMISSIONS DATABASE, *A global Database of large stationary CO2 sources.*, http://www.ieaghg.org/index.php?/20091223127/co2-emissions-database.html.

[45] *See supra* notes 18-22 and accompanying text.

[46] IEA GREENHOUSE GAS R&D PROGRAMME, *supra* note 44.

[47] Timothy Searchinger et al., *Use of U.S. Croplands for Biofuels Increases Greenhouse Gases Through Emissions from Land-Use Change*, 319 SCIENCE 1238, 1238–39 (2008).

[48] For analysis of those effects of corn-based ethanol, see CONGRESSIONAL BUDGET OFFICE, USING BIOFUEL TAX CREDITS TO ACHIEVE ENERGY AND ENVIRONMENTAL POLICY GOALS 16 tbl. 6 (2010).

DIREITO COMPARADO / COMPARATIVE LAW

ing corn-based ethanol for gasoline has effects on global warming that are even worse than the effects of substituting coal for petroleum products.

B. *We Should Replace Our Present Tools with a Carbon Tax*

Once we focus on the single goal of mitigation of global warming, we can then identify and implement ways of taking the most important step to further that goal – reduction of CO_2 emissions by at least 80 percent by 2050. The present mix of tools used to further that goal is expensive, ineffective, and unsustainable. The Supreme Court has provided the foundation for EPA to use the CAA to reduce CO_2 emissions,[49] and the Obama administration has taken a few modest steps in that direction,[50] but there is a broad consensus that CAA is poorly designed to reduce CO_2 emissions. In the context of the other pollutants EPA has regulated, it was possible to install pollution control devices that significantly reduced emissions produced by use of hydrocarbons, while continuing to consume the fuels. That is not an option in the case of CO_2. It is an inevitable byproduct of the process of using hydrocarbons. EPA can reduce CO_2 emissions only by reducing use of hydrocarbons. It is not clear how EPA could accomplish that result. The CAA is not designed to accomplish a result of that type.

Subsidies for carbon-free domestic fuels are extremely expensive, largely ineffective, and ultimately unsustainable. The subsidies needed to induce enough substitution of carbon-free fuels to reduce CO_2 emissions by 80 percent are enormous. Thus, for instance, since energy from windmills is almost twice as expensive as energy from coal or gas, wind farms would have to be assured of subsidies equal to the current price of coal or gas. Similarly, producers of solar energy would have to be assured of subsidies equal to three to four times the current price of coal or gas in order to induce a large scale transition to carbon-free fuels.[51] We simply cannot afford carbon-free fuel subsidies of that magnitude.

Mandates to electric utilities to add enough carbon-free generation to mitigate global warming would be equally expensive, but the cost would

[49] Massachusetts v. EPA, 549 U.S. 497, 556–60 (2007).

[50] For a description of the steps EPA has taken to date, see ROBERT GLICKSMAN, ENVIRONMENTAL PROTECTION: LAW AND POLICY (2011).

[51] These cost estimates and all others in this essay are from U.S. ENERGY INFO. ADMIN., 2016 LEVELIZED COST OF NEW GENERATION RESOURCES FROM THE ANNUAL ENERGY OUTLOOK 2010, at 3 (2009) [hereinafter U.S. ENERGY INFO. ADMIN., 2016 LEVELIZED].

be borne by consumers. The average price of electricity would increase significantly if utilities engaged in the massive fuel switching needed to reduce CO_2 emissions by 80 percent. Of course, consumers would revolt long before mandates could accomplish that result. For example, more modest increases in the price of electricity spawned a consumer revolt in the 1970s and 1980s.[52]

There has long been a broad consensus that the massive reductions in CO_2 emissions needed to mitigate global warming can be attained through only one of two means – a global cap and trade system or a large global carbon tax.[53] The failure of the Copenhagen meeting has left even many of the strongest proponents of a cap and trade system in despair.[54] It seems highly unlikely that an effective global cap and trade system can be designed and implemented. That leaves a large carbon tax as the only potentially viable means of mitigating global warming.

Given the present political climate, it is hard to imagine the United States adopting a large carbon tax. Democrats are unwilling to increase taxes on people who earn less than $250,000 per year, while Republicans are unwilling to increase taxes on anyone.[55] That aspect of the political environment must change in the near future, however, if the United States is to avoid the fate of Greece. Unless we make major changes in fiscal policy, we will experience large deficits for the indefinite future.[56] Deficits of that magnitude are unsustainable.[57] At some point in the near future, we must reduce spending and increase taxes.

A carbon tax is superior to an increase in income taxes or a value-added tax – the only alternatives to a carbon tax that offer the prospect of increasing revenues to the point at which our budget deficit will be toler-

---

[52] *See supra* notes 23-32 and accompanying text.

[53] Richard J. Pierce, *Energy Independence and Global Warming*, 37 ENVTL. L. 595, 600–01 (2007).

[54] *See, e.g*, Robert Stavins, *Another Copenhagen Outcome: Serious Questions About the Best Institutional Path Forward*, BELFER CENTER (Jan. 5, 2010, 8:11 PM), http://belfercenter.ksg.harvard.edu/analysis/stavins/?p=496; *C-Roads Analysis of Final Copenhagen Accord*, SUSTAINABILITY INSTITUTE (Dec. 19, 2009), http://www.sustainer.org/?p=1465.

[55] Editorial, *A Real Debate on Taxes*, N. Y. TIMES, Aug. 24, 2010, at A22.

[56] The Obama Administration proposes a budget deficit of between 533 billion dollars and over one trillion dollars for the indefinite future. OFFICE OF MANAGEMENT AND BUDGET, A NEW ERA OF RESPONSIBILITY 119 (2009).

[57] *See* INTERNATIONAL MONETARY FUND, FISCAL MONITOR: NAVIGATING THE FISCAL CHALLENGES AHEAD (2010), *available at* http://www.imf.org/external/pubs/ft/fm/2010/fm1001.pdf.

able. Taxes discourage the taxed activity. Thus, income taxes discourage work, while a value added tax discourages purchases of all types of goods and services. By contrast, a carbon tax discourages only what we need to discourage to mitigate global warming – emissions of CO_2.

A carbon tax is superior to subsidies for carbon-free energy sources in two important respects. First, it has the opposite effect on the budget deficit. While subsidies increase the deficit, a carbon tax would decrease the deficit. Second, it is much easier to design and to implement. To be effective, a carbon tax need only deter consumption of hydrocarbons. Consumers are left with complete discretion with respect to the ways in which they reduce their consumption of hydrocarbons. For example, by increasing the efficiency of their use of energy or by substituting for hydrocarbons some mix of carbon-free fuels like wind power, solar power, or nuclear power. It is important to give consumers that flexibility, both because the alternatives will be more or less attractive to different consumers in a variety of different situations, and because we cannot predict which of the alternatives to hydrocarbons will become more attractive in the future as a result of technological breakthroughs. By contrast, subsidies must be set at levels that are adequate to encourage optimal substitution of each subsidized alternative. By definition, they are always too high or too low, both because of the varying circumstances of consumers and because of the dynamic and unpredictable pace of technological progress.

C. Will a Carbon Tax Be Effective?

I am confident that a large carbon tax is the best policy the United States can implement in an effort to mitigate global warming. I am less confident, however, that a carbon tax implemented by the United States will be effective in mitigating global warming, given the daunting nature of the task. The climate experts tell us that we must reduce *global* CO_2 emissions by 80 percent by 2050. I am skeptical that there is anything the United States can do that can accomplish such a result. My skepticism has two sources – the likely behavior of some other countries, and the extreme difficulty of meeting this goal even in the United States. It is reasonable to assume that most other developed countries, for example, the members of the European Union and Japan, would join the United States in an effort to reduce their CO_2 emissions by 80 percent. But it is not realistic to make such an assumption with respect to most developing countries, for example, China, India, and Russia. If the developed countries reduce their CO_2 emissions by reducing their consumption of hydrocarbons, developing countries are likely to *increase* their emissions by *increasing* their consumption of hydrocarbons. Any significant reduction in the quantity of hydrocarbons consumed in developed countries will reduce the global price of hydrocarbons. That, in turn, will yield increased consumption of hydrocarbons in the developing countries that already account for almost all of the increases in global CO_2 emissions in recent years.[58]

The extent to which increased hydrocarbon consumption and increased CO_2 emissions in developing countries will offset decreased hydrocarbon consumption and decreased CO_2 emissions in developed countries, will depend on the price elasticity of demand for hydrocarbons in developing countries over the next forty years. Estimates of that metric range from 29 percent to 70 percent,[59] so increased emissions in developing countries will offset about one-half of the decreased emissions in developed countries unless developing countries impose meaningful limits on their own emissions. That is why efforts must continue to implement an international agreement that imposes meaningful limits of some type on the emissions of GHGs in developing countries.[60] Without such limits, nothing the United States does is likely to be effective in mitigating global warming.

Even a U.S. effort to reduce our CO_2 emissions by 80 percent would be extremely expensive and time-consuming. It also would produce uncertain and adverse effects on the environment. To illustrate the difficulty of the task, I will describe briefly each of the potential steps the United States might take to reduce CO_2 emissions in the electricity sector by 80 percent and a few of the obstacles to implementation of each of those steps.

The electricity sector accounts for 40 percent of U.S. emissions of CO_2.[61] The present composition of our sources of electricity are: 46 percent coal, 21 percent gas, 20 percent nuclear, 2 percent oil, 7 percent hydropower,

---

[58] Searchinger et al., *supra* note 47, at 1238-39; CONGRESSIONAL BUDGET OFFICE, *supra* note 48, at 16 tbl. 6.

[59] STEVEN STOFT, GLOBAL ENERGY POLICY CENTER, RENEWABLE FUEL AND THE GLOBAL REBOUND EFFECT 2 (2010).

[60] SHEILA OLMSTEAD AND ROBERT STAVINS, HARVARD KENNEDY SCHOOL, THREE KEY ELEMENTS OF POST-2012 INTERNATIONAL CLIMATE POLICY ARCHITECTURE 3 (2010).

[61] ENVTL. PROT. AGENCY, INVENTORY OF GREENHOUSE GAS EMISSIONS AND SINKS: 1990-2008, at 2–15 (2010).

DIREITO COMPARADO / COMPARATIVE LAW

and 4 percent other renewable sources.[62] Since coal consumption produces twice as much CO_2 emissions as gas consumption,[63] we would need to eliminate completely all emissions attributable to coal to reach the goal of an 80 percent reduction in CO_2 emissions in the electricity sector. That statistic illustrates a major political obstacle. Coal is mined throughout Appalachia and the Powder River Basin. Any effort to eliminate coal mining will face strong opposition from the many members of the House of Representatives and Senate who represent states and districts in which coal accounts for a significant part of the economy. There are many paths we can take to move toward elimination of CO_2 emissions from use of coal in generating plants, but there are many obstacles on each of those paths. I will begin by describing the generic obstacles to the kinds of changes we need to make to reduce CO_2 emissions from electricity generation by 80 percent.

First, all carbon-free sources of electricity are more expensive than coal or gas.[64] Thus, inducing consumers to switch sources will require either large subsidies or a large carbon tax. Second, electricity cannot be stored economically. That is important because some of the carbon-free sources of electricity are unpredictable in their availability. Thus, for instance, wind power is available only when the wind velocity falls within a particular range, and solar power is available only when the sun shines. This characteristic would be much less important if we could generate electricity in one period, store it economically, and consume it in another period. Since electricity cannot be stored economically, we can add only a modest amount of wind or solar energy to the grid without significantly impairing reliability.[65] Third, the United States has traditionally relied on state and local governments to regulate the most important activities that are needed to generate, transmit, and distribute electricity. Some state and local governments are not likely to share the national government's interests in taking the actions needed to mitigate global warming, and even

---

[62] U.S. Dept. of Energy, Net Generation by Energy Source: Total (2011), *available at* http://www.eia.doe.gov/cneaf/electricity/epm/table1_1.html.

[63] *Id.*

[64] U.S. Energy Info. Admin., 2016 Levelized, *supra* note 51.

[65] For a comprehensive discussion of the relationship between various carbon-free energy sources and reliability of electricity service, see North American Reliability Council, Reliability Impacts of Climate Change Initiatives: Technology Assessment and Scenario Development (2010), *available at* http://www.nerc.com/files/RICCI_2010.pdf.

those that do are likely to have divergent preferences with respect to the best means to further that goal. No national plan to mitigate global warming can succeed if California and Oklahoma are free to adopt different policies with respect to the actions needed to mitigate global warming.[66] Fourth, increased reliance on carbon-free sources like wind or solar will require large additions to our transmission grid. Most such additions provoke strong opposition on aesthetic grounds,[67] and there is an ongoing controversy over the manner in which such expansions should be financed.[68] Fifth, the United States is extremely litigious. Most of the projects needed to mitigate global warming will provoke opposition at regulatory agencies and in courts. The resulting litigation will slow the rate at which we can achieve the mitigation goal and increase the cost of achieving that goal.

(a) Conservation

Turning to particular steps that can be taken to mitigate global warming, I will begin with the step most people believe to be the most promising – conservation/increased efficiency of use. Price is the most reliable and effective means of encouraging conservation and increased efficiency. If consumers confront electricity prices that reflect accurately the cost of electricity, including external costs like those attributable to global warming, they will decrease their consumption of electricity and increase the efficiency with which they use electricity. A large carbon tax would move the price of electricity in the right direction, but it is not enough.

Demand for electricity varies greatly over time. Since electricity cannot be stored economically, that widely varying demand must be met with contemporaneous variations in supply. The cost of supplying a kilowatt hour (kWh) of electricity to a particular location can vary by as much as a factor of twenty to one depending on the time when the electricity is

---

[66] For an excellent analysis that demonstrates the problems created by state-based attempts to mitigate global warming, see Lincoln Davies, *Power Forward: The Argument for a National RPS*, 42 CONN. L. REV. 1339 (2010).

[67] Richard J. Pierce, *Environmental Regulation, Energy, and Market Entry*, 15 DUKE ENVTL. L. & POL'Y. 167, 176–183 (2005).

[68] FERC wants to spread the cost of expanding transmission capacity across all consumers in a region, but the Seventh Circuit has rejected that approach. *See* Ill. Commerce Comm'n v. Fed. Energy Regulatory Comm'n, 576 F.3d 470, 474 (7th Cir. 2009).

supplied.[69] Yet, most consumers pay a price for each kWh that does not vary as the cost of a kWh goes up or down.[70] We can encourage consumers to engage in optimal efforts at conservation and efficiency enhancement only by changing the methods used to bill consumers. To accomplish that goal, we must install smart meters for all consumers. Smart meters allow consumers and utilities to observe the constantly changing cost of electricity and to measure consumption at each cost level. Smart meters will have no effect, however, unless we also change the method of billing all consumers so that the price they pay for each kWh varies greatly depending on the constantly changing cost of meeting their demand for electricity.

The federal government is attempting to implement a smart grid that would include smart meters and new billing methods.[71] However, this attempt lacks the power to make the needed changes. Both the decision whether to authorize a utility to install smart meters, and the decision to change the method of billing consumers is subject to state regulation. The federal efforts to implement a smart grid have made little progress because many consumer advocacy groups and state regulators have objected on a wide variety of grounds.[72] Unless consumer advocacy groups or state regulators change their attitudes dramatically, or Congress gives the federal government the power to require installation of smart meters and changes in billing methods, and the federal government exercises that power, the highly touted attempt to install a smart grid will go nowhere.

Some people believe that price provides an inadequate incentive for consumers to conserve because of various imperfections in the market.[73] In order to overcome those imperfections, they urge adoption of state regulatory systems that reward utilities for using their customers' funds to make large payments for energy conservation purposes on behalf of their customers. Under a system of this type, a utility would pay for additional home insulation, high efficiency light bulbs, and high efficiency appliances, and add the cost of those acquisitions, plus a reward for their conservation-enhancing efforts, to their customers' bills.

---

[69] For an overview of this controversy, see Michael T. Burr, *Summer of Discontent: Smart Grid Planners Feel the Heat*, PUBLIC UTILITY FORTNIGHTLY, Aug. 2010, at 4.

[70] *Id.*

[71] *Id.*

[72] *Id.*

[73] Black & Pierce, *supra* note 26, at 1362–78.

Several states implemented regulatory systems of this type in the late 1970s and early 1980s with unfortunate effects.[74] The new systems replaced one arguable market imperfection with another – utilities that are rewarded for making purchases on behalf of their customers do not have an incentive to insure that the purchases are cost effective. Audits of the customer-funded conservation acquisition programs consistently found that the efficiency enhancing claims for the goods and services purchased by the utilities were overstated. Ultimately, all of the state agencies that authorized programs of that type were forced by consumer backlash to abandon them.

(b) Switching to Natural Gas

The United States can achieve some part of our global warming mitigation goal by encouraging utilities to switch from coal to gas. At present, gas is available in abundance at about the same price as coal, and it emits only half as much CO_2 per kWh of electricity produced as coal. There are limits on our ability to switch to gas as a mitigation strategy, however. In the short term, only about 10 percent of generating capacity that uses coal can switch to gas. Over a longer period, of course, we could substitute gas for all of our present coal capacity. It is highly likely, however, that the price of gas will increase, perhaps significantly, as a result of increased regulation of hydraulic fracturing and increased demand attributable to fuel switching. Moreover, even a complete replacement of coal with gas would decrease emissions of CO_2 attributable to electricity generation by only about 45 percent – far short of the 80 percent needed to mitigate global warming.

(c) Switching to Nuclear

The United States could pursue a strategy of switching from coal to nuclear power. The obstacles to success in pursuing that strategy include: nuclear energy is approximately 20 percent more expensive than coal or gas;[75] nuclear is controversial with the public; we have made no progress in solving the permanent nuclear waste disposal problem; nuclear generating plants are difficult to finance; and prospective investors remember the $100 billion dollars in losses investors in nuclear plants suffered in the 1980s.[76]

---

[74] Joskow & Marron, *supra* note 26.
[75] U.S. ENERGY INFO. ADMIN., 2016 LEVELIZED, *supra* note 51.
[76] *See supra* notes 28-30 and accompanying text.

(d) Switching to Hydro

The United States could pursue a strategy of switching from coal to hydro-electric power. The obstacles to success in pursuing that strategy include: hydro is about 20 percent more expensive than coal or gas;[77] the United States has limited untapped hydro potential; and hydro has become unpopular with the public because of the effects of dams on fisheries resources.

(e) Switching to Geothermal

The United States could pursue a strategy of switching from coal to geothermal. The obstacles to success in pursuing that strategy include: geothermal is about 16 percent more expensive than coal or gas;[78] there are limited viable sites and many are in environmentally sensitive areas such as Yellowstone National Park; geothermal induces category 3 plus earthquakes;[79] earthquakes closed the large geothermal project in Basel,[80] resulted in the criminal indictment of the Basel project manager, forced cancellation of a large project in California,[81] and created serious NIMBY (i.e., not-in-my-backyard) problems for any potential geothermal project in the United States.

(f) Switching to Wind

The United States could pursue a strategy of switching from coal to wind. The obstacles to success in pursuing that strategy include: wind is 50–90 percent more expensive than coal or gas;[82] wind farms kill large numbers of birds and bats;[83] wind farms raise serious issues under the Endangered Species Act;[84] windmills are extremely noisy; wind farms are aesthetically

---

[77] U.S. ENERGY INFO. ADMIN., 2016 LEVELIZED, *supra* note 51.

[78] *Id.*

[79] Adam Gabatt, *Swiss Geothermal Power Plan Abandoned After Quakes Hit Basel*, THE GUARDIAN, Dec. 15, 2009, *available at* http://www.guardian.co.uk/world/2009/dec/15/swiss-geothermal-power-earthquakes-basel; James Glanz, *Geothermal Project in California Is Shut Down*, N. Y. TIMES, Dec. 12, 2009, at A10.

[80] Gabbat, *supra* note 79.

[81] Glanz, *supra* note 79.

[82] U.S. ENERGY INFO. ADMIN., 2016 LEVELIZED, *supra* note 51.

[83] Robert Bryce, *Windmills Are Killing Our Birds*, WALL ST. J., Sept. 8, 2009, at A19; Catherine Brahic, *Wind Turbine Makes Bat Lungs Explode*, NEW SCIENTIST, Aug. 25, 2008, *available at* http://www.newscientist.com/article/dn14593-wind-turbines-make-bat-lungs-explode.html.

[84] A federal judge ordered the shut down of a large wind farm because it was killing endangered bats. *See* Animal Welfare Inst. v. Beech Ridge Energy, LLC, 675 F. Supp.2d 540 (D. Md. 2009).

controversial; windmills have a low load factor; it takes about 1,000 windmills to equal the output of one standard-sized generator; wind power is unreliable because its availability depends on wind velocity; and because of its unreliability and low load factor, wind power requires construction of a disproportionately large number of new transmission lines.

(g) Switching to Solar

The United States could pursue a strategy of switching from coal to one of two forms of solar energy – central station thermal or decentralized photovoltaic. The obstacles to success in pursuing a solar thermal policy include: solar thermal is about 160 percent more expensive than coal or gas;[85] it requires new transmission lines; and it requires a large amount of land that is rendered useless for any other purpose. The obstacles to success in pursuing decentralized photovoltaic include: photovoltaic is about 300 percent more expensive than coal or gas;[86] it requires states to approve feed-in tariffs to allow solar producers to sell their excess electricity to the grid at generous prices;[87] it is unpopular with many zoning boards and neighborhood associations;[88] and it is unreliable because it is available only when the sun shines.

(h) Switching to Clean Coal

The United States could pursue a strategy of switching from coal to "clean coal" by implementing a program of carbon capture and storage (CCS). The obstacles to success in pursuing that strategy include: it has never been done on a large-scale basis; it would increase the cost of generating energy with coal by about 30 percent;[89] it would take decades to construct the required pipeline network and underground storage caverns;[90] safe storage

---

[85] U.S. ENERGY INFO. ADMIN., 2016 LEVELIZED, *supra* note 51.

[86] *Id.*

[87] WILSON RICKERSON, FLORIAN BENNHOLD, & JAMES BRADBURY, FEED-IN TARIFFS AND RENEWABLE ENERGY IN THE USA – A POLICY UPDATE 4 (2008), *available at* http://www.wind-works.org/FeedLaws/USA/Feed-in_Tariffs_and_Renewable_Energy_in_the_USA_-_a_Policy_Update.pdf.

[88] Troy Rule, *Renewable Energy and the Neighbors*, 2010 UTAH L. REV. 1223.

[89] U.S. ENERGY INFO. ADMIN., 2016 LEVELIZED, *supra* note 51.

[90] David Biello, *Carbon Capture and Storage: Absolute Necessity or Crazy Scheme?*, SCI. AM. (Mar. 6, 2009), http://www.scientificamerican.com/blog/post.cfm?id=carbon-capture-and-storage-absolute-2009-03-06.

of CO_2 may be more difficult and risky than safe storage of spent nuclear fuel; a natural CO_2 leak in Cameroon killed 1,700 people in 1986;[91] public awareness of the risks of CO_2 storage will cause major NIMBY problems;[92] and no one will embark on such a project without federal legislation that limits the project sponsor's liability in the event of a catastrophic leak.

III. Conclusion

I hope that my description of the limited options available to us to reduce CO_2 emissions by 80 percent and the formidable obstacles to success in attaining that goal persuade you both that the task is daunting and that a large carbon tax provides the best prospect for success in attaining the goal. A large carbon tax would offset to some extent the difference between the cost of continuing to rely primarily on hydrocarbons to generate electricity and the cost of switching to primary reliance on carbon-free sources of electricity. It would also spur investment in the research and development needed to enhance the efficiency with which we use electricity, reduce the cost of using carbon-free sources, improve the reliability of sources like wind and solar, and develop methods of storing electricity at tolerable cost. Perhaps most important, given the high variability of circumstances and the uncertain pace of technological progress, producers and consumers may be able to take steps needed to mitigate global warming, and at the same time take advantage of the evolving options that are best suited for them.

Our only hope of mitigating global warming lies in major technological breakthroughs. With the economic incentives created by a large carbon tax, we are likely to attain significant improvements in the technology needed to mitigate global warming. It is impossible to predict, however, whether the major advances will take place in the context of conservation/enhanced efficiency, reduced costs and/or increased reliability of specific carbon-free sources, or improved ability to store electricity economically. If we imple-

---

[91] *Nature Untamed: Death Fog* (National Geographic television broadcast), *available at* http://channel.nationalgeographic.com/series/nature-untamed/4671/Overview#tab-Videos/07528_00.

[92] The most likely cause of a CO2 leak in the US will likely come from a backhoe that hits a high pressure pipeline in a populated area. While spent gas reservoirs are promising sites for storing CO2, they require a large amount of geologic and geophysical work before they can be used for that purpose.

ment a large carbon tax, we do not have to engage in the hazardous process of predicting technological advances. If they take place primarily in the context of solar power, the tax will automatically channel most of our mitigation efforts in that direction. Conversely, if they take place primarily in the context of some other source – such as conservation/efficiency enhancement, cost of storage, wind, geothermal, clean coal, or nuclear – the tax will automatically channel most of our efforts down whatever path has become the most economic route to mitigate global warming.

Why the U.S. Does Not Have a Renewable Energy Policy

E. Donald Elliott[*]

Portugal is one of the world leaders in renewable energy. Many in the United States feel there is much to learn from Portugal. The *New York Times* recently reported that about 45% of the electricity in the grid in Portugal comes from renewable energy sources.[1] That compares with only 12% in the United States, and of that total, about 10% is hydro, so we in the United States are actually in the range of only about 2% of our electricity coming from non-hydro renewable energy sources, as opposed to 45% in Portugal. A number of other countries in the European Union also have renewable energy numbers comparable to Portugal's.[2]

On the surface, the renewable energy gap between the United States and the European Union is surprising in that every U.S. president since Richard Nixon has declared as a national goal the ending of our addiction

---

[*] Professor (adj) of Law, Yale Law School and Partner, Willkie Farr & Gallagher LLP, Washington, DC. I am grateful to Matthew Christensen, Yale Law School class of 2012, for his excellent research assistance. Of course, I alone am responsible for the errors that remain. An earlier version was presented at the 10th Conference on European Union, Portuguese and American Law: Developments in Energy Law at The Catholic University of America, Washington, DC, April 7, 2011.

[1] Elisabeth Rosenthal, *Portugal Gives Itself a Clean-Energy Makeover*, N.Y. Times, Aug. 10, 2010, at A1.

[2] Promoting Sustainable Electricity in Europe: Challenging the Path Dependence of Dominant Energy Systems 286 (Williams M. Lafferty & Audun Rund eds., 2008) (Table 10.1).

DIREITO COMPARADO / COMPARATIVE LAW

to imported petroleum.[3] President Obama in his 2011 State of the Union address made moving to a clean energy economy one of the signature aspects of his presidency.[4] What I will try to *explain* – but not necessarily to *justify* – is why we have no effective national renewable energy policy in the United States.

We must first distinguish between a policy and a plan. We do have a *plan* – or more accurately, a long series of plans. Under the 1977 law that created our national Department of Energy, every two years the President and the Department of Energy are required by law to put together a "national energy policy plan."[5] The latest one was announced March 30, 2011.[6] For 35 years, these semi-annual national energy plans have been ignored. They are written, announced and go directly into the dustbin of history. Unlike the Renewable Energy Directive in Europe,[7] which creates binding obligations on the member states, our "national energy policy plan" is merely a semi-annual essay by the energy experts in the federal government that few read and no one follows.

One could see our failure to implement an effective renewable energy policy as a symptom of a more general breakdown in the ability of national political institutions in the United States to address environmental, as well as many other, pressing policy issues.[8] This paper seeks to understand the absence of a U.S. renewable energy policy not simply as a failure to

---

[3] MICHAEL J. GRAETZ, THE END OF ENERGY: THE UNMAKING OF AMERICA'S ENVIRONMENT, SECURITY AND INDEPENDENCE 250-251 (2011); DAVID SANDALOW, FREEDOM FROM OIL: HOW THE NEXT PRESIDENT CAN END THE UNITED STATES' OIL ADDICTION (2008).

[4] President Barack Obama, 2011 State of the Union: Winning the Future (Jan. 25, 2011), *available at* https://www.whitehouse.gov/the-press-office/2011/01/25/remarks-president-state-union-address.

[5] Title VIII of the Department of Energy Organization Act of 1977, 42 U.S.C. § 7321, requires that the President propose and submit a National Energy Policy Plan every two years. Congress then reviews it and may propose changes. 42 U.S.C. § 7322.

[6] THE WHITE HOUSE, BLUEPRINT FOR A SECURE ENERGY FUTURE (2011), *available at* http://www.whitehouse.gov/sites/default/files/blueprint_secure_energy_future.pdf.

[7] Directive 2009/28/Ec of the European Parliament and of the Council of 23 April 2009 on the promotion of the use of energy from renewable sources and amending and subsequently repealing Directives 2001/77/EC and 2003/30/EC, http://eur-lex.europa.eu/LexUriServ/LexUriServ.do?uri=OJ:L:2009:140:0016:0062:EN:PDF.

[8] *See generally* E. Donald Elliott, *Politics Failed, Not Ideas*, 28 ENVTL. F. 42 (Sept./Oct. 2011) ("The same period in which the American national political system has become dysfunctional on environmental issues is also one in which it hasn't done so well on many other important

develop an effective policy, but also as a deeper expression of our political structure and political culture, and perhaps to suggest that there may be some wisdom, as well as some obvious disadvantages, to our hesitancy to be a leader in the renewable energy parade.[9]

I. Structural Impediments: The Coordinate Model of Authority in the United States

A perceptive nineteenth century European, Walter Bagehot, the first editor of *The Economist* and the founder of political science, wrote many years ago:

> The English constitution, in a word, is framed on the principle of choosing a single sovereign authority, and making it good: the American, upon the principle on having many sovereign authorities, and hoping that their multitude will atone for their inferiority.[10]

A leading contemporary expert on comparative law, my colleague at Yale Law School, Mirjan R. Damaška, has made a similar point in a modern context. Damaška says a defining feature of the U.S. legal system is its "coordinate model of authority" in which multiple power centers all address the same issue.[11] That political structure makes it extremely difficult to develop a coordinated national policy, which can only be done by reaching consensus among many different power centers.

A. *Federalism as an Impediment to a National Renewable Energy Policy*
One aspect of this coordinate model of authority is what we call *federalism*. Each of our 50 states regulates electric utilities, often with different

---

issues, such as managing our financial affairs, reforming Social Security and the income tax system, or keeping us out of elective foreign wars.").

[9] Elsewhere I have suggested more generally that legal systems may be at an advantage when they are not the first to experiment with new devices, but can learn from the experience of others. E. Donald Elliott, *U.S. Environmental Law in Global Perspective: Five Do's and Five Don'ts from Our Experience*, 5 NAT'L TAIWAN UNIV. L. REV. 144, 146-47 (2010) (discussing "third-mover advantage"), *available at* http://digitalcommons.law.yale.edu/fss_papers/2717/.

[10] WALTER BAGEHOT, THE ENGLISH CONSTITUTION AND OTHER POLITICAL ESSAYS 296 (Paul Smith ed., Cambridge Univ. Press 2001) (1867).

[11] MIRJAN R. DAMAŠKA, THE FACES OF JUSTICE AND STATE AUTHORITY: A COMPARATIVE APPROACH TO THE LEGAL PROCESS (1986); Mirjan R. Damaška, *Structures of Authority and Comparative Criminal Procedure*, 84 YALE L.J. 480 (1975).

policies, whereas the wholesale transportation of electricity is regulated by the federal government.[12] One of the few bright spots with regard to renewable energy policy in the United States is the many "renewable portfolio standards" (RPSs) that have been adopted at the state level. These are state laws that require local utilities to supply a certain percentage of the electric power that they distribute from renewable sources. What counts as a renewable source varies from state-to-state, as do the target percentages. Seven states that have so-called voluntary RPSs, and 29 states, plus the District of Columbia and Puerto Rico, have enacted mandatory RPSs.[13] The most ambitious is California, which recently announced a goal of 33 percent of the state's electricity from renewable sources by 2020.[14]

Thus, even our most ambitious state is well behind Portugal and most other EU countries, but in over half our country, state governments are doing something to promote electricity from renewable energy, even though to-date we have been unable to pass a federal RPS that would apply nationally. In sum, we have a diversity of policies that are set at the state level, with over half of the states mandating some generation from renewables, but the others not choosing to make that a priority.

B. Separation of Powers as an Impediment to a National Renewable Energy Policy

The second example of how the coordinate model of authority stands in the way of our developing a national renewable energy policy is what we call *separation of powers*. Unlike the Portuguese parliamentary system in which the executive and the majority of the legislature are of the same party, a much more typical situation in the United States is one in which one party controls one house of the Congress and the Presidency, but the other house of the Congress is controlled by the other party. We call this "divided government," with different political parties in control of different parts of the government, and it has been a recurring feature of American political life.

Divided government is particularly important for national renewable energy policy because a strong wing of one of the two major political par-

---

[12] Joseph P. Tomain & Richard D. Cudahy, Energy Law in A Nutshell 264 (2004).
[13] *RPS Policies*, DSIRE: Database of State Incentives for Renewables & Efficiency, http://www.dsireusa.org/summarymaps/index.cfm?ee=1&RE=1 (last updated March 2011).
[14] *Brown Signs 33 Percent California RPS*, Energy Daily, Apr. 13, 2011 at 2.

ties is generally opposed to government action to promote renewables. *New York Times* columnist David Brooks perceptively summarized this central schism in American politics:

> Democrats tend to be skeptical that dispersed consumers can get enough information to make smart decisions. ... Democrats generally seek to concentrate decision-making and cost-control power in the hands of centralized experts. ... Republicans at their best are skeptical about top-down decision-making. They are skeptical that centralized experts can accurately predict costs. They are skeptical that centralized experts can predict human behavior accurately enough to socially engineer new programs. ... They are skeptical that political authorities can, in the long run, resist pressure to hand out free goodies. They are also skeptical that planners can control the unintended effects of their decisions. They argue that a decentralized process of trial and error will work better, as long as the underlying incentives are right. ... Democrats have much greater faith in centralized expertise. Republicans ... believe that the world is too complicated, knowledge is too imperfect. They have much greater faith in the decentralized discovery process of the market.[15]

While Brooks was writing specifically about health care policy, much of what he wrote also applies to energy policy. Many Republicans, like former Bush White House adviser David Frum, argue that we should leave energy choices to the market:

> Th[e] command-and-control method has been tried and tried again, always with conspicuous lack of success, and for all the obvious reasons: Because government favors big "imagination-capturing" technologies over incremental adjustments. Because government makes a bad venture capitalist. Because democratic governments (rightly) cannot decree the kinds of lifestyle changes that price signals will induce voluntarily. What government will order empty nesters to move from the exurbs to downtown? But a 60-minute commute and $5 gas will persuade people to do what no bureaucrat would dare command.[16]

---

[15] David Brooks, *Where Wisdom Lives*, N.Y. TIMES, June 6, 2011, http://www.nytimes.com/2011/06/07/opinion/07brooks.html?r=1.

[16] David Frum, *Obama's Doomed Green Jobs Plan: Just Tax Oil and Let Markets Do The Rest*, THEWEEK.COM http://theweek.com/bullpen/column/211455/obamas-doomed-green-jobs-plan.

C. *Changing Policies as an Impediment to a National Renewable Energy Policy*

A closely-related aspect of our politics that has made it difficult for the national government to promote renewable energy is frequent changes in control of government by our political parties and the *shifting policies* that result. A good example is our national policy to promote an alternative to gasoline-powered automobiles. Our two major political parties generally agree on this objective, but they differ on the means to accomplish it, with the result that mixed and inconsistent signals are sent to industry. In 2003, President George W. Bush in his State of the Union speech announced an initiative to devote billions of dollars to develop the *hydrogen-powered* car.[17] When President Obama came into office five years later in 2008, he cut 80% of the funding for the hydrogen car that had been sponsored by his predecessor.[18] In his 2011 State of the Union address, Obama announced that now we are going to promote *electric-powered* cars instead.[19]

Shifting policies and changing priorities as different parties come to power in the United States has been one of the major difficulties that we have had in promoting renewable energy. In a 2009 report, the U.S. National Academy of Sciences identified "lack of *sustained* policies" as one of the three top barriers to promoting renewable energy.[20] The Germans have made a long-term commitment to buy renewable energy, which facilitates developers in financing their projects. Our policies tend to come and go. And they tend to come and go on shorter time horizons than those

---

[17] George W. Bush, President of the United States, State of the Union (Jan. 28, 2003) ("Tonight I'm proposing $1.2 billion in research funding so that America can lead the world in developing clean, hydrogen-powered automobiles.").

[18] *Obama Puts Breaks on the Hydrogen Car*, WALL ST. J., http://blogs.wsj.com/washwire/2009/05/07/obama-budget-puts-brakes-on-hydrogen-car/ (last visited April 11, 10:00pm).

[19] Barack Obama, President of the United States, State of the Union (Jan. 25, 2011). The American Reinvestment and Recovery Act, Pub. L. 111–5 (2009), also known as the stimulus bill, included approximately two billion dollars for grants to support 30 factories that produce batteries, motors, and other electric vehicle components. See DEPARTMENT OF ENERGY, ONE MILLION ELECTRIC VEHICLES BY 2015: FEBRUARY 2011 STATUS REPORT 5 (2011).

[20] National Research Council, America's Energy Future Panel on Electricity from Renewable Resources, Electricity from Renewable Resources: Status, Prospects, and Impediments Executive Summary at 3 (2009) ("The current primary barriers are [two others and] the lack of sustained policies.").

that are necessary to make the long-term capital investments in the kind of infrastructure changes that Dick Pierce was talking about earlier in his contribution to this symposium.[21] One of our key structural problems to implementing a national renewable energy policy is that we have difficulty maintaining policies and sending consistent signals to the market over the long time periods required to replace capital stock.

D. Unrepresented Future Generations as Impediment to a National Renewable Energy Policy

In addition, there is not a strong political constituency for renewable energy or energy efficiency in America. There is some support, of course, but the core difficulty in organizing around these issues is that the putative beneficiaries are largely future generations and they are by definition unrepresented in our current political process.[22] This may be more of our problem in our system in which politicians are subject to frequent re-election. Promoting renewable energy is the kind of issue to which our political institutions are particularly ill-suited, because it would require an economic commitment over a sustained period to achieve benefits that are not obvious today but inure largely to future generations that are not represented in our current politics.

II. Cultural Impediments: Cheap Energy Now vs. Future Generations

In addition to these structural features of the U.S. political system, there are also important cultural differences between the United States and Europe that also help to explain why U.S. attitudes toward developing a national renewable energy policy are so different.

A. The "Right" to Cheap Energy as an Impediment to a National Renewable Energy Policy

We have deeply embedded the expectation of *cheap energy* in the expectations of our citizens. People complain mightily when gas reaches four dollars a gallon in the United States. Some analysts even suggest that President

---

[21] *See* PIERCE, *supra* p. 279.

[22] *See* ANDREW DOBSON & ROBYN ECKERSLEY, POLITICAL THEORY AND THE ECOLOGICAL CHALLENGE 186-88 (2006); Matthew W. Wolfe, Note, *The Shadows of Future Generations*, 57 DUKE L.J. 1897, 1901-02 (2008).

DIREITO COMPARADO / COMPARATIVE LAW

Obama's bid for re-election could be threatened by rising gasoline prices, pointing out that in America there is a stronger correlation between low prices of gasoline and presidential popularity than there is with unemployment rates.[23]

Some studies claim that the fully loaded-in social cost of gasoline is in the range of 6 to 15 dollars a gallon[24] and yet the U.S. public is very upset when the price rises as high as 4 dollars a gallon, which is about half the price in Europe. This is a bi-partisan problem. One of the few things that the George H.W. Bush administration and the Clinton administration agreed on is that energy prices in the United States were too low. The George H.W. Bush administration proposed an increase in the gasoline tax; the Clinton administration proposed a BTU tax.[25] Both of them had to back down as a result of public outcry. We have created a fundamental expectation in our democratic voters that energy prices must remain low.[26]

Some of this is a result of history and our large domestic supplies of fossil fuels. The United States is one of the world's largest fossil energy producers, unlike many countries that have led the way in developing renewable energy sources. The United States is either blessed (or cursed, depending upon ones' perspective) with large domestic supplies of oil, coal, and natural gas. In 1917, the United States wast he largest oil producer in the world and produced two-thirds of the world's oil.[27] Oil production peaked in the United States about 1970, but the United States is still the third largest producer of petroleum in the world (after Saudi Arabia and Russia), producing roughly twice as much petroleum as the fourth largest producer, Iran.[28] The United States produces on the order of five million barrels a day but consumes 14 million a day, so the United States is

[23] David Paul Kuhn, *Could Gas Prices Sink Obama's Reelection?*, Real Clear Politics, Mar. 9, 2011, http://www.realclearpolitics.com/articles/2011/03/09/could_gas_prices_sink_obamas_re-election_2012_study_president_approval_gas_price_109157.html.

[24] International Center for Technology Assessment, The Real Price of Gasoline: An Analysis of the Hidden External Costs Consumers Pay to Fuel Their Automobiles (1998), www.icta.org/doc/Real%20Price%20of%20Gasoline.pdf.

[25] SALVATORE LAZZARI, CONG. RESEARCH SERV., RL 33578, ENERGY TAX POLICY: HISTORY AND CURRENT ISSUES 6 (2008).

[26] For the sources and consequences of this expectation, see generally GRAETZ, *supra* note 3.

[27] DANIEL YERGEN, THE PRIZE 160-63 (1991).

[28] Top World Oil Producers, Exporters, Consumers, and Importers, 2006, http://www.infoplease.com/ipa/A0922041.html.

also by far the largest importer of oil.[29] But historically, we have had large domestic sources of energy and have gotten used to cheap energy prices. This assumption is now built deeply into the structure of our society, so that, for example, the average American worker drives 32 miles (53 kilometers) round-trip each day to and from work, and some drive over 100 miles (160 kilometers) each way.[30] And because of the layout of our cities, many of them do not have any alternative but to drive.

Because we have multiple sources of fossil energy within easy reach, as new supplies are discovered or new recovery techniques developed, energy prices can change dramatically. For example, in the last few years, the expectation of low natural gas prices from the huge new shale gas supplies in the United States have caused a number of developers who were making big investments in wind projects to delay or pull the plug on those projects.[31]

B. Free Market Ideology as an Impediment to a National Renewable Energy Policy

The second cultural factor is that we have a very strong *free market ideology* in the United States. Perhaps it is even stronger here than in most countries in Europe. Many of our leading conservative think-tanks in the United States, such as the Cato Institute, the Heritage Foundation, and the American Enterprise Institute, are attacking the concept of government promoting green energy and a green energy future.[32] It is not so much that they are opposed to renewable energy *per se*, but rather to the heavy hand of government to mandate it. But it is an interesting anomaly that conservatives in Europe generally support renewable energy,[33] but conservatives in the United States generally oppose it.

---

[29] U.S. Energy Information Administration, Petroleum Statistics (2009 data), http://www.eia.gov/energyexplained/index.cfm?page=oil_home#tab2.

[30] http://www.ehow.com/facts_7446397_far-americans-drive-work-average_.html.

[31] Keith Johnson, *Ill Winds Blow for Clean Energy: Cheap, and Abundant, Natural Gas Diminishes Alternative Projects' Appeal*, WALL ST. J.,July 9, 2009, http://online.wsj.com/article/SB124710043333415571.html.

[32] ANDREW P. MORRISS, WILLIAM T. BOGART, ROGER E. MEINERS, ANDREW D. DORCHAK, THE FALSE PROMISE OF GREEN ENERGY (Cato, 2011), http://www.cato.org/store/books/false-promise-green-energy.

[33] *See, e.g.,* [UK] Conservatives, Where We Stand: Climate Change and Energy Policy, http://www.conservatives.com/Policy/Where_we_stand/Climate_Change_and_Energy.aspx ("We are committed to optimising energy from renewable sources.").

A good example is an article that appeared by two senior fellows at the Cato Institute, Jerry Taylor and Peter Van Doren, in *Forbes,* an influential business magazine run by a conservative former presidential candidate, Steven Forbes. They wrote "renewable energy is quite literally the energy of yesterday."[34] (Actually they claimed it was "the energy of the 13th Century"[35] to be exact.)

> If green energy is so inevitable and such a great investment why do we need to subsidize it? ... If and when renewable energy makes economic sense, profit hungry investors will build all that we need without government needing to lift a finger. But if it doesn't make economic sense, all of the subsidies in the world won't change that fact.[36]

In addition, as Pat McCormick referred to in his presentation at the symposium, the U.S. electricity system is dominated by private ownership of electric utilities and some of them, along with some oil and coal companies, are a powerful lobbying force against fundamental changes in the U.S. energy structure.

C. *Less Concern with Climate Change as Impediment to a National Renewable Energy Policy*

The last point, to which Pat McCormick also referred, is that there is less concern with global climate change in the United States than there is in Europe. McCormick's point was well-taken that people from Europe tend to mention global climate change first and energy security second. In the United States, it is generally the other way around. A Gallup poll in March of 2011 said that global climate change was the *lowest* concern among environmental issues among Americans.[37] They ranked every other environmental problem higher than they ranked global climate change. And only 51% of Americans regarded global climate change as a "serious problem."[38]

---

[34] Jerry Taylor & Peter Van Doren, *The Green Energy Economy Reconsidered,* FORBES Mar. 29, 2011, http://www.forbes.com/2011/03/28/green-energy-economics-opinions-jerry-taylor-peter-van-doren.html.

[35] *Id.*

[36] *Id.*

[37] http://www.gallup.com/poll/146810/water-issues-worry-americans-global-warming-least.aspx.

[38] *Id.*

That is not enough to legislate. Our political structure was set up so that one could only legislate if there was a strong consensus.

To sum up, let me quote from the *New York Times*, which wrote in August, 2010:

> If the United States is to catch up to countries like Portugal, the United States must overcome obstacles like a fragmented, outdated energy grid poorly suited to renewable energy, a historic reliance on plentiful and cheap supplies of fossil fuels, especially coal, powerful oil and coal industries that often oppose incentives for renewable development and an energy policy that is influenced by individual states.[39]

III. A Half-Hearted Defense of the American Approach

After portraying this pessimistic picture about the prospects for a national renewable energy policy in the United States, let me try to make a brief, half-hearted, and only partial defense of the American approach. Admittedly, the U.S. system of government is not good at government-led transformations of the economy, such as mobilizing trillions of dollars of capital to re-make our energy infrastructure. At least unless there is a really strong and sustained popular consensus as the United States had around environmental issues in the 1970s and 1980s. The Framers intended it that way. The goal of the U.S. political system is to prevent government from leading us into misadventures. The Framers seemed to believe that it was better for government not to act than to act wrongly. Many Americans think that the government is not all that smart. They are more concerned about government picking and subsidizing losers than about missing the boat for lack of a strong centralized energy policy. Thus, current U.S. renewable energy policy is not to have a single national policy, but to allow states and private companies to experiment with different approaches and ultimately to let the market decide what works best.[40]

---

[39] Rosenthal, *supra* note 1.

[40] The great fallacy in our current "let the market decide" approach is that we already have significant government subsidies that distort the competition. *See generally* Envtl. Law Inst., Estimating U.S. Government Subsidies to Energy Sources: 2002-2008 (September 2009), http://www.eli.org/Program_Areas/innovation_governance_energy.cfm. This has led one of our political figures to call for the elimination of all energy subsidies. *Sarah Palin Calls To Eliminate Energy Subsidies*, http://www.politico.com/news/stories/0511/55970.html; *see also*

There are some theoretical justifications for the conservative position that the best national renewable energy policy may be not to have a single national one but a diversity of policies at the state level. This cautious approach can be seen as a version of what is called the "maxmin" strategy in game theory.[41] If you are a very risk-adverse player, and you think you are not very smart, the best way to play the game may be to try to ameliorate the worst possible outcome by cutting your losses. In other words, try to avoid being totally and disastrously wrong. Hedge your bets; invest some in renewable energy, but do not invest too much in something that may turn out to be wrong.

This is also closely akin to what is called "portfolio theory" in economics, diversifying and investing in multiple approaches,[42] as opposed to putting 45% of your electric power into renewables (or 75% into nuclear power in the case of France[43]). Walter Bagehot had it right that the essence of American government is hoping that the multitude of our institutions will atone for their inferiority. And at the core, that's why we don't have an effective national renewable energy policy.

But having said that, the United States is still third worldwide in renewable energy investment.[44] And the United States still invest more in clean energy research and development than Europeans do on a per capita basis.[45] But, as on many other issues of social and economic policy, the United States is playing an inelegant, untidy, diverse, more *laissez faire* strategy that is different than the more centralized strategy that Europe is pursuing. It will be interesting to see which will end up being more successful in the long run.

RICHARD H. K. VIETOR, ENERGY POLICY IN AMERICA SINCE 1945: A STUDY OF BUSINESS-GOVERNMENT RELATIONS (Cambridge, 1984).

[41] For a quick summary, see http://www.quickmba.com/econ/micro/gametheory/.

[42] For an introduction to basic portfolio theory, see generally HARRY M. MARKOWITZ, PORTFOLIO SELECTION: EFFICIENT DIVERSIFICATION OF INVESTMENTS 4-8 (1970). For a discussion of the value of a portfolio approach in energy policy, see Michael Grubb, Lucy Butler, and Paul Twomey, *Diversity and Security in UK Electricity Generation: The Influence of Low-Carbon Objectives*, 34 ENERGY POL'Y 4050 (2005).

[43] World Nuclear Ass'n, *Nuclear Power in France*, http://www.world-nuclear.org/info/inf40.html.

[44] *Behind China and Germany*, http://www.reuters.com/article/2011/03/29/us-renewables-report-pew-idUSTRE72S0T620110329.

[45] Paul Klempere, *What is the top priority on climate change?* (Dec 13, 2007), http://www.voxeu.org/index.php?q=node/803.

Another distinguished European, Otto von Bismarck, the inventor of the modern activist welfare state, once reportedly said, with apparent frustration, "God looks after drunkards, fools, and the United States of America."[46] Bismarck just could not understand how the misguided and misgoverned Americans manage to do as well as they do without an enlightened Prussian bureaucracy to guide them. With all due respect to Bismarck, it may not be God after all. It may be that the United States typically follows inelegant, muddled, untidy, diversified strategies that are never right, but also rarely end up being totally wrong.

---

[46] SAMUEL ELIOT MORISON, THE OXFORD HISTORY OF THE UNITED STATES 1783-1917 413 (1927) (*quoted at* http://en.wikiquote.org/wiki/Talk:Otto_von_Bismarck).

Developments in Mergers and Restructuring in the U.S. Energy Sector

KEITH D. LARSON[*]

The focus of this paper is on recent merger and restructuring activity in the energy sector in the United States, viewed from a commercial and not regulatory perspective. Other papers presented at this Conference have addressed important competition issues related to energy sector merger activity, particularly in the European Union, where large, state-owned utilities possess significant market power. Conditions in the United States are quite different, and in fact merger activity involving public utilities is rarely opposed by relevant antitrust authorities. To the contrary, given the fragmentation within individual industries across the United States, consolidation is actively encouraged by investors and generally supported by regulators. In that context, it is important to evaluate the commercial and regulatory drivers underlying merger and restructuring activity in the U.S. energy sector.

In my view there are two fundamental market developments that are presently shaping merger and restructuring activity in the United States. These are: (1) regulatory and other developments in the electricity industry that impact the choice of technology for new power generation and (2) developments in domestic natural gas production. As this paper will explain, these two fundamental developments are, to some degree, inter-related.

---

[*] Partner, Hogan Lovells, Washington D.C.

DIREITO COMPARADO / COMPARATIVE LAW

There are, of course, a number of other important issues in the U.S. energy industry that one could focus on. For example, the potential for further offshore oil and gas drilling, the potential for offshore wind power, developments in solar power generation technologies, the economic feasibility of natural gas pipelines running from Alaska to the lower 48 states, developments in energy efficiency and demand-side management, and even the promotion of electric automobiles each have become part of the national discourse regarding U.S. energy security. But these factors, although noteworthy, influence merger and restructuring activity to a much lesser degree. Ten or twenty years hence that may change – particularly as renewable or "clean energy" technologies become more cost competitive with conventional generation.

Natural Gas Expansion

The first critical factor to understand in evaluating the recent developments in U.S. energy merger and restructuring activity is the rapid discovery and development of shale gas resources in the Southwest and Northeast United States. According to recent estimates, over eight hundred trillion cubic feet of natural gas lies in shale formations beneath the surface of several U.S. states.[1] So prevalent is this resource base – which alone is sufficient to satisfy all U.S. gas demand for twenty-five years – that industry analysts expect shale gas to account for fifty percent of U.S. gas supply by 2035. In less than a decade, shale gas has transformed the U.S. energy landscape, reversing the fortunes of several complementary and competing industries.

The market for liquefied natural gas (LNG) in the United States exemplifies the impact of shale gas. Not long ago, the United States was viewed as the most promising long-term market in the world for LNG. Predictions were that stable economic growth would continue, natural gas demand would increase, and domestic gas supplies would start to deteriorate over time – leaving LNG to fill the widening gap. Additionally, natural gas prices were robust, creating an attractive forward curve. As such, every oil major and a host of independent developers began developing LNG import

---

[1] *See* Chris Nelder, *What the Frack?*, SLATE (Dec. 29, 2011, 6:37 AM), http://www.slate.com/articles/health_and_science/future_tense/2011/12/is_there_really_100_years_worth_of_natural_gas_beneath_the_united_states_.html.

facilities up and down the east and west coasts of the United States. In the east, LNG would come from such markets as Nigeria, Angola, Qatar, and Trinidad & Tobago, while in the west, LNG would come from Sakhalin and Australia, among other markets.

The LNG business was at that time and remains today a "value chain" business where large supply projects are developed with a view to supplying certain targeted markets with substantial gas demand. Unlike crude oil, LNG does not benefit from a fully developed spot market, and therefore one relies on long-term contracts to generate stable revenues that support the financing of highly capital-intensive liquefaction projects. Previously, any supply project in the "Atlantic-Basin" region that did not have guaranteed capacity at a U.S. import terminal was considered to be poorly structured and unfinanceable. Today, LNG remains a vibrant global business, but due to evolving supply forecasts from shale gas, the United States has transitioned from the most admired target market to among the most bleak. Import terminals that were built in the United States with high expectations in the last decade now accept less than half a dozen cargoes of LNG per year, and the owners of those facilities are seeking regulatory clearances to actually export LNG from the United States.

Of course, shale gas is not the silver bullet to energy independence in the United States that certain industry participants would like us to believe. Those who are familiar with the natural gas industry, or who have watched the documentary *Gasland*,[2] will know that the expansion of U.S. shale gas reserves has focused the attention of federal, state, and local governments on the horizontal drilling techniques used by producers to extract shale gas. Known as hydraulic fracturing, the process involves the creation or expansion of cracks, or fractures, in shale formations underground into which water, sand, and other (largely chemical) additives are pumped under high pressure. Once fractures are created or expanded, natural gas can more easily flow from the rock through the well to the surface at economic rates.

Many U.S. states have implemented and continue to consider rules and regulations that affect the way hydraulic fracturing activities are conducted and disclosed, with several imposing or threatening a temporary drilling moratorium until more studies can be performed. A recent well blowout

---

[2] GASLAND (HBO Documentary Films 2010).

in Bradford County, Pennsylvania resulting in a spill of hydraulic fracturing liquids has not inspired confidence among critics of the procedure.[3] Industry participants will be particularly focused on an initial report on hydraulic fracturing to be issued by the Environmental Protection Agency before the end of 2012, and whether its preliminary recommendations will dampen investment plans in U.S. shale gas during the critical retirement period from 2015-2020.[4]

Regardless of the regulatory uncertainty, shale gas production continues to drive merger and restructuring activity, both in the upstream exploration industry and in industries that complement the increase in domestic gas supply, or that because of market and regulatory developments may rely more heavily on natural gas as opposed to other fuel sources or technologies. With respect to the latter, shale gas is proving to have a significant influence over the U.S. electricity sector in particular.

Electricity Dynamics

If natural gas appears to be the dominant and abundant U.S. fuel source over the next several decades, what effect does that have on the U.S. electricity markets? To answer that question, one needs to consider what the nation's generation needs are, and the relative cost of competing technologies. While U.S. electricity demand is not anticipated to grow substantially for several years, the nation's generation fleet is poised to undergo a dramatic restructuring later this decade. In particular, most analysts predict that looming federal regulations that control the emission of sulfur dioxide, nitrogen oxide, particulates, and hazardous air pollutants are expected to put between 50-55 gigawatts of coal-fired generating facilities out of business between 2015-2020.[5] None of these facilities, many of which are over 30 years old, have any emissions control equipment. The

---

[3] Mike Soraghan, *Pa. Well Blowout Tests Natural Gas Industry on Voluntary Fracking Disclosure*, N.Y. TIMES, May 4, 2011.

[4] *See* ENVTL. PROT. AGENCY, EPA 601/R-12/011, STUDY OF THE POTENTIAL IMPACTS OF HYDRAULIC FRACTURING ON DRINKING WATER RESOURCES: PROGRESS REPORT (2012).

[5] *See* INST. FOR ENERGY RESEARCH, IMPACT OF EPA'S REGULATORY ASSAULT ON POWER PLANTS: NEW REGULATIONS TO TAKE 34 GW OF ELECTRICITY GENERATION OFFLINE AND THE PLANT CLOSINGS ANNOUNCEMENTS KEEP COMING... (2012), *available at* http://instituteforenergyresearch.org/wp-content/uploads/2012/04/Power-plants-to-close-because-of-EPAs-regs-April-20-update.pdf.

capital costs to retrofit them and extend their operating lives – particularly amidst the uncertainty regarding the cost of compliance with future carbon regulation – are better directed towards constructing new and more efficient generating plants.

While many technologies could be deployed to replace decommissioned coal-fired generation, natural gas-fired power generation should prove most attractive. Indeed, for a utility seeking to clean up its portfolio at the lowest overall cost, gas-fired generation is, at current gas prices, considerably more competitive than wind, solar or nuclear. As the ongoing development of the nation's shale gas reserves creates a huge fuel stock for new natural gas plants, independent power producers will recognize additional opportunities to deliver gas-fired power to key regional markets currently served by coal facilities. In fact, the longer gas prices remain low and carbon regulation prices remain uncertain, even more coal facilities may be retired in favor of gas-fired generation than expected.

Gas-fired generation also faces fewer challenges than competing technologies. With no near-term prospects for a federal policy regulating carbon dioxide, developers cannot accurately estimate and model the price of carbon regulation, making the financing of new coal-fired power generation unlikely. Renewable energy projects will continue to represent a measurable and important portion of the average utility's portfolio. However, as they have low-capacity factors and are in many cases limited by significant transmission constraints, such projects are not ideal candidates to replace sizeable retired coal facilities.

Finally, notwithstanding the ramifications of the accident at Fukushima in Japan,[6] capital intensive nuclear projects are not considered to be financeable absent billions of dollars in federal government loan guarantee assistance. Even with that support, the lack of a national solution for storage of spent fuel and radioactive waste, as well as the potential for stricter safety and compliance requirements, are certain to make some utilities more reticent to take on a nuclear project. Another problem for nuclear energy is that it cannot yet be deployed as an "incremental" technology. Other fuel sources, including renewable energy sources, are attractive in an era of moderate demand growth because they can be developed to scale

---

[6] *See generally* Evan Osnos, *The Fallout: Seven Months Later – Japan's Nuclear Predicament*, NEW YORKER, Oct. 17, 2011.

to match demand. Nuclear power, on the other hand, is a displacing technology, meant to replace large pieces of generating capacity with a single facility. Plans for smaller, modular reactors are underway, but the Nuclear Regulatory Commission has not yet approved a design, and it may be 2020 before the first such product is commercially deployed.[7]

As such, the U.S. energy market is focusing on a shift away from nuclear energy and renewable energy to gas-fired power generation. Merger and acquisition activity surrounding both generating assets and owners of generating assets has accelerated substantially. The likelihood of low, stable electricity and gas prices over the near term is making it easier for sellers and buyers to find mutually agreeable valuations. In addition, utility consolidation continues to advance at a rapid pace.

Trends and Examples

Against that background regarding the current dynamics in the U.S. energy market, this paper will next examine three recent mergers and/ or restructurings which embody some of the themes outlined above. The largest and most significant of such transactions is the Duke Energy-Progress Energy merger.

(a) Duke / Progress

On January 10, 2011, Duke Energy and Progress Energy – both large, regulated utilities headquartered in North Carolina – announced their merger and the creation of the nation's largest utility.[8] The combined Duke-Progress entity, which will be known as Duke Energy, will have 57 gigawatts of installed generation, including the largest nuclear fleet in the United States, and seven million customers across North Carolina, South Carolina, Florida, Indiana, Kentucky, and Ohio.[9]

Completion of the merger is conditioned upon, among other things, the approval of the shareholders of both companies, as well as expiration or

---

[7] *See* Memorandum from Michael R. Johnson, Dir., Office of New Reactors, Nuclear Regulatory Comm'n to Nuclear Regulatory Comm'rs, Staff Assessment of Selected Small Modular Reactor Issues Identified in SECY-10-0034 (Aug. 12, 2011), *available at* http://pbadupws.nrc.gov/docs/ML1104/ML110460434.pdf .

[8] Press Release, Duke Energy, Duke Energy and Progress Energy to Merge (Jan. 10, 2011), *available at* http://www.duke-energy.com/news/releases/2011011001.asp.

[9] *Id.*

termination of any applicable waiting period under the Hart-Scott-Rodino Antitrust Improvements Act of 1976.[10] Other necessary regulatory steps include filings with and/or approvals of the Federal Energy Regulatory Commission, the Nuclear Regulatory Commission, the North Carolina Utilities Commission, and the South Carolina Public Service Commission. Other state regulators, including the Florida Public Service Commission, the Indiana Utility Regulatory Commission, the Kentucky Public Service Commission, and the Ohio Public Utilities Commission, have detailed reporting requirements regarding the merger. Although the merger is expected to be approved, these filings set the stage for regulatory reviews on multiple fronts that could delay completion. In North Carolina alone, regulators are expected to devote several months to investigating the merger's potential harms and benefits to customers.

The companies have themselves acknowledged that the merger would fail several anti-competitive standards, but claim the violations are minor and pose no significant problems to consumers. As an accommodation, Progress and Duke have each committed to a five-year promise not to pass on merger-related costs to their wholesale customers, largely to avoid having to sell-off power plants or transmission lines as a condition to regulatory approval. The companies are also using their North Carolina connection to convince regulators to approve the deal, arguing that a single giant utility is far less likely to be acquired by an out-of-state rival, which might be accompanied by a loss of jobs in North Carolina.

The Duke-Progress merger offers a few important lessons in light of the developments in the U.S. electricity market:

- Scale is becoming important for a variety of reasons, most importantly stability. Indeed, in the utility sector, the conventional wisdom is that "bigger is better; bigger is safer." Scale is also important in raising financing for increasing capital expenditure requirements, as utilities reposition their generating portfolios.
- New nuclear energy projects will only come about through utility sponsors combining into larger entities with more significant balance sheets, particularly as federal nuclear regulators do not disfavor such combinations.

---

[10] *Id.*; *see also* Hart-Scott-Rodino Antitrust Improvements Act of 1976 §§ 101-106, 15 U.S.C. §§ 1311-1314 (2012).

- The procedure for rate recovery of capital costs associated with new nuclear power generation is critical to predicting where such projects are built. The Duke-Progress merger makes it likelier that a new nuclear reactor would be built in the Carolinas in the next ten years, provided that state legislation which requires utilities to request rate increases annually can be waived or modified to permit a one-time approval for recovery of all capital costs of a new nuclear station prior to commencing construction.
- Utilities are keen to grow at a time when they enjoy financial strength. As evidence, the regulated electricity index has outperformed all other sectors on the NYSE from 2000 to 2010, outperforming U.S. Treasury bonds and, by a large margin, the S&P 500 over that period.

(b) ExxonMobil / XTO

If in 2009 one was interested in embracing the shale gas revolution, there was perhaps no better target than XTO, the largest producer of natural gas in the United States. The company had grown very fast in 2007 and 2008 through acquisitions of reserves from Dominion Resources and by acquiring Hunt Petroleum.[11] In 2009, XTO was acquired by ExxonMobil in an all stock deal valued at around $31 billion (about a 25% premium) plus the assumption of approximately $10 billion in debt.[12] The acquisition immediately gave ExxonMobil the equivalent of about 45 trillion cubic feet of natural gas throughout the United States, and made it the third largest leaseholder in the promising Marcellus Shale.[13]

Although ExxonMobil was interested in diversifying its domestic business through taking a meaningful position in the U.S. natural gas market, the transaction was largely focused on the potential growth in shale

---

[11] *See XTO Energy Acquires $2.5 Billion in Select Producing Properties from Dominion and Increases Annual Production Growth Targets to 15% in Both 2007 and 2008*, HOUS. CHRON., June 4, 2007, http://www.chron.com/news/article/PRN-XTO-Energy-Acquires-2-5-Billion-in-Select-1803532.php; Clifford Krauss, *XTO Agrees to Buy Hunt Petroleum for $4.2 Billion*, N.Y. TIMES, June 11, 2008, http://www.nytimes.com/2008/06/11/business/11deal.html?_r=0.

[12] Press Release, ExxonMobil, Exxon Mobil Corporation and XTO Energy Inc. Announce Agreement (Dec. 14, 2009), *available at* http://news.exxonmobil.com/press-release/exxon-mobil-corporation-and-xto-energy-inc-announce-agreement.

[13] *Id.*

gas resources. In fact, ExxonMobil introduced a provision into the merger agreement permitting it to terminate the agreement prior to closing if hydraulic fracturing was outlawed or so severely regulated that the drilling of shale wells became "commercially impracticable."[14] However, the transaction can also be viewed as a technology play, insofar as ExxonMobil has ambitions to become a leading developer of shale gas resources around the world. Outside the United States, potential reserves of shale gas have been identified in countries from Mexico to Argentina to Algeria, not to mention at least 55 unconventional gas plays in Europe.

The ExxonMobil-XTO transaction has been the largest but is by no means the only significant merger and acquisition transaction in the shale gas sector, which, being comprised of dozens of small, independent operators holding acreage in the various shale basins, is ripe consolidation. Foreign investors have also shown strong interest in U.S. shale resources. In March 2011, one of the sector's leading companies, Chesapeake Energy Corporation, closed a $4.75 billion sale of its Fayetteville shale resources to global mining giant BHP Billiton.[15] In January 2011, it accepted a $570 million investment from China National Offshore Oil Corporation,[16] and in 2010, it into a $2.25 billion joint venture with French oil major Total.[17]

(c) Dynegy

Dynegy, Inc. is an interesting example of both merger and restructuring activity in the U.S. energy industry. In the late 1990s, the company was born out of a combination of the former Natural Gas Clearinghouse and the former natural gas business of Chevron. It modeled itself as emerging economy energy company – somewhat similar to the business model of its

---

[14] Elaine Meyer, *Exxon, XTO Say Fracking Regs Would Threaten Merger*, LAW360 (Jan. 20, 2010, 7:16 PM), http://www.law360.com/articles/144135/exxon-xto-say-fracking-regs-would-threaten-merger.

[15] Press Release, Chesapeake Energy Corp., Chesapeake Energy Corporation Announces Sale of Fayetteville Shale Assets to BHP Billiton for $4.75 Billion in Cash (Feb. 21, 2011), *available at* http://phx.corporate-ir.net/phoenix.zhtml?c=104617&p=irol-newsArticle&ID=1530960.

[16] Chris V. Nicholson, *Cnooc Adds to Chesapeake Energy Stake*, N.Y. TIMES DEALBOOK (Jan. 31, 2011, 4:21 AM), http://dealbook.nytimes.com/2011/01/31/cnooc-takes-further-chesapeake-stake/.

[17] Marcel Michelson & Tom Bergin, *Total in $2 Billion Shale Gas Tie-up with Chesapeake*, REUTERS (Jan. 4, 2010, 3:40 PM), http://www.reuters.com/article/2010/01/04/us-total-idUS-TRE60322520100104.

neighbor Enron – introducing electronic trading platforms for natural gas and electricity and increasing its long term exposure to the power market. In 2001, Dynegy actually entered into merger discussions with Enron, just as Enron was teetering on the edge of bankruptcy.[18]

Despite going through a significant restructuring over the last decade, including its own near-bankruptcy, Dynegy is one of several U.S. power companies whose market capitalization is now less than the aggregate value of its assets. This condition is reflective of the significant losses it has incurred over the last two years, largely due to out-of-market, long-term gas and power positions, as well as its substantial debt burden. Having projected negative cash flows of $1.6 billion over the next 5 years, its auditors recently warned that it may seek Chapter 11 bankruptcy protection.[19] So, naturally, everyone wants to buy the company.

In August 2010, Dynegy agreed to be acquired by The Blackstone Group for $4.50 per share.[20] The company underwent a customary "go shop" period thereafter to solicit better offers. At the same time, Seneca Capital, a hedge fund, acquired a large shareholding of Dynegy stock and formally solicited votes to block the Blackstone acquisition. It argued that shareholders should receive a higher price of $6.50 per share, or that Dynegy should reject the Blackstone offer and instead pursue a strategy of asset sales.[21] Unfortunately, Dynegy's lenders – sensing a bankruptcy might be imminent – would not consent to asset sale transactions unless they were repaid in full. In November 2010, Carl Icahn entered the fray, acquiring shares and offering a new credit facility to Dynegy to help it refinance existing debt in exchange for effective control of Dynegy. Two days later Blackstone raised its offer to $5.00 per share, in exchange for a $16 million break-up fee if the deal did not go through.[22] Dynegy also

---

[18] *Dynegy Scraps Enron Deal*, CNNMONEY (Nov. 28, 2001, 5:27 PM), http://money.cnn.com/2001/11/28/companies/enron/.

[19] *See* Press Release, Dynegy, Dynegy's Board of Directors Recommends Stockholders Vote FOR the Merger Agreement with Blackstone at November 17, 2010 Special Meeting of Stockholders (Nov. 8, 2010), *available at* http://phx.corporate-ir.net/phoenix.zhtml?c=147906&p=irol-newsArticle_Print&ID=1493146.

[20] Annalyn Censky, *An Enron-era Name Acquired by Blackstone*, CNNMONEY (Aug. 13, 2010, 10:38 AM), http://money.cnn.com/2010/08/13/news/companies/dynegy_shares_surge/.

[21] *See* Press Release, Dynegy, *supra* note 19.

[22] *See* Press Release, Blackstone, Statement of Blackstone on the Termination of its Merger Agreement with Dynegy (Nov. 23, 2010), *available at* http://www.blackstone.com/news-views/

adopted a "shareholder rights plan" that would prevent any shareholder from gaining de facto control of Dynegy unless it offered a premium to all shareholders.[23] Any cash offer for Dynegy of $5.00 per share or higher was exempt from the protections of the plan.[24]

When Dynegy's shareholders did not approve the improved Blackstone offer, Dynegy commenced an "open strategic alternatives process" led by a special committee of its board to consider alternative bids, including those from Icahn and Seneca. Three weeks later, on December 15, 2010, its Board of Directors approved an agreement to be acquired by Icahn Enterprises at $5.50 per share, or $665 million.[25] Unfortunately, the Icahn acquisition was also not approved by Dynegy's shareholders, and the merger agreement expired pursuant to its terms on February 18, 2011.[26] Dynegy's prospects do not appear promising, and if anything, its story is indicative of the repercussions arising out of the confluence of factors impacting the natural gas and electricity industries in the United States.

press-releases/details/statement-of-blackstone-on-the-termination-of-its-merger-agreement-with-dynegy; Michael J. De La Merced, *New Fight at Dynegy as Seneca Takes on Icahn*, N.Y. TIMES DEALBOOK (Dec. 20, 2010, 9:27 AM), http://dealbook.nytimes.com/2010/12/20/new-fight-at-dynegy-as-seneca-takes-on-icahn/.

[23] Dynegy Adopts Stockholder Protection Rights Plan, BUSINESSWIRE (Nov. 23, 2010, 7:05 AM), http://www.businesswire.com/news/home/20101123005687/en/Dynegy-Adopts-Stockholder-Protection-Rights-Plan#.VRcUQfnF-So.

[24] *Id.*

[25] Michael J. De La Merced, *Icahn Offers to Buy Dynegy for $665 Million*, N.Y. TIMES DEALBOOK (Dec. 15, 2010, 7:37 AM), http://dealbook.nytimes.com/2010/12/15/icahn-to-buy-dynegy-for-665-million-in-cash/.

[26] Press Release, Dynegy, Dynegy Announces Board and Management Restructuring (Feb. 21, 2011), *available at* http://phx.corporate-ir.net/phoenix.zhtml?c=147906&p=irol-newsArticle_Print&ID=1530976.

The Geopolitics of Oil in Africa

RICHARD S. WILLIAMSON[*]

Africa has attracted new interest, new investors, and new interlopers due, in part, to its substantial oil reserves. What will this mean to Africa and to global geopolitics? In his volume *Africa: Altered States, Ordinary Miracles*, Richard Dowden notes, "[i]n the past outsiders imposed the wrong things in Africa in the wrong way at the wrong time."[1] Will the new Africa oil rush usher in more of the same?

This article will address the geopolitics of oil in Africa. It will discuss the growing importance of African oil as its production rises and as other sources become less reliable. It will also address the question of oil production and more generally resource extraction effects on the economies and politics within African nations. Finally, it will discuss China's growing role in African oil and in Africa's economies more generally: its competing development and economic model.

I. Growing Importance of African Oil

Since the late 1990s, Africa has been an increasingly important source of American oil imports. World production has peaked, and, as production from older oil fields decline, there are few areas where significant new fields

---

[*] The late Ambassador Richard S. Williamson (1949-2013) served as U.S. Ambassador to the UN and Special Envoy of President George W. Bush to Sudan. He was a Partner at Winston & Strawn and a Visiting Scholar at Seton Hall's Whitehead School of Diplomacy.

[1] RICHARD DOWDEN, AFRICA: ALTERED STATES, ORDINARY MIRACLES 514 (2009).

may come into production in the years ahead. Africa is the most prominent among areas of potential growth. Africa holds nine percent of the world's known oil reserves but it is the least explored region.[2] Furthermore, African oil is "cheaper, safer [(sweet oil)] and more accessible than its competitors."[3] And the shipping lanes from Africa are more reliably secure than those going through the Persian Gulf.

Africa already supplies more oil to the United States than the Middle East. It currently provides between 15 and 20 percent of total United States oil imports and is expected to provide at least 25 percent by 2015.[4] Nine years ago, the Bush administration declared access to African oil supplies as a "strategic national interest" of the United States. Since that declaration, Africa's status in United States national security policy and military affairs has risen.

In 2001, Africa oil use was 3.06 million barrels per day.[5] In 2011, African oil use is 3.90 million barrels per day.[6] And by 2015, it is projected that Africa oil use will be about 4.40 million barrels per day.[7] Meanwhile, oil production in Africa was 7.93 million barrels per day in 2001.[8] It was 10.18 million barrels per day in 2010.[9] And it is projected that African oil production will rise to approximately 12.08 million barrels per day by 2015.[10] That means that African oil exports have been growing and will continue to do so. In 2001, Africa's average export of oil was 4.87 million barrels per day; in 2010, 6.36 million barrels per day; and in 2015 Africa's average export of oil is projected to grow to 7.68 million barrels per day.[11]

The Gulf of Guinea and West Africa more generally are where most oil rich countries are located. Angola has the greatest production growth

---

[2] David H. Shinn, Ctr. for Strategic & Int'l Studies, *Africa, China, the United States, and Oil* (May 8, 2007), http://csis.org/story/africa-china-united-states-and-oil.

[3] John Ghazvinian, Untapped: The Scramble for Africa's Oil, Slate (Apr. 3, 2007, 1:35 PM), http://www.slate.com/articles/news_and_politics/foreigners/features/2007/untapped_the_scramble_for_africas_oil/does_africa_measure_up_to_the_hype.html.

[4] See Shinn, *supra* note 2.

[5] BUSINESS MONITOR INT'L, NIGERIA OIL AND GAS REPORT Q1 2011 (2010).

[6] *Id.*

[7] *Id.*

[8] *Id.*

[9] *Id.*

[10] *Id.*

[11] *Id.*

potential with Nigeria exports also set to climb if it can resolve its various political stability issues. And with its parliamentary elections postponed for the second time just days ago, it is clear that Nigeria continues to face challenges.

However, is East Africa the next frontier for oil? There are some who think so. Seismic tests over the past 50 years have shown that countries up the coast of East Africa have natural gas in abundance. Some of the data compiled by oil industry consultants also suggest the presence of massive off-shore oil deposits. This has led to oil explorers dropping more wells in East Africa. In the past, few have wanted to pay the cost of searching for oil or gas in East Africa, or risk drilling wells in volatile countries. But, as one expert has written, "[b]etter technology, lower risk in some of the countries and higher oil prices in recent years have changed the equation."[12] Both wildcatters and majors have moved into East Africa including Italy's Eni, PETRONAS of Malaysia, and the China National Offshore Oil Corporation (CNOOC). Of course, this activity still is much smaller than North Africa and West Africa.

Global demand for oil continues to rise, the Middle East turmoil of the "Arab Spring" uprisings has brought renewed attention to the need to diversify global sources of oil, a rising Shia Iran continues to bring into focus the vulnerability of Persian Gulf shipping lanes, and the rise of oil prices all contribute to making African oil more and more attractive. And a side note, the current turmoil in the Arab world may create unexpected opportunities. For example, the pipeline being constructed from Elderot, Kenya, to Kampala to bring oil to Uganda has reverse flow capabilities. Eventually it could provide outflow of oil from the African Great Lakes, locking up production from Uganda and potentially Southern Sudan. This is a Libyan project. Given events in Libya and the possible need for Libya to get money, China is poised to buy this project along with other Libya infrastructure programs that might be for sale. So events in the Arab Spring not only will impact the reliability of oil flows from North Africa and the Middle East, they may open a scramble for existing African oil projects that will go on the auction block.

[12] *Id.*

II. Oil: A Curse or a Blessing?

But as elsewhere, will oil become a curse for Africa, not a blessing? The United States needs oil. The United States wants countries that sell oil to us to be stable. But oil itself can destabilize them. Some of the most dangerous and dysfunctional nations in the world produce oil. It is a sad tale of greed, corruption, and violence.

Journalist Nicholas Shaxson writes, "[f]acts reveal the central and dangerous role that African oil states now play."[13] Oil is a poison not only to the continent but "to liberty, democracy and free markets."[14]

Elsewhere, Ricardo Soares de Oliveira writes,

> The [Gulf of Guinea's] large petroleum reserves allow the elites of Angola, Equatorial Guinea and Nigeria to reap the benefits of international investment and expertise regardless of their reckless conduct. While the populations of these countries suffer and starve. ... Corrupt regimes can essentially behave how they want, joining with groups that guarantee protection and dominance, and the edifice of the state while largely moribund, is sustained in order to keep oil flowing.[15]

He labels these countries rich in oil in the Gulf of Guinea "successful failed states."[16]

In his book *Untapped: The Scramble for Africa's Oil*, John Ghazvinian discusses the situation in oil rich Nigeria. He writes:

> The problem, in a nutshell, is that for fifty years, foreign oil companies have conducted some of the world's most sophisticated exploration and production operations using millions of dollars' worth of imported ultra modern equipment, against a backdrop of Stone Age squalor. They have extracted hundreds of millions of barrels of oil, which has been sold in the international market for hundreds of billions of dollars, but the people of the Niger Delta have seen virtually none of the benefits. While successive military regimes have used oil proceeds to buy mansions in Mayfair or build castles in the

[13] Nicholas Shaxson, Poisoned Wells: The Dirty Politics of African Oil (2008).
[14] *Id.*
[15] Ricardo Soares de Oliveira, Oil and Politics in the Gulf of Guinea (2007).
[16] *Id.*

THE GEOPOLITICS OF OIL IN AFRICA

sand in the faraway capital of Abuja, many in the Delta live as their ancestors would have done hundreds, even thousands of years ago – in hand built huts of mud and straw. Though the Delta produces 100 percent of the nation's oil and gas, its people survive with no electricity or running water. Education is patchy, with one secondary school for every 14,000 people.[17]

Also writing about Nigeria, Martin Meredith observes in his excellent book *The Fate of Africa*:

> The Nigerian example showed how quickly oil wealth could be dissipated. For a brief period its finances were transformed, with annual revenues soaring from $4 billion to $26 billion. But such riches set off a massive spending spree. Patronage politics and corruption reached new heights. Grand industrial projects were launched – an integrated steel complex, an automotive industry, a petrochemical sector. Contracts were signed for new infrastructure – roads, schools, housing, a new capital city at Abuja. Huge salary increases were awarded to public servants. Vast sums were spent on imported consumer goods. Import scams proliferated. Fraud and corruption cost billions of dollars. Meanwhile, export crops were virtually abandoned; subsistence farming was neglected; local manufacturing suffered; inflation soared.[18]

Is a country rich in natural minerals that seeks to develop a resource extraction business, whether oil or other minerals, doomed to a growing gap between the governing elite and the people? Is it doomed to become yet another country that is so dependent on resource extraction that it fails to develop a broad, robust, and healthy economy that creates jobs, opportunity and wealth for the many? Is it destined to have an authoritarian government unresponsive to the people because it does not need the people due to wealth from oil? Of course, it is not inevitable, but it may be likely. And so far oil rich nations such as Angola, Nigeria, and Sudan do not encourage much optimism.

To summarize this issue, resource rich nations often have suffered from too great a dependency on resources extraction. These countries often fail

[17] JOHN GHAZVINIAN, UNTAPPED: THE SCRAMBLE FOR AFRICA'S OIL 19 (2007).
[18] MARTIN MEREDITH, THE FATE OF AFRICA: A HISTORY OF THE CONTINENT SINCE INDEPENDENCE 284 (2011).

DIREITO COMPARADO / COMPARATIVE LAW

to develop a broad based and diversified economy. It helps prop up a narrow power elite and thwarts normal progress to broaden participation in society economically and politically. It can create a false sense of stability as we are witnessing today in Libya and elsewhere. It can contribute to failed or near failed states, which become breeding grounds for terrorists which are a direct threat to the United States and others.

Looking at the situation in Sudan, oil wealth has helped prop up an extreme regime that has engaged in a broad range of horrific atrocities in the long North/South civil war and in Darfur in order to stay in power. The oil wealth has been concentrated in a small minority in Khartoum and not benefited the broader population. And in both the North and the South, oil wealth is a primary reason why the economies have not diversified nor developed.

III. China in Africa

The final significant geopolitical consequences of Africa's oil to be discussed is China's rush into Africa. It is one of the most important geopolitical shifts since the fall of the Berlin Wall. Of course, it is not only oil that Beijing seeks in Africa. In order to feed its rapidly rising economy, China is in search of the full range of mineral resources all over the world. But certainly one of China's biggest plays is in Africa and among the most desired natural resources is petroleum.

Under Deng Xiaoping, China began a "second China revolution." As Piers Brendon writes, Deng "permitted capitalist free enterprise while keeping a Communist grip on political power."[19] Brendon continues, "[t]he result was annual growth rates of nearly 10 percent over the next three decades."[20] Brendon goes on to explain why the Communist Party of China is so committed to continued economic expansion. He writes:

> China's leaders seem dedicated to augmenting prosperity in order to secure stability. Having been racked by internal convulsions for generations, the country evidently prefers tyranny to anarchy, even to democracy. ... As Deng Xiaoping insisted, 'Stability supersedes all.'[21]

[19] Piers Brendon, *China Also Rises*, NAT'L INTEREST (Oct. 20, 2010).
[20] *Id.*
[21] *Id.*

THE GEOPOLITICS OF OIL IN AFRICA

Or as Professor Susan Shirk has written in her book *China Fragile Superpower*, "[t]he (Chinese) Communist Party considers rapid economic growth a political imperative because it is the only way to prevent massive unemployment and labor unrest."[22] To continue its rapid economic growth, China needs raw materials from abroad. And Africa has become a prime source of current and future Chinese raw materials.

In many ways Africa is benefiting from China's mixture of aid and investment. China is providing multi-billion dollar, resource-backed loans for infrastructure (which will be built by Chinese companies with Chinese workers). China's economic support is provided absent the pre-conditions of United States, other Western countries, the World Bank, and so on. China freely engages with bad actors shunned by others such as the governments of Sudan and Zimbabwe. China provides competition to the West.

In 2008, the Centre for Conflict Resolution, a highly respected think tank in South Africa, collected essays from several leading African intellectuals and published a book titled *Crouching Tiger, Hidden Dragon? Africa and China*. The opinion uniformly expressed in this volume is that "China's interest in the continent ... is refreshing and therefore laudable, compared to what many view as the often paternalistic, patronizing and culturally prejudiced attitudes of the West and Japan towards Africa."[23] And agreement, as Adam Habib writes, that "(a) new scramble for Africa is underway... (And) Asia looks set to become the dominant economic presence in Africa in the years to come."[24]

What does this growing Chinese footprint in Africa mean for Africans and for global geopolitics? One concern is that growing Chinese exports to Africa that have accompanied the growing imports of African natural resources, including oil, is crushing African manufacturing. Chinese low-end products such as textiles that are mass produced with cheap labor are crowding out economic space that could provide development opportunities for African businesses and employment opportunities for African labor. Another major concern is that the Chinese investments and aid to Africa will weaken the influence of conditional Western develop-

---

[22] SUSAN L. SHIRK, CHINA: FRAGILE SUPERPOWER 54 (2007).

[23] CROUCHING TIGER, HIDDEN DRAGON?: AFRICA AND CHINA 4 (Kweku Ampiah & Sanusha Naidu, eds. 2008).

[24] Adam Habib, *Western Hegemony, Asian Ascendancy and the New Scramble for Africa in* CROUCHING TIGER, HIDDEN DRAGON?: AFRICA AND CHINA, *supra* note 23, at 259.

ment funding, which mandates conduct deemed necessary for long term economic development and political stability such as transparency, good governance, the rule of law, good education, good health systems, and accountability. As Ted Fishman writes in his book *China Inc: How the Rise of the Next Superpower Challenges America and the World*, "[t]he worldwide competition for the good graces of the Chinese government (including in Africa) means that there can be no unified front for the rule of law, compliance with the World Trade Organization, or sanctions against a government that muscles companies to transfer their patents."[25] China not only does not require these sorts of reforms which we believe are building blocks of sustainable economic growth and stability, China provides a different model for economic growth. It is a model made attractive due to China's continuing rapid economic growth and made more attractive during the global financial crisis seen as having been caused by unfettered financial speculation in the West. While the United States, Europe, and Japan continue to gradually climb out of the great recession caused by the global financial crisis, China has remained relatively unscathed with continuing double-digit economic growth. As Stephan Halper writes in his fascinating book *The Beijing Consensus: How China's Authoritarian Model Will Dominate the Twenty-First Century*:

> As growing numbers of countries in Africa and Latin America embrace relationships with China, one can see how Beijing's example illuminates a path around the West. It is making the West less relevant in world affairs. In effect, China is shrinking the West."[26]

Martin Jacques in his book *When China Rules the World: The End of the Western World and the Birth of a New Global Order* elaborates on this phenomenon by writing:

> A nation that comprises one-fifth of the world's population is already in the process of transforming the workings of the global economy and its structure

[25] TED. C. FISHMAN, CHINA, INC.: HOW THE RISE OF THE NEXT SUPERPOWER CHALLENGES AMERICA AND THE WORLD 293 (2006).
[26] STEPHAN HALPER, THE BEIJING CONSENSUS: HOW CHINA'S AUTHORITARIAN MODEL WILL DOMINATE THE TWENTY-FIRST CENTURY xi (2010).

of power. A country that regards itself for both cultural and racial reasons, as the great civilization on earth will, as a great global power, clearly in time require and expect a major reordering of global relationships. ... A state that has never shared power with any other class, group or institution, which has never been subject to popular sovereignty, which operates on a continental scale and which, to this day, is suffused with a Confusion outlook, albeit in a distinctive and modernized Communist form, stands in sharp contrast to the credo that informs Western societies and which has hitherto dominated the global community.[27]

And clearly a growing venue for this global competition is in Africa, fueled in large part by China's need for oil and other mineral resources.

Does this mean, as Richard Bernstein and Ross Munro have written in their book *The Coming Conflict with China* that this geopolitical shift will inevitably lead to conflict?[28] Will, as James Mann writes in *The China Fantasy*, "a huge, permanently undemocratic, enduringly repressive China ... a Chinese autocracy persisting into the mid-twenty-first century ... cause large problems for American policy elsewhere in the world"?[29] Perhaps. But a full exploration of this dynamic goes well beyond my topic. Suffice it to say that China's rise, which is playing out in many areas including African oil, is a dominant geopolitical shift with broad and challenging repercussions.

IV. Conclusion

In conclusion, Africa's oil is of growing geostrategic importance. As more of this valuable resource is discovered and large extraction industries further develop, it will bring great wealth into those countries fortunate enough to have oil deposits. But history shows that this is not always a benefit to most of the people and can be a curse contributing to inequities, impediments to broad based economic development, corruption, poor governance, and false stability. And as the world's need for oil grows, Africa will increasingly be an arena of competition between consumer countries that may dramatically shift geopolitical balances.

---

[27] Martin Jacques, When China Rules the World: The End of the Western World and the Birth of a New Global Order 431 (2012).
[28] Richard Bernstein & Ross H. Munro, The Coming Conflict With China (1998).
[29] James Mann, The China Fantasy (2007).

International Petroleum E&P Contracts in Africa: The Rise of Risk Service Agreements?

AGOSTINHO PEREIRA DE MIRANDA[*] & RITA MOTA[**]

1. Introduction

Facing the challenges of today's petroleum investment environment requires an effective and adequate management of change and volatility. The ability to respond, to adapt to the surrounding environment, in life as much as in the petroleum industry, is pivotal. To paraphrase Charles Darwin:

> *It is not the strongest of the species that survives, nor the most intelligent; but the one most responsive to change.*

Change and volatility are a part of everyday life in the petroleum industry. Governments and companies alike need to have a measure of adequate responsiveness. Rigidity, while promoting standardization and certainty, means equally less ability to adjust to change and volatility. There is a competitive edge (and ensuing rewards) in the ability to respond to said change and volatility: riding the roller coaster of competing petroleum investment opportunities.

Petroleum regimes, as a whole, must have a measure of flexibility. Flexibility allows governments (and companies) to respond to challenges, in

---

[*] Chairman, Miranda Correia Amendoeira & Associados
[**] Associate, Miranda Correia Amendoeira & Associados. The authors acknowledge and thank Nuno Antunes, Of Counsel to the Firm, for his decisive analytical input.

particular when economic uncertainty, and unwillingness to take over-bearing risks, gives rise to a capital scarcer market. Competition for petroleum investments requires innovative and tailor-made solutions. Petroleum contracts may then become the key to suitably addressing specific risk and benefit issues of a specific acreage.

Much to the credit of its prolific basins, some of the most renowned petroleum provinces are located in Africa. Significant petroleum investment opportunities continue to emerge on a regular basis, even in a scenario that is characterized by change and volatility, as it happens today.

2. The origins of Risk Service Agreements

Risk Service Agreements (RSAs) were first used in Latin America in the 1950s and in the Middle East in the 1960s. Their adoption and development was closely related to specific political and social conditions in the Host Countries (HCs), which, by that time, did not want to grant ownership of mineral resources to international oil companies (IOCs). By adopting RSAs, HCs were able to resort to the expertise and experience of the IOCs without giving them the ownership of the oil produced. Furthermore,

> *(...) it is not surprising that [RSAs] are mostly used in Latin American and Middle Eastern countries, where nationalist sentiments concerning hydrocarbons are the fiercest and where the monopoly for petroleum exploration and exploitation is generally entrusted to an NOC.*[1]

On a different note, it is also commonly accepted that RSAs are used mostly in net importing countries. As the HCs want to freely dispose of their petroleum, they adopt contractual systems that do not put production into the hands of the IOCs.[2]

One of the most significant historical examples in this regard is the Mexican experience. In 1938, President Lázaro Cárdenas took control of the country's oil industry by ordering its expropriation. This was seen by Mexican citizens as a *"great symbolic and passionate act of resistance to foreign*

---

[1] Claude DUVAL, Honoré LE LEUCH, André PETRUZIO and Jacqueline Lang WEAVER (2009), "International Petroleum Exploration and Exploitation Agreements: Legal, Economic and Policy Aspects", Barrows, 2nd Edition, page 100.

[2] Daniel JOHNSTON (1994), "International Petroleum Fiscal Systems and Production Sharing Contracts", PennWell Books, page 87.

control.[3] Nevertheless, this act of fervent nationalism had serious consequences on the petroleum industry: a national oil company (NOC) was created ("Petróleos Mexicanos", or "PEMEX"), but Mexico's lack of capital, technology and skills was evident. Furthermore, its production ceased to focus on exports and became directed to the domestic market.[4] It took Mexico only one year to realize that it needed foreign participation; as early as 1939, the government entered into service contracts with smaller European and American oil companies (thus avoiding the presence of the expropriated companies).[5] It was the only way of combining the constitutional and political requirements of State ownership with the need for foreign capital and expertise.

The first countries that made use of RSAs were, therefore, Mexico, Argentina, Bolivia, Brazil and Venezuela, followed by Iraq and Iran. A study conducted in 1990 shows that *"of a total of 106 developing countries that had oil legislation or agreements in force in 1987, 48% proposed production-sharing contracts for new exploration permits, 38% concessions, and only 7% risk service contracts"*.[6]

IOCs do not easily accept RSAs. This contractual form is relatively ineffective in attracting foreign investment,[7] and that has led several governments to introduce incentive clauses in their RSAs. Such is the case of the Philippine RSA, which establishes the "Filippino Participation Incentive Allowance", reverting to the Contractor group.[8]

---

[3] Daniel YERGIN (2009), "The Prize – The Epic Quest for Oil, Money and Power", Free Press, page 259.

[4] *Idem*, page 261.

[5] Marcelo BUCHELI (2006), "Economic Nationalism, Political Constituencies, and Multinational Corporations: The Impact of the Mexican Oil Nationalization in Colombia", University of Illinois at Urbana-Champaign Working Papers, available at: http://www.business.uiuc.edu/Working_Papers/papers/06–0123.pdf

[6] Victor RODRIGUEZ-PADILLA (1991) "Sovereignty Over Petroleum Resources: The End of an Era?," *Energy Studies Review*: Vol. 3: Iss. 2, Article 3, page 111, citing his earlier study of 1990, "Lois, contrats et fiscalité pétrolière: une retrospective", mimeograph (Grenoble: Institut d'Economie et de Politique de l'Energie).
Available at: http://digitalcommons.mcmaster.ca/esr/vol3/iss2/3

[7] Cfr. Carole NAKHLE (2010), "Petroleum fiscal regimes – Evolution and Changes", in "The Taxation of Petroleum and Minerals: Principles, Problems and Practice", Routledge and IMF, page 104.

[8] Daniel JOHNSTON (1994), "International Petroleum Fiscal Systems and Production Sharing Contracts", PennWell Books, page 88.

3. The general design of Risk Service Agreements

In an RSA, the IOC is hired by the HC to perform the role of a contractor for petroleum activities. The IOC bears the entire financial risk, providing the capital associated with E&P activities; the costs will only be reimbursed and the IOC will only be remunerated, in the event of a commercial discovery.[9] The difference between Production Sharing Agreements ("PSAs") and RSAs is thus virtually nonexistent[10] – the only relevant distinction lies in the nature of the remuneration offered to the contractor (though even that difference disappears when the RSA provides for payment in kind). A fundamental feature of both RSAs and PSAs reveals their similarity: in both cases, the IOC assumes the risk until a commercial discovery occurs, and only then will it be remunerated.

As for other legal effects of RSAs, it is important to note that the IOC does not become the holder of mineral rights, the production thus belonging to the HC.

A very common provision in RSAs provides for the change of operators from the IOC to the NOC at a certain point during the validity of the contract, which is coherent with the nationalistic trait usually accompanying the adoption of this type of agreement.

The ability of an IOC to book reserves under an RSA depends entirely on the way the agreement is drafted. If the remuneration and reimbursements due under the contract are to be paid in cash, that ability is basically voided; if, however, the contract provides for said payments to be made in kind, the IOC is entitled to an economic interest which allows it to book a part of production and reserves.[11] Solutions may vary depending on the choices made when negotiating the agreement.

a. RSAs and Pure Service Contracts

Even less common than RSAs, Pure Service Contracts entail a particular regime. The Contractor is paid an invariable fee for a defined work program, regardless of a commercial discovery. This means that, contrary to what happens under an RSA, the HC bears all financial risks. In common

[9] Cfr. Claude DUVAL, Honoré LE LEUCH, André PETRUZIO and Jacqueline Lang WEAVER (2009), above cited n1, page 86.

[10] Daniel JOHNSTON (1994), above cited n8, page 88.

[11] Claude DUVAL, Honoré LE LEUCH, André PETRUZIO and Jacqueline Lang WEAVER (2009), above cited n1, page 87.

with RSAs, Pure Service Contracts have two main features: they allow for the HCs to resort to the expertise and experience of the IOCs, and to keep the ownership of all the oil produced, since remuneration is paid in cash.

b. RSAs and Concessions

Historically, concession agreements were largely unfavorable to the HC: they covered large parts of the territory, without any minimum work requirements; the duration of the agreements was typically very long (sometimes 60 and 70 years); ownership of the petroleum reserves was exclusively granted to the concessionaire; the HC only received royalties as payment; and the concessionaire controlled all aspects of petroleum operations.

Not surprisingly, early concessions were subject to strong criticism from developing countries, given that the HC only got the minimum financial benefit out of the agreement and it enjoyed little, if any, control over petroleum operations.

In the 1950s, at first, and especially in the 1970s, HCs began using new, more sophisticated concession agreements – sometimes connected to other types of agreements. These "modern concessions" improved the position of the HC through an enhanced involvement in petroleum operations, more favorable fiscal terms, minimum work requirements and, most importantly, IOCs were not granted title over natural resources.

Under modern concessions, the contract area and duration are limited; there are local content requirements; the IOCs pay royalties, tax on "excess" profits and, very often, other taxes, fees and bonuses; the HCs regain control over, and access to information on, petroleum operations.[12]

It is interesting to note that many countries adopted concessions together with other forms of contracts (e.g., Angola, Algeria, Nigeria, Kazakhstan and Russia).[13]

Either motivated by the will to preserve ownership and control of natural resources indispensable to energy self-sufficiency, or because oil is the most significant export of a given country, the fact is that concessions are still broadly adopted.[14]

---

[12] *Idem*, pages 63-68.
[13] *Idem*, page 63.
[14] Ernest E. SMITH, John S. DZIENKOWSKI, Owen L. ANDERSON, John S. LOWE, Bruce M. KRAMER and Jacqueline L. WEAVER (2010), "International Petroleum Transactions", Rocky Mountain Mineral Law Foundation, 3rd Edition, page 442.

c. RSAs and Production Sharing Agreements

As mentioned above, RSAs and PSAs are hard to distinguish and their basic difference lies in the type of remuneration offered to the IOC.[15] Both contractual formats first started being used by countries which had, until then, adopted traditional concession agreements. In fact, PSAs became popular in the 1960s, in Indonesia,[16] as a reaction to a particularly complicated moment in economic and political terms.[17] In order to attract foreign investment and to revitalize its petroleum industry, the Indonesian State adopted more efficiency and flexibility and offered the new contractual model to potential foreign investors.

One of the main features of PSAs is that the IOC bears the entire risk of the operations. It conducts its activities under the monitoring of the NOC or a State-appointed entity. All production is property of the State, except for the part which can be lifted for cost recovery and as a result of profit sharing. This, together with the joint management of the activities by the NOC or the State and the IOC, is, in fact, the most relevant difference with regard to concessions, in which all petroleum lifted belongs to the licensee[18] and the latter acts alone throughout the duration of the agreement.[19]

Traditional PSA terms provide for all the investment in equipment and facilities to be made by the IOC,[20] but they also establish that their property be transferred to the State either immediately or at a determined moment. After the contract expires, the State may require the removal of all those facilities and equipment.

PSAs are currently the most widely accepted form of petroleum agreement, adopted all over the world, particularly by developing countries.[21]

---

[15] See section 3.

[16] Claude DUVAL, Honoré LE LEUCH, André PETRUZIO and Jacqueline Lang WEAVER (2009), above cited n1, page 69.

[17] Robert FABRIKANT (1973), "Oil discovery and technical change in Southeast Asia: legal aspects of production sharing contracts in the Indonesian petroleum industry", Institute of Southeast Asian Studies, 2nd Edition, page 16 et seq.

[18] Claude DUVAL, Honoré LE LEUCH, André PETRUZIO and Jacqueline Lang WEAVER (2009), above cited n1, page 70.

[19] Ernest E. SMITH, John S. DZIENKOWSKI, Owen L. ANDERSON, John S. LOWE, Bruce M. KRAMER and Jacqueline L. WEAVER (2010), above cited n14, pages 448 and 464.

[20] *Idem*, page 464.

[21] Claude DUVAL, Honoré LE LEUCH, André PETRUZIO and Jacqueline Lang WEAVER (2009), above cited n1, page 69.

d. A note on Participation Agreements

For the sake of completeness, a few words must be dedicated to participation agreements, their main features and roles. The first inevitable comment on this issue is that participation agreements are actually not, per se, petroleum agreements; they are included in such agreements or their annexes, with a view to allow the HC to enter into petroleum activities, either directly or through an NOC.[22] In practice, participation agreements trigger the formation of a joint venture between the HC and the IOC(s) that is(are) a party(ies) to the main petroleum agreement.[23] The intensity of State participation varies from case to case, depending on the contractual phase, the specific conditions of the country and, in many cases, the initial negotiations with the IOC.

It is possible to find participation agreements in the context of virtually all types of international petroleum agreements, namely concessions, PSAs and RSAs (although their pertinence is discussed in these two cases). It normally reflects the intensity of the HC's desire to closely control the activities and to take advantage of the IOC's expertise to develop its own.

e. A word on hybrids

Petroleum agreements are generally an attempt to balance the HC's interests (e.g., sovereignty; profitable exploitation of natural resources; economic, social and technological development; environmental protection) and the IOC's incentives (e.g., return from the investment, cash-flow, political and fiscal stability). The structure of each type of agreement and the choice of one model may also vary according to the oil and gas markets.[24] Furthermore, there are endless examples of hybrid contractual forms. As it has been pointed out,

> [...] One should not be misled by the various labels affixed to [international petroleum agreements], since they all share many basic features and can be made to achieve the same economic results. In fact, at least 80% of the contents of most [international petroleum agreements] consist of the same clauses, irrespective of their label.[25]

---

[22] *Idem*, page 103.
[23] Ernest E. SMITH, John S. DZIENKOWSKI, Owen L. ANDERSON, John S. LOWE, Bruce M. KRAMER and Jacqueline L. WEAVER (2010), above cited n14, page 492.
[24] Claude DUVAL, Honoré LE LEUCH, André PETRUZIO and Jacqueline Lang WEAVER (2009), above cited n1, page 53.
[25] *Idem*, page 54.

DIREITO COMPARADO / COMPARATIVE LAW

It is not, therefore, surprising that the distinction between RSAs and other modern contractual forms becomes increasingly difficult.

4. Risk Service Agreements in Africa

In order to understand how and when RSAs are applied, we have sought to assess the practice adopted in four countries: Libya, Algeria, Nigeria and Angola. These countries were selected for their relevance in the context of African oil-producing States.

a. Libya

Libya has used, throughout the years, concessions, participation agreements and production sharing agreements. The early concessions were limited to a legally determined maximum size, in order to ensure that Libyan oil production would not be exclusively held by a few majors.[26]

In 1970, a NOC was created and the government started a revision of the existing concessions, demanding 51% participation in favor of the NOC. Companies that did not agree with the new terms had the corresponding 51% in their concession nationalized.

In 1973, Libya started using exploration and production sharing agreements (known as EPSA I), under which the IOCs were entitled to a fixed tax-free share of oil production but could not allocate costs to any part of production. In the late 1970s, the Libyan government forced the relinquishment of unexploited blocks, which were then subject to a second generation of exploration and production sharing agreements (EPSA II). The terms of these contracts were even less favorable to IOCs than the first generation and that fact was reflected upon reduced production.

In the late 1980s, a third generation of contracts was introduced (EPSA III), allowing for the first time the deduction of costs against part of the production.

Only in 2004 did Libya create an instrument following the structure of traditional PSAs – the EPSA IV. No record of use of RSAs in Libya has been found. Given the recent political events in the country, the future of E&P contracts in Libya is anybody's guess.

---

[26] Bassam FATTOUH (2008), "North African Oil and Foreign Investment in Changing Market Conditions", Centre for Financial and Management Studies, SOAS and Oxford Institute for Energy Studies.
Available at: www.oxfordenergy.org/pdfs/WPM37.pdf

b. Algeria

The 1986 Hydrocarbon Law allowed the use of production sharing agreements, joint ventures and risk service contracts and set out strict requirements for IOCs. It was, however, extensively amended in order to establish more attractive conditions for foreign investors. There are records of an RSA having been signed in 2000 for the Ohanet region, between Sonatrach and a group led by BHP Billiton Petroleum of Australia.

In 2005, the Hydrocarbon Law was reformed, establishing new royalty/tax contracts instead of the PSAs that were usually used until then. No record of RSAs was found after the enactment of the new law.

c. Nigeria

The 1969 Petroleum Act repealed previous colonial legislation without, however, dramatically changing the licensing regime. The duration of licenses was decreased and relinquishment of one half of the area after 10 years became mandatory.[27] The type of arrangements with IOCs shifted to joint ventures entered into with the government. More recently, PSAs were adopted, as well as RSAs, although the latter more rarely.

RSAs can most frequently be found where indigenous oil companies are involved.[28] These companies are granted a number of benefits under the Nigerian Oil and Gas Industry Content Development Act, such as a 'first consideration' right in the award of oil blocks, as well as 'first consideration' for employment and training.[29] Furthermore, they are given *'exclusive consideration' 'to bid on land and swamp operating areas of the Nigerian oil and gas industry for contracts and services contained in the Schedule to [the] Act'*, if they *'demonstrate ownership of equipment, Nigerian personnel and capacity to execute such work'*.[30]

---

[27] Jedrzej George FRYNAS (2000), "Oil in Nigeria: conflict and litigation between oil companies and village communities", LIT Verlag Münster, page 81.

[28] See Soji AWOGBADE, Sina SIPASI and Gloria IROEGBUNAM (2008), "Oil Regulation: Nigeria", AÉLEX Legal Practitioners and Arbitrators; and the NNPC official website (http://www.nnpc-nigeria.com/nnpc.htm):
[In 1990], a reinvigorated indigenous operatorship programme was introduced through the allocation of blocks to indigenous companies, who presently operate on sole risk basis.

[29] Cfr. Articles 3(1) and 28 of the *2010 Nigerian Oil and Gas Industry Content Development Act*, hereinafter referred to as "the Act", available at: http://www.ncdmb.gov.ng/index.php?option=com_content&view=article&id=54&Itemid=59

[30] Cfr. Article 3(2) of the Act.

Nigeria is on the verge of completely restructuring its petroleum industry, a change that has been in the offing since 2000, when the Oil and Gas Sector Reform Implementation Committee was set up. The Senate is currently considering the Petroleum Industry Draft Bill ("PIB"), a far-reaching project; it covers such topics as institutional structure, regulation of both upstream and downstream activities, transparency, environmental protection, local content and taxation. The government refers to it as *"one of the most modern and forward looking petroleum laws in the world, incorporating the best international practices from a large number of countries"*. Its 495 articles are exhaustive and ambitious, with the announced purpose of improving efficiency and government revenue. It appears obvious, however, that its approval and entry into force will be anything but easy due to the opposition of many stakeholders, who have been trying to influence the shape of its provisions ever since congressional review began.

The Minister of Petroleum Resources formed an Inter Agency Team ("IAT"), subsequent to the presentation of the report prepared by the Oil and Gas Sector Reform Implementation Committee, which further reviewed the PIB. As of time of writing, there is no certainty as to which version will be passed as law. However, some comments may be advanced with regard to the texts that are presently available.

According to the IAT version, oil companies holding a license or a lease granted by the Minister will have the power to enter into the following contracts for the exploration, prospecting, production and development of oil and/or gas: (i) PSAs; (ii) RSAs; (iii) concession contracts; and (iv) any variation thereto, so long as it is in harmony with international practice. The description of RSAs in the PIB leaves virtually no room for distinction from PSAs; it is defined as a contract under which *"the financial risk-bearing party shall be reimbursed for costs where a discovery is made and shall be entitled to payment in cash or in kind from petroleum produced from the contract area"*. The only difference with regard to the definition of a PSA is the expression *"payment in cash or in kind from petroleum produced"*, since the description of a PSA refers to *"a share of production as established in the contract"*. As we have noted above, whenever the possibility of payment in kind exists, there is a quasi identity between both types of contract. It will be interesting to see how these RSAs are drafted in practice, so as to assess their specificities (if any).

d. Angola

Angola launched a licensing round at the end of 2007 ("2007/2008 Licensing Round"). On offer were "old" onshore and offshore blocks, as well as "new" ultra-deepwater blocks. For various reasons, domestic and international, the 2007/2008 Licensing Round has not been completed yet. However, in the meantime Blocks 9 and 21, which were initially included in the 2007/2008 Licensing Round, have been awarded.

The granting of these two blocks for exploration was hallmarked by the emergence of a "new kid on the block" of Angola petroleum contracts: the risk service agreement ("RSA"). The concession decrees, as will become apparent hereinbelow, provide little information on many of the variables of the Blocks 9 and 21 petroleum investment regime. No doubt, a more in depth analysis will only be possible if and when details on the RSAs become public.

An RSA may *à vol d'oiseau* be theoretically distinguished from a petroleum sharing agreement ("PSA") by reference to the means of payment for the services provided. Whereas a PSA (widely used in Angola) entails a payment in kind, an RSA (unresorted to until 2009 in Angola) provides for a payment in cash, both contract types reflecting an element of risk.

The Angolan Petroleum Activities Law[31] ("PAL") and Petroleum Taxation Law[32] ("PTL") both allude to RSAs. Article 14 of the PAL lists the contractual instruments that may be used as a basis for the undertaking of petroleum operations. As this provision's heading – "Types of Association and Risk Service Agreement" – implicitly indicates, an RSA does not appear to be viewed as a "type of association" between the National Concessionaire (*Sociedade Nacional de Combustíveis de Angola, Empresa Pública – Sonangol E.P.*) and petroleum companies. Weight is lent to this view, first, because the forms of association listed in article 14 are (i) corporation, (ii) consortium, (iii) production sharing agreement; and, second, because it is provided that "[t]he *National Concessionaire* shall also be allowed to carry out petroleum operations **by means of risk service agreements**" (emphasis added).

This interpretation – that RSAs are not a "type of association" –, in and of itself reasonable in light of the letter of the law, seems to be confirmed

---

[31] Law no. 10/04, of 12 November 2004.
[32] Law no. 13/04, of 24 December 2004.

by the conduct of the Angolan authorities in the few instances in which RSAs were resorted to. But what does it boil down to?

In article 46, the PAL further provides that "open tender procedures" for the awarding of "the status of associate of the National Concessionaire" are to be established by regulations. Enacted pursuant to said article 46, Decree 48/06, of 1 September 2006 (the "Tender Decree") sets forth *inter alia* the rules for the acquisition of the status of associate of the National Concessionaire through competitive tender. Since an RSA does not confer upon petroleum companies the status of associate of the National Concessionaire, their signing consequently does not have to be preceded by a competitive tender.

The release of Blocks 9 and 21 for exploration was not carried out through open tender procedures, but rather through direct negotiation with the operating company. Because of constitutional requirements concerning taxation, a National Assembly Resolution had to be passed, authorizing the Government to legislate on tax matters respecting the petroleum concessions for Blocks 9 and 21.[33] Two Concession Decrees were subsequently enacted.[34] They grant the petroleum mining rights to the National Concessionaire, and allow it to enter into an RSA with a consortium that includes *Cobalt International Energy, LP* (operator), *Sonangol Pesquisa e Produção S.A.*, and *Nazaki Oil and Gas*.

One of the key arguments put forward in this process, expressly mentioned in the National Assembly Resolution 23/09 (the "Enabling Resolution") and in the Concession Decrees, which apparently seems to be the main grounds for the "direct negotiation procedure" followed in the granting of Blocks 9 and 21, was that such blocks had been unsuccessfully explored in the past. It is not clear whether "new" blocks, such as the ultra-deepwater Blocks 46 to 48, which were equally on offer in the 2007/2008 Licensing Round, could have been or may in the future be granted through such procedure.

With regard to taxation, RSAs bring several changes when compared to PSAs. Firstly, the rate of the Petroleum Income Tax ("PIT") is 65.75%, instead of the PSA's rate of 50%. Secondly, Petroleum Production Tax ("PPT") at a standard 20% rate and a "rent-skimmer" Petroleum Trans-

---

[33] Resolution no. 23/09, of 2 April 2009.
[34] Decree-Laws 14/09 and 15/09, both of 11 June 2009.

action Tax ("PTT") at a 70% rate apply to RSAs, which does not occur with PSAs. Thirdly, in RSAs, the ring-fencing principle covers the concession area, instead of the development area as in the case of PSAs. Fourthly, production and/or investment allowance deductions for PTT purposes may be granted to the contractor.

The Enabling Resolution 23/09 authorized the Government to approve (i) tax exemptions and (ii) reduced tax rates, both of which may extend to customs rights and duties. In the Concession Decrees, however, the only provisions on taxation cover taxes applicable to the National Concessionaire. A reduced 50% PIT rate and a full exemption of PPT and PTT are provided for the National Concessionaire. No provision sets out the tax position of the members of the consortium. It appears though that they will be subject to PIT and PTT at the standard rates. Assuming that production is to belong fully to the National Concessionaire, no PPT can be levied in respect of the members of the consortium. In respect of PTT, finally, the government enacted last year Decrees 3/10 and 4/10, of 21 January 2010. A Production Allowance (deduction) was granted, based on a sliding scale set by reference to the after-tax nominal rate of return ("ROR") (from 95% of gross production for a ROR lower than 10%, down to 55% of gross production for a ROR higher than 40%). No Investment Allowance (deduction) was granted.

5. Conclusion

RSAs are not common, in Africa or elsewhere. Moreover, they have become quite similar to PSAs, the type of agreement that is presently most resorted to in the petroleum industry. Because PSAs are more widely accepted by the IOCs, it is natural that HCs use them more often.

It should be noted that RSAs not only allow for the protection of sovereignty of mineral rights, but also constitute an outstanding opportunity for NOCs to acquire scientific and technical knowledge as a result of the cooperation with experienced IOCs. This is a strong point in their favour, yet not entirely decisive, since, as mentioned above, similar goals may be achieved by means of more popular contractual instruments.[35]

---

[35] Cf. Ernest E. SMITH, John S. DZIENKOWSKI, Owen L. ANDERSON, John S. LOWE, Bruce M. KRAMER and Jacqueline L. WEAVER (2010), above cited n14, page 482.

As to the Angolan case, the recourse to RSAs for purposes of carrying out petroleum operations was perhaps the last untapped "contract province". The question to be answered is whether the procedure followed for Blocks 9 and 21 is an approach that came to stay, to be applied in the future in the granting of other blocks. If that is the case, it may become the new trump card in the Angolan practice, whose flexibility will offer plenty of opportunities. Acreage will be possible to release without recourse to open tender procedures. Tailor-made solutions, which consider the specific circumstances of the investment project in question, as well as the surrounding economic environment, will be easier to set up. Most significantly, such flexibility will include tax and customs regimes and related incentives.

Lisbon, April 2011

Petroleum Arbitration

DÁRIO MOURA VICENTE[*]

I. The relevance of arbitration as a means of settling international petroleum disputes and the problems it raises

International contracts concerning the production of petroleum have a high potential for disputes. They are frequently complex, long-term contracts, involving private companies and States or State agencies, which implicate high commercial and political risks, *inter alia* due to the frequent variations of crude oil prices in international markets[1]. Public interests are often at stake, since these contracts concern the exploitation of the contracting State's non-renewable natural resources. An equally relevant interest is, however, to ensure foreign investors fair and equitable treatment.

This interest, as well as the desire to avoid a submission to the jurisdictional power of the contracting State, has often led foreign investors to prefer arbitration as a means of settling disputes concerning petroleum contracts.

Several other reasons also account for this preference. Among them are: (a) The highly technical nature of those disputes, which requires adjudicators with expert knowledge; (b) The need for confidentiality, which is often crucial in order to preserve the parties' image and trade secrets; (c) The fact that arbitration awards are frequently easier to enforce abroad than judgments; and (d) The widespread exclusion of an appeal on the merits of arbitral awards, which ensures a speedier settlement of disputes.

---

[*] Professor of Law, University of Lisbon.
[1] See Manuel A. Abdala, «Key Damage Compensation Issues in Oil and Gas International Arbitration Cases», *American University International Law Review*, 2009, pp. 539 ff.

Although the *Calvo doctrine* – according to which foreign nationals are mandatorily subject to the jurisdiction of national courts, which may not be excluded by an arbitration agreement – is still prevalent in some parts of the world (notably in South America), States have increasingly overcome their traditional reluctance in regard of submitting petroleum disputes to arbitration[2].

Nevertheless, such arbitrations present some difficult problems. First and foremost is that of the applicable law. Unlike courts, arbitral tribunals do not have a *lex fori*, since they do not administer justice on behalf of a State. Therefore, they are not directly bound by any particular choice of law rules. The question thus arises, how should arbitral tribunals determine the applicable law? Secondly, when States are involved as parties to such arbitrations, one may ask if and to what extent should International Law prevail over their domestic laws? Thirdly, if the law of an Islamic State is applicable, the question also arises, whether arbitrators may apply the Sharia, which is in force in many oil-producing countries. Fourthly, one may ask what effect, if any, should be given by arbitrators to other supranational legal criteria, such as the usages and customs of the petroleum industry (the so-called *lex petrolea*)? And fifthly, the problem comes to notice of whether and to what extent stabilisation clauses inserted in petroleum contracts should be enforced by international arbitral tribunals.

Over the past 60 years, several arbitral awards concerning petroleum disputes have dealt with these issues at length. Petroleum arbitration has thus given an important contribution, which we'll examine in this paper, to the theory of international arbitration. Before going into that contribution, however, we'll give a brief outlook of the legal and institutional framework of international petroleum arbitration.

II. The legal and institutional framework of international petroleum arbitration

a) A major step forward in creating an efficient legal framework for international arbitration of investment disputes was taken in 1965, when the Washington *Convention on the Settlement of Investment Disputes Between States*

---

[2] See Pieter Sanders, *Quo Vadis Arbitration?*, The Hague, 1999, pp. 40 ff.; Gary B. Born, *International Commercial Arbitration*, 3rd ed., Alphen aan den Rijn, 2009, p. 144; and Bernardo M. Cremades, «State Participation in International Arbitration», *Revista Internacional de Arbitragem e Conciliação*, 2011 (forthcoming).

and Nationals of Other States was concluded under the auspices of the World Bank[3]. As of January 2011, 157 States had ratified it[4].

This Convention provides for the settlement of those disputes by persons chosen by the parties or appointed from the panel of arbitrators of the International Centre for the Settlement of Investment Disputes (ICSID). The jurisdiction of this Centre is set out in article 25 (1) of the Convention, according to which it extends to:

> «any legal dispute arising directly out of an investment, between a Contracting State (or any constituent subdivision or agency of a Contracting State designated to the Centre by that State) and a national of another Contracting State, which the parties to the dispute consent in writing to submit to the Centre.»

Two hundred and twenty cases were decided within ICSID through April 2010. Currently, there are 121 cases pending, 47 of which (or 39%) are related to energy disputes. Several of these concern petroleum issues.

Although the authority and influence of the World Bank may render voluntary compliance with ICSID awards more likely than in the case of awards rendered by other arbitral tribunals, the Washington Convention also provides for the recognition and enforcement by its member States of arbitral awards made under its provisions. Such enforcement must take place, according to article 54 (1), «as if [the award] were a final judgment of a court of that State».

b) Another important forum for the arbitral settlement of disputes concerning foreign investments is the Iran-United States Claims Tribunal[5].

---

[3] See, on the Convention, Aron Broches, «The Convention on the Settlement of Disputes Between States And Nationals of Other States», *Recueil des Cours de l'Académie de La Haye de Droit International,* vol. 136 (1972-II), pp. 331 ff.; Andreas R. Lowenfeld, «The ICSID Convention: Origins and Transformation», *Revista Internacional de Arbitragem e Conciliação,* 2008, pp. 37 ff.; Luís de Lima Pinheiro, «A arbitragem CIRDI e o regime dos contratos de Estado», *Revista Internacional de Arbitragem e Conciliação,* 2008, pp. 75 ff.; and Christoph H. Schreuer, Loretta Malitoppi, August Reinisch & Anthony Sinclair, *The ICSID Convention: A Commentary,* 2nd ed., Cambridge, 2009.

[4] See http://icsid.worldbank.org/ICSID.

[5] On which see David Caron, «The Nature of the Iran-United States Claims Tribunal and the Evolving Structure of International Dispute Resolution», *American Journal of International*

DIREITO COMPARADO / COMPARATIVE LAW

This Tribunal was established in The Hague in 1981 on the basis of the so-called *Claims Settlement Declaration* of the Government of Algeria, to which the United States and Iran subsequently adhered. Its jurisdiction is limited to claims by nationals of one State Party against the other State Party and to certain claims between the State Parties. Arbitrations under the Declaration are conducted in accordance with a modified version of the UNCITRAL Rules.

Over the past 30 years, the Tribunal's three chambers have delivered 600 awards, several of which concerning petroleum disputes.

Unlike the awards rendered in ICSID arbitrations, however, the Iran-U.S. Claims Tribunal's awards do not benefit from a specific enforcement mechanism. Article IV (3) of the Claims Settlement Declaration merely states in this regard that:

> «Any award which the Tribunal may render against either government shall be enforceable against such government in the courts of any nation in accordance with its laws.»

In *Dallal v. Bank Mellat*[6], decided in 1986, the English High Court held that an award of the Iran-U.S. Claims Tribunal was not enforceable in England under the New York Convention. But in *Gould Marketing Inc. v. Ministry of Defence of the Islamic Republic of Iran*[7], decided in 1992, the United States Court of Appeals for the Ninth Circuit found that the same Convention was applicable to that Tribunal's awards and considered that an award «need not be made under a national law for a Court to entertain jurisdiction over its enforcement pursuant to the New York Convention». The problem is still unsettled among commentators[8].

Law, 1990, pp. 104 ff.; George H. Aldrich, *The Jurisprudence of the Iran-United States Claims Tribunal: An Analysis of the Decisions of the Tribunal*, Oxford, 1996; David Caron & John R. Crook (editors), *The Iran-United States Claims Tribunal and the Process of International Claims Resolution*, Ardsley, New York, 2000.

[6] Reported in *Yearbook of Commercial Arbitration*, 1986, pp. 547 ff. See also, on this case, P. F. Kunzlik, «Public International Law – Cannot Govern a Contract, Can Authorize an Arbitration», *The Cambridge Law Journal*, 1986, pp. 377 ff.

[7] Reported in *ibidem*, 1990, pp. 605 ff.

[8] For a discussion, see e.g. Jean-François Poudret & Sébastien Besson, *Droit comparé de l'arbitrage international*, Zurich, etc., 2002, pp. 866 ff.

c) A more specific and highly innovative international agreement was concluded in Lisbon in 1994, providing for the arbitration of petroleum and other energy disputes: the *Energy Charter Treaty* (ECT)[9].

This multilateral treaty was entered into between 51 European and Asian countries, as well as the European Union, and came into force in 1998. A number of countries, including the United States, have acquired observer status[10].

The Treaty seeks to open up energy markets in its member States, in order to promote efficiency. It also aims at protecting investments in the energy sector and at ensuring investors a level playing field.

Article 26 of the ECT provides for the settlement of disputes between investors and member States, as well as the European Union, by conciliation or arbitration. Disputes not settled amicably may be submitted, at the choice of the investor, to one of three different arbitration venues mentioned in article 26 (4): (a) ICSID, insofar as the Contracting Party of which the investor is a citizen or according to which it was organized and the Contracting Party to the dispute are both parties to the ICSID Convention (arbitration under the Additional Facility Rules of ICSID may also apply if the Contracting Party of the investor or the Contracting Party to the dispute, but not both, is a member of ICSID); (b) *Ad hoc* arbitration under the UNCITRAL Arbitration Rules; or (c) The Arbitration Institute of the Stockholm Chamber of Commerce.

Unlike the ICSID Convention, the ECT doesn't require an arbitration agreement in order that the dispute may be submitted to arbitration. By entering into the Treaty, Contracting Parties have, according to article 26 (3), given their «unconditional consent to the submission of a dispute to international arbitration». For States and the European Union, arbitration under the ECT is, in this sense, compulsory.

---

[9] On the arbitration provisions of this Treaty, see Thomas W. Wälde, «Investment Arbitration Under the Energy Charter Treaty – From Dispute Settlement to Treaty Implementation», *Arbitration International,* 1996, pp. 429 ff.; Matthew D. Slater, «The Energy Charter Treaty: A Brief Introduction to its Scope and Initial Arbitral Awards», *in* Association for International Arbitration (ed.), *Alternative dispute Resolution in the Energy Sector,* Antwerpen/Apeldoorn/Portland, 2009, pp. 15 ff.; and Paul Oxnard & Benoit Le Bars, «Arbitration of Energy Disputes: Practitioners' Views From London and Paris», *in ibidem,* pp. 55 ff.

[10] For the present list of ratifications, see http://www.encharter.org.

This dispute settlement system is, however, limited by article 26 (1) of the Treaty to alleged breaches of the obligations of Contracting Parties under Part III of the Treaty, which concerns investment promotion and protection.

According to article 26 (8) of the Treaty, each Contracting Party undertakes to carry out without delay any arbitral award rendered in conformity with its rules and to make provision for the effective enforcement in its area of such award.

Disputes between Contracting Parties of the ECT may also be settled by an *ad hoc* arbitral tribunal, whose members shall be appointed, according to article 27, by the parties or by the Secretary-General of the Permanent Court of International Arbitration. The Arbitration Rules of UNCITRAL apply.

III. The law applicable to the substance of the dispute

a) What law should arbitral tribunals apply to the substance of petroleum disputes?

Common rules of Private International Law usually provide for the application of the law of one of the parties in international contracts, e.g., failing a choice of that law by the parties, that of the country where the party that is required to effect the characteristic performance of the contract has its habitual residence[11].

Such rules are, however, ill-adapted to disputes arising from international petroleum contracts between States and foreign companies.

In fact, parties to such contracts are not on equal footing, since States exercise sovereign powers under which they may change the laws and regulations applicable to the contract, as well as nationalise or expropriate the foreign investor's assets. Private investors that enter into those contracts thus require special protection against the possibility of States using their legislative powers in order to evade their contractual obligations.

But, as mentioned above, public interests are also at stake in those contracts and must be taken into consideration in the settlement of disputes arising from them, including in the determination of the applicable law.

---

[11] See article 4 (2) of Regulation (EC) No 593/2008 of the European Parliament and of the Council, of 17 June 2008, on the Law Applicable to Contractual Obligations («Rome I» Regulation), published in the *Official Journal of the European Union*, no. L 177, of 4 July 2008, pp. 6 ff.

b) A possible solution for this problem is to apply Public International Law[12]. This solution substantially strengthens the position of private parties, since according to it the obligations of States under those contracts are treated as international commitments, from which States cannot exempt themselves by invoking their own internal laws.

However, concerns have sometimes been raised that a full «internationalisation» or «delocalisation» of State contracts may unduly restrict the right of peoples and nations to the permanent sovereignty over their natural wealth and resources[13].

Furthermore, Public International Law often contains no rules on specific issues raised by contractual obligations. The *Convention on the Law of Treaties*[14], for example, doesn't provide for damages owed for the breach of contractual obligations. In such cases, applying Public International Law in international petroleum arbitrations may therefore be an impractical solution.

It is therefore no surprise that arbitral awards finding for the exclusive applicability of Public International Law to petroleum disputes are scarce. This does not mean, however, that Public International Law is irrelevant

---

[12] As was advocated *inter alia* by Alfred Verdross, «Die Sicherung von ausländischen Privatrechten aus Abkommen zur wirtschaftlichen Entwicklung mit Schiedsklauseln», *Zeitschrift für ausländisches öffentliches Recht und Völkerrecht*, 1957/58, pp. 635 ff.; F.A. Mann, «The Proper Law of Contracts Concluded by International Persons», *British Yearbook of International Law*, 1959, pp. 34 ff.; Prosper Weil, «Problèmes relatifs aux contrats passés entre un État et un particulier», *Recueil des Cours de l'Académie de Droit International de La Haye*, vol. 128 (1969-III), pp. 95 ff. (pp. 148 ff.); and Karl-Heinz Böckstiegel, *Der Staat als Vertragspartner ausländischer Privatunternehmen*, Frankfurt a.M., 1971, pp. 119 ff. See also, in Portuguese literature, Dário Moura Vicente, *Da arbitragem comercial internacional*, Coimbra, 1990, pp. 227 ff. and 286 ff.; *idem*, «Direito aplicável aos contratos públicos internacionais», *in Estudos em homenagem ao Professor Doutor Marcello Caetano no centenário do seu nascimento*, Lisbon, 2006, vol. I, pp. 289 ff.; Fausto de Quadros, «Direito Internacional Público I – Programa, conteúdos e métodos de ensino», *Revista da Faculdade de Direito da Universidade de Lisboa*, 1991, pp. 351 ff. (p. 445); *idem, A protecção da propriedade privada pelo Direito Internacional Público*, Coimbra, 1998, p. 55; André Gonçalves Pereira & Fausto de Quadros, *Manual de Direito Internacional Público*, 3rd ed., Coimbra, 1993, p. 181; and Luís de Lima Pinheiro, *Contrato de empreendimento comum (joint-venture) em Direito Internacional Privado*, Lisbon, 1998, pp. 507 ff.

[13] Which the United Nations have recognized in several resolutions as a basic constituent of the right to self-determination: see, e.g., General Assembly Resolution 1803 (XVII) of 14 December 1962.

[14] Done at Vienna on 23 May 1969 and entered into force on 27 January 1980. Published in the United Nations *Treaty Series*, vol. 1155, pp. 331 ff.

DIREITO COMPARADO / COMPARATIVE LAW

in regard of these disputes. As we shall see, it may operate either as a constituent part of the contracting State's law or as a limit to its applicability.

c) An alternative approach, which also aims at denationalising petroleum arbitrations, consists in applying general principles of law[15].

This path was followed, for example, in *Sapphire International Petroleum Limited v. National Iranian Oil Company (NIOC)*[16], decided in 1963. The Swiss Judge Pierre Cavin, sitting in Lausanne as sole arbitrator, held that the substantive law applicable to the agreement at stake was the principles of law generally recognized by civilized nations, to the exclusion of Iranian law, although Iran was the place of execution of the contract and of its performance. On this basis, the arbitrator established that NIOC, by having refused to properly cooperate with Sapphire, had breached the generally recognized rule of *pacta sunt servanda* and decided that this breach gave Sapphire the right to be compensated.

This precedent was subsequently invoked, *inter alia*, in *Deutsche Schachtbau- und Tiefbohrgesellschaft mbH (DST) et al. v. The Government of the State of R'as Al Khaimah and the R'as Al Khaimah Oil Company (Rakoil)*[17]. This case concerned a concession agreement concluded between the Government of R'as Al Khaimah and a number of companies for the exploration of oil and gas in the territorial waters of that Arab Emirate. The arbitral tribunal, composed by Pierre Folliet, Bjorn Haug and Cedric Barclay, found that reference to the law of any one of the companies or of the State was inappropriate. It decided instead to refer to «what ha[d] become common practice in international arbitrations particularly in the field of oil drilling concessions and especially to arbitrations located in Switzerland». The tribunal stated that such practice, «which must have been known to the parties», should be regarded as «representing their implicit will». It therefore held «internationally accepted principles of law governing contractual relations to be the proper law applicable to the merits of this case».

---

[15] See Lord McNair, «The General Principles of Law Recognized by Civilized Nations», *British Yearbook of International Law,* 1957, pp. 1 ff.; Philippe Fouchard, *L'arbitrage commercial international,* Paris, 1965, pp. 423 ff.; René David, «L'arbitrage en droit civil, téchnique de régulation des contrats», in *Mélanges dédiés à Gabriel Marty,* Toulouse, 1978, pp. 383 ff.; and Peter Nygh, *Autonomy in International Contracts,* Oxford, 1999, pp. 192 f.

[16] Reported in *The International and Comparative Law Quarterly,* 1964, pp. 1011 ff.

[17] ICC arbitration no. 3572, of 1982, reported in Sigvard Jarvin, Yves Derains & Jean-Jacques Arnaldez (eds.), *Collection of ICC Arbitral Awards 1986-1990,* Paris, etc., 1994, pp. 154 ff.

This line of thought was also followed in *Mobil Oil Iran Inc. v. Islamic Republic of Iran,* decided by the Iran-United States Claims Tribunal in 1987[18]. The claimants had brought proceedings against the Government of Iran and the National Iranian Oil Company (NIOC), seeking to recover damages for respondents' alleged breach and wrongful termination of a Sale and Purchase Agreement entered into in 1973 for the supply and purchase of petroleum products. The agreement contained a choice of law clause under which it should be interpreted in accordance with the laws of Iran. Nevertheless, Chamber 3 of the Iran-U.S. Claims Tribunal held that, given the agreement's international character, it would not be appropriate to apply the law of one party. Accordingly, it decided that Iranian law would only be applicable to issues of interpretation of the contract and that the general principles of Commercial and International Law would be applied to all other issues. Among these principles was, according to the tribunal, that of *force majeure* as a cause of suspension or termination of a contract. In the circumstances of the case, however, the tribunal did not find that on the date of the alleged termination of the contract by NIOC (10 March 1979) the situation was such that the agreement could be considered as frustrated or terminated on grounds of *force majeure.*

Notwithstanding its ingenuity, this approach has not remained exempt from criticism. Often, one finds no universally accepted general principle on major legal issues posed by international contracts. Take, for example, liability for the breach of pre-contractual duties of conduct arising from the principle of good faith. While the German and the Portuguese Civil Codes impose such a liability in the case of the so-called *culpa in contrahendo,* and thus offer each party a high degree of protection for their reliance on the other party during the contract's preliminaries, English law, which takes a much more liberal stance in this regard, rejects such a rule[19].

But even if a general principle can be found on a specific point of law, its indeterminate nature inevitably gives arbitrators a high degree of discretion, which may be detrimental from the point of view of legal certainty[20].

---

[18] Reported in the *American Journal of International Law,* 1988, pp. 136 ff.

[19] See, on this, Dário Moura Vicente, *Da responsabilidade pré-contratual em Direito Internacional Privado,* Coimbra, 2001, pp. 239 ff., with further references.

[20] This was stressed, *inter alia,* by Wilhelm Wengler, in «Allgemeine Rechtsgrundsätze als wählbares Geschäftsstatut», *Zeitschrift für Rechtsvergleichung,* 1982, pp. 11 ff.

DIREITO COMPARADO / COMPARATIVE LAW

Let us consider, for example, *BP v. Libya*, decided in 1973 by Justice Gunnar Lagergren as sole arbitrator[21]. The choice of law clause contained in the contract that governed the concession awarded to BP in Libya adopted a «two-tier system», according to which the dispute was primarily governed by the principles of law common to Libyan and International Law and, in the absence of such common principles, by the general principles of law. In the light of these principles, the arbitrator held the nationalisation of BP's concession, decreed in 1971 by the Libyan Government, to be a breach of contract, as it was arbitrary, discriminatory and confiscatory. The arbitrator found, however, that no specific performance of the contract was to be allowed in the instant case, since English, American, Danish and German laws varied on the availability of that remedy. Accordingly, he decided that Libya should only be liable to pay damages to BP, to be determined in subsequent arbitral proceedings. The case was settled for UK £ 17.4 million.

Precisely the opposite conclusion was reached in a similar case, *Texaco v. Libya*, decided in 1977 by Professor René-Jean Dupuy as sole arbitrator[22]. The choice of law clause in this case was identical to the one in *BP v. Libya*. Texaco's claims were also based on the nationalisation of an oil concession, occurred in 1973 and 1974, which the arbitrator found to be a breach of the contract entered into by the parties. He further established that under both Libyan and International Law *restitutio in integrum* was the principal remedy available for the breach of contractual obligations. The concession therefore remained binding on the parties, and Libya was held to be bound to perform the contract. The case was subsequently settled for US $152 million.

Still another conclusion was reached on the basis of the same choice of law clause in *Libyan American Oil Company (LIAMCO) v. Libya*, decided in 1977 by a Lebanese jurist, Dr. Sobhi Mahmassani, acting as sole arbitrator[23]. LIAMCO, an American company, had entered into concession agreements for the exploration and production of petroleum in Libya, which

---

[21] Reported in *Yearbook of Commercial Arbitration*, 1980, pp. 143 ff., and in *Revue de l'arbitrage*, 1980, pp. 117 ff.

[22] Reported in *Clunet: Journal de Droit International*, 1977, pp. 319 ff., and in *Yearbook of Commercial Arbitration*, 1979, pp. 177 ff. See also, on this award, Jean-Flavien Lalive, «Un grand arbitrage pétrolier entre un Gouvernement et deux sociétés privées étrangères», *Clunet : Journal de Droit international*, 1977, pp. 319 ff.

[23] Reported in *Revue de l'arbitrage*, 1980, pp. 132 ff.

were nationalised in 1973 and 1974. It subsequently commenced arbitration proceedings against the Libyan Republic claiming the restoration of its concession rights or the payment of damages. The arbitrator found that the nationalisation of LIAMCO's concession was not unlawful, but that the company was nevertheless entitled to compensation. He held further that the standard of compensation should be determined according to the general principles of law, given the fact that there was no conclusive evidence that there were common principles in this respect in Libyan and International Law. According to the arbitrator, one of those general principles was equity. It would therefore be reasonable and just to adopt the formula of equitable compensation as a criterion for the determination of the damages. In light of this criterion, damages should correspond to the market value of the LIAMCO's assets at the time of the nationalisation. Lost profits should also, under the same the criterion, be compensated. LIAMCO was thus awarded approximately US $80 million plus interest and costs.

These cases make it clear that the application of general principles of law to petroleum arbitrations may lead to great uncertainty as to their outcome[24].

d) A third approach regarding the proper law of petroleum arbitrations has therefore gained ground. It consists in applying the rules chosen by the parties or, failing such a choice, those of the contracting State. The applicability of the domestic law of the contracting State is nevertheless limited by International Law, in the sense that the former's rules will not apply if they are inconsistent with the latter.

This system of concurrent laws adequately balances the different interests at stake. On the one hand, the reference to the law of the contracting State gives due importance to the sovereign interests of that State. On the other hand, the applicability of International Law provides the necessary protection to the interests of the private party.

It corresponds, in essence, to the rule contained in article 42 (1) of the ICSID Convention, which states that:

---

[24] For a comparative overview of the three awards, see Brigitte Stern, «Trois arbitrages, un même problème, trois solutions. Les nationalisations pétrolières libyennes devant l'arbitrage international», *Revue de l'arbitrage*, 1980, pp. 3 ff.

«The tribunal shall decide a dispute in accordance with such rules of law as may be agreed by the parties. In the absence of such agreement, the tribunal shall apply the law of the Contracting State party to the dispute (including its rules on the conflict of laws) and such rules of international law as may be applicable.»

According to this rule, if the domestic law applicable to the contract allows the contracting State to expropriate or nationalise the other party's assets without compensation, the customary principle of International Law that requires such compensation shall prevail.

This was the essential finding in *AGIP v. Congo,* the first petroleum arbitration conducted under the ICSID Convention[25]. AGIP's assets in Congo were nationalised in 1975 and transferred to a local company by an ordinance expressly providing that it created no right to any compensation. In an award rendered in 1979, the tribunal, composed by Jogen Trolle, René-Jean Dupuy and Fuad Rouhani, examined the validity of this ordinance from the point of view of International Law and concluded that the act of nationalisation was inconsistent with it. Accordingly, the Government of Congo was ordered to compensate AGIP.

An award rendered in 1988 in *Wintershall AG v. The Government of Qatar*[26], by an *ad hoc* arbitral tribunal composed of John Stevenson, Bernardo Cremades and Ian Brownlie followed the same path. The case concerned an Exploration and Production Sharing Agreement (EPSA) under which Qatar granted the claimant and other companies the exclusive right to explore, drill and produce petroleum in a defined area offshore Qatar, as well as the right to store, transport and sell petroleum in Qatar and to export petroleum. The claimants claimed that Qatar had breached the agreement by denying them access to a part of the contract area. The contract had no choice of law clause. The tribunal held that the law applicable to the dispute should be that of Qatar, due to the close link between the contract and that country. Public International Law would, however, also be applicable, the tribunal stated; but it was not held relevant in regard of the issues under consideration.

[25] Reported in *Yearbook of Commercial Arbitration,* 1983, pp. 133 ff.
[26] Reported in *International Legal Materials,* 1989, pp. 795 ff.

In this respect, the Iran-U.S. Claims Settlement Declaration gives the arbitral tribunal a larger discretion by stating in article V:

«The Tribunal shall decide all cases on the basis of respect for law, applying such choice of law rules and principles of commercial and international law as the Tribunal determines to be applicable, taking into account relevant usages of the trade, contract provisions and changed circumstances.»

Anyway, the reference to choice of law rules in this provision suggests that the applicability of a national law should always be considered by the Tribunal.

A greater restraint in what concerns the applicability of the host State's law may be noted in article 26 (6) of the Energy Charter Treaty, according to which:

«A tribunal established under paragraph (4) shall decide the issues in dispute in accordance with this Treaty and applicable rules and principles of international law.»

It seems, however, that this provision should not be interpreted as excluding the applicability of a contracting State's national law, at least in disputes with private investors. This is so for several reasons.

On the one hand, because the applicability of national law is expressly provided for in the conflict of laws rules of the ICSID Convention (article 42), the UNCITRAL arbitration rules (article 33) and the arbitration rules of the Stockholm Chamber of Commerce (article 22), to which, as we have seen, article 26 (4) of the ECT refers.

On the other hand, because whenever the contract from which the dispute arises contains a choice of law clause the arbitrators cannot disregard it, as this expression of party autonomy is protected by International Law itself. This was expressly admitted, e.g., in the award on the *LIAMCO* case.

Finally, as already mentioned, International Law will often provide no answer to the legal problems posed by the contracts or concessions under examination by the arbitral tribunal. The legally binding nature of a contract, for example, should be judged, first and foremost, in accordance with national law.

The provision cited above must therefore be understood, we submit, as meaning solely that, whenever national law applies, this law should be in conformity with International Law.

IV. The applicability of the Sharia

a) In many oil-producing countries, Islamic Sharia is the main source of the law. Such is the case, *inter alia*, of Libya and Nigeria, in Africa, and of Saudi Arabia and Kuwait, in the Middle East. This poses the problem of whether, and to what extent, should Sharia rules be applied to international arbitrations concerning petroleum disputes[27]. Arbitrators have dealt with this problem in some major petroleum arbitrations. Two patterns of decision have emerged from the awards rendered in those arbitrations.

b) In *Petroleum Development Ltd. v. Sheikh of Abu Dhabi*, decided in 1951 by Lord Asquith of Bishopstone[28], the Umpire wrote on the issue of the proper law applicable in construing the contract:

> «This is a contract made in Abu Dhabi and wholly to be performed in that country. If any municipal system of law were applicable, it would *prima facie* be that of Abu Dhabi. But no such law can reasonably be said to exist. The Sheikh administers a purely discretionary justice with the assistance of the Koran; and it would be fanciful to suggest that in this very primitive region there is any settled body of legal principles applicable to the construction of modern commercial instruments.»

The Umpire then invoked a clause of the contract that, in his view, prescribed «the application of principles rooted in the good sense and common practice of the generality of civilised nations – a sort of modern law of nature». He then proceeded to state that:

[27] See, on this, Pieter Sanders, *op. cit. supra* (note 2), pp. 51 ff.; Alan Redfern & Martin Hunter, *Law and Practice of International Commercial Arbitration*, 3rd ed., London, 1999, pp. 110 ff.; Julian D. M. Lew, Loukas A. Mistelis & Stefan M. Kröll, *Comparative International Commercial Arbitration*, The Hague/London/New York, 2003, pp. 447 ff.; Ali Mezghani, «Le droit musulman et l'arbitrage», *Revue de l'arbitrage*, 2008, pp. 211 ff.; Mary B. Ayad, «Harmonisation of International Commercial Arbitration and *Sharia*», *Macquarie Journal of Business Law*, 2009, pp. 93 ff.; Abdul El-Ahdab, *Arbitration With the Arab Countries*, 3rd ed., Alphen aan den Rijn, 2011.

[28] Reported in *The International and Comparative Law Quarterly*, 1952, pp. 247 ff., and in *International Law Reports*, 1957, pp. 144 ff.

«Albeit English Municipal Law is inapplicable as such, some of its rules are in my view so firmly grounded in reason, as to form part of this broad body of jurisprudence – this "modern law of nature".»

A similar problem arose in *Ruler of Qatar v. International Marine Oil Company, Ltd.*, decided in 1953 by Sir Alfred Bucknill[29]. After hearing the evidence of two experts in Islamic law, he concluded that «there is no settled body of legal principles in Qatar applicable to the construction of modern commercial instruments» and that «[Islamic] law does not contain any principles which would be sufficient to interpret this particular contract». Furthermore, he stated, «certain parts of the contract, if Islamic law was applicable, would be open to the grave criticism of being invalid». In his opinion, therefore, «neither party intended Islamic law to apply». Instead, they «intended that the agreement was to be governed by "the principles of justice, equity and good conscience"».

c) Thus, in both cases mentioned above the arbitrators excluded Islamic law as the law applicable to the substance of the dispute. This negative choice of law has, however, not been repeated in subsequent cases.

In *Aramco v. Saudi Arabia*[30], decided in 1958 by an arbitral tribunal composed by a Swiss law professor, Georges Sauser-Hall, and by two Egyptian jurists, Mohamed Hassan and Saba Habachi, the arbitration agreement expressly stated that the dispute should be settled in accordance with Saudi Arabian law in what concerned matters within the jurisdiction of Saudi Arabia; and by the law that the arbitral tribunal deemed applicable in the remaining matters. Saudi law was, according to the same agreement, «Muslim law (a) as taught by the School of Imam Ahmed Ibn Hanbal; and (b) as applied in Saudi Arabia». The concession at stake in the dispute was thus considered by the arbitral tribunal to be subject to the Sharia as in force in Saudi Arabia. However, this law contained, according to the tribunal, no precise rules on the exploitation of petroleum fields. Therefore, insofar as doubts remained on the content or on the meaning

---

[29] Reported in *International Law Reports*, 1953, pp. 534 ff.

[30] Reported in *Revue critique de droit international privé*, 1963, pp. 304 ff. See also on this case Suzanne Bastid, «Le droit international public dans la sentence arbitrale de l'Aramco», *Annuaire français de droit international*, 1961, pp. 300 ff. ; and Henri Batiffol, «La sentence Aramco et le droit international privé», *Revue critique de droit international privé*, 1964, pp. 647 ff.

DIREITO COMPARADO / COMPARATIVE LAW

of the contract, the tribunal decided to apply the general principles of law. These would, according to the tribunal, also supplement the rights and obligations of the parties.

A much greater effort in order to determine the existence of Sharia rules applicable to a petroleum concession and to the consequences of its termination was made in the *Liamco* case. Citing the Koran, the Sunna and the Ottoman Madjalla, the sole arbitrator endeavoured to demonstrate that the Sharia, which was a part of Libyan law, enshrined rules on the binding nature of contracts, on the specific performance of contractual obligations and on damages for the breach of contracts, which were consistent with International Law. He thereby distanced himself from the greater internationalisation of the dispute carried out by the arbitrators in the other Libyan cases mentioned above.

The ICSID Convention doesn't expressly deal with the problem of the applicability of religious sources of law, such as the Sharia. But article 42 (1) of that Convention seems incompatible with the approach followed in the *Abu Dhabi* and *Qatar* arbitrations. For two reasons: firstly, by providing for the applicability of «rules of law as may be agreed by the parties», the Convention seems to allow the choice by the parties of religious rules to govern the dispute; secondly, by determining the applicability of the «law of the Contracting State party to the dispute» failing such a choice by the parties, the Convention also leads to the application of Sharia rules insofar as they are part of the law in force in that State. These may only be excluded by the arbitrators if it is proven that they are inconsistent with International Law.

V. The emergence of a *lex petrolea*

a) One may further ask what role should be reserved in this context to the usages and customs of the petroleum industry, which some authors have characterised as a new, emerging *lex petrolea*, or as a branch of the so-called *lex mercatoria*[31].

In arbitral case-law, the notion of *lex petrolea* seems to have been mentioned for the first time in *Kuwait v. American Independent Oil Company (Aminoil)*, decided in 1982[32]. This case concerned the nationalisation of the company's oil concession in Kuwait, which had been granted in 1948 for

[31] See, on the concept of *lex petrolea*, R. Doak Bishop, «International Arbitration of Petroleum Disputes: The Development of a *Lex Petrolea*», *Yearbook of Commercial Arbitration*, 1998, pp. 1131 ff.
[32] Reported in *Yearbook of Commercial Arbitration*, 1984, pp. 71 ff.

60 years. According to the tribunal, Kuwaiti law and Public International Law, as a constituent part of the former, applied.

In its pleadings, the Government of Kuwait invoked a number of previous awards concerning nationalisations of oil concessions occurred in the Middle East. These awards had allegedly generated a customary rule valid for the oil industry – a rule of *lex petrolea* – according to which compensation should be limited to the «net book value» of the concessionaire's assets.

The tribunal, composed by Professor Paul Reuter, Professor Hamed Sultan and Sir Gerald Fitzmaurice, Q.C., didn't follow this view. It stressed that the «net book value» method advocated by Kuwait had been used in negotiations rather than in arbitrations; that the consent of investors thereto had been given under very strong economic and political constraints; and that it was not an expression of *opinio iuris* and therefore could not be seen as a rule of International Law. Thus, the tribunal awarded Aminoil a compensation that purported to reflect its legitimate expectations in conducting its business according to the circumstances that prevailed during the period that preceded the nationalisation of its assets in Kuwait.

b) Anyway, the question may be asked, what should be the status of *lex petrolea* in international arbitration?

It is doubtful that the usages and customs of the oil industry can appropriately be characterized as a *lex* – that is, as an autonomous legal system – which can be applied in petroleum disputes as an alternative to domestic laws.

To a large extent, those usages and customs have not been codified (contrary to what happened in other branches of the so-called *lex mercatoria*, such as those covered by the International Chamber of Commerce's *Incoterms* and *Uniform Rules on Contract Guarantees and Documentary Credits*). The comparatively more indeterminate nature of petroleum industry's usages would therefore generate, should they be taken as the sole criterion for the settlement of disputes, a considerable degree of uncertainty.

Finally, it seems highly unlikely that States would agree to be exclusively bound by such usages and customs in disputes concerning the exploitation of their natural resources.

c) The role of such usages and customs is thus, from our point of view, essentially a supplementary one: they should apply whenever parties refer to them, insofar as they are not contrary to the mandatory rules of the otherwise applicable domestic law, and also in order to fill in the gaps of that law.

This was the effect granted to those usages, e.g., in *Aramco v. Saudi Arabia*. According to the arbitral tribunal, in matters of private law the gaps of the domestic applicable law (which was, as mentioned above, Saudi Arabian law) should be filled in by the «customs and usages established in the world for the industry and trade of petroleum».

The ICSID Convention is silent on this point. Article 42 (1) may be interpreted as allowing a choice by the parties of the customary rules complied with by the petroleum industry. But failing such a choice it is doubtful that arbitrators may refer exclusively to such rules[33].

A more specific reference to trade usages may be found in the UNCITRAL Model Law on International Commercial Arbitration[34], which provides in article 28 (4):

> «In all cases, the arbitral tribunal shall decide in accordance with the terms of the contract and shall take into account the usages of the trade applicable to the transaction.»

A similar rule is contained in article 35 (3) of the UNCITRAL Arbitration Rules (as revised in 2010)[35]; and the Iran-U.S. Claims Settlement Declaration also determines, in article V, that the Tribunal shall take into account relevant usages of the trade.

VI. Stabilisation clauses

a) One last question is raised by the subject-matter of this paper. In long-term petroleum contracts, *stabilization clauses* are sometimes used in order

---

[33] See, in the sense that «[t]he mandate given to an ICSID arbitral tribunal is thus clear, and the rules relevant to the process of determination are those found in the traditional systems of law, to the exclusion of the *Lex Mercatoria*», Georges Delaume, «Comparative Analysis as a Basis of Law in State Contracts: The Myth of the Lex Mercatoria», *Tulane Law Review,* vol. 63 (1988-1989), pp. 575 ff. (at p. 591).

[34] Available at http://www.uncitral.org/uncitral/en/uncitral_texts/arbitration/1985Model_arbitration.html.

[35] Available at http://www.uncitral.org/uncitral/en/uncitral_texts/arbitration/1976Arbitration_rules.html.

to avoid modifications of the applicable rules by a unilateral act of the contracting State (including administrative or judicial rulings that interpret the existing law) or to preserve the economic *statu quo* at the time of contracting[36].

Such clauses may stipulate that the applicable State law comprises only the rules that were in force at the time of conclusion of the contract, thereby excluding all modifications subsequently introduced in it. For this reason, they are also called *freezing clauses*.

For example, in the Libyan concession contracts that gave rise to the abovementioned arbitral awards those clauses read as follows:

> «The concession shall throughout the period of its validity be construed in accordance with the petroleum law and the regulations in force on the date of execution of the agreement [...].»

As an alternative, stabilization clauses may require the private party to comply with new laws enacted by the contracting State, but provide that this party shall be compensated for the additional cost of complying with them (e.g., by way of adjusted tariffs, extension of the concession, tax reductions, monetary compensation, etc.). They are then called *economic equilibrium clauses*.

b) The validity and effects of these clauses are controversial.

Article 3 of the Resolution of the Institut de Droit International on *The Proper Law of the Contract in Agreements Between a State and a Foreign Private Person,* adopted in 1979[37], allows them without reservations. According to that provision:

---

[36] See, on these clauses, René David, «Les clauses de stabilité dans les contrats pétroliers», *Clunet: Journal de Droit international,* 1986, pp. 79 ff. ; Margarita T.B. Coale, «Stabilization Clauses in International Petroleum Transactions», *Denver Journal of International Law and Policy,* vol. 30:2, 2001/2002, pp. 217 ff. ; Andrea Giardina, «Clauses de stabilisation et clauses d'arbitrage: vers l'assouplissement de leur effet obligatoire ?», *Revue de l'arbitrage,* 2003, pp. 647 ff.; Zeyad A. Alqurashi, *International Oil and Gas Arbitration,* 2005, pp. 179 ff.; Ahmed El-Kosheri, «International arbitration and petroleum contracts», *in Encyclopaedia of Hydrocarbons,* vol. IV, *Hydrocarbons: Economics, Policies and Legislation,* Roma, 2005, pp. 879 ff.; and Stefan Leible, «Private International Law: Contracts for the Delivery of Gas», *German Yearbook of International Law,* 2009, pp. 327 ff. (at p. 331 f.).

[37] Available at http://www.idi-iil.org.

«The parties may agree that domestic law provisions referred to in the contract shall be considered as being those in force at the time of the conclusion of the contract.»

States' liability for the breach of a stabilisation clause should be assessed in accordance with the law applicable to the contract. This is also enshrined in the same Resolution, article 6 of which states:

«The rules of law chosen in accordance with the preceding provisions shall govern the incidence of contractual liability between the parties, in particular those raised by the State's exercise of its sovereign powers in violation of any of its commitments toward the contracting partner.»

But arbitral case-law is ambivalent in this regard.

In *Texaco v. Libya*, the arbitrator held that the stabilisation clause inserted in the concession contract prevented the State from nationalising it. According to him:

«The recognition by international law of the right to nationalize is not sufficient ground to empower a State to disregard its commitments, because the same law also recognizes the power of a State to commit itself internationally, especially by accepting the inclusion of stabilization clauses in a contract entered into with a foreign private party.»

However, in *Kuwait v. Aminoil* the tribunal found that the purpose of a stabilisation clause inserted in the contract entered into by the parties was merely to inhibit nationalisations of confiscatory nature, that is, without proper indemnification. Nationalisations were *per se* not excluded by the clause. The tribunal admitted, however, that stabilisation clauses create expectations that must be taken into account when determining the amount of damages.

The Institut de Droit International's 1991 Resolution on *The Autonomy of the Parties in International Contracts Between Private Persons or Entities*[38] also takes a more restrictive stance regarding such clauses, by stating in article 8:

---

[38] Available at *ibidem*.

«If the parties agree that the chosen law is to be applied as it is in force at the time when the contract was concluded, the provisions of that law shall be applied as substantive provisions incorporated in the contract; if, however, the chosen law has been amended or repealed by mandatory rules which are intended to govern existing contracts, effect shall be given to those rules.»

c) Be that as it may, case law specifically enforcing a State contract on the ground of a stabilisation clause is extremely rare.

Stabilisation clauses essentially operate as *additional financial guarantees* for investors entering into petroleum contracts with States or other public entities; not as limitations to their sovereign powers.

The main effect of these clauses is thus to generate a higher likelihood of obtaining damages in case a unilateral act of the State adversely affects the legal environment or the economic balance of the contract[39].

In any event, the validity of stabilisation clauses is subject to their conformity with International Law: a State cannot validly exclude the applicability of mandatory rules of International Law through such clauses. This is particularly important in what concerns rules on human rights and the protection of the environment.

Lisbon/Washington, D. C., April 2011

[39] See Eduardo Jiménez de Arechaga, «International Law in the Past Third of a Century», *Recueil des Cours de l'Académie de Droit International de La Haye*, vol. 159 (1978-I), pp. 1 ff. (at p. 307).

Applicable Law in the 2010 UNCITRAL Arbitration Rules: a Comment on Professor Vicente's Petroleum Arbitration

David D. Caron[*]

I basically agree with Professor Vicente. But, I would add that this area is a complicated subject and one in which there is some uncertainty. Indeed, it would be a miracle if the two of us agreed on everything, I don't think that would be possible. I will emphasize a few things and then offer one main comment.

First, it should not be a surprise that this area is both complicated and debated. And that is because petroleum arbitration is different from other arbitration for the same reason that energy is different from other sectors. It is just too valuable, too sensitive to national interests, and too fought about every step of the way.

Second, uncertainty in the law piles back into negotiation. First of all, if clarity is not possible because negotiating positions are so different, then ambiguity is intentionally slipped into agreements as much as possible as to what is the applicable law. Each side will try to find their little way to make it a little unclear for later arbitrations. All this also leads to games about not only what the profits are, but also as to when they are to be realized. So it is unfortunate that this unpredictability at the end actually leads

---

[*] President, American Society of International Law; C. William Maxeiner Distinguished Professor of Law, University of California at Berkeley; and Member of Chambers, 20 Essex Street.

DIREITO COMPARADO / COMPARATIVE LAW

to distortions at the front end. For example, if one thinks one will lose if you are an investor and you think you are going to lose your contract half way through the investment period, then you will look to frontload the profits coming out so you can get ahead of that problem.

There were two broad main comments I intended to offer, I will pass over the first set for brevity's sake. The first main comment sought to provide a historical overlay to the doctrinal framework that Professor Vicente has given us in his paper. In the cases cited and developments mentioned, it is important to place them on a timeline divided so that private transnational disputes are below the timeline while the public international arbitration is above. A critical observation is that there is a relationship below and above the line with their being a choice as to whether a private-state dispute is characterized as one below the line or as an interstate matter above. The value of lining up the cases in these fashions is that the push for internationalization of applicable law in the 1970s reflects in part a corrective to the characterization of the dispute. The broad insights to take out of this timeline's trajectory is (a) an increased characterization of disputes below the line so what in the past would have been a public international dispute is more and more in a private international setting through a waiver of state immunity; and (b) a main driver of this trajectory, particularly if you look at the Energy Charter Treaty or the bilateral investment treaties (BITs), is to protect legitimate expectations of the investor. And in terms of applicable law, a fundamental expression of legitimate expectations is the contract itself. It may be possible to have legitimate expectations without a contract, but a contract is a key expression.

As to my main comment, I focus on the thrust of Professor Vicente's discussion – applicable law. He discussed a number of issues in the abstract, and I want to turn that around by taking a particular case and grounding it for a moment so to view the topic of applicable law in a different way.[1]

Let us assume there is an arbitration between an oil company and an oil producing state taking place in Geneva under the UNCITRAL rules of arbitral procedure. For that Tribunal, an analysis of applicable law would start with Article 33 of the 1976 UNCITRAL Rules that provides:

---

[1] I should disclose this is one of my things, my being a coauthor of one of those doorstop commentaries from Oxford University Press, mine on the UNCITRAL Rules of Arbitral Procedure.

1. The arbitral tribunal shall apply the law designated by the parties as applicable to the substance of the dispute. Failing such designation by the parties, the arbitral tribunal shall apply the law determined by the conflict of laws rules which it considers applicable.
2. The arbitral tribunal shall decide as *amiable compositeur* or *ex aequo et bono* only if the parties have expressly authorized the arbitral tribunal to do so and if the law applicable to the arbitral procedure permits such arbitration.
3. In all cases, the arbitral tribunal shall decide in accordance with the terms of the contract and shall take into account the usages of the trade applicable to the transaction.[2]

Why look at Article 33? The three arbitrators properly view themselves as contractual agents of the contract. The contract has told them to use these rules and those rules tell how to decide a dispute. In particular, they are instructed in Article 33(1) that "[t]he arbitral tribunal shall apply the law designated by the parties as applicable to the substance of the dispute."[3] So in the first sentence the clear emphasis is that the intent of the parties is key – again, the legitimate expectations of the parties in the contract are at the center of analysis. If the parties state in the contract that the law of the oil-producing state is the applicable law, then that is a very explicit instruction to the arbitral tribunal. Although contested by some, that is a very clear statement.

Now, let us make it more complicated. Above, I quote to the 1976 Rules, but those Rules were revised in 2010. The 2010 rule corresponding to Article 33 is Article 35. It provides:

1. The arbitral tribunal shall apply the rules of law designated by the parties as applicable to the substance of the dispute. Failing such designation by the parties, the arbitral tribunal shall apply the law which it determines to be appropriate.
2. The arbitral tribunal shall decide as amiable compositeur or ex aequo et bono only if the parties have expressly authorized the arbitral tribunal to do so.

---

[2] UNCITRAL Arbitration Rules art. 33 (1976).
[3] *Id.* art. 33(1).

3. In all cases, the arbitral tribunal shall decide in accordance with the terms of the contract, if any, and shall take into account any usage of trade applicable to the transaction.[4]

The first sentence was changed to state that the tribunal "shall apply the *rules of law* designated by the parties."[5] This change tracks a point made by Professor Vicente – that is, the tribunal is not applying a *legal system*. They are not a court of that oil-producing state. Rather, they are a tribunal who just happens to read the text of whatever *rules of law* the parties designate and then apply them. And this change of language was intended precisely to emphasize that (a) the tribunal is not a court of a given legal system and (b) that the parties can choose just a couple of rules of law, not an entire system, nor only draw upon only one system. The parties can just choose, for example, the contract interpretation rules of the oil-producing state. Thus this language makes clear that the parties may break the applicable law apart quite dramatically into rules of decision – an emphasis particularly important to European thought regarding arbitration.

The second sentence is also important because for another change. This sentence begins "failing such designation," that is the parties are silent in the contract as to the applicable rules of law.[6] Again, bear in mind that the parties in an oil contract have probably fought about this. If they are silent, it is because they cannot agree. It is not that they have not thought about it. The second sentence makes clear that if the contract is silent, the parties have given the question of determining the applicable rules of law to the arbitral tribunal.

The older generation of arbitration rules (for example, Article 33 of the 1976 Rules) instruct the tribunal to use a conflict of laws analysis to determine the law to be applied. The new tendency (for example, Article 35 of the 2010 Rules) states "failing such designation the arbitral tribunal shall apply the law which it determines to be appropriate."[7] Unlike Article 33 of the 1976 Rules, Article 35 does not say anything about conflict of laws. Why was that change made? One reason is the belief that

---

[4] UNCITRAL Arbitration Rules art. 35 (2010).

[5] *Id.*

[6] *Id.*

[7] *Id.*

conflicts analysis is a game that takes a lot of time. Rather than spell out the possible conflict of laws rules, the choice is to let the tribunal determine the law that is appropriate, to have trust in the tribunal's judgment. Moreover, as suggested by Professor Vicente, it is not entirely clear that conflict-of-laws rules lead to the right answer in this situation. It is not clear because often such rules would, following a real property approach, lead to the law of the place where the oil is extracted. But in the situation envisioned, it is clear that neither party trusts each other. After all, they could not agree in the contract because the oil company, in all likelihood, did not want that law. Ironically, conflict of laws might lead to a choice the parties clearly did not jointly agree upon. It may be that some parts of the law of the place where the oil is extracted would be desired by both parties, but not necessarily all of that law.

An important and subtle caveat to the instruction in first sentence of Article 35(1) to "apply the law designated by the parties" can be found at the outset of Article 35(3). Look only at the first half of Article 35(3): "in all cases, the arbitral tribunal shall decide in accordance with the terms of the contract."[8] In *all* cases, you shall decide in accordance with the terms of the contract. The question that arises is what is the hierarchy between the first part of the third paragraph and the first sentence of first paragraph. The hierarchy is actually that you apply the law designated by the parties as provided in paragraph one, and – because the parties have chosen the UNCITRAL Rules – they are also telling the tribunal in paragraph three that they are designating, making an implicit designation, to always apply the contract. The contract, in essence, is the best expression of what the parties think the relationship is. In petroleum arbitration, a challenge is that one party potentially controls the content of the law applicable to the contract. Thus, for example, assume the contract had a clause that provided "revenues may be freely transferred out of the country in accordance with Law 20 of the oil-producing country." But years later, the country passes a new law that states "Law 20, and any contract provision adopted in reliance on it, is null and void." If applicable law is governed solely by article 35(1), the tribunal is potentially led into a loop where it applies the law that changes the contract. Article 35(3), on the other hand, instructs the tribunal value the terms of the contract more. Thus through Article

---

[8] *Id.* art. 35(3).

DIREITO COMPARADO / COMPARATIVE LAW

35(3) an importance is given to the terms of the contract, the document that best manifests the relationship between the parties.

Finally, I draw your attention to the last half of Article 35(3) which provides that the tribunal "shall take into account" usages of the trade applicable transaction, a point discussed by Professor Vicente.[9] The meaning of "usages" can be looked at in a number of ways. But notice the distinction: the first part of Article 35(3) provides that the tribunal "shall decide in accordance with" (a mandatory phrasing), while the second part of Article 35(3) provides that the tribunal "shall take into account" (a discretionary phrasing). Thus, the lesser role given to trade usages only serves to emphasize the primacy given to the terms of the contract.

The rules of arbitral procedure one chooses can be very important, and as Professor Vicente points out, the UNCITRAL Rules, along with ICSID, is an option of the investor to choose in many bilateral investment treaties.[10]

---

[9] *Id.; see* Vicente, *supra* p. 368.

[10] Following Professor Caron's presentation of this paper, the following Question-Answer dialogue followed:

 Question: I don't want to over determine language, but it does seem to me that this is a shift towards the arbitrator and away from some notion of rule of law. That is to say, "appropriate" has a lot to do with the notions an arbitrator may hold regarding equity. Anyhow, I just want to know what you say to that.

Answer by Professor Vicente: If I may, I'd say that in any instance, the tribunal has to give reasons for applying a given law. Whether these reasons are stated on the basis of conflicts reasoning or on the basis of other criteria. So I don't think we are moving away from the rule of law in any of the cases. I think that this 2010 version of the arbitration rules of UNCITRAL just give arbitrators some scope for other considerations, but still arbitrators will have to justify how they reached a given conclusion on the applicable law.

Answer by Professor Caron: There was a tension in the negotiation of the revisions to the UNCITRAL Rules as to whether to constrain the discretion of the arbitrators and thereby they think give the parties more control or whether to trust in the arbitrators and that actually the value of arbitration is maintained by giving them that discretion. This is one of the few examples in the 2010 revision where the negotiators actually favor the arbitrators. But I think part of the reason is that the first sentence provides "do exactly what the parties say." And I think what most of the pro-party control advocates would say is that if the parties are silly enough to not designate the applicable rules of law, then it should be in the hands of the arbitrators and that rules should allow that action by the tribunal to be as efficient as possible.

Regulation of the Energy Sector in the EU[1]

Luís Silva Morais[*]

1. Introduction and Preliminary Considerations

The European internal energy market, serving about half a billion people in 27 Member States is the largest integrated energy market in the world. It is true that electricity and natural gas consumption are higher in the United States than in the European Union (EU) but, differently from what is happening in Europe, energy systems in the United States tend to be physically and legally separated into several sub-systems and a significant part of energy consumers is not free to choose suppliers. Conversely – and representing somehow a contradictory or even incoherent feature – the EU is still battling to establish and consolidate truly supranational regulatory institutions like the Federal Energy Regulatory Commission (FERC) in the United States, a fact which is due to the rather peculiar EU institutional architecture (peculiarities which influence sovereign debt market turmoil that we are experiencing today but are also present in the domain of energy regulation).

Beside these specific European challenges involved in providing an adequate regulatory framework to an internal energy market only recently

---

[*] Professor at Lisbon Law University (FDL) – Jean Monnet Chair on EU Economic Regulation. Attorney at Law.

[1] This Article is essentially based on the Presentation made at INTERNATIONAL CONFERENCE – The Tenth Conference on European Union, Portuguese and American Law, held in WASHINGTON, D.C. – April 7 – 8, 2011 – Columbus School of Law, Catholic University of America – in the 1st/Opening Session – 7 th April 2011. *Accordingly it is essentially updated until April 2011.*

created in the EU, my other 'leitmotif' in this brief analysis has to do with the acknowledgement that the energy systems of the twenty-first century will be extremely different from the energy systems of the previous century, which, in turn, will require a true *reinvention* of energy regulation. I shall argue that the EU regulatory framework, despite barely *"invented"* ten or fifteen years ago, in the context of the liberalization of national energy markets of the Member States, and notwithstanding its numerous gaps, is somehow in a pivotal position to lead the way towards the adoption of new regulatory policies to the energy sector (because it is new, very adaptable and based in multiple building blocks).

The general theme of regulation of the energy sector in the EU may be covered from several different perspectives. Due to the limited scope of this analysis, I shall focus my attention on three main interlocked topics: (i) On the one hand, I shall briefly refer to the issue of EU energy dependency and the way it may seriously condition European sustainable economic growth. (ii) On the other hand, I shall cover a set of issues related with the gradual building of an *internal energy market in the EU* aimed towards competitive and efficient energy markets – assessing in the process its regulatory pillars. (iii) Finally, in the context of the regulatory pillars of the internal energy market, I shall very briefly refer to some elements of possible *reinvention* of energy regulation in the EU oriented towards market restructuring and introduction of new technologies and new energy infrastructures.

2. EU energy dependency and the gradual building of an internal energy market in the EU

Despite the fact that from the start of the European integration process the energy sector was considered as a vital area, demanding some form of coordinated action – which was duly reflected by the Treaties concerning certain aspects of the energy sector (European Coal and Steel Community and the European Atomic Energy Community)[2] – the more broad and fundamental of these supranational communities in which such European integration process has been anchored [*the original European Economic Community (EEC), now European Union*)] somehow surprisingly did not contain

---

[2] On these Communities, both from an historic persepctive and considering more recent developments, see, *inter alia*, MICHELLE CINI (Ed.), *European Union Policies*, Oxford University Press, 2006; D.G.VALENTINE, "Amendment of the European Coal and Steel Community Treaty", in International and Comparative Law Quarterly, 2008.

any original provisions on energy policy (we refer obviously to the original Treaty of Rome).

That omission had far reaching consequences. In fact, the lack of provisions in the EEC Treaty on energy prevented the formation and the consolidation of any form of global common policy on energy, from the adoption of the Treaty till the first oil shock of the seventies. In that context, there was no actual EEC reaction to such oil shock. Essentially, the Member States acted on a unilateral basis. Some common reaction to the core issues associated with the supply of energy to the EEC markets was envisaged after the second oil crisis, but it was only with the internal market program that broad legislative initiatives in the electricity and gas sectors were implemented. Furthermore, it was only with the Maastricht Treaty that measures in the sphere of energy were listed among the different activities of the Community and that new articles were added on the promotion of trans-European networks, comprehending namely energy infrastructures. Among other things, these omissions and the lack of a clear legal basis for energy policy has resulted in the absence of a true EU-wide energy regulator in charge, namely, of developing interconnectors even after the liberalization process begun. It also somehow prevented the European Commission from holding powers to alter property rights in the Member States and to carry a more active policy of de-integration of energy groups.

This situation has changed, albeit on a limited basis, with the Lisbon Treaty and the new Article 194 of the Treaty on the Functioning of the European Union (TFEU) through which it was attempted a consolidation of the existing goals and instruments of European energy policy. However, this new provision does not fundamentally grant new competences to the Union and paradoxically could even weaken the current foundations of EU energy policy (for instance, and in theory, we can not entirely rule out that a decision of the Commission under the competition rules could be challenged on the basis of this new Article 194 TFEU for not duly considering national security of supply or other concerns).

The project of the European Union (formerly European Community) to liberalize and integrate energy markets and – in the process – to regulate such internal energy market has repeatedly been characterised as unique in its scale and in its extremely complex allocation of competences between Member States and the European Union.

DIREITO COMPARADO / COMPARATIVE LAW

The adoption of the Directives on the internal market for electricity and gas gave a definite shape to the Community energy policy. We should refer here to the *first generation of Directives on electricity and gas*, starting in 1996 – including EC Directive 1996/92 (common rules for the internal market on electricity)[3] and EC Directive 1998/30 (common rules for the internal market on gas)[4] – and the *second generation of Directives in this field*, of 2003, including Directive 2003/54/CE[5] (electricity) and Directive 2003/55/CE[6] (gas).

Notwithstanding this liberalization effort, which was globally oriented towards creating open and more competitive energy markets, there remained a basic challenge of energy supply security in the EU, particularly considering that we are nowadays confronted with what may be termed as a third energy shock (quite different on several points from its predecessors on account, *inter alia* of a set of more structural and permanent factors underlying this energy crisis).[7]

This situation of growing dependence of the EU on external energy sources has led the Commission to publish in 2000 a Green Paper designated *"Towards a European Strategy for the Security of Energy Supply"*,[8] which was to be followed by another one in 2006, entitled *"A European Strategy for Sustainable Competitive and Secure Energy"*[9] (and by other discussion and policy papers that I shall not quote exhaustively).

Above all, these crucial issues – associated with ensuring Europe's energy supply – are underlying the current *EU third legislative package on energy*, presented in September 2007 and finally approved after a difficult negotiation process in the first semester of 2009.[10]

---

[3] EC Directive 1996/92 – OJ L 27 – 30/1/97.
[4] EC Directive 1998/30 – OJ L 204 – 21/7/98.
[5] EC Directive 2003/54 – OJ L 176/37 – 15/7/2003.
[6] EC Directive 2003/55 – OJ L 176/57 – 15/7/2003.
[7] On the current third energy shock, see, *inter alia*, Mamdouh G. Salameh , "A Third Oil Crisis?", in Survival, Volume 43, Issue 3, September 2001, pp. 129 ss.; C.J. Campbell, *Oil Crisis*, Multi-Science Publishing, 2005.
[8] *"Towards a European Strategy for the Security of Energy Supply"* – Green Paper – European Commission, 29 November 2000 – COM (2000) 769 Final.
[9] *"A European Strategy for Sustainable Competitive and Secure Energy"* – Green Paper – European Commission, 8 March 2006 – COM (2006) 105 Final.
[10] On the main components of the *EU third legislative package on energy*, of September 2007 see *infra*, 3.2.2.).

Despite these recent analysis of different scenarios regarding energy supply and also even more recent political initiatives concerning the interplay of the EU with other economic areas in order to promote energy efficiency internationally – as the so called *"international partnership of energy efficiency cooperation"* agreed in the context of the G8 ('Group of the eight more industrialized countries')[11] upon an EU proposal – *the basic underlying problem of EU energy dependency has not been solved and, on the contrary, the creeping and apparently structural oil crisis has aggravated it.*

This new awareness of the negative prospects in terms of energy supply has, however, paved the way to some new significant initiatives at the EU level beside the aforementioned third legislative package on the energy internal market and its regulation. On the whole, a significant part of those initiatives are aimed towards a more diverse energy mix, diversifying energy sources and transit routes, which implies considering the nuclear option and the renewable energy sources. In this context, the Commission has put forward proposals for a long-term *renewable energy* road map which brings about binding energy targets to the Member States in terms of *renewable forms of energy*, thus creating what may come to represent a more robust common energy policy and less of a soft policy limited to statements of intentions. This *renewable energy* road map implies the adoption of several EU Directives, on which the present paper will not expand *(since that would require an autonomous 'ex professo' analysis which considerably exceeds the purposes of the paper).*

> *Without denying the importance of these ad hoc initiatives, it should be emphasized that the bulk of the progress in order to tackle the fundamental problem of EU energy dependence lies in ensuring more efficient energy markets. That structural broad goal, in turn, is essentially related with the deepening of the EU energy internal market and on establishing the proper equilibrium to its functioning. I shall argue that such desirable outcome, in turn, largely depends on a proper regulatory structure for the energy sector* (and with that assumption in mind, some essential topics should be considered in the field of liberalization and regulation of energy markets).

---

[11] *"International partnership of energy efficiency cooperation"* discussed at the G8 Heiligendamm Summit of June 2007 and very recently agreed on June 2008 in the context of the 2008 G8 presidency, involving also in that process beside the G8 countries, China, India, South Korea (and, of course, the EU as such).

3. The regulatory pillars of the internal energy market

In this crucial field of liberalization and regulation – and as several commentators have already emphasized – the energy sector may be somehow in an intermediate position between two extreme situations as regards EU liberalization processes.[12] One of those extremes is represented by telecoms – a sector in which the wired and wireless technological and economic 'revolutions' meant that little remains of the past natural monopolies. One of the other extremes may be represented by the water sector, as an industry where natural monopoly elements remain to a large degree in place. Energy may be in some sort of middle ground and, therefore, EU liberalization and regulatory measures concerning the energy sector are somehow at a critical and sensitive crossroad.

This is an economic sector in the EU to which applies particularly well the much quoted conditions defined by authors such as MICHAEL BEESLEY and STEPHEN LITTLECHILD about the *regulation of former monopolies*.[13] Clearly, the focus here lies on *facilitating the durable entry of new competitors*, which may imply a three step approach, comprehending, namely: (a) focusing on likely patterns of market entry; (b) identifying options which are open to the regulator; and finally (c) choosing options which are likely to have the greatest positive impact on entry.[14]

Considering this perspective, the second generation of EC energy Directives (of 2003) were intended to accelerate the market liberalization and to create truly open and competitive energy markets. With that overriding goal the 2003 Directives identified some fundamental barriers to energy sector

---

[12] On this point, and for a comparative perspective about liberalization of the energy sector *vis a vis* other sectors, considering also concomitant regulatory and competition problems, see, *e.g.*, J. FAULL, A. NIKPAY, *The EC Law of Competition*, (2end edition), Oxford University Press, Oxford 2007.

[13] See MICHAEL. E. BEESLEY and STEPHEN C. LITTLECHILD, "The Regulation of Privatized Monopolies in the United Kingdom", in The RAND Journal of Economics, Vol. 20, No. 3 (Autumn, 1989), pp. 454-472 ; *Ibidem, The regulation of privatized monopolies in the United Kingdom*, in *Privatization, regulation and deregulation*. London: Routledge, 2nd edition, pp.58-83; STEPHEN LITTLECHILD, *Beyond Regulation*, IEA/LBS Beesley Lectures on Regulation series XV, 4 October 2005, Institute of Economic Affairs – London – SW1P 3LB – www.iea.org.uk

[14] See in particular on the aforementioned conditions, MICHAEL. E. BEESLEY and STEPHEN C. LITTLECHILD, *The regulation of privatized monopolies in the United Kingdom*, in *Privatization, regulation and deregulation*, (quoted above), pp. 58-83; See, also specifically quoting such conditions, PHILIP LOEWE, *The Liberalization of EU Energy Markets*, (SPEECH), The Beesley Lectures, Institute of Economic Affairs, the Royal Society, London, November 2006, (available at the DGCom website).

liberalization and competitiveness and attempted to find solutions for those issues. In particular, reference should be made here to key issues, such as:

(i) the vital importance of energy network operators and the need for at least a legal and financial unbundling of these operators;
(ii) The need for a transparent, non-discriminatory and predictable system of access to energy networks and related infrastructure;
(iii) the requirement established in the Directives that Member States should create national regulatory authorities with a sufficient degree of autonomy and effective powers of intervention in the market in order to address the two previous aspects [(i) and (ii)].

However, after the implementation of the 2003 Directives the recent *European Commission Inquiry into competition in gas and electricity markets* – whose final conclusions were presented in January 2007 – clearly implied that the measures and powers put forward by such second generation Directives were not sufficient to ensure actual open, competitive and efficient energy markets.

In short, the main negative findings of this energy inquiry were namely:

(1) Excessive market concentration and slow development of wholesale energy trade;
(2) Vertical integration of incumbents and foreclosure of markets barring new entrants – these markets being characterized by long-term contracts and lack of liquidity and the resulting lack of available gas and electricity that could be acquired by alternative providers;
(3) Little cross-border integration – with gas and electricity markets remaining still largely national – and difficulty to secure transit capacity in key routes (*e.g.*, Argelia-Russia) in gas and insufficient interconnector capacity in electricity;
(4) Lack of transparency and high barriers to market entry;
(5) Lack of fair competition in the functioning of the wholesale markets (probable anti-competitive practices).[15]

---

[15] For a critical and systematic assessment of those findings of the Sector Inquiry concluded in 2007, see MARTHA ROGGENKAMP, ULF HAMMER (Eds.), *European Energy Law Report V –* Energy & Law Series, Intersentia, 2007.

DIREITO COMPARADO / COMPARATIVE LAW

Furthermore, a (6) sixth overriding deficiency identified in the Inquiry referred to a *"gap in the regulatory environment: a persistent regulatory gap particularly for cross border issues. The regulatory systems in place have loose ends which do not meet"*.

These negative findings, arising from the Commission Inquiry into competition in gas and electricity markets *have directly influenced the new regulatory step arising from the 'third legislative package on the energy sector'* of 2009.[16]

On strictly formal terms, the main components of this third EU legislative package of July 2009 on the electricity and gas markets, include a (i) *Regulation Establishing an Agency for the Cooperation of Energy Regulators,*[17] a (ii) *Directive amending Directive 2003/54/CE – Common Rules for the Internal Market on Electricity,*[18] and a (iii) *Directive amending Directive 2003/55/CE – Common Rules for the Internal Market on Gas.*[19]

> The limited scope of this short paper does not allow any kind of extensive elaboration on this revised legislative framework. I shall merely concentrate on two focal points. The first one corresponds to a *trend towards the reinforcement of the separation of energy supply and production activities from network operations, including transport and distribution of energy* (which implies a preferred option of ownership unbundling of those two types of activities). The second point concerns the *establishment of a new EU agency for the cooperation of energy regulators.*

On the first point, it is clear that the best approach envisaged in the September 2007 proposals corresponded to the *ownership unbundling* of, on

---

[16] See in this field, *inter alia*, F.P. SIOSHANSI (ed.), *Competitive Electricity Markets: Design, Implementation, Performance* – Elsevier Global Energy Policy and Economic Séries, Elsevier, 2008.
[17] Regulation 713/2009, of the European Parliament and of the Council, of 13 July, 2009, establishing an Agency for the Cooperation of Energy Regulators, OJ, 14.8.2009, L 211/1.
[18] Directive 2009/72, of the European Parliament and the Council of 13 July 2009, amending Directive 2003/54/CE and concerning Common Rules for the Internal Market on Electricity, OJ 14.8.2009, L 211/55.
[19] Directive of the European Parliament and the Council, amending Directive 2003/55/CE and concerning Common Rules for the Internal Market in Natural Gas, OJ 14.8.2009 L 211/94. Other elements of this 2009 third regulatory package comprehend Regulation 714/2009, of 13 July 2009, on conditions for access to the network for cross-border exchanges in electricity, OJ 14.8.2009, L 211/15 and Regulation 715/2009, of 13 July 2009, on conditions for access to the natural gas transmission networks, OJ 14.8.2009, L 211/36.

the one hand, *energy supply and production activities* and, on the other hand, *network operations, including transport and distribution of energy* (following the preceding 2003 option of a mere *legal and financial unbundling* of such activities). Notwithstanding that preferred solution, the final compromise reached in 2009 allowed the Member States to choose between several alternative arrangements in terms of restructuring vertically integrated groups. In particular, the revised 2009 framework allowed for a so called *alternative option*, which would largely correspond to a derogation from the ownership unbundling approach (a solution identified as the establishment of an *independent system operator*).

What is essentially at stake under this *independent system operator* option is the possibility for vertically integrated energy companies – comprehending large French and Germany energy groups with substantial market power –[20] to retain the ownership of network assets with the proviso that such networks would be managed by an *independent transmission operator system (under detailed rules on autonomy, independence and investment plus a specific revision clause which can lead to legislative proposals in the future by the Commission)*. While there are undeniably some legal issues associated with a full ownership unbundling option – *e.g.*, related with the *proportionality principle* –[21] this has, above all, become a politically contentious and sensitive issue and the final compromise solution may owe more to political than to technical considerations. As things stand, on the basis of the compromise solution at stake the idea of dissociating ownership and day-to-day management decisions concerning network grids and infrastructures may prove hard to implement. Particular hardship will involve the establishment of actual monitoring procedures that may assess the autonomy levels of the management of those infrastructure and assets. The governance structures and procedures to be actually developed in order to ensure the effective independence of the *transmission system operator* will probably involve a too complex and elaborate regulatory machinery (so it can be argued that the potential for failure associated with very elaborate *ex novo* regulatory machineries is great). In this context, while there are disadvantages in adopting solutions perceived by the market as

---

[20] We are referring here to large energy groups and former state monopolies such as EDF or GDF in France or E.ON and RWE in Germany.
[21] On these issues see, *inter alia*, SABRINA PARDUROUX, KIM TALUS, "The third legislative package and ownership unbundling in the light of the European Fundamental Rights Discourse", in Competition and Regulation in Network Industries, March 2008, pp. 3 ss.

non-definitive or non-stable it may be convenient to leave open the option of a later review of the *independent transmission operator system* to check its actual efficiency (on the basis of the specific revision clauses included in the new 2009 framework).

On the second point, involving the establishment of an EU new Agency for Cooperation of Energy Regulators (ACER) – also independent from the Commission – this initiative is related with two main areas: (i) the establishment of some kind of regulatory oversight of the cooperation between transmission operators systems (oriented towards cross-border integration of networks) and (ii) the attribution of a certain degree of decision power to a new supranational body focused on cross-border issues (in the event of disputes on cross-border issues this body should resolve conflicts within a reasonable time frame).

The ACER corresponds essentially to what we have been qualifying, under EU law and soft law, as a "network agency" providing an institutional basis to foster closer regulatory convergence between Member States and moving beyond the mere coordination of procedures and the exchange of information and best practices related with the regulatory network of national agencies that were established due to impositions contained in the 2003 legislative framework. This regulatory model carries with it considerable risks and uncertainties because it brings into existence a multi-level regime with different lines of responsibility running between the Commission, the ACER, the Member States and their National Regulatory Authorities (NRAs). Furthermore, at another level the ACER may lack some effective powers when confronted with another new institutional reality, corresponding to the *European Network of Transmission System Operators for the gas and electricity networks*, which will act in connection with remaining vertically integrated companies. In fact, such European Network of Transmission System Operators will be entrusted with large powers to approve *market and technical 'codes'* (in some cases prevailing over NRAs). It seems that, as regards these extensive powers of the *Transmission System Operators*, the ACER would basically have a mere advisory role, which may prove insufficient to counter those powers.

4. Conclusive Remarks

Coming now to a final and more positive note, it should be recognized that the EU regulatory framework for energy, despite its complexity related with the originality of the institutional architecture of the EU and regardless of its remaining regulatory gaps after the third legislative package of 2009, has, conversely, some advantages arising from its dynamic nature and adaptability. As referred at the beginning of this Paper, those advantages may place the EU model in a pivotal position for leading the way internationally towards a true reinvention of energy regulation. A reinvented energy regulatory policy must go beyond the traditional goals of promoting consumer rights and economic efficiency in energy markets. It must involve – in response to a new global environment – at least two more demanding objectives:

(1) To provide appropriate incentives to the modernization of energy infrastructures aiming especially at improving energy efficiency at all levels (generation, transmission/distribution and use), increasing the penetration of renewable sources and facilitating the development of new services. This absolutely requires a new proactive regulatory approach to infrastructure planning and operation.

(2) To actively encourage the use of available funds and financial instruments by energy undertakings in order to accelerate investments necessary to modernise the energy infrastructure through the massive introduction of information and communication technologies, to increase the connectivity of electricity and gas networks or to diversify and decentralise supply sources. I am referring 'inter alia' to processes widely known as "smartening the energy grids". The existing grids or networks are ageing which will lead to more power outages and a decline in reliability (in Europe the majority of the assets in the energy networks date back to the period from 1960 to 1990 with a peak in the 1970s, this being caused by a structural growth in energy consumption in that period). In this context, new regulatory policies and techniques should play a central role to maintain or enhance the reliability of ageing grids through appropriate replacement strategies (which will not involve necessarily major grid expansions but may, to a large extent, by achieved through the smartening of the grids, based on the introduction of communication technology elements that can facilitate and control a significant part of the flexible demand for the fluctuating distributed supply of energy). This, in turn, requires investments and medium and long

term strategies. *One of the key dimensions of a reinvented energy regulation lies in providing regulatory constraints and incentives to those types of investments and strategies.*

ANNEX

We have deliberately avoided to overburden this article with excessive information references about energy regulatory policies and national regulatory policies and structures.

Extensive information on these issues can be easily obtained through the SITE of the International Energy Regulation Network (IERN) – http://www.iern.net/portal/page/portal/IERN_HOME/REGULATION_COUNTRY. IERN is a CEER (Council of European Energy Regulators) initiative launched in 2005 which is managed and supervised by the Florence School of Regulation.

The United States' Experience With Market-Based Emissions Regulation

GEORGE GARVEY[*]

The topic of this paper is an increasingly popular form of pollution regulation, one that relies primarily on the private market to achieve an appropriate balance between a clean environment and the pollutants resulting from industrial production.

A short overview of the history of environmental regulation may help to better appreciate the current practice. In the Anglo-American system, the "regulation" of air pollution had its genesis in the law of private nuisances.[1] Until the mid-nineteenth century there was no comprehensive system of air quality regulation in England. Private nuisance law was the only available remedy and it provided very limited relief to a party whose right to use or enjoy property was adversely effected by the use of another's property. An action could lie only for a substantial interference with the property interests of a complainant.[2] Non-physical or "aesthetic" injuries could not be remedied.[3] Most importantly, the law was subject to a territorial principle that provided virtually no relief for persons living in agricultural or industrial areas where malodorous and toxic emissions

---

[*] Professor of Law, Columbus School of Law, Catholic University of America.

[1] *See generally* Noga Morag-Levine, *The Problem of Pollution Hotspots: Pollution Markets, Coase, and Common Law*, 17 CORNELL J.L. & PUB. POL'Y 161 (2007).

[2] Restatement (Second) of Torts § 821F (1979).

[3] Morag-Levine, *supra* note 1, at 187.

were likely to be present.[4] The law, therefore, was subject to ad hoc judicial determinations and relief tended to be available only for those fortunate enough to live in areas that did not have undesirable industrial or agricultural activities in the vicinity. In short, nuisance law protected only those who could afford to avoid the undesirable, perhaps even toxic, consequences of poorer neighborhoods. It was not until the mid-nineteenth century that the English established a comprehensive regulatory regime to deal with at least one form of particularly noxious subject, the alkali pits used by tanneries.[5]

The United States naturally followed the English Common Law tradition. Nuisance law in the United States, however, has several variants, two of which reflect the main competing approaches to private nuisance law. One line of cases will find an actionable nuisance if the injury to another's tangible property is more than "nominal."[6] Particularly if the jurisdiction considers an abatement order (injunction) to be the preferred or required remedy for a private nuisance, the law can have devastating consequences for those engaged in otherwise legal productive activities. Moreover, this approach to nuisance law ignores the fact that there are social interests in industrial and other forms of productivity and their consequences that go beyond the parties to private litigation.

The competing model, adopted by the Restatement (Second) of Torts, explicitly requires an economic balancing of the injuries, both to determine if a nuisance exists and to decide if an injunction is the proper remedy.[7] If the cost of abating an alleged "nuisance" would exceed the benefits of continuing the offensive practice, the activity is not "unreasonable" and therefore not a nuisance.[8] When a nuisance is found to exist, the particular

---

[4] *Id.* at 179.

[5] Ben Pontin, *Integrated Pollution Control in Victorian Britain: Rethinking Progress within the History of Environmental Law*, 19 J. ENVTL. L. 173, 173 n. 2 (2007).

[6] *E.g.*, Jost v. Dairyland Power Coop., 172 N.W.2d 647, 651 (Wis. 1969). The Court held that "We conclude that the injury was substantial as a matter of law, since under the reasoning of Pennoyer ... and the Restatement, the injury was obvious injury to tangible property. Moreover, it was, in fact, of such a nature that *the jury placed more than a nominal value upon the injury done.*" *Id.* (emphasis added). The jury in *Jost* had, in fact, found the damages not to be "substantial," but the trial judge changed the finding and the Wisconsin Supreme Court affirmed the trial court. *See id.* at 650-51.

[7] *See generally* Restatement (Second) of Torts §§ 821-831 (1979).

[8] *Id.* § 829.

jurisdiction may also require the use a "balancing of the equities or utilities" to determine if an injunction is appropriate.[9]

The two models presented above should be viewed as the extremes of a continuum rather than a binary formula for nuisance law. The law is complex and many variations are found in principle and practice. Courts and legislatures have implemented policies and procedures that mitigate perceived problems with both extremes. This brief and necessarily superficial overview of nuisance law, however, serves a couple of purposes. For one thing, the development of nuisance law, particularly in the United States, rehearses the economic debates that have informed the development of modern approaches to the problem of pollution regulation. Also, nuisance law remains a potent tool in the development of environmental policies. Actions have been brought by states, for example, against private polluters, other states, and even the federal government for emitting or permitting the emission of pollutants that harm the complaining state or states.[10] Given the inherently interstate and even international nature of major environmental issues, such as acid rain and global warming, preemptive federal laws or international conventions may be necessary and appropriate, but nuisance law may provide an effective, although limited and variable, tool as long as pertinent regulation is left to individual states.

In the second half of the twentieth century, the need for a more comprehensive approach to the problem of environmental degradation became clear. The United States responded by creating an administrative body, the Environmental Protection Agency (EPA) that largely followed the prevailing regulatory norms. This regulatory body, like others of that time, was built on the Progressive and the New Deal eras' confidence in the judgment, expertise, and objectivity of a professional bureaucracy. Accordingly, a traditional system of "command-and-control" regulation was established to deal with environmental pollution. In the context of noxious emissions, the Clean Air Act of 1970[11] gave the EPA considerable authority to regulate the emissions of environmentally hazardous gases and particulates. Initial efforts under the command-and-control regula-

---

[9] *Id.* § 941.

[10] *See* J.R. DeShazo & Jody Freeman, *Timing and Form of Federal Regulation: The Case of Climate Change*, 155 U. Pa. L. Rev. 1499, 1521-29 (2007).

[11] 42 U.S.C.A., 1857c-2–c-9 (1970).

tory scheme attempted to deal with serious emissions problems through source-specific, technology-based regulations. That is, major producers of air pollutants, primarily electrical generating plants, were ordered to reduce their output of hazardous emissions often through the use of the best available technology (BAT).[12] The complexity of the task proved to be overwhelming. Old plants, which were most likely to be generating large amounts of pollutants, were grandfathered, creating disincentives to establish new, more efficient (and likely more costly) plants. Access to cleaner forms of energy (e.g., low-sulfur coal, oil, gas) varied among firms and between geographic locations. Technology was changing. Regulators could not anticipate all of the possibilities that would minimize levels of emissions at any given time, location, technology, or technique. Eventually, many policy makers and commentators believed that command-and-control regulation could not achieve the desired balance between a clean environment and efficient production.[13]

The perceived failure of command-and-control regulation led to the most current regulatory technique, market-based regulation (MBR). The experience, at least in some contexts, with this new method of regulation has proven to be very promising, which is the topic of this paper.

Just as the law has evolved in the area of environmental controls, economists have changed their thinking with time. A.C. Pigou provided the framework of welfare economics that many economists followed for decades.[14] Building on the work of his mentor and predecessor, Alfred Marshall, Pigou distinguished between private and social welfare. Maximizing private welfare, he observed, does not necessarily maximize social welfare. "Externalities," i.e., the costs of production which are not fully borne by the producer, are imposed by one party on others.[15] Since costs are not fully

---

[12] Cass R. Sunstein, *Administrative Substance*, 1991 DUKE L.J. 607, 627-629.

[13] The phenomenon of "deregulation" was certainly not limited to environmental regulation. To varying degrees virtually all regulated sectors of the U.S. economy have been freed from rigid regulatory controls over the past several decades.

[14] *See Arthur Cecil Pigou*, The Concise Encyclopedia of Economics, LIBRARY OF ECONOMICS & LIBERTY, http://www.econlib.org/library/Enc/bios/Pigou.html (last visited Mar. 22, 2015).

[15] Pigou was also concerned with "positive" externalities, i.e., others derive the benefits of a producers work without compensating him or her. The result of positive externalities is a reduction in the production of such goods. The actor will not invest in the production of a good that others can take without compensation. Pigou's remedy for positive externalities is

borne by the producer, too much of the product will be produced. If, on the other hand, others obtain the benefits of a producer's actions without compensation (positive externalities), too little of the good will be produced. In both cases, society's welfare is less than it would be if production costs and benefits were fully internalized. Stated simplistically, Pigou's remedy was a system of taxes and subsidies that would better ensure the maximization of social welfare. From this perspective, externalities are a "market failure" that must be corrected by governmental intervention. As one commentator has summarized the situation under the model associated with Pigou as applied to the issue of pollution, "industrial sources, irrespective of circumstances, [must] either take precautions not to harm others or pay for any harm they inflict."[16] Prominent economists, such as the University of Chicago's Frank Knight, challenged Pigou's model,[17] but most economists found his conclusions to be sound.

One of the more dramatic shifts in economic and related legal thinking, however, occurred when Ronald Coase demonstrated that Pigou's paradigm was fundamentally flawed.[18] Externalities were not simply costs imposed by one actor on another. The nature of the relationship between two parties seeking to use their property in ways that cannot be reconciled is reciprocal. The industrialist generating offensive odors interferes with the right of the homeowner to enjoy her garden. The assertion by the homeowner of her right to garden, however, if enforced, interferes with the industrialist's right to use his property in the way he feels is most beneficial to him and hopefully to society. Moreover, Coase hypothesized that, in the absence of transaction costs, the way that society assigned the property right (to the industrialist or the gardener) did not matter. The parties would negotiate a transfer of the property right, if necessary, to the user who valued it most highly. In other words, mitigate or eliminate transaction costs and the market would resolve the problem of externalities.

---

subsidies, i.e., compensating producers for their work. For purposes of this paper, however, the focus will remain on negative externalities.

[16] Morag-Levine, *supra* note 1, at 174.

[17] Robert L. Formaini, *Frank H. Knight – Origins of the Chicago School of Economics*, ECON. INSIGHTS (Fed. Reserve Bank of Dallas), Vol. 7 (2002), *available at* http://www.dallasfed.org/assets/documents/research/ei/ei0203.pdf.

[18] R. H. Coase, *The Problem of Social Cost*, 3 J.L. & ECON. 1 (1960).

Economists of either persuasion share a common belief in the ultimate ability of freely operating markets for private goods to efficiently allocate societies resources. Pigou and his adherents, however, saw the existence of "externalities" as a market failure that had to be corrected by government. That intervention could come in the form of taxes, nuisance law, or administrative fiat, but the existence of externalities meant that the private market mechanism could not achieve the most efficient outcome. The parties imposing harm on others or obtaining benefits without paying for them were reducing social welfare for their own gain. The emphasis of Coase, by contrast, was on recognizing and mitigating the flaws in the proper functioning of the market, which could be done by minimizing transaction costs. If transaction costs could be reduced to zero, property and its uses would always end up with the highest valued user.

It is of course noteworthy that Coase did not advocate an unqualified commitment to markets, nor did he deny the existence of the limitations of markets. His great insight was that many perceived failures of the market are the result of transaction costs, some of which may be reduced through sound policies, laws and enforcement. Policy makers and regulators, therefore, should facilitate the market mechanism by minimizing the costs that make efficient transactions too costly. Only when the costs inhibiting private transactions cannot be removed, should a court or administrator attempt to mandate the socially "best" outcome.

As already noted, the modern trend in regulation has been away from administrative command and control towards a system that employs the market when possible to best allocate resources. Many examples exist of previously regulated industries switching to market-based models. Most sectors of the transportation industry, for example, have shifted from rigid command-and-control structures to competitive environments.[19] None of these changes, however, signaled the death of government regulation. Public health and safety still require government to set and enforce appropriate standards. Those regulatory regimes that were intended to foster the efficient or otherwise socially-desirable allocation of resources, however,

---

[19] *E.g.*, Shipping Act of 1984, Pub. L. No. 98-237, 98 Stat. 67; Bus Regulatory Reform Act of 1982, Pub. L. No. 97-261, 96 Stat. 1102; Airline Deregulation Act of 1978, Pub. L. No. 95-504, 92 Stat. 1705; Railroad Revitalization and Regulatory Reform Act Amendments of 1976, Pub. L. No. 94-210, 90 Stat. 31.

became suspect over time and the trend is to let markets do what markets typically do best.

This rather abstract discussion applies to the particular matter of air emissions regulation. The issue of acid rain prompted the first major market-based regulatory regime in the United States.[20] Congress amended the Clean Air Act in 1990.[21] Among other things, the amendments established a "cap and trade" program to control and reduce the major source of acid rain, sulfur dioxide (SO_2).[22] Rather than continue to attempt to order the reduction of each producers' emission on a facility-by-facility basis, usually by requiring the use of the best available technology (BAT), the cap and trade program provides "allowances" that permit the holder to emit a specific amount of SO_2. Each allowance permits the holder to emit a unit (currently one ton) of sulfur dioxide during a year. At the end of each year, the emitter must produce allowances equal to the amount of pollution emitted. The allowances may be used, banked (held for future use), or traded. Any party may purchase allowances, which includes environmentalists – who wish to retire them without use – and brokers – who are speculating on price changes.

The major perceived benefit of the system of allowances is that it provides flexibility to those in the target industries. Those who are producing and emitting SO_2 have an incentive to reduce their emissions, but they can decide when and how that reduction can best be achieved. A firm, again generally firms that operate electrical generating plants, can either reduce emissions in a given year or acquire allowances from others to increase their emissions. A firm that can reduce emissions at relatively low cost will have the incentive to do so. That company will then have excess allowances to trade in the market. Moreover, each firm will decide which methods best suits its situation. Some firms can shift to cleaner burning fuels, e.g., low-sulfur coal or natural gas, while others can install technology (scrub-

---

[20] The cap and trade program established by the 1990 Amendments to the Clean Air Act is generally referred to as the Acid Rain Program. *See* U.S. ENVTL. PROT. AGENCY, OFFICE OF AIR & RADIATION, CLEARING THE AIR: THE FACTS ABOUT CAPPING AND TRADING EMISSIONS, (2002), *available at* http://www.epa.gov/airmarkets/presentations/docs/clearingtheair.pdf.

[21] Clean Air Act Amendments of 1990, Pub. L. No. 101-549, § 401, 104 Stat. 2399, 2584 (codified as amended at-42 U.S.C. §§ 7651-7651o).

[22] For general information about the cap and trade system, see *Cap and Trade*, U.S. ENVTL. PROT. AGENCY, http://www.epa.gov/captrade/ (last visited Mar. 22, 2015).

DIREITO COMPARADO / COMPARATIVE LAW

bers) to reduce emissions. Multi-plant firms can shift output from less clean to cleaner facilities and then trade or bank the allowances not required because of the overall reduction in its emissions. In short, the allowances become one more factor in the cost equation and the decision about how best to reduce overall emission levels is driven by rational business decisions rather than regulatory fiat.

As previously indicated and as the name implies, the cap and trade program is not a license for polluters to continue to emit pollutants unabated. There is a "cap" and the system anticipates ongoing reductions in the overall level of the undesired emissions over a stated period of time, although this may translate into reduced levels of anticipated growth.[23] A firm that keeps a plant operating with high emission levels would likely simply be using up the resource. At some point, the cost of the necessary allowances would make it unprofitable to continue operating the polluting plant. But the decision to exhaust a facility before closing it is neither economically nor environmentally unsound.

Experience with the SO_2 and other similar market-based systems have shown them to be effective, at least to date,[24] but they do not promise to eliminate the need for regulatory oversight. As is often the case with regulatory reform, new regulatory skills must be brought to bear. The market for allowances, for example, must be made to operate honestly and efficiently. Markets require a certain amount of liquidity and activity in order to properly price commodities. If the market for emission allowances does not properly price the product, there will be either too much or too little emissions. Also, the amount of emissions must be accurately measured to ensure that the emitters are producing the proper amount of allowances, or paying the resulting fines, at year's end.

At this point, let me identify some of the issues that make the creation and administration of a market-based regulatory system challenging. The paradigms of Pigou and Coase deal with the efficient allocation of resources – the pricing mechanism – which is the stuff of neoclassical economics. At least two other schools of economic thought help to further

---

[23] The Clean Air Act Amendments of 1990 set the cap for SO_2 emissions by 2010 at 50% of the emissions in 1980.
[24] *See* U.S. ENVTL. PROT. AGENCY, CLEAN AIR MARKETS DIVISION, ACID RAIN PROGRAM 2004 PROGRESS REPORT: 10 YEARS OF ACHIEVEMENT (2005).

THE UNITED STATES' EXPERIENCE WITH MARKET-BASED EMISSIONS REGULATION

our understanding of the limitations of a market-based regulatory regime: public choice and behavioral economics. These approaches to economic analysis do not usurp the neoclassical paradigm, one that relies on the pricing mechanism to efficiently allocate resources through transactions between rational utility maximizers. Rather they add to and enrich the neoclassical canon. Remember that Coase's model shifts the analytical focus to transaction costs— minimize them and the market will allocate private resources more efficiently. Public choice theory adds a political component and behavioral economics adds the psychological sphere. Each, however, address some variant of costs related to transacting efficient market outcomes. The first has particular significance to decisions made by public bodies. The second has more general application.

One of the most critical elements in the establishment of a market for emissions or other pollution allowances is the initial allocation of the allowances. When government is involved, the process naturally takes on a political as well as economic dimension. These allowances are very valuable, which invites "rent seeking" or opportunistic behavior. Market-based regulation requires at the very least that property rights be fixed and protected. Although the cap and trade system has taken government largely out of the business of dictating the methods firms must use to reduce harmful emissions, the initial process of allocating the property interests (allowances), which was essential for the operation of market-based regulation, was done by Congress and was subject to considerable pressure politics. The allocation itself could have been done through a more or less "pure" market approach, i.e., auction off all of the allowances to the highest bidders, but that would have presented its own set of problems because a new government-created commodity was being offered. Congress selected in the context of the SO_2 cap and trade program, however, not to utilize that device. The result was a process that allocated allowances in part on the basis of influence. Paul Joskow and Richard Schmalensee have demonstrated rather compellingly that the establishment of air control standards, both those predating the market-based approach of 1990 and those of the 1990 amendments, has been subject to the influence of powerful members of Congress and strong economic constituencies.[25] The

---

[25] Paul L. Joskow & Richard Schmalensee, *The Political Economy of Market-Based Environmental Policy: The U.S. Acid Rain Program*, 41 J.L. & ECON. 37 (1998).

DIREITO COMPARADO / COMPARATIVE LAW

high-sulfur coal producing states, the low-sulfur coal producing states, the states with "dirty" production facilities and the states with up-to-date clean generating plants, among many others, all sought special protection or benefits. Many of them prevailed by getting special allowances and sometimes exceptions.

Public choice theory can perhaps best explain how political considerations often trump purely economic consideration when decisions are made in a political forum concerning the regulation of economic matters. This is a predictable consequence of the political processes that should not defeat the exercise of establishing sound market-based regulatory programs. It does, however, demonstrate that establishing such programs may be impeded and will surely be distorted by politically powerful special interests. The withdrawal of the United States from the Kyoto Protocol may reflect just this type of political dilemma.[26] International pollution control policies have implications across many sectors of national economies. While some nations claim rights to have higher emissions in order to develop (either more allowances/credits or generous national caps), and some developed nations—the United States—resist "discriminatory policies" that would put their industries and workers at a competitive disadvantage, establishing an international market-based system will remain difficult.

There are many practical problems with the allocation of the original allowances that go beyond the pressure to satisfy the "rent seeking" goals of constituents. The options include allocations based on existing levels of emissions. This essentially assigns property rights based on existing outputs of pollutants. An allocation system based on current levels of emissions, however, penalizes firms that have recently invested in new technology or made other changes to reduce emissions. They will receive fewer allowances and have fewer options to make emission reducing changes. In short, their progressive investments put them at a disadvantage with their "dirtier" competitors under a cap and trade system if the initial allocations are based on current pollution levels. When applied internationally, an allocation system that provides credits based on existing levels of emissions is the bane of undeveloped nations. Providing allow-

---

[26] Eric Shaffner, *Repudiation and Regret: Is the United States Sitting out the Kyoto Protocol to its Economic Detriment?*, 37 ENVTL. L. 441, 442 (2007).

ances or credits based on pollutants emitted during times of low industrial output will impede undeveloped and underdeveloped nations from achieving their goals of industrial growth. Nascent industries in these nations will have to purchase emission allowances, adding perhaps substantially to their start-up costs. Moreover, a system that awards the right to pollute based on existing levels of pollution will reward those nations that have recently and aggressively industrialized, and that are adding significantly to worldwide pollution. The point is that the most direct and obvious way of allocating newly created allowances to pollute – property interests in toxic emissions – presents difficulties and they are compounded in an international setting.

In spite of the previously discussed issues, the U.S. acid rain program allocated allowances free of charge to the emitters based on their heat inputs over a three-year period.[27] Special allowance reserves were also set aside for firms that installed highly effective technology or that induced substantial reductions in consumer demand. The program also initially withheld a small percentage of allowances to be sold at auction. The auctions were intended to ensure the establishment of a market for the allowances.[28] The auctions are held annually and the proceeds from these sales returned on a pro rata basis to the emitters.[29]

Another perceived problem with a market-based system for the right to pollute is the issue of "hot spots." The cap and trade system exemplified by the U.S. SO_2 system is intended to systematically reduce harmful emissions in the aggregate. Depending on the nature of the pollutant, however, a policy that permits firms to continue or even increase emission levels can result in areas that suffer relatively more than other areas, i.e., "hot spots." When harmful effects are not geographically specific, that is they do their harm in the atmosphere (global warming), the source of emissions should not matter.[30] When the trading system, however, authorizes producers to purchase the right to damage the local environment, the problem is thornier. The trading system that the U.S. government imple-

---

[27] For a concise description of the process used for allocating allowances, see *Allowance Markets*, U.S. ENVTL. PROT. AGENCY, http://www.epa.gov/airmarkets/participants/allowance/index.html (last visited Mar. 22, 2015).

[28] *See id.*

[29] *Id.*

[30] Morag-Levine, *supra* note 1, at 163.

DIREITO COMPARADO / COMPARATIVE LAW

mented for emissions containing mercury[31] is controversial and the subject of litigation for this reason.[32]

Initial evidence shows that the U.S. acid rain program was very successful, particularly when measured by the reduction in emission levels. Most of the gains, however, came from reductions in the levels of SO_2 production. That part of the intended congressional message – reduce the levels of harmful emissions – got through to the major producers. The role of the allowance trading market, however, was less obvious. Emission reductions seemed to have been the product of production decisions and new technologies. The market for allowances did not materialize as was expected.[33] Few allowances were sold, and the demand for them did not generate prices that would stimulate more interest. Most allowances that could have been marketed due to reductions in emission levels were banked. The trading that did occur was between a relatively small numbers of firms.

The relatively slow creation of an active market for SO_2 allowances is caused in part by the management culture of the regulated utilities. The management of a pervasively regulated firm does not engage in the same types of cost analysis that is true in competitive, market-driven industries. There is, for example, a somewhat perverse incentive to increase costs that can be added to the utility's "rate base" which provides the basis for the firm's permissible rate of return. In short, the market-based regulation of emission outputs must be incorporated into a more comprehensive system of traditional regulation, often by multiple governmental bodies, and the transition has not been entirely smooth. Again, it should be emphasized that the main goal of the new regime – reduction in the overall amounts of pollution – has been successful. The development of an active, effective market for allowance, however, is taking place more slowly than expected.

It seems fairly clear that market-based regulation works well in the context of emission controls. It enjoys much support, both nationally and

---

[31] *See* Standards of Performance for New and Existing Stationary Sources: Electric Utility Steam Generating Units, 70 Fed. Reg. 28606, 28,608-10, 28,614-15, 28,619, 28,622 (Clean Air Mercury Rule). The Clean Air Mercury Rule has recently been overturned by a federal court, *New Jersey v. EPA*, 517 F.3d 574 (D.C. Cir. 2008).

[32] Morag-Levine, *supra* note 1, at 161-63.

[33] JEFFREY L. HARRISON, THOMAS D. MORGAN & PAUL R. VERKUIL, REGULATION AND DEREGULATION: CASES AND MATERIALS 482 n.3 (2d ed. 1997); *New Strategies for a New Market: The Electric Industry's Response to the Environmental Protection Agency's Sulfur Dioxide Emission Allowance Trading Program*, 47 ADMIN. L. REV. 469, 481 (1995).

internationally. Europe, of course, has opted for market-based regulation in the context of greenhouse gas emissions and it is fairly clear that the United States will follow suit in the not so distant future. There have been multiple proposals in the past couple of Congresses to do just that. One or two of these proposals would have established a tax-based system, but none had suggested returning to a command-and-control regime.

This paper cannot address all of the complexities of market-based regulatory systems. Regulatory reform often results in failures that prompt re-regulation.[34] Market-based regulatory regimes in the context of environmental pollutants, however, have not prompted demands for a return to older regulatory techniques. Leadership may have shifted from the United States (acid rain) to Europe (greenhouse gases) and the international community (the Kyoto Protocol), but the utility of cap-and-trade-based pollution controls seems to be widely acknowledged. The future promises more creative uses of such systems, particularly of carbon emissions controls. Carbon allowances, for example, may be allocated to non-polluters in order to protect environments that help to neutralize carbon pollution. Most notably, carbon allowances could provide compensation to South American nations to preserve the Amazon rain forest. Selling the allowances would compensate these nations and their citizens for sparing indigenous forest lands. The overall effects of reducing harmful greenhouse gas emissions and simultaneously preserving natural resources that naturally convert the emissions to beneficial substances would be great indeed.

In conclusion, environmental regulations utilizing market-based programs have proven themselves to be more effective at reducing the output of harmful emissions than traditional command-and-control regimes. They hold the promise of addressing the great environmental problem of the day, global warming, in ways that will reduce greenhouse gases and simultaneously help to preserve the forest lands that reduce the harmful effects of carbon-based pollution. Like all governmental regulation, however, market-based programs may be complex and plagued by political, economic, and technological barriers. Hopefully, the United States,

---

[34] Sidney A. Shapiro and Joseph P. Tomain make a compelling case for a "life cycle of government regulation" which suggests a repeating cycle of market failure, regulation, regulatory failure, deregulation, market failure, and re-regulation. REGULATORY LAW AND POLICY: CASES AND MATERIALS 27 (3d ed. 2003).

where this regulatory model was first implemented, will join Europe and the rest of the international community to create a politically acceptable model applicable to the nations of the world. The concerns of developed nations, newly developed nations (e.g., India and China), and underdeveloped nations are all valid. A well-equilibrated, market-based regulatory regime must moderate the adverse economic impact on developed nations; not stymie the success of newly industrialized economies nor permit such newly developed nations to pollute at little cost over time; grant sufficient allowances for underdeveloped economies to grow; and compensate nations with great forests to forgo otherwise desirable development. The task is obviously daunting, but the need is great. The best evidence available today suggests that the problems of environmental degradation cannot be solved without government intervention, but that tradition forms of regulation do not work well. The problems of command-and-control regulation are magnified in the international context, where the governmental structures for such detailed regulatory management do not exist. Market-based regulation holds the most promise for meaningful progress. Once caps are determined for all participating nations – no simple task – and allowances are distributed among emitters – again, a challenging job – markets will facilitate the regulatory goals. Exchanges already exist for carbon and other greenhouse gases[35] so the structure is in place for the private market to employ the economic self-interest of generators of greenhouse gasses, environmentalists, and even speculators in the task of cleaning the environment. Governmental structures will still be needed to monitor emissions and to enforce national caps, but the bulk of the "regulation" will be market-driven. In sum, market-based regulation has already demonstrated its capacity to deal effectively with environmentally hazardous industrial emissions. The consequences of these emissions, global warming, present an increasingly critical problem for the world community. This calls for renewed efforts by all of the major industrial powers of the world, as well as those nations that do not have substantial industrial bases, to establish a workable market-based international system of emission controls. Non-regulation and traditional command-and-control forms

---

[35] *See, e.g.*, CHI. CLIMATE EXCHANGE, http://www.chicagoclimatex.com (last visited Mar. 22, 2015); *European Union Emission Trading System*, EUROPEAN COMM'N, http://ec.europa.eu/clima/policies/ets/index_en.htm (last visited Mar. 22, 2015).

of regulation will not effectively address this issue. Given current knowledge and recent experience, an international market-based system holds the best hope for successfully reducing the emissions that are exacerbating the critical problem of global warming.

PLANO DA OBRA / TABLE OF CONTENTS

Dário Moura Vicente, Marshall J. Breger   5
Introdução / Introduction

I PARTE / PART I
IMIGRAÇÃO
IMMIGRATION
(8ª conferência, Washington, 2009
8th conference, Washington, 2009)

1. Stephen Legomsky   11
   Refugees and Asylum in the United States

2. Maryellen Fullerton   21
   Portugal and European Union Asylum Policy

3. Donald Kerwin   33
   Creating an Effective, Humane United States Immigration Policy As a Pillar of Comprehensive Reform

4. Carlos Ortiz-Miranda   63
   Employment Eligibility and Mobility of Workers in the United States

5. Carla Amado Gomes   75
   The Administrative Condition of Immigrants: General Aspects and Topic Remarks

DIREITO COMPARADO / COMPARATIVE LAW

II PARTE / PART II
CRISE FINANCEIRA
FINANCIAL CRISIS
(9ª conferência, Lisboa, 2010
9th conference, Lisbon, 2010)

1. Harris Weinstein   107
   Easy Money, High Leverage, and the Burst Bubble

2. David Lipton   123
   *The Financial Meltdown Crisis – Does The Nature of the Regulatory Failure
   Presage the Unlikelihood of Effective Solution?*

3. Andrea Boyack   147
   Cooking Up a Crisis: the Capital-Valuation Connection in U.S. Real Estate Markets

4. Michael Taylor   185
   *Balancing on One Leg: The International Standard Setting Response
   to the Global Financial Crisis*

5. Miguel Moura e Silva   213
   Antitrust in Distress: Causes and Consequences of the Financial Crisis

III PARTE / PART III
DESENVOLVIMENTOS DO DIREITO DA ENERGIA
DEVELOPMENTS IN ENERGY LAW
(10ª conferência, Washington, 2011
10th conference, Washington, 2011)

1. Antonio de Lecea   233
   Scope of Energy Law

2. Joseph Kelliher   245
   Regulation of the Energy Sector in the United States

3. Richard J. Pierce   279
   The Past, Present, and Future of Energy Regulation

PLANO DA OBRA / TABLE OF CONTENTS

4. E. Donald Elliott   301
   Why the United States Does Not Have a Renewable Energy Policy

5. Keith D. Larson   315
   Developments in Mergers and Restructuring in the United States Energy Sector

6. Richard Williamson   327
   The Geopolitics of Oil in Africa

7. Agostinho Pereira de Miranda & Rita Mota   337
   International Petroleum E&P Contracts in Africa: The Rise of Risk Service Agreements?

8. Dário Moura Vicente   351
   Petroleum Arbitration

9. David D. Caron   373
   Applicable Law in the 2010 UNCITRAL Arbitration Rules: a Comment on Professor Vicente's Petroleum Arbitration

10. Luís Silva Morais   379
    Regulation of the Energy Sector in the EU

11. George Garvey   391
    The United States' Experience with Market-Based Emissions Regulation